Silent Speedways of the Carolinas

Silent Speedways of the Carolinas

The Grand National Histories of 29 Former Tracks

Perry Allen Wood

McFarland & Company, Inc., Publishers
Jefferson, North Carolina, and London

All photographs in this book were either taken by, or at the direction of,
Perry Allen Wood and are his property.

LIBRARY OF CONGRESS CATALOGUING-IN-PUBLICATION DATA

Wood, Perry Allen, 1952–
Silent speedways of the Carolinas : the Grand National histories
of 29 former tracks / Perry Allen Wood.
p.   cm.
Includes bibliographical references and index.

ISBN-13: 978-0-7864-2817-5
(softcover: 50# alkaline paper) ∞

1. Automobile racing—North Carolina—History.
2. Automobile racing—South Carolina—History.
3. Racetracks (Automobile racing)—North Carolina—History.
4. Racetracks (Automobile racing)—South Carolina—History.
I. Title.
GV1033.5.G73W66   2007   796.7209756—dc22   2006037792

British Library cataloguing data are available

©2007 Perry Allen Wood. All rights reserved

*No part of this book may be reproduced or transmitted in any form
or by any means, electronic or mechanical, including photocopying
or recording, or by any information storage and retrieval system,
without permission in writing from the publisher.*

On the cover: Columbia Speedway, Columbia, S.C.; Checkered flag ©2006 PhotoSpin

Manufactured in the United States of America

McFarland & Company, Inc., Publishers
Box 611, Jefferson, North Carolina 28640
www.mcfarlandpub.com

I sincerely dedicate this book to my parents, Naomi A. and Jesse L. Wood, Jr., for their love and for exposing me to stock car racing from birth, enabling me to witness it first-hand. To Smoke and Anne Wood: him for being a witness, a supporter, and more than a big brother; and her for support and letting him relive the races with me. To Donnie Allen for being a witness, a supporter, and closer than a cousin could ever be. To Mike Clements, Joe Littlejohn, Jr., Brent Moore, Daryl Moore, and Greg Moore for sharing with me their families' racing stories which they experienced first-hand. To Buck Baker, Louis Clements, John McCarthy, Bud Moore, Cotton Owens, Mario Rossi, and Jack Smith for letting me touch and sit in their racecars. To David Ball, Cleve Brown, Jack Burnett, Bill Dickerson, Sam Forry, Billy Pratt, and Bill Shoolbred, who are life-long pals and witnesses to much of this history. To Wachovia Bank and Mike Musgrave for time off to find the tracks, Bill Campbell and Joanna Flanagan for time off to make the deadline, David Bridges and Lisa Hartsell for proofreading, Charles Baker for his connections, and Sherrill Barnes and David Burton for tech advice. To Shawn Coxson for invaluable photographic assistance. And finally, I dedicate this book to my family for their love. Particularly Yaneth for losing me almost every night to the computer and many days for archeological trips without complaint and with total support. To Allen Jake, *a.k.a.* A.J., for those same reasons, for defending me, and often going with me on my journeys. And to Hannah Naomi for her smiles, her laughs, and for waiting on me to finish this book before growing up. *Thank you all!*

Acknowledgments

When I started this project, I had no idea how much help I would need as the size of the undertaking continued to grow. I knew that the best possible book would include "then and now" photos of the 29 tracks in North and South Carolina that hosted Grand National races, and I had all the "now." Acquiring the "then" was the hard part, though I had a few from races I attended in Columbia and Spartanburg decades ago. So in an effort to finish this book, and it is four years and counting as I write this in 2006, I decided not to pursue old photos from Spring Lake, Hillsborough, Jacksonville, and the other tracks. Maybe if this book flies, I can do it again with a little help from the public.

When I decided to write the story of each race at these old tracks, it was obvious that my personal recollections of a handful of races in Columbia and Spartanburg would be woefully lacking. There is only one source for the complete history of the sport and that is three of my four volumes of *Forty Years of Stock Car Racing* by Greg Fielden, plus *Rumblin' Ragtops*, also by Fielden. I conducted my research with the help of his accounts of the races and their final results. His accounts are not always in agreement with what I saw for myself or heard from eyewitnesses, and I cannot say I believe everything I read anywhere, but Fielden's books are as accurate as stock car racing has. Many times, I read the write-ups of these races in the local papers at the appropriate libraries, often as a sideline of my effort just to find where the track was located.

I present these chapters chronologically, based on when I made my visits to the tracks. *Almost.* Spartanburg's Piedmont Interstate Fairgrounds is first because I got the idea for this book there during Christmas 1997. I took video, but no photos, unfortunately. My official visit there was in October 2002. I placed Charlotte Speedway second because that's where it all started on June 19, 1949, with the first ever "Strictly Stock" race. I actually found the site after much difficulty in January 2004, which would have put it somewhere in the middle of the book, and that just did not seem right. Otherwise, the order of the chapters is as I found time to journey to the tracks.

Truthfully, my mind is so crammed with 54 years of reading stock car racing news and stories, which now qualify as ancient history, that it is impossible for me to attribute it accurately to any particular source without trying to include everything I have ever read. Here I have listed what I know I used as a reference source.

Another extremely valuable tool was racing-reference.info.com, which made it possible to easily find and determine trends, streaks, firsts, lasts, and many other statisticals that make for fascinating storytelling. I found mistakes there, too, but it is a fantastic source.

I talked to countless locals, librarians, and law enforcement officers to get track locations and racing stories. Unfortunately, I don't have the full names of all of these individuals. The most valuable, make that priceless, contributions of all are the thousands of conversations I had and overheard with the people I grew up with in Spartanburg. Folks there told me stories, tall tales, and eyewitness reports of stock car racing happenings from as far back as I can remember off and on until I moved to Chicago in December 1982. That is about 30 years of information absorbed in front yards, back yards, schoolyards, kitchens, dens, bars and garages.

I guess my first real data source was my father, Jesse L. "Smoky" Wood of the Spartanburg City Police Department. He would hear it from Bud Moore, or Buck Baker, or Joe Littlejohn, or Jack Smith, or Pop Eargle, or Cotton Owens, or any of a dozen other experts around town, and then tell me. I soaked everything up like a sponge. When I got older, I gathered my own news from Bud Moore's sons. There was Daryl, five years older and seen almost daily when he stopped by on his red Honda 50 at Bill and Anne Dickerson's house. Anne is now my sister-in-law. He would come to see Anne, and I would come to talk racing with him, from about 1961 to 1966. Brent is two years older and I got to know him in the last half of the '60s as we played and talked as normal teenagers do. Then there was Greg, or "the baby," as Bud and Betty Moore called their youngest. He was a few years younger and Brent and I used to run off and hide so we would not have to play with him. Man, did that change later!

Another huge source of news in the mid–1960s was Mike Clements, son of Louis Clements, the 1960 Grand National Champion car owner and top wrench for Rex White and later J.T. Putney. Mike's uncle is Crawford Clements, who built many top-notch stockers. Along with Brent Moore, Mike carried me through the years at Evans Junior High School with daily tales of life on the Grand National scene. And to add an occasional anecdote was Joe Littlejohn, Jr., a good friend, but not quite with the same frequency as Brent and Mike when it came to racing gossip. Then the 1970s hit, college came and went, and we all lost touch.

We came out on the other side of 1974 and Daryl was married with children. He was building engines for Bud and not a regular acquaintance any longer. Brent was married and working for FPL in Tampa, I think. Louis Clements moved his family to Arizona to test cars for GM, I heard. Joe Littlejohn, Jr., and I rarely crossed paths, losing the infrequent contact we had. But by the '70s, "the baby" was no baby anymore. He was a full-blown drinking buddy and that we did. Greg was now at least six inches taller than me, handing out business cards announcing "General Manager, Bud Moore Engineering." He made up for the lack of racing gossip in spades and provided dozens of pit passes, many of which he secreted to me through a chain link fence wrapped in a red shop rag. Another master of pit pass prestidigitation was Danny Fowler who often secreted that valuable document to me, and then performed his jackman duties on Bud Moore's pit crew without one in the 70's and early 80's.

These people were the sources of a huge amount of the information presented between these covers. Told to me as truths, embellishments, or outright lies, I present them all here, woven into the fabric of the history of stock car racing in the mind of Perry Allen Wood, aka *Silent Speedways of the Carolinas*.

Table of Contents

Acknowledgments	vii
Preface	1
1. Piedmont Interstate Fairgrounds, Spartanburg, South Carolina	5
2. Charlotte Speedway, Charlotte, North Carolina	32
3. Columbia Speedway, Columbia, South Carolina	41
4. Hartsville Speedway, Hartsville, South Carolina	86
5. Cleveland County Fairgrounds Speedway, Shelby, North Carolina	90
6. Harris Speedway, Harris, North Carolina	96
7. Occoneechee Speedway, Hillsborough, North Carolina	100
8. Newberry Speedway, Newberry, South Carolina	125
9. Salisbury Super Speedway, Salisbury, North Carolina	131
10. Starlite Speedway, Monroe, North Carolina	134
11. Harris Speedway, Concord, North Carolina	137
12. Spindle Center Fairgrounds Speedway, Gastonia, North Carolina	144
13. North Carolina State Fairgrounds Speedway, Raleigh, North Carolina	149
14. Raleigh Speedway, Raleigh, North Carolina	153
15. Wilson County Fairgrounds Speedway, Wilson, North Carolina	159
16. Dog Track Speedway, Moyock, North Carolina	167
17. Harnett County Speedway, Spring Lake, North Carolina	172
18. Forsyth County Fairgrounds, Winston-Salem, North Carolina	176
19. Coastal Speedway, Myrtle Beach, South Carolina	180
20. Jacksonville Speedway, Jacksonville, North Carolina	184
21. Champion Speedway, Fayetteville, North Carolina	190
22. Southern States Fairgrounds, Charlotte, North Carolina	194
23. Tar Heel Speedway, Randleman, North Carolina	203
24. Tri-City Speedway, High Point, North Carolina	210
25. McCormick Field, Asheville, North Carolina	213

26. Asheville-Weaverville Speedway, Asheville, North Carolina	218
27. New Asheville Speedway, Asheville, North Carolina	231
28. Greensboro Agricultural Fairgrounds Speedway, Greensboro, North Carolina	237
29. North Wilkesboro Speedway, North Wilkesboro, North Carolina	240
Sources	283
Index	285

Preface

Everything that stock car racing is today germinated at these venues, long gone, of the Carolinas: Charlotte Speedway, Occoneechee Speedway, North Wilkesboro Speedway, Columbia Speedway, Piedmont Interstate Fairgrounds. Some of the traces of these silent speedways are easy to find. Many are fading fast. Some take a vivid imagination to see. And saddest of all, some have disappeared completely.

Silent Speedways of the Carolinas is defined by a few simple rules. First, the speedways have to be in North or South Carolina. Second, they must have hosted at least one NASCAR Grand National race—not the recent Grand National Busch Series, but the division that started in 1949 as the Strictly Stock Division, was renamed from 1950 through 1970 as the Grand National Division, was renamed the Winston Cup Series from 1971 through 2003 and was renamed the Nextel Cup Series in 2004. Since 20 of the 22 years covered here took place during the Grand National period, that term is generally used. Third, the track must be dead. No weekly races, no occasional races, no driving schools, but completely dead. This requirement eliminated circuits such as Greenville-Pickens Speedway, Gamecock Speedway in Sumter, Lancaster Speedway, Bowman-Gray Stadium in Winston-Salem, Hickory Speedway, and North Carolina Speedway in Rockingham. One venue returned briefly in Spartanburg. It is dead now, for good!

I have followed stock car racing all my life. Actually, I have lived and breathed it and why I never became a real part of it with the chances I had is a mystery. I was not around at the very beginning, but I was around early enough to appreciate what it used to be. I was born in Spartanburg, South Carolina, in 1952. My father, Jesse L. "Smoky" Wood, was a city cop. He knew all the drivers and mechanics in town, and from the 1940s into the 1970s, Spartanburg had far, far more than its share. My earliest memory is being with my mother Naomi and older brother Smoke at the Piedmont Interstate Fairgrounds when the Fabulous Flocks, Tim and Fonty, finished one-two in those big white Kiekhaefer Chryslers in a 100-miler. Tim drove number 300, Fonty 301. What burns it into my memory is that somehow after the race, we were all down in front of the grandstand at the finish line with the Flocks. I remember my mother holding me up so I could see. Smoke and I went home with brand-new electric replica Kiekhaefer Mercury Outboard motorboats and our parents got decks of cards. I was three and a half and remember sitting on my bed playing with that boat the next morning. My gift from the Flocks! That race took place on July 6, 1955, a muggy Wednesday night.

The Piedmont Interstate Fairgrounds is a half-mile red clay track near the Southern Shops Haynes Freight Yard in Spartanburg. The track is still there, and it was the seed for this book. Christmas 1997 found my wife Yaneth, two-year-old son Jake, and I visiting my mother, as we had driven up from Miami for the holidays. Donnie Allen, my cousin who is more like a best friend, was also in town from Columbia and remembers almost as much about the old days as I do. We decided to drive around town on a cold and cloudy winter's day and videotape what was left of the landmarks of our youth. The highlight was a trip to "The Fairgrounds," as we and most locals called the track there. The Piedmont Interstate Fair is still held at the fairgrounds every October as it has been forever. As we drove onto the deserted midway toward the track, we kept finding open gates and continued on our way. It was not long before we were on the track. It was in terrible shape. In fact, the main straightaway, the first and most of the second turn were gone and grass covered. Except for the concrete grandstand, still used for shows staged where the start/finish line and pits used to be, there was no sign of the track until we reached turn two. There the old guardrail was, still right where it was when Buddy Baker bounced off it and flipped in 1964 during the greatest race I ever saw. As Donnie drove around the track, I hung out the passenger side window videotaping what we claimed had to be the fastest lap turned there in over a decade. Outside the backstretch you could still see the high clapboard fence that separated roaring stock cars from residences no more than 20 feet away, if that. More than once, I saw a hobby or sportsman car go through that fence and re-enter the track through the gate sporting somebody's hedge or rosebush on its nose. The backstretch was littered now with light poles fallen outward from the infield where they once lit the red, dusty air. There was still a string of caution lights sagging about ten feet above the backstretch, some broken, some whole and yellow, like weird fruit that needed to be picked, but too high to reach. The third and fourth turns were still pretty much intact except for old tires, more light poles, tree limbs, and so on. The guardrail was there, although beaten badly. Then out of number four we drove and ... nothing. No main straightaway existed where everybody that was anybody in Grand National racing's childhood pounded their machines southward toward the finish line 22 times from 1953 until 1966. We did the best we could to finish the lap as close to the old surface as possible. Then we took a long last panoramic look and reluctantly drove away. I did not take any still shots, just video. Big mistake!

That holiday lap around the Fairgrounds gave me the idea, during our long drive back to Miami, to write a book on old abandoned racetracks. What was insignificant to others, I could not get out of my mind. In early 2002, when it became apparent that I was moving to Charlotte for a new job, my dream was rekindled. I could not wait to get back to the Carolinas and find old racetracks and maybe even interview some of the legends, my heroes. However, I arrived in Charlotte on April 28, and my all-time favorite driver took his final checkered flag 14 days earlier. His name is Buck Baker.

After I moved into temporary quarters, I found that aside from settling into my new job and finding a permanent address, I had time on my hands. Yaneth, Jake, and new daughter Hannah stayed back in Miami to finish school, sell the house, pack the stuff, and join me in late June. I used that spare time looking for these old tracks and found some of them. Once the family was reunited, it was very difficult to find the time to chase the rest of the ghosts. However, I did, and this book is the result. I spent many, many long hours in libraries, talking to older-timers than me, driving back roads, and tromping through the hot, critter-infested jungles that were once the Occoneechee and Hartsville Speedways. It was in Hartsville that I received a spider bite that got real, real ugly and stayed with me for the summer of '02.

So here they are. *Silent Speedways of the Carolinas*. All 29 of them. They did not deserve to die, but did neither my dad or your Aunt Agnes or Fireball Roberts. Their time just came and they passed into memory. When the big corporate dollars came in, first as a trickle, then as a flood, it was inevitable. Some of these tracks had little chance to survive and are lucky to have held a Grand National race at all. There are seven one-shot wonders that for a single fleeting day, or night, were the seeds of the mega-sport we know today. The top drivers knew about these races and showed up. Newspapers reported them and the spotlight shone briefly on Harnett Speedway in Spring Lake, NC (1953), Newberry Speedway in SC (1957), McCormick Field in Asheville, NC (1958), Salisbury Super Speedway in NC (1958), Spindle Center Fairgrounds in Gastonia, NC (1958), Hartsville Speedway in SC (1961), and Starlite Speedway in Monroe, NC (1966). All have a story to tell, but not all left a trace to see. This book will at least give these tracks one last moment in the sun, bring back memories to the old-timers who may have been there, and educate the novices that know nothing of what happened before last week.

For some folks, like me, the former tracks just cannot be forgotten. Not yet. Not while a bony hand still reaches out of a dilapidated ticket booth to take your two-dollar admission at Harris. Not while you can still see the faint outline of the track where Bob Flock out-distanced Gober Sosebee at Occoneechee in the third Strictly Stock Car race ever held. Not while the guardrail in Columbia, part wood and part steel, still dares Buck Baker to push Lee Petty into it one more time. Not while the grandstands that once held thousands of screaming spectators are still protesting the roots of pine trees that are so big they must have started growing the day after the last fanny left. Not while bullet-riddled light fixtures still stare blindly down, pretending to illuminate Herb Thomas in Victory Lane 50-plus years ago. Not while museums still house the actual Hudson Hornets, Olds 88s, Ford Fastbacks, and the uniforms of their brave chauffeurs. Not while one can remember how it was when stock car racing was a child. *A wild child!*

This book is not full of spooky pictures because I want to show these venues in broad daylight so one can see what is left of them. It takes a quite an imagination to see some traces of races themselves. Winter is the best season to seek these haunted grounds because the critters are mostly hibernating, as is nature's camouflage. These battlefields, and that is what they are, are racing back to nature and Occoneechee is a great example of a track going from one extreme to the other at 60 seconds a minute.

If you love stock car racing's roots, you will love this book. Embrace it and absorb the early days. These are places of unimaginable extremes in emotion, from the sheer excitement of the spectators, the exaltation of the victors, the hilarity of the improbable, the amazement of the unbelievable, to the anger of the cheated and wrecked, the despair of the losers and the injured, and the grief of friends and family that had their loved ones leave beneath a white sheet. The tales here were perhaps witnessed by you or your neighbors. Cherish the faint, fading arenas where Byron, Rexford, the Flocks, Roberts, the Bakers, Turner, the Pettys, Pearson, the Thomases, Isaac, Paschal, Jarrett, White, Smith, Johnson, Figaro and other great, fading names raced and bled and died. I will not forget them and I do not want history to, either. This book is about those places ... *Silent Speedways of the Carolinas*.

1

Piedmont Interstate Fairgrounds, Spartanburg, South Carolina

It was always called "the Fairgrounds," not the "Hub City Speedway." It is the genesis of this book. With 22 races, it is the fifth most prolific of the *Silent Speedways of the Carolinas*. On October 19, 2002, there was a legends race held there to raise money for a racing museum, which the city and county richly deserve. David Pearson, Bud Moore, Cotton Owens, Rex White, sports car champ Roger Mandeville, Dick Brooks, James Hylton, Joe Littlejohn, Jr., Louise Smith from Greenville, Fireball's ex-wife Doris, Jack Smith's widow Betty, Tim Flock's widow Frances, and many others were there. Joe Littlejohn, Sr. promoted the Fairgrounds from its first race in 1939 until that sad day in 1966 when the last Grand National wheels turned. Joe Sr., raced and sat on those sandy Daytona poles before and after World War II. He was the first man to trip the timers on the hard, white sand at over 100 miles per hour in a stock car in 1950. He was one of the chosen 35 attending the meetings Bill France held in the Ebony Room of the Streamline Hotel in Daytona the week of December 14, 1947, when NASCAR was formed and got that name. Joe is clearly recognizable with his dark, husky, handsome features in all the photos of the meetings. Joe Littlejohn, Sr., a true stock car pioneer, started it all for Spartanburg, and is its undisputed Father of Racing. So they got out the bulldozers in 2002 and made this old track raceable again.

Fans entered the Fairgrounds through these turnstiles for 22 Grand National races.

But by 2005, the Spartanburg museum idea died and the Fairgrounds was once again very unraceable. The silent speedway is back as home to the memory of those brave Grand National teams that started scattering red Carolina dust in 1953. The schedule-makers could not have expected drivers in the Friday night 100-miler in Rochester, NY, to trek down for another century the next night. Nevertheless, four men tried it and three competed. The first of 22 Grand National races held over the next 13 years at Joe Littlejohn's Piedmont Interstate Fairgrounds half-mile of South Carolina red clay landed a plum date, the Saturday night of Independence Day, 1953. A crowd of 7,000 race fans arrived early to see warm-ups, time trials, and the big race. However, they got a shock to learn that one of those making it down from Rochester was in Spartanburg General Hospital in critical condition. Race and fan favorite Tim Flock flew down from New York City and was snoozing in a shady spot of the infield with some other drivers and crewmen. Tim sat on the pole and finished fourth, one lap down, the night before. As they rested up for the night's grind, the unthinkable occurred. A representative for some automotive part backed his car on top of Tim Flock's head! He was surely driving some massive '50s Detroit iron when he parked it on Flock's coconut. The chaotic situation under the hot Fourth of July sun must have been incredible. There is not much use in flying down early to have nap time if it lands you in the hospital for the next few months. Tim was in bad shape and his championship hopes as flat as his gourd.

Fun with Flocks was not over. No doubt bolstered by his brother's calamity and who knows what else, Fonty Flock went out and qualified second in the field of 19. Then NASCAR said he and pole-sitter Buck Baker made their runs too late and both had to start at the rear of the field. Baker retreated and strapped himself in while Fonty had a conniption, maybe two. Probably he had been at Spartanburg General watching over Timothy, who had a major headache. Whatever the reason, Fonty was going home before going to the rear. He demanded second spot! Fonty stood out on the track in front of the grid and made them drive around him. No doubt, all 18 had something to say as they rolled past. However, Truman Fontello Flock, one of the real showmen in all of racing history, decided to give the crowd what they came to see. He fired up the Frank Christian–owned, Red Vogt–wrenched, 1953 Hudson 14 and decided to show 'em what the Flock Boys were all about. When Fonty picked up shotgun on the field, Official Starter Alvin Hawkins waved the green and the Fairgrounds' 2200 miles of Grand National history was underway. Poleman by default Curtis Turner put his Olds out front and stayed there until he had to make two long stops just before halfway and Herb Thomas' Smokey Yunick Hudson led. Thomas won the night before in Rochester. On lap 174, Herb pitted for fuel and Buck took over first, even after being penalized to the rear. Five laps later, he had to gas up, too, and Lee Petty in a '53 Dodge led the final 21 circuits for his 11th career win. Lee was a cinch to win all along because he was so fresh at the start. No, he did not fly down from Rochester like Tim Flock. Lee drove! He ran all 100 miles for third up there, drove his racer 830 miles to the Fairgrounds, and did another 100 miles for the victory. His two-day earnings were $1,450. Actually, that was not bad for someone who likes to drive. It was the job Petty faced and it was the natural thing for him to do. Never let it be said Lee Petty was not tough. As it turned out, he was near indestructible! Second was Baker, third Thomas, Fonty "I'll show 'em" or "This one's for Tim" Flock fourth, with Johnny Patterson in H.B. Ranier's Hudson fifth. Other notables were hometowner Joe Eubanks in Bud Moore's Hudson sixth, old time moonshiner Gober Sosebee eighth, pre-race favorite Dick Rathmann, the fourth Rochester racer from the night before, tenth, Otis "Bib Overalls" Martin 11th, Gene Comstock 12th, Paschal 15th, Turner 16th, and Liguori 17th. That hot, dusty Fourth of July came to an end and anyone who lived it from start to finish had to be mentally and physically exhausted.

Amazingly, Tim Flock did not do months of sheet time. He returned to sit on the pole at Hickory on August 29th, exactly eight weeks later leading the first five laps. If the next 21 races at the Fairgrounds were to be as wacky as the first, this was going to be a long, strange trip.

The return date was 364 days later on a blazing hot July Saturday, this time on the afternoon of the third. There were no fireworks, no funny Flock fiascos, no Flocks at all, and not much of a race. Hershel McGriff took the pole, finishing 11 laps behind in tenth. The day belonged to the Fabulous Yunick Hornet and Herb Thomas who won by more than a half-mile over Jimmy Lewellen's Mercury. It was three wins in the last four races for the streaking Thomas. Petty was third, Baker fourth, Eubanks fifth, Paschal sixth, Rathmann seventh, Blair 14th, and Thompson 21st and last. That first race here in '53 was tough to top and the 1954 edition was not close.

The next day an event registering completely off the weird scale took place before the 100-miler at Asheville-Weaverville. Spartanburg promoter Joe Littlejohn wrangled a passenger seat fitted to the Hudson of Herb Thomas and rode with him as they qualified at a new track record of 67.771. The circumstances of why and how that occurred remain unknown. In addition, why in the world Joe did not do it a day earlier at his own track is especially baffling. Something must have happened in Spartanburg on the third and paid off on the fourth in Weaverville.

The third installment took place on July 4, 1955, and was a Monday nighter. A day race would have been better because summer thunderstorms rumbled in and washed out the event after only 50 laps. Those first fifty laps were action packed as the star-studded field of 27 took the green, led by lap record-holder Tim Flock and Brother Fonty in Carl's Chryslers that started on the front row. Dirt flew early when on lap one, second row starter Lewellen, last year's runner-up here, flipped his new Olds in the first turn, drove it away, and parked in the pits. No caution waved. It did one lap later, though, when Arden Mounts rolled his Hudson in the second turn landing on his lid facing traffic. The West Virginian scampered out and tried to get it righted in vain. After a lengthy delay, the green fell and Tim got away again. However, a war was raging for second between Fonty Flock and Junior Johnson's Olds. Fonty led down the straights and Junior passed him in the turns. Then Speedy Thompson, subbing for Herb Thomas, who was still recovering from his Charlotte crash in April, spun his Smokey's Buick for a caution, but rejoined the fray. A few laps later, the rumble of thunder was heard over the racecars, nature's fireworks lit the sky behind the field lights, the heavens opened, and that was it for Independence Day night. The cautions undoubtedly kept 100 laps from being completed, which would have constituted an official race. So everyone had to come back on Tuesday night and miss Uncle Miltie's *Texaco Star Theater* on Channel 4.

If you were smart, you did not miss Uncle Miltie because it rained again Tuesday night and the race was reset for Wednesday night. If you were real smart Wednesday night, you bet the farm on Tim Flock. Again, he sprinted away in the powerful Chrysler 300 unchallenged. Johnson's engine soured and Fonty captured second in 301. Petty bid for second place briefly, but settled for third in his Chrysler. Baker made it a big Mopar sweep bringing Kiekhaefer's 303 in fourth. It was Buck's first ride for Kiekhaefer and he primarily raced there until the end of 1956. Others were Owens fifth in a Chevy, Matthews sixth, Donald Thomas seventh in another Yunick Hudson, Eubanks ninth, Welborn tenth, Thompson 13th, Rathman 14th, Staley 16th, Johnson 19th, Paschal 20th, Carden 22nd, and Lewellen 27th.

The Grand National Tour visited Spartanburg twice in 1956, the first time on Saturday night, July 7th. The event was moved from the prestigious Independence Day for a 250-

miler on the Raleigh asphalt, won by Fireball. On the dirt, 18 cars entered with Kiekhaefer rolling out two high-powered Chryslers for Buck and Speedy and a Dodge for Herb. It was Roberts in one of three De Paolo Fords on the pole with a new track record of 58.900 with Baker's Chrysler 300 outside. Only seven cars finished as Staley's Chevy slowed in the groove entering the first turn with a sour engine and Thomas, in an effort to avoid him, creamed the boards in his Dodge 500D. They settled for last and next to last. Johnny Allen's Plymouth lost a drive shaft for 15th, Baker went out after halfway with steering failure for 13th, Brownie King crashed his Chrysler in turn three for 12th, and Moody's De Paolo Ford lost an oil line for 11th. Tim Flock, the winner here last year, popped the grandstand wall in his Chevy as factory boss and three-time Indianapolis 500 winner Mauri Rose watched disgustedly from the pits, settling for tenth, where he started. A much-chagrined Kiekhaefer witnessed Thompson crash his Chrysler with 34 left for seventh. Roberts ran hard all night, but could not catch the streaking Petty, who took the $850 first prize in his Dodge. Californians Panch and Amick were third and fourth in Fords, Spartanburg's Joe Eubanks fifth in a Ford, and Billy Myers sixth in a Guy Wilson Mercury.

After the race, in a major development, Herb Thomas bid a bitter bye-bye to Commandant Kiekhaefer's Chrysler carnival and announced that he would field his own Chevrolet for the rest of the season. It had been seven races since his last win on June 3rd in Merced, CA, which was his third for Mr. K and Herb's last anywhere. It left point-leader Baker and henchman Thompson to handle the big Chryslers until that fateful and tragic meeting with Herb in Shelby on October 23rd. Thomas' career passed the point of no return at the Fairgrounds as he unknowingly—and slowly, at first—started his slide into history.

Ten races later, on the muggy Thursday night of August 23, 1956, the boys returned in the midst of another of those maniacal scheduling streaks of four races in five days. This was the second of the four after Billy Myers had topped 13 others in Norfolk the night before. There were only two leaders this night: Speedy Thompson, who maybe had a one-race spat with Kiekhaefer and drove one of three De Paolo Fords, and Ralph Moody, his Ford teammate. Moody took his second pole in a row and led the first 126 before Thompson took over looking like a sure winner. Then with three and a half miles remaining, Speedy's speedster sputtered to a stop and Moody motored to his third checkered flag of the season by two laps over the red and silver-lettered C U Later Alligator Mercury of Paschal. Rex's Chevy, number (rather letter) X, finished third. Fourth was Thomas in his own Chevy and Thompson salvaged fifth smoldering in the pits. Always in the top ten at home was Eubanks sixth, and Baker, in the only Kiekhaefer entry, was sent to the rear at the start as in 1953, winding up seventh. Fireball spun and continued, finishing eighth. Johnny Allen took tenth, Petty 14th, Jimmy Pardue was 15th in his second start, and Billy Myers went to worst from first the night before. It took less than two hours to decide this one.

A Fairgrounds event worth mentioning occurred on Saturday afternoon, September 29, 1956, when the ragtops ran the first of two races there. Jim Donavan crashed on lap eight and the caution flew with Curtis Turner leading. However, his best friend and teammate Joe Weatherly outran him back to the flag stand and was awarded first place. It was the first recorded incidence of racing back to the caution flag and taking the lead.

Saturday afternoon, April 27, 1957, the factory battle raged at the Fairgrounds and nearly all the big names entered. There were 20 entries, but hardly a stiff in the crowd. Speaking of crowds, over 8,500 jammed the stands and infield on a gorgeous day to watch Thompson blister to a new track record in Bud Moore's 1957 Black Widow Chevy 46 at 61.538. Lund surprised the fans, timing outside row one in the Brushy Mountain Motors Pontiac. The quick race saw numerous lead changes between Panch, Roberts, Thompson, Owens,

1. Piedmont Interstate Fairgrounds

The battered rail and red clay of Turn Two remains as it was 40 years ago.

and Petty. When it ended, it was a sweep even topping Kiekhaefer's of 1955, with Panch beating his De Paolo Ford mates Roberts and Moody, the only guys to complete all 200 laps. Petty's Olds was fourth, and Greenville's Allen fifth in Spook Crawford's Plymouth. On back was Lund sixth, and Baker tenth in a Moore Chevy. Jack Smith's Chevy was 12th, Goldsmith in Smokey's Ford 13th, Earnhardt in a Petty Olds 14th, Thompson blew for 15th, Billy Myers in Bill Stroppe's Mercury 17th, Cotton Owens in the Daytona-winning Ray Nichels Pontiac spouted oil after 27 laps for 19th, and Stroppe's other Merc with Paschal up was last.

Nine weeks later was the hot, simmering, summer Saturday night of June 29, 1957. Earlier in the month, the factories pulled out due to bad publicity and outside pressure. Gone were the big Detroit dollars, but the big names were still around, fueled by deal money from NASCAR and promoters, under-the-table bucks from factories and vendors, and funds raided from piggy banks and mattresses all over the country. Twenty-two stockers lined up and saw a whale of a show for 187 laps. Bud Moore had two Chevrolets out front with 13 laps to go when leader Buck Baker and teammate Speedy Thompson dueled neck and neck into that high board fence outside the first turn that gets blasted almost every race. The red flag flew to clean up two demolished '57 Chevrolets, lots of whitewashed kindling, and put Bud in a straight jacket after seeing his personal hometown sweep vanish in a cloud of dust and splinters. They hit it at about 11:30 p.m. and there was no time to make repairs and finish the 200-lapper before the Sunday morning curfew. In 1957, there was no racing in the Palmetto State on the Sabbath. Officials declared Petty the winner, even though Baker led the last lap completed. Petty was parked before the finish line and never completed the 188th lap, but was declared the winner anyway, his third at the Fairgrounds.

Amick was runner-up in a Ford, while Buck and Speedy crashed their ways to third and fourth, with Jack Smith fifth. Sixth was Allen, Mercurys of Myers and Paschal were seventh and eighth, Fireball ninth, Owens 17th, Panch 19th, Lewellen 20th, and Lund 21st. Postscripts to this one were that with the 187th lap red-flag finish, the Grand Nationals actually only ran 2193.5 miles over 13 years, not 2200, and the great Fireball Roberts was winless in four races there.

The lone visit to the Fairgrounds for 1958 was also the middle of three races in four days and took place on Saturday afternoon, April 12th. Thompson beat Smith on Thursday night in Columbia and they were back along with 25 others in a big field under the springtime sun. In fact, Thompson had the pole in Bud Moore's year-old Southern 500 winner, with Owens outside in last year's Daytona-winning Pontiac. And as in Columbia, it was The Speedy and Jack Show with Speedy on top and Jack runner-up again. In his second race since release from stir, Junior Johnson repaired his '57 Ford, involved in Thursday night's Capital City crash, finishing third, Eddie Pagan was fourth in a '57 Ford, and Possum Jones fifth in a year-old Chevy. Notables further back were Reds Kagle seventh, Petty 12th, Herman Beam in his Fairgrounds debut 14th, Blackie Pitt had the highest finishing 1958 model, a Studebaker, 16th, Lund 19th, Buck 22nd, Carden 24th, and Owens broke a fan belt for 26th. The third of the four-day trifecta was the next afternoon at Lakewood in Atlanta, where Holman-Moody Fords swept with Fairgrounds absentees Turner and Weatherly.

The Grand Nationals returned only once in 1959, too, a balmy Friday night, June 5th. Twenty drivers arrived with the locals faring well. Cotton sat on the pole with a new track record of 63.180, with Tiny outside. Cautions were rare as it took only an hour and 48 minutes for the Spartanburg combo of Jack Smith in his Bud Moore–tuned '59 Chevy to dispose of the other 19 for the $1,000 first prize. Second was homegrown Joe Eubanks in his familiar 82 What-A-Burger '58 Ford. Junior Johnson took third for the second year in a row in the same old Paul Spaulding '57 Ford as last year. Fourth was G.C. Spencer from up the road in Inman, and fifth Roy Tyner. Also on hand were the Turtle ninth, Baker 11th, Petty 12th, last year's winner Thompson 14th, pole-starter Owens lost a fan belt for the second year in a row for 15th, and Pardue, Lund, Rollins, and Welborn took the last four places.

Spartanburg was solidly the center of stock car racing as far as the number of owners, builders, and drivers were concerned, and it stayed that way through the decades into the seventies. They came and went as lots of out-of-towners arrived, joining the locals to chauffeur and win, becoming champions in Spartanburg cars.

May 28, 1960, was the first of two trips the big time made to the Fairgrounds that season. It was Saturday afternoon with a dynamite field on hand to sling dirt, swap fenders, and crack that battered old first turn fence again. Twenty-two teams made the scene as Jack Smith put Moore's beautiful candy-apple red 1960 Boomershine Pontiac 47 on the pole with a scorching time of 64.220. Outside was Baker in his white Thor Chevy 87. Row two saw Owens in his white 1960 Hedges Pontiac with the DayGlo red 5s, flanked by Rex in Louis Clements' spectacular gold and white 1960 Piedmont Chevy with the red 4s. Fifth was Inman's Tommy Irwin in a yellow '59 T-Bird sporting red 36s. The first five qualifiers were all Spartanburg drivers in Spartanburg cars. Further back more stars lurked, with Johns seventh in a blue and white '59 T-Bird with red 93s and Larry Frank eighth in the '59 Thor Chevy of Tom Pistone. Defending National Champion Lee Petty in the famous Petty-blue 1960 Plymouth was ninth and local sportsman hero, rookie David Pearson, in Jack Smith's old '59 race-winning Chevy of the year before, tenth. Richard Petty started 11th, Curtis Turner in an increasingly rarer appearance sat 12th, and Joe Lee Johnson, three weeks from winning the first World 600 was 13th. Spencer's pink '58 Chevy was 14th, Buddy Baker started a '58 Chevy 15th, Jarrett had a red 1960 Courtesy Ford with white 11s 16th; and Bunkie Blackburn drove Spook Crawford's '58 Ford from 17th. The tail-enders were Crawfish Crider in a '58 Ford 19th, Gerald Duke in a mean-looking black and gold '59 T-Bird with red 92s 20th, Paul Lewis had a new Chevy 1 in 21st, and last, but never least, crowd-pleasing Herman "The Turtle" Beam. Turtle cruised around in his spotless, dent-free, powder blue-bodied, white-topped, 1960 Elizabeth City Motors Ford with DayGlo orange 19s adorning it. Twenty-two stock cars were all lined up and gleaming under a brilliant South Carolina late-spring Saturday afternoon sun.

The green fell, off they dashed, and five laps later Johns exited with a steamy radiator. Turner burned out his rear end in ten and Buddy Baker and Larry Frank crashed in turn two as the track started to take its toll. The frame on Smith's leading Pontiac broke near halfway and Owens, Petty, Pearson, and Jarrett dueled for the lead. Ned fell ill just after halfway and luckily, Jim Massey was hanging out in the pits with a helmet, but no car, and got in the 11. Paul Lewis crashed on lap 167 and Joe Lee was next with a rear-end failure on lap 170. Richard Petty tangled with a slow car, crashing in turn four on lap 186, and parked. Remarkably, Jimmy Massey hustled the Ford in front of three-time Spartanburg winner Lee Petty for the win in relief, only the fifth time a pinch-hitter ever found Victory Lane in a Grand National. A lap back in third was Owens, Irwin fourth, and Pearson fifth, the best finish of his 17-race career. Others were Spencer sixth, Duke seventh, Doug Yates eighth, Buck Baker ninth, Blackburn tenth, White 12th, Turtle 13th, and Crawfish 14th. It was a splendid day and the 8,000 that watched went home happy, especially Jim Massey and Ned Jarrett.

It was Friday, August 12, 1960, raining, and the race was postponed. Because there was a 100-miler at Asheville-Weaverville on Sunday afternoon the 14th, this rainout would be squeezed in after that one and before Columbia's 200-lapper on Thursday night the 18th. As it turned out, it was shoehorned between a pair of Rex White wins, too. So Tuesday night, August 16, 1960, the Grand Nationals battled on that strangest of all race days. The field of 21 was minus hometowners Smith and Bud Moore. However, another local took up the slack as owner, driver, and racetrack neighbor Cotton Owens destroyed the field, taking the pole and leading most of the way in his white 1960 Hedges Pontiac 5. The "King of the Modifieds" won by about a second over Lee's high-finned Fury in what turned out to be Papa's final Spartanburg appearance, which included three wins and five top fives in 11 starts. Third was Junior Johnson in a 1960 Daytona Beach Kennel Club Chevrolet, two back. Fourth was previous winner Jarrett in a '60 Ford, and fifth came Spartanburg's Rex White and Louis Clements enroute to the National Championship. Others were Irwin sixth, Duke seventh, Greenville's L.D. Austin in a dilapidated '58 Chevy eighth, Buck ninth, and Pardue's Lowe's '59 Dodge 54 tenth. The Turtle crawled in 11th, Crawfish 12th, Richard 13th, Possum 14th, Buddy Baker 15th, Eubanks in an uncharacteristic 16th, Pearson heading for Rookie of the Year 18th, Spencer 19th, and Bobby Johns had the dubious distinction of finishing last in both Spartanburg races of 1960, this time 21st.

Owens hired Johns, who ran fourth two days earlier at Asheville-Weaverville in the same Fairgrounds-winning Pontiac 5. Johns experienced good finishes in pick-up rides all year long beginning at Daytona. He finished second in his Daytona qualifier, nearly winning the 500 in Yunick's year-old Pontiac until the back glass blew out with ten left, forcing him to settle for second. Johns was sixth at Darlington in the Rebel 300 in the T-Bird, third in the first World 600 in a third Petty Plymouth, fourth for Yunick again at Atlanta's first Dixie 300, eighth in the T-Bird at Bowman-Gray, then the Grim Reaper sidled up to him. On September 5th in the Southern 500, Johns was near the front in Cotton's white Bonneville when he locked bumpers in turn two while lapping Ray Tyner's old Olds. He careened into the backstretch pit wall and flipped. The barrier exploded on impact, sending big chunks of concrete sailing through the air. Mowed down in the blast were famed crew chief Paul McDuffie of World 600 winner Joe Lee Johnson and another of his crewmen, Charles Sweatlund. Johnson's car was withdrawn following the deaths. A NASCAR official was also killed and three others injured. Johns slithered from the wheels-up 5 dazed and bloodied, but otherwise OK. Buck Baker won that 500, driving the Boomershine Pontiac the final lap on the left rear rim. Owens repaired the Darlington car and Johns drove it again to fourth in the inaugural National 400 in Charlotte. The potent Pontiac pair ended the year with Johns driving the 5 Justus Pontiac of Rock Hill, SC, to Victory Lane in the first Atlanta 500 on Halloween Eve. Johns nipped Spartanburg driver Buck Baker for third in the final point standings. Bobby Johns did it in 19 starts compared to 40 for hometown champion Rex White and Richard in second, Baker fourth with 37, Jarrett fifth with 40, and Lee Petty sixth with 39. It was Bobby Johns' best season as he hung his hat at the Sun 'n Sand Motel on I-85 and Highway 221 in Spartanburg for the Cotton Owens months of his career. Johns, White, Baker, and Petty never did as well in the standings again as they did in 1960. Tragedy and all, it was a great year for Spartanburg racing and the Fairgrounds.

Saturday afternoon, March 4, 1961, the Fairgrounds held the first race after the Daytona 500. Only 18 entries lined up as three giants declined to race in their hometown. Weatherly's Bud Moore Pontiac that ran second to Panch at Daytona failed to show. Bud was not running for the title in his first year as a car owner and kept it in its St. Johns Street shop. Jack Smith was sixth at Daytona in his Pontiac and stayed in his Reidville Road garage. And on the morning of the race, Buck Baker, ninth at Daytona, told promoter Joe Littlejohn that he did not have the time to get the powerful 1961 Chrysler 87 ready and it stayed in its second floor Broad Street home with Buddy's 86. It was the first race there Buck missed since the big time came in '53. Buck's old '60 Chevy was parked in there, too, with a "For Sale" sign on it. Other locals Elmo Henderson, 23rd at Daytona, Joe Eubanks, and G.C. Spencer stayed off the Piedmont clay that day, too. That is seven Spartanburg racecars not running at home.

Recovering at Halifax Hospital from a death-defying sub-orbital flight at Daytona was Lee Petty. He had not missed a race in ages until the Daytona 500, and now his season was over and the masses felt his absence. It made Richard the sentimental favorite everywhere. He even had to bring a 1960 Plymouth because both '61s were used up at Daytona. A couple of "new" old cars were on hand as Cotton had just finished rebuilding the '60 Pontiac torched on lap six of the first World 600 nine months earlier. He got to the track ten minutes before practice ended, getting only two laps on the clay before time trials. The other "new" old car was a '60 Chevy 67 for Pearson, also completed race morning. Pearson was about 90 days from super-stardom. Another interesting racer was the 1960 Holly Farms Pontiac that Junior Johnson brought. He had to use it and led the 500 in it for seven laps until blowing. Junior came from 43rd to first in 34 laps. No wonder it blew! He destroyed his new Pontiac in the crash that sent Richard Petty over the rail in the first Daytona qualifier. The kicker is that Johnson bought old Pony from Owens, the same car Cotton dominated in here last August.

However, the most important pre-race story of all got no ink and involved that old used up '60 Chevy of Buck's. A veteran Virginia short-tracker needed a car to get started in Grand National racing and Baker's old Impala was perfect. The man did not have a lot of money to spend, but he made up for that on the track with mountains of guts and skill gained as a driver and mechanic transporting moonshine around the Blue Ridge Mountains after his hitch in the Army. He was 39 years old. He was black. He was Wendell Oliver Scott of Danville, VA, and he ran his first big-time race at The Fairgrounds on March 4, 1961. He did not have time to paint Buck's old car or even change the number. Some thought it was Buck Baker out there that day.

Jarrett won the pole in the red '60 Ford he and Jimmy Massey shared for the win last May. Junior had his "used" Pontiac outside. Petty and Owens made up row two, White and Pearson the third, Crider and Harb in row four, and Wendell Scott and Ernie Gahan took the fifth. The green fell and Johnson roared away literally in a cloud of dust. It seems NASCAR told Mr. Littlejohn to stop with the water truck already and he did so against his own better judgment. The result was the dustiest Fairgrounds 100-miler ever! Harb, driving a dent-covered white 1959 Ford 17, overheated for last. First-timer Scott made it just past the quarter mark before overheating and settling for 17th. By the time he made his next start a month later in Hillsborough, Wendell had that Chevy painted red with white 34s on the panels. Jarrett lost oil pressure for 16th and a young Hoosier placing 15th at Daytona had an engine fire in turn one for a caution. That rookie was Charlie Glotzbach, finishing 15th again. Irwin dropped out for 13th and Crawfish took 12th. Sailing along with 18 to go, Johnson's gas line broke and the streaking Pontiac was through, finishing tenth. Petty had a long pit stop and spun trying to catch up with 30 laps to go. Harry Leake looped his Chevy in turn three for a late yellow and got ninth. Herman the Turtle was 13 laps behind for eighth and Rex White had a disappointing day in seventh, a lap ahead of Herman. Pardue and Gahan rattled around the fourth turn fighting for third with two remaining, but still managed fourth and sixth. Doug Yates copped fifth in a two-year-old Plymouth and Pearson was third, the highest he would ever finish at home. With the wrong gear that had him pegging the tach coming off the corners, Owens sped to his second straight Fairgrounds win by a lap over Richard. As Del Shannon's number-one hit of the day noted, Owens' victory that dusty day was a "Runaway."

Friday night, June 2, 1961, could not have been more joyous at Joe Littlejohn's Piedmont Interstate Fairgrounds. Only five days earlier, Whitney Mills' pride and joy, David Gene Pearson, completed as unlikely a climb to the top as was imaginable. He won the World 600 in Ray Fox's Pontiac 3 over Fireball, limping the last lap a la Buck Baker on a tireless rim, showering sparks under the checkers. It was Littlejohn's recommendation that got Pearson the hot ride, the shocking win, and the homecoming of a lifetime. At the very least, Pearson's days at John Sewell Heating and Roofing were over. He climbed off that ladder and onto another where he stood on the top rung. So what could David do for an encore but take his own light-blue Chevy 67 and smoke 'em at the Fairgrounds, right? Hardly! There was a real good field of 21 waiting that perfect late spring evening on the clay and none of the locals kept their machines in their garages this time. Pearson's win and the hoopla surrounding it energized the whole town. The pole-winner was the story of the last three races. Although he did not win them all, Cotton Owens had a white '60 Pontiac 5 always at or near the front with two wins and a third. This day, Weatherly won the pole in Bud Moore's '61 Pontiac with Cotton outside. Third was Buck in Buddy's '61 Chrysler 86 and alongside him was Jack Smith's '61 Pontiac 47. Notables further back were Jarrett fifth, Johnson sixth, White seventh, Richard eighth, Dieringer tenth, Paschal 11th, Pardue 12th, hometowners Spencer 13th and Elmo Henderson's T-Bird 14th, Charleston's Crawfish 15th, Man of the Hour Pearson 17th, Maurice Petty 19th, and the Turtle last. Great hometown grid, with all Spartanburg cars and three drivers in the first two rows and four more further back, including the Grand National champion.

The field took off under the lights, kicking up that boiling red dust as Weatherly and

The long backstetch under a string of yellow light bulbs that flashed on often.

Petty fought it out for first, banging fenders and knifing through traffic. Dieringer only made it a lap, Johnson a dozen more, and Crawfish boiled over, too. Then Pearson overheated and parked, after which he removed his cape and tights. Entering turn three on lap 70, Joe and Richard bumped one too many times and crashed hard enough to DNF. Elmo Henderson edged his white '59 T-Bird 55 over the rail and into the bushes and darkness between turns three and four 14 laps later for 12th and an impromptu safari. Cotton was out front, in control, and seemingly unstoppable. Buck lost a rear end just past halfway for 11th, and in four laps, White's suspension snapped, giving the champion tenth. With 20 to go, a wheel broke on the big Bonneville and Cotton wobbled to the pits for a quick replacement, but it was too late. For the first time since July 12, 1958, at Asheville's McCormick Field, Jim Paschal of High Point hustled home by two laps over the disappointed Owens. Third for a career-best finish was Maurice Petty in Lee's old Plymouth, three behind. Showing again that he was a lot better than people thought, Herman Beam brought in his spotless '60 Ford 19 unscratched fourth only 12 laps down, and look whom he beat. Fifth was Jarrett, sixth Pardue, seventh Harb, eighth Spencer, and Jack Smith ninth. It took only an hour and 48 minutes for the festive Friday night crowd of 6,000 to see an exciting, action-packed 100-miler.

Saturday night, May 19, 1962, the Fairgrounds 100-miler was the only race held between Nelson Stacy victories in the Rebel 300 on May 12th, NASCAR's final convertible race, and the World 600 on May 27th. It seems that would have attracted more than 15 entries, but it did not. Seven of those 15 had a legitimate shot to win and the locals had some absentees again. Cotton brought a 1961 Pontiac for a change and this one was number 6. He broke the track record in time trials at 64.423 with Jarrett outside in a '62 Chevy. A very famous car was surprisingly entered that night as the year-old Ray Fox Pontiac 3 of David Pearson that had been "The Giant Killer" the year before, winning the World 600, Firecracker 250, and Dixie 400, qualified third. Smith was outside in his Pontiac and fifth was Weatherly in Bud Moore's year-old Pontiac 8 that was set up especially for dirt tracks and appropriately called "The Dirt Dauber." It was a great car and had everything to do with Joe winning the 1962 Grand National Championship. Outside Joe was winner of the last race here, Jim Paschal, in a Pontiac. Row four found Petty still hustling a high-finned '60 Plymouth for the fifth straight here, and Charleston's Curtis "Crawfish" Crider in a new red Mercury 62. The meager pack roared away and with Cotton leading for 20 laps until the engine blew. Jarrett took over and on lap 30, Pearson's Pontiac blew, too. Paschal and Petty chased Ned's Chevy all night and kept it close, completing all 200 laps, but could not catch him. Spencer was fourth, Weatherly fifth, Tom Cox sixth, Smith seventh, consistent Herman Beam in his dent-free '60 Ford eighth, Sgt. George Green ninth, and Crawfish tenth. There were no cautions and Ned covered the ground in just under 100 minutes for a record average of 60.080. Jarrett's win shared the sports pages Sunday morning with Greek Money winning the Preakness and Stan the Man breaking Honus Wagner's National League base hit record of 3,431.

The return for '62 was on Tuesday night, August 21st. One cannot expect much of a crowd on that oddest of race nights. The last five races had been won by either Petty or Paschal in a Plymouth and 14 other cars came to Spartanburg to put a stop to it. The news leading up to this was that a California hot shot named Dick Getty was coming to town and the race was actually going to be for second. One way or the other, a Petty or a Getty was going to win. Of the 16 entries, maybe six had a chance at victory. Richard took the pole without a '60 Plymouth to do it. However, Cotton did revert to his trusty, obsolete, 1960 Pontiac and stuck it outside of row one with a special deal. Since the car would not be eligible for the Grand National tour much longer, Owens put it up for sale before the race for $1,000, would drive it for the new owner, and split the winnings 50/50. He got no takers. Jarrett put his B.G. Holloway Chevy 11 third with Spencer outside in fourth. Potent Spartanburg Pontiacs of Weatherly and Smith made up row three. Qualifying those stockers by power sliding through the first and second turns was a thing of beauty. They came thundering down the homestretch and right before it ended, cut the power and cocked the car left, setting the rear end out toward the boards. Dead silence for just a beat. Then accelerator to the floor while turning back hard right, wide open through one and two, and down the backstretch with the engine roaring, car drifting around searching for grip and firing dust from the screaming rear tires. G.C. Spencer was different. After that beat of dead silence, he would feather the throttle, a BRAAM ... BRAAM ... BRAAM style that let you know who it was. You could pick Spencer out with your eyes closed. Spencer was much underrated and real good! He had some good rides and definitely should have won some races.

As in the past, Weatherly and Petty duked it out at the front in an electrifying display the entire race. Dick Getty was a Californian colossal flop as his '62 Chevy 00 broke after nine miles for 16th and last place. He started last, finished last, and double zeroes were the perfect digits for him. Crawfish made it past halfway before his Mercury lost a rear end for 14th. Spencer's Inman neighbor Tommy Irwin was putting on a spectacular show in Mel Bradley's red '62 Chevy 27 giving the leaders all they could handle. Then, with everybody in the house watching, Tommy got into that big wooden fence in turn one and wound up on the dirt bank where the fence ended. He was done for the night, finishing 13th. Wendell

Scott had demolished his number 34 at Nashville 16 days earlier and was driving his old '60 Chevy again, now 89, and wound up 11th after clutch failure. Jarrett was fighting for the win when he got crossed up in front of the grandstand and stuffed his Impala into two telephone poles about four feet high that protected the Pagoda. Ned got tenth. Making it six straight races in his light-blue 1960 Ford 19, Herman took eighth for an average finish of 8.67 and did not touch another car or obstacle of any kind in all those races. Never a scratch! Newcomer Larry Thomas was sixth and Spencer drove Floyd Powell's '60 Chevy to fifth. One hour and 40 minutes after the start, Richard Petty won his third and the team's sixth in a row, beating Weatherly by half a lap. A mile and a half back were Spartans Smith third and Owens fourth. Too bad nobody bought Cotton's car before the race. He would have had to split a hefty $300.

There was an extra air of excitement on the cool clear Saturday morning of March 2, 1963. As in 1961, this was the first race after the Daytona 500 and it always brought more anticipation than usual. The cars had been used only at Daytona and were not yet beat up through miles and miles of racing. One of the most famous racecars of all time was on hand, as Junior Johnson brought the white 1963 Holly Farms Poultry Chevrolet 3 fresh from his shop. It was a spotless white with red lettering, black trim, and a red stripe with gold ones on each side of it running from nose to tail of the Impala. As if not to be outshined, Tommy Irwin, from up Highway 176 in Inman, came to race and he was loaded for bear. Irwin had a sparkling new candy-apple red 1963 Ford Fastback 44 sponsored by Lafayette Ford and backed by the bucks of zillionaire sportsman Briggs Cunningham. Irwin had received everyone's attention during the last race here with the spectacular style in which he was power sliding through the turns and running with the leaders before crashing. Tommy had just finished tenth out of 50 in the 500 and the sky was the limit for this young charger who had matured just enough to be ripe for stardom. Johnson and Irwin were practicing hard that clear, crisp morning when the Reaper took a swing. As the red Ford dove into turn one, its left front fender caught the dirt bank on the inside. Number 44 was thrown sideways and began to roll side over side for what seemed like forever, but was actually only three or four times. Irwin flopped out the driver's window with every roll, coming to rest in the middle of the track, wheels down, facing the infield. The new Galaxie was destroyed with the roof flattened almost to the body. When the rescuers arrived, Tommy was slumped over on the floor shift, not moving at all. They worked on him awhile trying to get him out, and when they did, he was limp, but there was no sign of blood. The white Brewington's Ambulance Service '58 Pontiac raced from the scene with a police escort to Spartanburg General Hospital with sirens howling. Later in the pits, the crumpled Ford gathered grisly gawkers, parked there the whole day. It even appeared on the front page of the *Spartanburg Herald-Journal* sports section Sunday morning.

As expected, Junior put that rocket ship on the pole at a new track record of 64.470 with Richard Petty in a new Plymouth outside. Row two found Daytona 500 hard-luck loser Jarrett in his light blue, red and white-numbered Fastback Ford inside. Bobby Isaac, in his first *Silent Speedways of the Carolinas* start and third overall, was outside in the '62 ex–Petty blue Plymouth Richard used to win here last August, but now sporting 99s for new owner Bondy Long. Fifth was Billy Wade in Cotton's new Dodge 5, and sixth was a surprising red '62 Chevy 33 of Sgt. Roy Mayne, up from his post at Shaw Air Force Base in Sumter. Paschal timed seventh in a '62 Petty Plymouth, with Gary Sain in a year-old Dodge 90 eighth. Row five held Wendell in a blue '61 Chevy, and making his Grand National debut was Johnny Clements of Mebane, NC, in a '61 Chevy 98. Weatherly went shopping for a ride after Bud Moore did not have "vital parts for dirt track racing" available for his Pontiacs. Joe cut a deal with local driver/owner Floyd Powell to drive a '62 Pontiac 70, which he clocked in for 14th. Failing to get to the qualifying line on time was Pearson in Owens' other new Dodge, which started 20th, and Pardue's '62 Pontiac 54 that started 21st. In addition to the 21 starters, there was a great field of drivers hanging out in the pits not participating, such as USAC Stock Car Champ Paul Goldsmith, locals Rex White, Jack Smith, Cotton Owens, Floyd Powell, Joe Eubanks, Elmo Henderson, Southern 500 winner Larry Frank, and Darel Dieringer.

The race started on what became a warm Saturday afternoon with Johnson jumping out front and the rest of the field in tow. Lap three saw Sgt. Mayne ride the top of the turn two rail and disappear into a ditch paralleling part of the backstretch. It took a while for Red Collins' Pierce Motor Company wrecker to extract Mayne's 33 from that gully for last. After Sain and Melton fell out, three crowd favorites parked in the dusty, grassy pit area for the day. Lap 34 was the last for Pearson as he tangled in turn four earlier with the Pontiac 104 of Atlanta rookie Bruce Brantley and hit the dirt bank. Brantley continued and on lap 42, the smoking differential of Junior's front-running Chevy made it really look like a rocket ship and he retired for 17th. Six laps later, Wade was running fourth, but lost the clutch, joining David and Junior. Jarrett held the lead with the Plymouths of Petty and Paschal in hot pursuit until lap 183, when rookie Johnny Clements spun that old Chevy right in the groove where Irwin landed that morning and was T-boned by another rookie, Frank Waites, of Tucker, GA, in an ancient Dodge 65. The leaders bore down on the scene and Jarrett slipped by high, but when Petty tried to follow, he rattled off that infamous board fence, damaging the right front fender and suspension. Clements crawled from his smashed racer, walked to the infield, and collapsed. Leroy Brewington put him in the back of the meat wagon and hauled him to Spartanburg General in shock with back injuries. Jarrett looked to be home free, but Petty pitted as Lee and Maurice hammered out the fender and added ten gallons of Pure Firebird without losing a lap. They restarted and Ned dashed away, but not far. With three to go, the baby-blue 11 sputtered out of gas, just like six days earlier in the 500 when it happened with nine laps left. Ned rolled in, got a splash, and barely nipped Paschal for second, a lap behind. Jarrett said after the race that from now on, anytime he pitted, he was going to get gas. Good idea! Fourth was Weatherly, and Wendell claimed a tough fifth, ten back. Others were Brantley sixth, Pardue eighth, the Turtle ninth in a "new" two-year-old Ford, Crawfish tenth, Isaac 11th, and Stick Elliott 13th.

Tommy Irwin made a name for himself in his brief time on the tour as a competent driver that never made it to the top. His rookie season of 1959 was his best with ten top fives including second at Columbia, third at Myrtle Beach, and fifth in the Southern 500. That year, Tommy Irwin beat Richard Petty handily in almost every single category, driving his own independent T-Bird against Petty Engineering's big bucks. Yet, Petty won Rookie of the Year honors in what should have been a rout for Irwin! Both actually started in 1958 and Tommy licked him then, too. Irwin got a lot of ink for crashing in the 1960 Daytona 500 and swimming to safety after making Lake Lloyd his own private T-Birdbath. In 1961 and '62, he plugged away, gaining experience and respect, until it looked like his ship had finally come in with the Cunningham deal for 1963. But it was never the same after March 2nd. The Grim Reaper just missed that day and Tommy Irwin did not die in that crash. However, he broke his left hand and left shoulder, and damaged his left eye. He came back on July 13, 1963, at Bowman-Gray Stadium in Winston-Salem in the same race as Lee Petty's return. Guess who got all the press that day. Irwin finished 16th, then took tenth at Bristol in Cunningham's 44 on July 28th in the race remembered for Fireball Roberts flipping. Finally on August 11, 1963, Irwin started third at Asheville-Weaverville and dropped out due

A single ribbon of steel held the thundering stockers in turn three, usually.

to a vibration for 19th. The next race was at Spartanburg on the 14th, but Tommy did not go and never raced in the big time again. Tommy Irwin had a load of talent, matched by a larger load of bad luck.

The Fairgrounds' second race of 1963 was on the sticky Wednesday night of August 14th. About 7,000 fans came, along with 17 race teams. It cannot be said that Cotton did not do his part, bringing three, count 'em, three Dodges the few blocks from his shop. One of them was an aircraft-carrier-sized 440 he drove, number 16. Owens had not driven in 51 weeks since finishing fourth here last August 21st. He also had Pearson in 6 and Wade in 5. The pole went to Weatherly in Moore's '63 Pontiac, breaking Junior Johnson's track record of March. Outside row one was Jarrett, back in a baby-blue Fastback. Rows two through five paired Petty and Pearson, Pardue and Isaac, Wade and Yarborough, and Spencer and Owens. Also on hand was Buck Baker for the first time since June of 1961 in his new Pontiac, along with Crawfish and Wendell. Weatherly was chasing his second straight championship and led the first 33 laps, but the engine dumped on the red and black 8. Ten laps later, an oil line broke on Pearson's Polara and he was done. On lap 65, Scott tried to dodge Castles' sliding ex–Buck Baker Chrysler and used that battered board fence in turn one like one of those motorcycle thrill shows at the fair. Wendell got the blue and white '62 Chevy 34 completely off the ground, rode in the air on that fence for 20 feet or so, then came crashing down on its side where it ended. He landed on his roof, wheels still spinning, and scrambled out to the wild cheers of the crowd. Wendell was a big favorite at the Fairgrounds. Isaac, this trip in a black Bowani '63 Ford with yellow 99s, retired, followed shortly by Sgt.

Mayne, Crider, Pardue, and Stick Elliott. Right at the beginning of the grandstand on lap 152, Bobby Keck somehow managed to get his purple Pete Stewart '63 Ford 57 impaled on a fence post, which left the nose buried and the rear end at two o'clock. It was quite a sight. With the race winding down, that enormous Dodge 440 of Cotton's crashed between the first and second turns, executing vicious side-over-side flips with glass flying everywhere. The car came to a stop rubber-side down with Cotton nowhere to be seen until he rose from the floor and climbed out. He appeared to be bleeding from every pore in his body, but it was equal parts Carolina dust and sweat ... lots of both! He was unhurt, but that Dodge was demolished. Ned passed Buck's white 87 with a handful of laps to go to take the win. Petty also slipped by Baker on the last lap for second. Buck was third, Wade fourth, Yarborough fifth, Castles sixth, Spencer seventh, and Cotton missed the last 30 laps, finishing eighth. It was a most memorable Grand National, even if it was on a Wednesday night, proving the old oval was still alive and well.

The schedule makers were just as mad in 1964 as they ever were. What is worse: four races in six days or five races in nine days? It was 100 miles in Asheville-Weaverville on Saturday afternoon, April 11th, 150 miles at Hillsborough the next afternoon, 100 miles in Spartanburg Tuesday night, 100 miles in Columbia on Thursday night, and 250 miles at North Wilkesboro on Sunday afternoon. Therefore, the Fairgrounds got the middle of the five, the worst date, and drew the smallest field. A crowd of 6,500 came out on a warm school night. There were two gates into the track area and across to the infield. One was the east gate near turn two, beside the old horse stables left over from the days when the track saw hay-burning horsepower. The other was the west gate at the beginning of that oft-battered first turn fence at the end of the front stretch. The arriving racers usually came in that gate because it led directly to the pits. The traffic pattern caused them to pass the east gate first en route to the first turn and the west gate. As the haulers, or trailers as most teams used, came onto the grounds off Bishop Street, they would go by the east gate and, if it was opened, the fans might get a glimpse of who it was. If practice was underway and that gate was closed, they might just be able to see enough to tell that there was a racecar out there by seeing only the very tiptop of the car over the fence. Or maybe looking out between the cracks in the boards of the fence. Then the racer would come in through the west gate and sometimes it would be Tommy Irwin, Ned Jarrett, or a couple of Petty cars. Sometimes it would be a racecar not recognizable, with the name of a driver unknown painted on the door or roof. Somebody like Bobby Keck, Gene Hobby, or Danny Byrd would arrive. Without fail, the greatest cheer heard was when Wendell Scott pulled through a gate because everybody loved him and his 34. The race at Asheville-Weaverville on Saturday saw Panch beat Johnson and Wade by a lap. Sunday at Hillsborough was Pearson by three over Hutcherson. Then Tuesday was Spartanburg's turn. The field of 19 was not without surprises. Popping in with the Wood Brothers' Ford was Marvin Panch, winner here back in April of '57. Hutcherson, the IMCA star from Keokuk, made his first start at Greenville on March 28th, won the pole, then broke his lugs and DNF'd. Hillsborough was next and he was second. The Fairgrounds was his third start and he made it count! Not only did he capture the pole, he obliterated the track record with a run of 69.044, four and a half miles an hour faster than Weatherly the previous August! Who would have thought that by the time the big boys came back, Joe would have already been dead for three months. Dick's car was a yellow Holman-Moody '64 Ford with red and black 1s on it. Since Wade and Moore had priority on that number, Dick's guys took some red tape and made the 1s into 7s. They would worry about Bobby Johns' priority later. Speaking of Wade, he had Bud's big black and red Marauder outside Hutch on the front row. Row two was Petty and

Jarrett. Three had Panch and Pearson. The fourth found Pardue and Fairgrounds first-timer LeeRoy Yarbrough. Jimmy Pardue's Burton-Robinson Racing Team red Fury was being unloaded from its hauler as the crew carefully rolled it down two very stout boards. When Car 54 got almost to the bottom, it slipped off the side, slinging the boards every which way. That car bounced and bounced. And bounced! And bounced! It would not stop resembling a raging bull spinning and bolting. When it finally tired, the crew snuck up behind it, got a firm hold, and eased it over to a spot on the grass. And row five paired Ken Rush and Spartanburg's Elmo Henderson. Also in the field was Buddy Baker, Castles, Scott, Stick Elliott, Crawfish as always, and Ralph Earnhardt in Tom Spell's surprising '63 Ford 31 that finished fourth at Hillsborough. The green fell and Hutcherson took off with Wade right behind him. After nine laps, Elliott retired for last, and a lap later the caution flew for Crawfish Crider's team cars. The white and gold '63 Mercury 01 of Bob Cooper sat in turn four with the rubber-side down, right beside the other white and gold '63 Mercury 02 of Crawfish, which had its rubber pointing up. Green again and Wade caught Hutcherson setting sail with the lead on lap 16. Eight later Earnhardt's motor cooked for 16th, Petty's rear end burned out for 15th, and LeeRoy's yellow '63 Plymouth 45 parked with a bad ignition for 14th. That car always had a red light burning on the dash and the radio commentators mentioned it every week as if they had never seen it before. Then on the 121st round, pole-sitter Hutcherson fried a wheel bearing for 13th. The axle snapped on Pardue's Plymouth, probably a result of bouncing around the pits before the race, for 12th. A big hole developed right in the middle of the track under a string of caution lights at the end of the backstretch, and Billy Wade would run right through it lap after lap. He had a healthy lead and could have avoided the crater easily, but never missed it. That is until he lost the lead on lap 162 to Jarrett as rear end trouble developed. Then with 15 left, Wade's Mercury gave up with a bent rear end housing and Jarrett romped home with only Panch in the lead lap. Third was Pearson three back, tying his best hometown finish, Rush was fourth, and Henderson had a good run in a two-year-old Pontiac fifth. Wade salvaged sixth, Castles in Buck's '62 Chrysler seventh, Buddy eighth, Scott ninth, and Trivette tenth.

The next one was held on Friday night, June 26, 1964, and fell into a twilight span of 39 days between the horrific crash on May 24th that had Fireball Roberts' life oozing away in a Charlotte hospital bed and his last breath on July 2nd. Nine races were held in those 39 days and Spartanburg had the ninth. The morning of the race, the *Spartanburg Herald* sports page had a caricature of Buck Baker labeled "The Old Pro" and told about his heroics. Buck was driving Ray Fox's Dodge 3 in which he had won three nights earlier at Valdosta and would win his third Southern 500, his 46th and final Grand National win ever, on September 7, 1964. Others racing that Friday night were Petty, Pearson, Henderson, Scott, Yarbrough, Yarborough, Buddy Baker, Crider, Putney, and the soon-to-be stars of the show, Billy Wade and Ned Jarrett. It was a picture-perfect, hot summer night with what turned out to be three of the top five winningest stock car drivers of all time in the field. (If Cale Yarborough had won one more career victory, it would have been the top three.) The pole went to the Spartanburg Dodge team of Pearson and Owens with Petty outside. The most victorious stock car drivers of all time sat on the front row. Paired behind them were Wade and Jarrett, Buck and LeeRoy having already won twice since May Day, and Doug Cooper and Cale Yarborough in Herman's 19 gold and white 1964 Ford. Thirteen others qualified to make a trim field of 21, and what a show they were going to put on.

It started innocently. David Pearson set a torrid pace. Rodney Bottinger in one of Crawfish's two '63 Mercurys lasted a lap, as did Jimmy Helms in Buck's '62 Chrysler. Henderson went ten laps before he blew and Worth McMillion made 27 laps and parked. The first contender to go was Buck, who was running fourth at 67 laps when he lost his brakes, finishing 17th in his last drive at the Fairgrounds, where he never won. Five laps later, Pearson snapped the axle for 16th and the Dodge Boys were gone. Promising Larry Thomas lost oil pressure on lap 87 and just past halfway, Buddy Arrington lost his rear end. At this caution-free point, Petty was leading Jarrett, Wade, and Yarbrough with Cale one back in fifth. On lap 115, Petty pitted for some Pure, lost a lap, and the others moved up one. There the routine 100-miler ended. On lap 127, Buddy Baker in an orange '63 Dodge 87 was four laps back in eighth and came upon Putney's blue '62 Chevy 46. Buddy caught him in the right rear as they powered through turn two, they slid backwards into the steel rail, and performed simultaneous acrobatic barrel rolls, landing wheels down. During this first caution, Jarrett pitted and Wade led a lap. Then Wade and Yarbrough stopped, falling to second and third with Jarrett in front again. That got Petty back on the lead lap in fourth, but almost a lap down right behind the pace car just ahead of Jarrett, Wade, and Yarbrough. The stage was set for the Fairgrounds' greatest and most enduring finish that the witnesses will never forget. Seventy of the most exciting, frantic laps imaginable were run with caution absolutely thrown to the wind. On the restart, Wade went after Jarrett with all he had as 6,000 spectators went wild. Billy was flailing away with that big Marauder at Jarrett's back chrome every chance he got. Wade would go high, Jarrett went higher. Billy went low, Ned chopped him lower. Lap after lap in all four turns and down each straight, it was back and forth using every inch of Spartanburg County clay. Wade never relented as he bobbed and weaved and pounded on Ned, but Jarrett held on. All the while, Richard and LeeRoy were closing ground. This continued for 25 laps until Wade went into turn three

Billy Wade removes his helmet and surveys the damage to his car after racing hard with Ned Jarrett in the June 26, 1964 race.

Ned Jarrett tries to get his 1964 Courtesy Ford started after Billy Wade took him out on June 26, 1964.

side-by-side with Ned, but bounced hard off the fourth turn steel after getting into the loose stuff in a failed outside pass. There was no smoke, no loss of speed, and no relenting. Billy gave it another banzai charge, and on lap 164 down the home chute, the big red and black 1 edged past the blue and white 11 and into the lead. The tables were turned and Ned gave it all back to Billy in spades. Darting and dashing, bumping and ramming, fainting and diving, Jarrett used it all. This was almost 50 laps of the absolute toughest, grittiest, dirt-slinging, metal-bashing stock car racing ever seen in Spartanburg before or since. Then it got serious! On lap 175, Jarrett dogged Wade out of turn four and popped him real hard, and all that red dust boiled up as Billy's Merc did a 360 ... and stalled. Caution number two flew as Wade got it rolling again and pitted since he landed right at its entrance. Then was uttered a line that was quoted in the *Spartanburg Herald* the next morning. Billy Wade vowed, "I'll get him if I have to wait on him!" It was probably first said after the first racer was ever spun out. Bud gave Billy the green light to destroy a couple of top-flight Grand National racecars with no regard for safety, Fireball Roberts notwithstanding. Nobody was going to get hurt and Jarrett was not going to win the race if it was up to Billy Wade. And it was! The green waved again over Jarrett with Petty second, Yarbrough third, and Wade fourth, two laps behind. Billy probably broke the track record catching Ned in traffic, no less. With 15 laps left, those two streaking stockers ripped down the main straightaway with only mere glimpses of them flashing between cars and trucks and the people standing on top, all in a horizontal ribbon of brilliant color against a backdrop of pure black. Since they were out front, Jarrett and Wade roared alone out of turn four, down the stretch, and readied to cut the throttles as they set up for the first turn. Only Billy never cut the throttle. As Ned cut and cocked his Ford into the turn, Wade blasted him. To this day, Texan Billy Wade still has his right boot buried in the gas. With 6,000 crazed spectators looking right at it, the middle of the Mercury's bumper met the Ford's left rear quarter way past the shut-off point. Wade kept going straight and was slowed only slightly by the blue Ford. Jarrett's racer lifted on the left rear, flipped a couple of times, glanced off that battered wooden fence, and landed glass up facing downwind on the side of the embankment at the end of the fence in turn one. The car was badly bent up and Ned was trying to get it going because a huge shower of sparks and smoke was pouring from beneath the Courtesy Ford as he revved the engine. Ned Jarrett wanted to race! As for Wade, he had enough speed left to pulverize that sorry plank fence and it is a wonder he was not launched into one of the parking lots across Bishop Street. Nevertheless, Wade stayed in the track, although he did a couple of rollovers himself, and parked with the tail of the Marauder up on the grassy infield berm. The infield fans rushed the scene screaming for Wade to climb back in, so he turned around and

Infield fans push off the battered racer of hometowners Billy Wade and Bud Moore during the June 26, 1964, race.

remounted the battered racer. The mob stormed the hometown Mercury to push it onto the clay. After Trivette, Yarbrough, and Scott passed, Billy Wade amazingly got the rolling wreck moving again. Most believably, though, he made it back to the pit area and retired for good. Ned gave up and trudged back to the pits on foot with an escort, smiling, covered with sweat and red dust. While those two were crashing the boards with splinters and dust flying, Petty drove under Wade's car as it was in mid-air. Yarbrough rode that wooden fence and dirt bank thrill-show style nearly on two wheels and chased Petty down the backstretch. Caution number three flew, but a showdown was not to be. Yarbrough had to pit and lost a half mile because his miraculous avoidance of the crash damaged something requiring a lap of attention. The last ten were raced in stunned silence and Petty cruised under the checkers by a half mile over Yarbrough in a Plymouth one-two sweep. Doug Cooper was third, crowd-pleasing Wendell Scott fourth, and Ned actually took fifth. Wade finished sixth, Cale faded to seventh, Gene Hobby eighth, Crawfish ninth, Trivette tenth, and the second ancient Buck Baker '62 Chrysler had Neil Castles aboard 11th. That night it was the Piedmont Interstate Battleground and for winner Richard Petty it was, as in the Beatles' number one song, "A Hard Day's Night."

That 100-miler was the last Grand National run while Fireball Roberts was alive. Popular word was that he was all through driving, but would survive. Thirty-nine days after his crash and six days after this Fairgrounds race, Fireball mercifully slipped away in Charlotte Memorial Hospital on July 2nd.

There was a four-way match race held at the Fairgrounds later in 1964 that is notable as Joe Littlejohn tried to catch lighting in a bottle again. As a preliminary to a major 100-mile sportsman race, Billy Wade, Ned Jarrett, Richard Petty, and David Pearson went head-

Cale Yarborough and Richard Petty wash under a spigot after 100 Spartanburg miles, June 26, 1964.

to-head-to-head-to-head for a 25-lap winner-take-all grudge match race. The announcer barked, "The winner gets a thousand dollars and the others go home kicking rocks!" Billy blew Bud's Marauder in practice, so they loaded it up and left. However, less than an hour later, back in they came, unloaded, and won the sprint from last place in a rout. Petty crashed just bad enough to retire and Jarrett easily beat Pearson for second. The race was a dud. Bud Moore swore that they swapped engines, not cars, when they left before the match. Bud never entered a car at the Fairgrounds again. The Pettys had a car qualify once, but it did not race. Buck Baker entered a heap once, but not with him at the wheel.

Saturday morning, February 27, 1965, the Grand Nationals returned for the first race after the Daytona 500. The Chrysler hemi ban meant no Pearson and Petty racing, but Richard was there on the eve of the second deadly tragedy to visit racing's first family. Bobby Myers' fatal crash in a Petty Olds during the '57 Southern 500 was the original. Petty was very outgoing that day, walking around, shaking hands, signing autographs, and sowing the seeds that made him The King. A bigger field was expected than the 16 teams that showed up. Considering the hemi ban and the infamous Rod Eulenfeld–triggered 13-car crash in the second Daytona qualifier, the slim field was predictable. However, there were some interesting entries. Berry Brooks ran a '64 Pontiac two laps for 16th and last in the third of four career starts. The next day, Brooks demolished the Bob Cooper Bonneville at Weaverville and retired. Two, maybe three, records

The author at 12 years old gets winner Petty's autograph; The King always had the time.

Junior Johnson warms up past the old horse stables in Turn Two on February 27, 1965.

were set that day. First, Hutcherson in a new Holman-Moody Ford rewrote his old track record by better than half a second, turning the first lap at the Fairgrounds at over 70 miles per hour. Sharing the front row with the Keokuk Comet was Junior Johnson in that powerful yellow Holly Farms '65 Ford 26. Paired behind them were Lund and Spencer, Jarrett and Moore, then Setzer and Scott rounded out the top eight. The first two laps were as good as it gets, with Hutcherson and Johnson glued side-by-side, banging sheet metal and slinging rooster tails of red Spartanburg dust against a cloudless Carolina blue sky. Junior paced the first two laps, then slipped high in turn four, but saved it, losing four positions. Driving like the Ronda Roadrunner, Junior charged back strong until the 427 overheated and he parked it at the one-quarter mark for 11th. He was beat to the sidelines by five others including Dieringer and Yarborough. Hutcherson sailed along for 110 laps, steadily widening his lead after staving off a serious challenge from Lund earlier. Tiny faded to ninth, the last man standing only 57 laps behind, and Paul Moore blew for tenth just after halfway. As the race sped to a quick conclusion, Ford 29 started trailing smoke and on lap 160, Hutch was done for fifth place. Because there were no cautions, the field never bunched up and Jarrett found himself with a 22-lap lead. Promoter Littlejohn allegedly was scared to death that Jarrett would fall out and the race would have to be extended another 20 laps

Dick Hutcherson's #29 still holds the track record of 70.644 mph. Long gone is the pagoda-style officials' and flagman's stand beside the multi-directional loudspeakers seen here on February 27, 1965.

Popular veteran Tiny Lund poses with Sam Forry under the adoring gazes of others, February 27, 1965.

or so. That did not happen and Ned won, setting the second record of the day: one hour 30 minutes and 26 seconds, for an average speed of 66.367 miles per hour. Winning by 22 laps was quite a feat and Ned did it again at Shelby on May 27th. Second was Spencer, the only Spartanburg County driver or car in the race, winning a torrid battle with third placer Bob Derrington, who came all the way from Houston and last starting spot. Fourth was Hobby, sixth came Setzer in a new Chevy, Doug Cooper claimed seventh, Wendell overheated and finished where he started in eighth. It was Jarrett's fifth Spartanburg win in five years.

The next day, Sunday, February 28, 1965, the Grand Nationals went to Asheville-Weaverville for another 100-miler. Richard, Lee, and Maurice Petty headed to the Southeastern International Dragway in Dallas, GA, to race a 1965 Plymouth Barracuda named 43 Jr. Outlawed. After a trial run, he lined up against Arnie Beswick and stalled at the line at the green. Beswick roared to the win, but Richard wanted to give the 10,000 fans what they came to see. He got away, then at mid-course, started swerving from lane to lane. Onlookers said a wheel came off and went high into the crowd. Petty's blue dragster darted toward the dirt embankment from which the spectators viewed the action, since there were no grandstands. The car hit the bank, flew high into the air over a wire fence, and came down nose first in the middle of the crowd. Petty was thrown from the Barracuda as thousands screamed, running in horror. An eight-year-old boy, Wayne Dye, was killed. Six others were injured and transported to area hospitals. Petty was treated for shock and left drag racing. It was Petty Tragedy II, with more to come.

In 1965, NASCAR still scheduled races on three consecutive nights. With the Interstate Highway System well underway, this schedule was not as bad as it used to be, but it was still pretty rough. The Fairgrounds played host to the middle of three that long, hot summer after a Friday night 100-miler in Maryville, TN, won by Hutcherson. Saturday night, August 14th, was the penultimate trip to Spartanburg and had real fan appeal. Curtis Turner was reinstated into the bosom of the NASCAR family on July 31st, but had been blown off by Ford, who thought him washed up at the ripe old age of 41. Even if he was not the Blond Blizzard anymore, he could still draw a crowd and inject great enthusiasm into a dismal 1965 that saw Ford dominate everywhere before meager crowds. As a matter of fact, that is why Bill France invited his return. Chrysler's hemi was allowed back in NASCAR on June 21st, but only in certain models on certain tracks. Ford had won all 34 races, including a Bud Moore Mercury win, until July 31st when Petty won at Nashville. Then he got another at Asheville-Weaverville and set the stage for Chrysler, Ford, and Turner to all converge in Spartanburg on Saturday night. It was hot, it was clear, and the fans were there.

It was twilight in Spartanburg's and in Curtis Turner's careers. Promoter Supreme Joe Littlejohn wanted Turner in a first-class ride for the comeback. So Joe got Curtis in the seat of Richard Petty's 1964 Plymouth Fury 43. Since Petty had already missed more than half the season anyway, he decided to sit this one out for the sake of Turner's return. In the dusty dusk of that sultry Saturday evening, Curtis Turner warmed up for 15 or 20 laps in one of the most electrifying displays of speed and control ever seen on dirt, or maybe anywhere for that matter. That Petty-blue Petty Plymouth thundered down the front stretch, clawing the track as Turner cocked the car for the first turn. When he came through, the nose of that Plymouth was all that was visible from the infield. With that hemi howling, Curtis' big bare hands gripped the wheel fully at right lock. Only when he went into turn two, the cockpit of Turner's 43 revealed his mighty left arm cranked as far to his right as it could go. With thick red plumes of dust billowing from the right-side tires, he swung wide and tore down the back chute, choreographing it the same way in three and four. If there were any other cars on the track, nobody noticed. Possibly, there were no others out there because their chauffeurs were lined up on the rails watching to see how the master did it. The jam-packed house roared its approval with every lap. Turner seemed to be making up for lost time, using as much skill and courage as he could muster. It was spine-tingling, heart-pounding, and breathtaking all at once, and was a stand-alone show without the 100-miler. The Dirtmeister was back! Factory Ford had five-time Fairgrounds winner Jarrett and track record holder Hutcherson with strong South Carolina independents Tiny Lund from Cross, G.C. Spencer from Inman, Cale Yarborough of Timmonsville, and LeeRoy Yarbrough of Columbia in their familiar old Fords. Elmo Langley and Wendell Scott had old Fords, too. Chrysler had hometowner David Pearson in his Cotton Owens Dodge and Turner driving for Petty. Notables scattered through the pits in non-competitive mounts were Dieringer, Putney, and Arrington. Twenty-four cars were set for time trials, the same number as in Maryville the night before. Notably absent were Buck Baker's three cars: his Chevy, Buddy's

Dodge, and Neil Castles' Olds that raced 24 hours earlier. They skipped the Fairgrounds and went on to Augusta. Buck and Curtis would have been amazing to see. Time trials got under way beneath the lights in what was now a hot, sticky summer dusk. Hutcherson was making his third start here and had a good speed, although far off his February record. Pearson had timed in for second spot when Curtis Turner pulled onto the clay. The stands roared, and for the first time since the World 600 on May 28, 1961, Curtis Turner took the track to compete in a NASCAR event, albeit time trials, not a race. With the same flair he had shown in the gloaming, Turner ripped through his warm-up and set what looked like an excellent first-lap time. Before the p.a. announcer could broadcast the speed, Curtis flew into the first turn determined to improve on his previous clocking and backed hard into the old wooden fence that had been pounded on for years, with the Fury's right rear spinning back around facing the wrong way. It did not look nearly as bad as it was. Curtis fired it up and limped directly back to the crew by going the wrong way down the slope to enter the pit exit as if he had driven in the west gate. It was announced that his first lap was good enough for third on the grid, and all were sure Maurice would beat out the fender and bumper and Turner would assume his spot on the inside of row two. To everyone's horror, Fury 43 was pushed onto its trailer for the trip back to Randleman. Major disappointment does not begin to describe what was felt by the 8,000 witnesses. A collective moan went up from the stands and infield after time trials when that wooden gate swung open right where Turner landed in turn one. The blue and silver half-ton with "Plymouth" painted in big blue letters on the side, pulling 43, rumbled, rattled, and squeaked up the slope of the bank, over the rim, and into the darkness. Lee Petty won the first Grand National there in 1953 and two others. Richard won the best race ever seen there in 1964 and two others. Maurice had his best career finish there, a third in 1961. The Pettys did better than most, always ran hard, and never came back.

The race got underway with a field of 23 and Pearson jumped ahead from the outside of the front row and ran away. He stretched it to three-quarters of a lap ahead of a torrid battle between Hutcherson and Jarrett rapping on his back bumper in third. Yarbrough spun his yellow '63 Ford 31 in turn four, but continued, as did Pearson after the brief caution it caused on lap 60. Then on lap 110, Wayne Smith looped his red '65 Chevy 38 and everyone pitted again. Jarrett was stewing in the pits with a miserably slow stop as Pearson, Hutcherson, Yarbrough, and Lund roared through the north end of the track heading for the restart. Unbelievably, Ned pulled onto the clay just as the leaders took the green on lap 113. Jarrett was a sitting duck as the pack engulfed him. Pearson got to Ned first and missed him, only to cream the steel rail in turn two, way past the crash behind him. LeeRoy, G.C., and Clyde Lynn bounced off Jarrett, each other, and the fence, and piled up in turn one as the yellow waved frantically. Pearson was towed to the pits and retired with front-end damage. Likewise Yarbrough and Lynn as they were tugged to their trailers. Spencer had damage, but kept going. Jarrett, the rolling chicane, sheepishly eased away with only cosmetic damage. Four guys could not do the job on Ned that Billy Wade did the previous summer in the very same spot all alone. From then on, it all swung Ned's way. Hutcherson developed an overheating problem while leading and it only took Ned a mile and a half to overhaul him on lap 121. It was another 22 rounds before the Keokuk Comet pulled his gold and red Holman-Moody 29 smoldering to the pits on lap 143 to stay. Jarrett cruised the final 57, beating a game Yarbrough in the gold and white Kenny Myler '64 Ford 06 by two laps. Third went to Langley, fourth Wendell, fifth Spencer, sixth Derrington, seventh Arrington, eighth Wayne Smith, ninth Hutcherson, and tenth Pearson. It was a double disappointment for the Spartanburg fans, first for Turner not racing, and second for Pearson's dominating performance dashed and bashed by the bonehead that sent Jarrett out of the pits in front of the lead pack. On the other hand, 8,000-plus saw an exhibition of driving by one of, if not the greatest, dirt track stock car driver of all time. Turner finally made his comeback at Darlington on Labor Day, starting eighth and finishing only 51 laps for 35th place in a non-competitive Red Vogt–tuned Plymouth. And when they loaded up and rattled through that wobbly first-turn gate late that night to go to Augusta, six-time Fairgrounds winner Ned Jarrett, three-for-three pole winner Dick Hutcherson, Cale Yarborough, LeeRoy Yarbrough, and G.C. Spencer never came back, and there was 100 miles yet to go.

There were originally going to be two races at the Fairgrounds in 1966, but the first one, right after the 500, was rained out and canceled. So on Saturday night, June 4, 1966, Promoter Joe Littlejohn hosted the final 100 miles of big-time stock car racing in Spartanburg. It was a perfect late spring night and a decent car count of 22 entered. Out of those 22, Pearson was far and away the favorite to break his winless jinx at home. His main challenger was James Hylton in his Fairgrounds debut. The others drove two-year-old Fords. Tiny Lund's orange 55, Tiger Tom Pistone's blue 59, and Elmo Langley's orange 64 also stood in Pearson's way. Three memorable things about time trials took place. First, Pearson took the pole, but could not break Hutcherson's track record. Second, Inman Rookie of the Year-to-be James Hylton turned in two real good qualifying laps, then proceeded to pull a Curtis Turner and clobbered that old wooden fence in turn one. Hylton said that he "just lost it," bent the A-frame, and did not have time to make repairs, watching the race in the pits from the roof of his yellow '65 Dodge 48. As a rookie, Hylton would ultimately finish second to Pearson for the Grand National Championship, edging out Richard Petty. Third was Richard Petty's absence. He had not raced in Spartanburg since winning the June 1964 epic due to the hemi ban, and then giving up his seat for Turner's comeback. This time, he had torn the front end off his Fury at Asheville-Weaverville two nights earlier and could not get it fixed in time. It was the two-year-old factory Dodge of Pearson, wrenched by Cotton Owens, against the independents, many of which were renegade Ford outcasts. FoMoCo withdrew from competition because of an engine dispute with NASCAR in April, therefore, no Jarrett, Hutcherson, Turner, Panch, or Isaac. The gates suffered badly, too, as only 7,000 paid to see the Rebel 400 at Darlington and 45,000 for the World 600 at Charlotte, both in May. The announced crowd at the Fairgrounds that final night was a measly 3,200. The field of 22 took the green and the Big Fisherman from Cross out-dueled Pearson into treacherous turn one from the outside front row and tore away. Pearson's night got worse when on lap 25, Wendell Scott, who started his big-league career on this clay five years earlier, spun in turn one. Six-time '66 winner Pearson slapped sides with him and was never the same. Wendell limped around for nine laps before parking. Numerous pit stops and laps behind later, Pearson's engine went sour and he retired with a damaged right rear to boot. Often the favorite and usually the leader, Pearson never led the last one and never won at home. One hundred and five career wins, but not in his own backyard. Pistone hung around in second or third for a long time, but overheated and packed it in on lap 120. Lund paced the field for 160 laps in a display of total dominance over Pearson and everyone. He had them on the hook with twenty miles to go when he dropped to the inside while streaking down the back chute and coasted to the pits, filling the late spring night air with the acrid odor of burning oil. Grease, to be exact, as Lund fried the Ford's rear end just like he would a Lake Santee bass over a campfire. Tiny ran hard there a lot of times and deserved a win as much as Pearson, Buck, Weatherly, or anybody. When Tiny failed, somebody was going to notch his first big-time win unless the earth opened up and swallowed Spartanburg. Veteran Virginian Elmo Langley, winless in nearly a gross of starts since his first in

Donnie Allen stands with Elmo Langley's first winner after final Grand National at the Fairgrounds on June 4, 1966. Wendell Scott, with helmet, is sitting on the hood chatting.

the 1954 Southern 500, inherited the point and romped the last 39 laps for a very popular, yet sad win. The only Buck Baker entry at The Fairgrounds in two years was Neil "Soapy" Castles piloting an ex–Owens '64 Dodge 88, finishing four laps back in second. In their best races ever, third went to Doug Cooper (he had some others) and fourth to Joel Davis. Fifth was cigar-chomping J.D. McDuffie, sixth Blackie Watt, seventh Henley Gray, eighth Tiny, ninth Sonny Lamphear, and tenth Max Ledbetter, the last car running 45 laps behind and 27 laps back of Gray. Others were Pistone 12th, Sears 13th, Putney 14th, Stick Elliott 15th, Pearson 16th, Tyner 17th, Scott 18th, and Buddy Baker 20th. Never again did big-time racing grace the historic clay of Spartanburg, and a huge part of the Piedmont died on sultry June 4, 1966. The last major-league stock car race in Spartanburg had about 3,200 fans in attendance, which is about 6,000 less than an average Spartanburg High vs. Dorman High School football game. NASCAR Grand National racing was close to its all-time low in the summer of '66. Even most of the local drivers and teams quit coming, but not Cotton

Owens. Of the 22 races run there, he drove and/or entered at least one car in 16 of them. The Pettys did even better. However, Promoter Joe Littlejohn could not save the Fairgrounds after 1966. High insurance costs, low attendance, factory boycotts, slim car counts, fixing that first-turn fence after every race, and who knows what else all contributed to the track's demise. Then in 2002, they planned regularly scheduled races and renovated the Fairgrounds so the racers could "wind it out." Two or three more events after that first legends race, the novelty wore off, foul rumors of mismanagement abounded, the celebrities left, the Spartanburg racing museum died, and so did the Fairgrounds ... again. But you know what? They have been winding it out all along for decades ... after hours.

Track History by the Numbers

RACES:	22
YEARS OF RACES:	1953–1955, 1956 (2), 1957 (2), 1958, 1959, 1960–1965 (2), 1966
WINNERS:	Jarrett (6), L. Petty (3), R. Petty (3), Owens (2), T. Flock, Langley, Moody, Panch, Paschal, J. Smith, H. Thomas, S. Thompson
MOST POLES:	3—Dick Hutcherson
RACE RECORD:	66.367 mph—Ned Jarrett, 1965 Ford (2/27/65)
QUALIFYING RECORD:	70.644 mph—Dick Hutcherson, 1965 Ford (2/27/65)
WINS BY MAKE:	Ford (8), Chevrolet (3), Plymouth (3), Pontiac (3), Dodge (2), Chrysler, Hudson, Oldsmobile
MOST STARTS:	Buck Baker—14
MOST LAPS LED:	403—Ned Jarrett
MOST TOP FIVES:	10—Ned Jarrett
BEST AVERAGE START:	6th—Buck Baker, 3.9—Cotton Owens (12)
BEST AVERAGE FINISH:	8.9—Buck Baker, 4th—Ned Jarrett (12)

2
Charlotte Speedway, Charlotte, North Carolina

Sunday afternoon, June 19, 1949, is when it all began. Charlotte Speedway was this great sport's Garden of Eden, but not because of its looks. Appearance-wise, it was anything but. The surface was rough and an even rougher high wooden fence that never saw the business end of a paintbrush surrounded the grounds. The crowd was estimated at over 20,000, but years later, it must have been an Indianapoliseque 100,000 because so many people claimed to have been there. The weather was hot and humid with a haze in the air you could almost touch. I guess Indy influenced the starting grid, too, because the race was opened to 33 starters, strictly stock cars all.

The day it really all began was on Saturday, when Bob Flock took the first pole in a three-year-old Hudson at a tick under 68 miles per hour on the three quarters of a mile of red Carolina clay. Brother Tim was outside in an Olds, Red Byron in a Raymond Parks' Olds was third, Otis Martin in his bib overalls fourth in a Ford, and the third Flock brother, Fonty, was fifth in another Hudson. Curtis Turner started a Buick beside Bill Blair, driving for Hubert Westmoreland. Jim Roper and a pal drove a Lincoln from Great Bend, KS, to

I-85 Frontage Road (Brady Drive) and Little Rock Road was the venue for Charlotte Speedway.

12th. Names synonymous with stock car racing and mainstays in the sport for years to come lined up. Drivers the likes of Jim Paschal, Buck Baker, Jack Smith, Lee Petty, Herb Thomas, Frank Mundy, Jimmy Thompson, and Jimmy Lewellen made that historic first start. A gutsy gal named Sara Christian started 13th in a Ford. There was a Slick, a Skimp, a Felix, and a Pee Wee that day. And they drove Lincoln, Hudson, Ford, Olds, Cadillac, Buick, Chrysler, Kaiser, and Mercury. Alvin Hawkins dropped that first green flag and Bob Flock's 7 led the sport into history. Bob paced the field for the first five laps until Blair put his Lincoln 44 out front. History and fate pointed a fickle finger at Lee Petty on lap 107 when his monstrous borrowed Buick Roadmaster sedan 38 blew a right rear tire that had been rubbing a spring and flipped four times in turn three. An unlikely thought, that NASCAR Strictly Stock/Grand National's first-ever caution flag would be brought out by a driver eventually becoming one of its very, very top drivers and patriarch of the sport's most famous family. Needless to say, better days were ahead for the Pettys. Blair paced the field until lap 150 when Glenn Dunnaway of Gastonia, NC, inherited the lead from Bill's liquid-spewing hot rod Lincoln. Dunnaway sailed home first with a convincing three-lap bulge over the hemorrhaging Lincoln of Roper. Glenn Dunnaway ... immortalized as the winner of the first NASCAR Strictly Stock race. Almost. The post-race inspection conducted by NASCAR Tech Chief Al Crisler revealed that the Hubert Westmoreland '47 Ford had "moonshiner springs" on it. That is, springs that had been stretched out in the rear to give a level appearance when the trunk was loaded with its cargo of contraband. It also gave the car more stability in the turns and on the washboard surface. Westmoreland and Dunnaway were disqualified and Hubert sued NASCAR for $10,000. However, it was no dice as the case was dismissed in a Greensboro courtroom, setting a precedent for future litigation against the sanctioning body.

So meet the winner, Jim Roper, who with his car-dealer pal Millard Clothier, took the cue from a Smilin' Jack cartoon strip note about this inaugural event and drove a pair of lumbering Lincolns east straight into history. One small catch, though. Roper's 34 only completed 197 of the scheduled 200 laps and was creeping along at the end. What if Dunnaway had been DQ'd earlier or not raced at all? Could third-placer Fonty Flock have run Roper down? There is a good chance he could have with three laps left. NASCAR tore Roper's engine down so completely after the race that his sponsor, Mecklenburg Motors, gave him a new one to get him on the road again. The old one was rather used up anyway. "Alfalfa Jim" took the hefty $2,000 pot back to Great Bend by way of one more race on August 7, 1949, in Strictly Stock race number three at Hillsborough. As for Christian D. "Alfalfa Jim" Roper, he lived until the ripe old age of 83, passing away at Friendly Acres Retirement Community in Newton, KS, on Friday, June 23, 2000. It was 51 years and four days after his historic Charlotte checkered flag. Roper started racing midgets in 1944 and became "Alfalfa Jim" after driving a sprinter through a wooden fence in Salina, KS, and into an alfalfa field. He spun it back around, re-entered the same way he got out, lost the race, but gained a nickname since the cockpit was full of the fluffy green stuff. Roper set the track record in 1950 on the high banks at Belleville, KS, in a sprint. He got national ESPN time on a couple of NASCAR telecasts, once as he was given a duplicate trophy at North Wilkesboro in 1993 because Millard Clothier kept the hardware he won in 1949 at Charlotte. In 1996, at age 80, he slung one of his old midgets around the banks at Belleville once more. He was recognized at Texas Motor Speedway in 1998, and the next year, he was honored at Atlanta Motor Speedway when the NAPA 500 trophy was named in his honor. Shortly before his death, he was quoted by a friend as saying, "Boy, I've had fun."

Sunday afternoon, April 2, 1950, was the second race of the second season and the second under the new banner of the Grand National Division. It was the tenth big-time race in stock car history. Thirteen thousand eager fans watched the dusty spectacle under a sunny spring sky. Twenty-five brave souls opened the doors of their hulking behemoths and stormed away chasing, as in 1949, pole-sitter Bob Flock's Olds. And as in '49, Bob led the first five laps before giving way to cigar-chomping Red Byron, the 1949 National Champion. Red held the point until Tim Flock roared by on lap 48, pushing the same Lincoln 21 that Harold Kite used to win at Daytona about two months earlier in the season opener. The scariest moment of the day went to the terrifying crash on lap 85 of June Cleveland, who flipped his Buick 55 and flattened it in the same place Junie Donleavy's modified driver Hank Stanley had been killed earlier in the year. Tim won easily ahead of brother Bob for the first checkers of a career that would see him win at the still all-time record and most assuredly unbeatable rate of 21.2 per cent of the time. Third went to Clyde Minter, fourth Byron, and Bill Snowden fifth. Others were the hard-luck guy from '49, Glenn Dunnaway sixth, Herb Thomas ninth, Frank Mundy 11th, Bill Rexford 13th, Curtis Turner 15th, Cotton Owens 16th, Lee Petty 18th, Bill Blair 19th, Fonty Flock 21st, Buck Baker 22nd, and Jim Paschal 23rd. It was quite a sight to see Flock's black winning Lincoln plastered with masking tape across the nose and other leading edges, masking tape numbers and sponsor, and white sidewall tires. That car won the first two races of 1950!

Hot, dirty, sticky, and perfect for racing describes Sunday afternoon, July 23, 1950. It was the second trip and final to Charlotte Speedway for the year and still only the 17th big-time stock car race ever. The field of 28 was the largest yet and a healthy $1,500 was the victor's spoils. In addition, for the second race in a row, handsome Roanoke daredevil Curtis Turner led every lap from the pole in his Eanes Motors Olds 41. He pulled exactly the same act three weeks earlier in Rochester, NY. It was Curtis' fourth win of the season and gave him a career total of five, three more than the closest drivers, Red Byron and Bob Flock. Other victims of Turner's tear were Chuck Mahoney second, Herb Thomas third, Jimmie Lewellen fourth, and Dick Burns fifth. Notables further back were Herb's brother Donald seventh, Mundy eighth, Tim ninth, Petty 11th, Dunnaway 12th, Baker 14th, Blair 16th, soon-to-be new champion Bill Rexford 19th, and Paschal 20th. A few of the boys made early runs at the Virginia lumberman, but all broke in the black Olds' wake.

Sunday afternoon, April Fool's Day, 1951, and a grand assortment of stock jockeys arrived for the second race of the season. Factory rides were bountiful and the faces behind the goggles were familiar. The Fabulous Hudson Hornet of Smokey Yunick was there with Marshall Teague fresh off his win on the Beach. Plymouths were represented by Lee Petty, Herb Thomas, Speedy Thompson, and 1949 Indianapolis 500 winner Bill Holland. Holland, from Miami, was booted off the AAA circuit for driving in an Opa-Locka, FL, charity race of a whopping three laps on November 15, 1950. Opportunistic Bill France arranged for the open-wheel superstar to drive the Hubert Westmoreland 1950 Plymouth number 98 Jr. in which Johnny Mantz had won the inaugural Southern 500. Bill Holland debuted resplendent in his crisp white driving suit, looking every bit the part of an Indianapolis 500 winner. Other top shoes on hand were the Oldsmobiles of Tim Flock, Roberts, Blair, pole-sitter Fonty Flock, sprint car ace Frank Luptow, and Paschal. Nash, armed with the most unracecar-like vehicle ever to hit the clay, showed with none other than the Blond Blizzard Curtis Turner pushing the buttons. Lincoln had Lewellen, a Mercury was managed by Bill Rexford, Lloyd Moore fielded a Julian Buesink Ford Police Special, Ray Pruitt drove a Dodge, Leo Schneider brought a Kaiser, Clyde Minter raced a Chevy, James Ward pushed a Packard, John Barker handled a Henry J, and a legitimate threat saw Frank Mundy in the potent Perry Smith Studebaker. Thirteen makes, 39 drivers, and the April Fool's joke was on 38 of them. After Fonty led the first 46, Turner's cockroach-looking Nash 41 took over for the final 104. Petty was the only other finisher on the lead lap with Marshall's Teaguemobile third, Herb Thomas fourth, and Luptow fifth. Holland was all but home with a top ten finish when he wiped the famous 98 Jr. in a vicious set of barrel rolls that flattened the historic Plymouth, but not terminally. He still finished 14th. The Henry J of Lloyd Dennis flipped early and he was unhurt.

For Curtis Turner, it was his Grand National–leading sixth career win and his first since leading every lap here in the last race. For the factory-backed Nash Ambassador Team, it was career victory number one in its second effort. At Daytona in the season opener, Nash had Turner, Holland, and Mantz driving and did well. Turner was seventh and Mantz ninth. Following that up with a dominating win at Charlotte, the ugliest stock car that ever raced had a bright future. April Fools again! Literally, by the end of the month, Nash was all but gone from the Grand National scene as Turner left for Olds. However, Mantz stayed and had a second and a third later in the year. Still, the threat of the Nash dynasty passed as quickly as it arrived, having its zenith on a spring Sunday in Charlotte. So when the ghosts come out in the Mecklenburg twilight around I-85 and Little Rock Road, you can bet Turner's in a Nash just for the laughs. No foolin'!

A funny thing happened on Sunday afternoon, September 23, 1951. Not only did NASCAR hold Grand National race 28 in Charlotte, but they also held Grand National race 29 at the half-mile high-banked blacktop at deadly Dayton. Twenty-six drivers went to Charlotte for 150 laps, while 31 others went north for 200. Which venue had the best drivers that afternoon? Probably Charlotte. Who had the best race? Definitely Charlotte! Wild crashes abounded at both sites, but amazingly, there were no serious injuries. Charlotte had Turner, Baker, pole-sitter Billy Carden, Lewellen, Paschal, Mundy, Shuman, Owens, Eubanks, Flock Brothers Tim and Bob, Thomas Brothers Herb and Donald, Blair, Shorty York, Billy Myers, and Bill Widenhouse. The Dayton contingent was pretty impressive, with winner Fonty Flock, Lloyd Moore, Petty, Tommy Thompson, Jim Reed, IMCA star Iggy Katona, Rathmann, and Jimmy Florian, the first driver to win a Grand National race in a Ford ... and shirtless! In the Queen City, Herb Thomas drove the Fabulous Hudson Hornet 92 to the win, his third straight, edging York, brother Donald, Blair, and Lewellen. Bill Miller tumbled a '51 Ford so completely that number 217 was unrecognizable. Carden had one of his best career outings, leading often, but fading to seventh at the end. Curtis' stranglehold on the place ended with a dismal 19th. Where was his Nash?

It turned out to be the last *Silent Speedways of the Carolinas* event for the Frank Mundy/Perry Smith Studebaker. Even though they had a dismal day in Charlotte, finishing last, they would be victorious two months and two days later in a 150-lapper in Mobile in the season finale. They finished fifth in the standings, showing well in the Studebaker 23. Then on December 8th, owner Smith was performing an air ambulance function in his personal plane, flying an old lady and her nurse from Columbia to Chicago. The single engine aircraft hit the ground near Greensburg, IN, killing all aboard. Studebaker died in that crash as a viable stock car option. It would have died before long anyway. Mundy hooked up with Hudson and later Kiekhaefer, taking many checkers, mostly in USAC stockers, where he was a champion.

The 1952 Grand National campaign saw only one visit to Charlotte Speedway, on Sunday afternoon, June 15th. A light field of 24 showed with some of the biggest dogs missing. After pole-sitter Fonty Flock's Olds 14 got passed by Hustlin' Herb's Hudson Hornet on lap 32, it was over. Fonty's brother Tim managed at least to finish on the lead lap followed by Blair, Petty, and Rathmann. Ray Duhigg destroyed a Petty Plymouth and Gober Sosebee flipped a new Chrysler 17 laps later. The crowd was as thin as the high overcast on the hot late spring Sunday.

Maybe the old modified track was falling out of favor because there was also just a solo appearance for big-time stock car racing in Charlotte in 1953. However, nearly 9,000 saw one of the best races in the 107-race history of the series. It was Sunday afternoon of course, April 5th. A very healthy roster of 28 stockers provided the thrills on an extremely dusty day as the Grand National record for lead changes occurred with 17, one about every nine laps for 150 rounds. Tim had Hudson 91 on the pole leading for the first 60 laps before Buck put Olds 87 in front for 17 circuits. Next it was Flock again, then Rathmann, then Flock, then Rathmann, then Flock, then Rathmann, then Flock, then Rathmann, then Flock, then Rathmann, then Flock, then Rathmann, then Herb Thomas, then rookie Pop McGinnis until his wheel fell off with three laps to go. Finally, the win went to, in his tenth start, Dick Passwater, driving an Oldsmobile for ill-fated Hoosier millionaire Frank Arford. Sosebee raced his famous Cherokee Garage Oldsmobile 51 into second, followed by Herschel Buchanan on the lead lap in one of those pesky Nashes that still seemed to run well at Charlotte two years after that only checkered flag. Tim Flock eased home fourth and three-wheeling McGinnis copped fifth. Others not faring too well were Petty 11th, Herb Thomas 12th, Rathmann 13th, Baker 14th, Blair 16th, Lewellen 18th, Eubanks 20th, Paschal 21st, Shuman 23rd, Curtis "The Magic Is Gone" Turner 24th, and Fonty 25th.

The exhausting lead changes between six men and their stirring duels were overshadowed somewhat by a nasty crash near midway of the event. It happened when Gene Comstock and Pop McGinnis slapped fenders, sending Gene into terrifying flips that culminated with the fans being showered with Hudson parts and the racer resting where a couple of spectators' laps were located. The two hardy souls were carted off to the hospital in Shelby, recovered, and never considered suing. Good old 1953!

Busy, busy, busy. That is what Memorial Day weekend 1954 was. On Saturday afternoon, May 29th, the big-dollar Raleigh 250 was run at the banked, paved mile, where Herb Thomas won. By the next afternoon, Decoration Day, 25 of those guys towed, hauled, or drove their stockers a few hours southwest to the Charlotte Speedway to line up for a 100-miler, the 15th race of the season. If that was not enough, a continent away in Gardena, CA, 32 more stockers were gridded for the circuit's 16th race of the season. In mid–America, on a big patch of Indiana real estate, 33 very brave men were holding the 38th Annual International Sweepstakes, also known as the Indianapolis 500. A weekend of four major races ... and on May 30, 1954, three events running at the same time, evenly spread across the country, involving 90 fearless throttle jockeys.

After the change of venue in North Carolina, the lone visit for the season was held. The pole went to AAA Big Car driver Al Keller in a Hudson, the only one of his career. Al would distinguish himself two weeks later by winning NASCAR's first road race in bandleader Paul Whiteman's Jaguar. (Then Al would spend the following five of six Memorial Days at Indianapolis, where the next year he was involved in Bill Vukovich's incineration. Al would not survive a Phoenix Big Car crash on November 19, 1961.) Keller was the only leader besides Baker, whose Olds V-8 exploded as he cocked it off the fourth turn with the checkers in sight. A fast-closing Lee Petty could not get there in time to prevent Buck's seventh career win, though. Third went to the Spartanburg duo of Joe Eubanks in a Bud Moore Hudson, fourth was Russ Helper in the Hudson 120 Rathmann had driven so well in 1953, and finishing fifth placed Blair. Others were Hershel McGriff tenth, Rathmann 13th, Keller 16th, Herb Thomas 19th, Sosebee 21st, and Lewellen 23rd.

Incidentally, on the left coast at the 16th race of the season, a field of mostly nobodies was beaten by John Soares in a Dodge for what was supposed to be a 250-miler and speedway finale. It was billed as "The Poor Man's 500" at the Carrell Speedway in Gardena, but confusion cost everyone four laps and it only went 496 on a half-mile of rich Golden State dirt. Twelve thousand fans came to say good-bye and did so for nearly five hours. Two days later, the wrecking ball smashed the famous speedway into memory. At that other race in the middle of the country, Vuky won by a lap for two 500s in a row.

Sunday afternoon, May 1, 1955, was a gorgeous spring day across the Piedmont as the number-one song in the land was Perez Prado's "Cherry Pink, Apple Blossom White." In Spartanburg, superstar Babe Zaharias won the LPGA Betsy Rawls Peach Blossom Invitation Golf Tournament. In Charlotte, a superstar was fighting for is life. Twenty-six stockers took the green, led by pole-sitter Herb Thomas in Yunick's new Buick. The white Kiekhaefer Chrysler of Tim Flock drove past and away. Broadsliding with wild abandon through the first turn on lap 41, Thomas' Buick hooked a rut and went airborne. It performed multiple flips and threw the Olivia, NC, veteran from its hissing, steamy remains. He was hauled to the hospital badly battered with a broken leg, a concussion, and a wide variety of cuts, gashes, and bruises. Meanwhile, Buck Baker set his sights on the point from back in 16th where he started and with 20 laps to go, made his move on Flock. He notched his 11th win, this one in a Buick. Flock wound up second, youngster Dave Terrell took third in an Olds, old Gober in an Olds was fourth, and Bob Welborn was fifth in a Chevy. Notables were Dink "The Concord Comet" Widenhouse 12th, Jim Ord in a Packard flipped during the race for 13th, Petty 15th, Speedy 17th, Rathmann 18th, Paschal 19th, Junior Johnson 20th, Thomas got 21st for his pain, Fonty 23rd, and Blair 25th. About 6,000 fans saw Baker pull off the win in just under two hours.

In 1956, the Grand Dame of the Grand National held a record three events at the rutted old three-quarter mile clayland. The City of Charlotte had two others at the Southern States Fairgrounds, and Concord held one of its own. The Queen City was a busy place on the circuit, a portent of things to come. The second race of '56 went for 100 miles, 134 laps on the nippy, overcast Sunday afternoon of November 20, 1955. It was Thanksgiving week and Fonty had plenty for which to be thankful. He was at the helm of one of the most powerful cars in the land, a Carl Kiekhaefer Chrysler, and little brother Tim had one, too. As they had already done four times earlier in the year, they finished one-two. They also started that way. It looked like a rout on paper, but the margin of victory was half a car length as the Brothers Flock battled side-by-side off the fourth turn and down the stretch to the line. Petty had the best seat in the house for the sibling rivalry, as he was third. Fourth followed Weatherly and Baker was fifth. Further back were Dink sixth, Curtis seventh, Gwyn ninth, Cotton tenth, Herb 11th, a youngster named Ned Jarrett in one of his first starts took 12th, Lewellen 16th, Thompson 17th, Blair 18th, a flipping Welborn got 20th, 21st placer Don Oldenberg's gas tank fell off, causing Welborn to crash, and Paschal captured 23rd. As if the skies weren't gloomy enough that day, heavy hearts filled the track because of the death of NASCAR modified great Louis "Buddy" Shuman the previous Sunday. Shuman, winner of one Grand National race on July 1, 1952, in Niagara Falls, Ontario, apparently fell asleep while smoking in a Hickory, NC, hotel room and burned to death. More on Buddy in the Southern States Fairgrounds chapter.

The middle event for '56 took place on May 27th, a Sunday afternoon. It was the 20th race of the season and the 21st was taking place 3,000 miles away in Portland. The southeastern affair had a field of 25 and the northwestern assembled 21. These were after a Friday night 100-miler on the dirt in Abbottstown, PA, won by Baker. Would it be possible for the Kiekhaefer team to keep its 11-race winning streak alive? Not only did they, but the big white monsters won them both, for 13 in a row! And it was not just a win. At Charlotte, it was a one-two-three sweep led by Thompson, new Kiekhaefer driver Junior Johnson second, and Baker third. Buck had it won until a stop for fuel with four laps left killed his chances. Fourth was Paschal and fifth Petty. Others were Weatherly sixth, Eubanks seventh, Staley eighth, Jack Smith ninth, and Billy Myers tenth. The big action started in turn three of lap one when Turner, Rex White, Bobby Johns, and Blackie Pitt tangled. Johns' '56 Chevy was sent bounding through the high board fence and down the steep backside of the banking. The Miamian was taken to the hospital with serious shoulder damage. Meanwhile, Commandant Kiekhaefer had ordered Herb Thomas to go out west, win the three races there, and meet up with the rest of the squadron in Lehi, AR, on June 10th for the 250-miler. At Portland, Herb captured his 46th career victory in a 75-miler over slim competition, even though John Kieper and Clyde Palmer finished on the lead lap. Thomas proceeded to California and at Eureka on May 30th, won number 47 in a 78-miler, and at Merced on June 3rd, took checkered flag number 48 in a 100-mile chase. Mission accomplished with 16 consecutive Kiekhaefer wins! Then he met the rest of the Great White Fleet in Lehi, where Ralph Moody broke the curse. Herb Thomas went winless for the next five races and quit Kiekhaefer in Spartanburg, never winning again.

Elvis Presley was shaking the airwaves on the cool autumn Wednesday night of October 17, 1956, with "Don't Be Cruel," "Hound Dog," and "Love Me Tender." At dilapidated Charlotte Speedway, the curtain went up for the last time. The literal birthplace of big-time

The view from trees was shared by hundreds at that first Strictly Stock race in 1949.

stock car racing held its twelfth and final installment before a modest gate of less than 7,000 and a solid field of 22. Baker, Paschal, Thomas, and Petty had been there on June 19, 1949, for the first and ran in most of the ones in between.

Moody took the pole and swapped the lead early with Thompson. Then on lap 30, Buck took over and that was it. He led the next 103 caution-free rounds and took his 12th win of the year and Carl Kiekhaefer's 26th. Moody was second, followed by Panch, Paschal, Amick, Thompson, Thomas, Petty, Lund, and Roberts. Baker was 246 points behind Thomas with three to go. But this where Kiekhaefer flexed his muscle and rented the Cleveland County Fairgrounds in Shelby for October 23rd, the following Tuesday night, and the rest is very ugly history.

The old Charlotte Speedway sat and decayed after that near Little Rock Road, Wilkinson Boulevard, and I-85. A Comfort Inn grew nearby, roads were widened and rerouted, and what should have been a true shrine for this great sport faded into oblivion. Then on May 17, 2006, North Carolina Lt. Governor Beverly Perdue did the right thing. Joined by Stock Car Hall of Famers Bobby Allison, Ned Jarrett, Humpy Wheeler, NASCAR President Mike Helton, Charlotte Mayor Pat McCrory, the family of C.C. Allison, who still own most of the land, and dozens of other interested citizens, she unveiled the long-overdue historical marker recognizing one of the most famous patches of real estate in auto racing history.

Its remains are long gone, but somewhere in that space between day and night, sound and silence, truth and illusion, and life and death, this nightly netherworld is filled with the unholy roar of Hudsons and Nashes, Fords and Chevies, and Kiekhaefer Chryslers spewing red Carolina dust into the void. Speedsters guided by the restless souls of men and women known and unknown, famous and infamous, and forever dead. Spectators by the thousands sit hipbone to hipbone screaming like banshees for Roper, Rathmann, and Roberts; Turner, Thomas, Teague, and Thompson; Byron, Baker, and Blair; Shuman, Staley, Smith, and Sosebee; Christian, Keller, and Carden; Lewellen, Liguori, and Dunnaway; Weatherly, Holland, and Eubanks; and the Three Fabulous Brothers Flock. Bony fingers gripping black steering wheels, hollow eyes peering through dirty goggles from beneath the bill of a leather-sided helmet. They open the doors, they strap themselves in, and they live!

Track History by the Numbers

RACES:	12
YEARS OF RACES:	1949, 1950 (2), 1951 (2), 1952, 1953, 1954, 1955, 1956 (3)
WINNERS:	Buck Baker (3), H. Thomas (2), Turner (2), F. Flock, T. Flock, Passwater, Roper, Thompson
MOST POLES:	3—Fonty Flock
RACE RECORD:	72.268 mph—Buck Baker, 1956 Chrysler (10/17/56)
QUALIFYING RECORD:	76.966 mph—Speedy Thompson, 1956 Chrysler (5/27/56)
WINS BY MAKE:	Chrysler (3), Oldsmobile (3), Hudson (2), Lincoln (2), Buick, Nash
MOST STARTS:	11—Lee Petty, Herb Thomas

MOST LAPS LED:	352—Tim Flock
MOST TOP FIVES:	6—Tim Flock
BEST AVERAGE START:	7th—Herb Thomas, 2.4—Tim Flock (9 starts)
BEST AVERAGE FINISH:	8.7—Lee Petty, 7.7—Tim Flock (9 starts)

3
Columbia Speedway, Columbia, South Carolina

Tied as most prolific of the *Silent Speedways of the Carolinas* is this West Columbia relic. The Grand National tour came here 41 times, then twice more in the first year of the Winston Cup. Cross the Blossom Street Bridge into West Columbia, bear left at the fork, go past Maurice's Piggy Park, and head out U.S. 176, the Charleston Highway, toward I-26. At the entrance to Congaree Mobile Home Sales is a shiny green city street sign with white letters reading "Old Speedway Circle." Turn left up the hill, through the mobile homes, off the asphalt, and into the weeds. Heavy brush leads to denser foliage and the road turns to a trail, getting tougher by the foot. In the oaks and pines rests the track and it is magnificent! Weeds grow tall through the cracks in the asphalt. Trees crowd and nudge the old railing, which still faintly carries the red and white colors of the speedway long passed into stock

In June 2002, evergreens and weeds crowded the long Columbia homestretch from both sides.

car history. On the main straightaway is the finish line, all cracked and faded. The pits have an infield scoring and concession stand all in one, now reduced to rubble. All that remains of the stands are the concrete pilings jutting a foot or so out of the weeds. At the crossover gate between the end of the grandstand and the first turn crumbles what remains of the office. Painted on it the words "Keep Out" whisper a warning in faded red where the teams checked in and picked up their share of the purse: $1,000 to win in 1951 and $1,500 twenty years later! The light poles stand blindly, riddled with bullet holes. These fixtures once shone down on the first night race in Grand National history.

An organization known as Carolina Velo took over this old lady, killed the weeds, trimmed back the trees, built walls, painted white stripes on the asphalt, and made a bicycle track out of it. But that is all right because the ghosts do not care one way or the other.

The Palmetto State's second Grand National race ever was on Saturday, June 16, 1951. The night before, Joe Louis knocked out Lee Savold on closed circuit television and on race day Ben Hogan claimed his second straight U.S. Open. At the Columbia Speedway, the inaugural 100-miler on the hard half-mile of sandy clay was ready to set off an amazing string of firsts. It was a hot Saturday in the Capital City and as the sun set, thunderstorms threatened the crowd of nearly 8,000. Soon the lightning was obscured by the incandescence provided by Carolina Power & Light, the thunder was drowned out by that of 34 stockers, and the 38th race in Grand National history, the first night event ever, got the green. On the pole for the first time in his career was "The Rebel," Frank Menendez. The half–Irish, half–Spanish refugee from Lucky Teeter's Hell Drivers came from Atlanta and was better known as Frank Mundy. His car owner, Columbia's Perry Smith, also got his first career pole with swift Studebaker 23. In addition, this was Studebaker's first pole, too. The Spartanburg duo of Joe Eubanks and Bud Moore had an Olds outside of row one. The large field glistened under the lights with stars like the Flock Brothers, Marshall Teague, Dick Rathmann, Herb and Donald Thomas, Gober Sosebee, Lee Petty, Buck Baker, Bill Blair, Jim Paschal, and Red Byron shining through the dust. The stellar field included Studebakers, Fords, Hudsons, Plymouths, Oldsmobiles, a Cadillac, a Mercury, a Buick, and five, count 'em, five Henry Js. The Rebel loused up the first 144 laps in night racing history by leaving the others choking on his dust. Eubanks fell out early for 33rd and Rathmann did not last much longer for 31st. Legendary Red Byron made his third from last of only 15 career starts, which included two wins and the 1949 Strictly Stock Championship. Limping badly from having his B-24 blasted out of the sky over the Pacific, Red crashed his Ford 83 early in the night and his last *Silent Speedways of the Carolinas* start only netted 30th. Byron ran the Big One a few weeks later in Detroit, finishing fourth, and called it a career after crashing out of the Southern 500 very late on Labor Day, claiming 25 out of 82 starters. Donald Thomas retired for 26th, Petty lasted a little longer for 20th, and Sosebee parked his Cadillac for 15th as Mundy orchestrated the rout. When Frank finally pitted, Paschal shoved his Ford to the front for 33 laps until he came in and the Rebel was gone again ... for good. Flashing under the lights in his Studebaker Commander, Frank Mundy cruised home first by a lap over Hubert Westmoreland's 1950 Southern 500–winning Plymouth 98 Jr. piloted by Bill Blair. The historic hemi was demolished by 1949 Indianapolis 500 victor Bill Holland at Charlotte in April, rebuilt, raced again by Holland, then turned over to the veteran Blair. Third was Teague in his Fabulous Hudson Hornet, fourth Herb Thomas in a Plymouth, as was Buck Baker in fifth. Other stars shining that first night were Paschal, who faded to sixth, Tim Flock in his Black Phantom Olds seventh, Fonty Flock in the Red Devil Olds 12th, and Bob Flock in the Gray Ghost Olds 13th. It was the first of three career wins for Frank Mundy, the first of two career wins for car owner Perry Smith, and the first of three career

Vines now overwhelm the board rails that once repelled the speeding two-ton stock cars.

wins for Studebaker. Finally, it was the first win for a car numbered 23. It was truly a night of firsts in the Capital City.

The racers returned beaten and battered for the tour's second trip to town on Friday night, September 7, 1951. Only four days earlier, most of them had limped and crawled from Darlington's blazing Labor Day sun after Herb Thomas' dominating win. Worth mentioning from that Second Annual Southern 500 was Columbia winner Frank Mundy, putting Studebaker 23 on the pole in record time only to retire after twelve laps, finishing dead last ... as in 82nd! That is the greatest loss of position in Strictly Stock/Grand National/Winston/Nextel Cup history. That is quite a feat since nobody will ever go from first to worst and lose more than 42 places today. Mundy's record loss of 81 positions in one race is safe for all time. In addition, infrequent competitor Buddy Shuman had a great third place in that 500. Red Byron was running well until tangling with Teague, then retiring, literally, with only a handful of laps left for 25th. This night, 29 Darlington survivors were on hand for a controversial finish. Tim Flock had the pole with brother Bob alongside, and it was the elder Flock who led the first 72 laps. Then Fireball took over and raced under the checkers for the win and 5,000 fans roared their approval. Second placer Tim Flock and Black Phantom owner Ted Chester lodged a protest and the scorecards were rechecked. Lo and behold, Flock was declared the winner. Roberts and car owner Ed Saverance went postal and told NASCAR where to stick their second-place money. It was career win number six for Tim instead of number two for Roberts. Third was Jimmy Lewellen, Bob Flock fourth, and Buck Baker fifth, again. Others were Donald Thomas sixth, Cotton Owens seventh, Fonty tenth, Mundy ran out of tires for 17th in the Studie, Petty was 18th, Herb crashed

Pit road angles left off the homestretch with a lone light pole still standing watch.

his Southern 500 winner for 20th, Eubanks was 27th, and last in 29th place was Darlington's sixth placer Harold Kite. It was a one-sided affair until NASCAR picked a different winner than the other 5,000 people witnessed.

Sidebars of joy and sadness ended the 1951 season with the direct involvement of two major players in Columbia Speedway stories. One was Studebaker, which won all three career Grand National victories that year. On October 28th on the half-mile dirt in Hanford, CA, Danny Weinberg drove a Studie to its second career win over Marvin Panch and Fonty Flock. In the season finale on November 25th, that dynamic duo of Perry Smith and Frank Mundy sat on the pole in number 23 and led all 150 laps at the three-quarter mile dirt track in Mobile, AL, whipping three Flocks, Thomas, Smith, Petty, and others. It was the third and final win for a Studebaker in Grand National racing, although Hank Grilliot tried it for one lap one last time on August 5, 1962, at Nashville. Mobile also proved to be the third and final career win for Mundy in Grand National racing. (Frank won number two at Martinsville on October 14th in Bob Flock's Gray Ghost Olds.) For car owner Perry Smith, his career total of Grand National wins stopped abruptly at two on December 8th when his single-engine plane piled into a wooded area near Greensburg, IN. On a mercy mission, Smith was flying an air traffic controller, an 83-year-old lady, and a nurse from Columbia to Chicago. It is an easy bet that Smith has Studebaker 23 on the ready most nights at Columbia Speedway, but old Frankie Menendez is not there to drive it ... yet.

On April 12, 1952, Columbia staged a Saturday night 100-miler under the lights in another night of firsts as the springtime crowd watched Hartsville native Buck Baker put B.A. Pless' Hudson 89 on the pole. A quality field of 22 lined up as darkness set in on the Capital City. Buck scratched away and led for the first 62 laps until Gober Sosebee took over the point, filling in for Fonty Flock, who was on the mend with a hurt shoulder. As the old moonshiner from Dawsonville, GA, displayed the rear of his Olds to the field, a rarity, and surely a first, occurred on lap 81. A drunk probably intending to join the race pulled his personal car out onto the track and was blasted by Greenville's E.C. Ramsey driving Louise Smith's Ford 94. Ramsey then proceeded to pummel the alky until cops came and restored order. Just past halfway, Dick Rathmann shoved his Hudson to the fore, but the Hartsville bus driver took back the lead for good and rumbled home the winner in the first of what was to be a stellar Grand National career for Elzie Wylie Baker, Sr. The young Buck edged Lee Petty with Rathmann third, New Jersey's Frankie Schneider fourth, and Joe Eubanks fifth. It was also the first Grand National win for car owner Pless. It was also the first win by a car numbered 89. Further back came Donald Thomas sixth, Shuman seventh, Paschal eighth, Jack Smith ninth, Sosebee 12th, Bill Widenhouse 15th, Herb 17th, Ramsey 20th, Fireball Roberts 21st, and Marshall Teague 22nd and last. The packed house saw more than they bargained for and Columbia was three for three in providing action, surprises, and excitement, always under the lights. However, the big boys would not be back for 13 months.

When they returned on Saturday night, May 9, 1953, something must have been wrong. Only 16 entries showed and the crowd was thin. Still, some top chauffeurs were on hand as Herb Thomas' Smokey Yunick–wrenched Hornet took the pole at nearly 59 miles per hour with the familiar black 51 of Sosebee outside in a brand new Cherokee Garage Olds. It was a three-way fight between those two and the streaking Baker who found himself tangling at the front of every race he entered. Big-timer Dick Rathmann's Hudson fell out first for last and was followed closely by Herschel Buchanan's Nash and Fonty Flock's Hornet. With the laps running out, Hustling Herb's Hudson expired for eighth, Blair parked for seventh, and Gober was the last man running in sixth. When the checkers fell after 200 laps, it was across the nose of the red and white Olds 87 of Buck Baker. He notched his third career win, second of the week after Langhorne, and second straight in Columbia. Runner-up went to Tim Flock, third to Lewellen, Ray Duhigg fourth, and Petty fifth. By the season's end, Buck Baker would add hardware from the Southern 500 and the finale at Lakewood in Atlanta to his trophy case.

One big-league stop was all for 1954, too, as Columbia got the call on June 6th. It was the season of the Army-McCarthy hearings, *The Creature from the Black Lagoon*, *The Caine Mutiny*, Willie Mays, and Vuky's second straight at Indianapolis. Big names were among those entered this Saturday night and high-flying Buck Baker put Ernest Woods' Olds 88 number 88 on the point for the 100-miler. Buck looked like he would back up his Memorial Day win on Charlotte's three-quarter mile clay a week earlier with another, but the engine went sour and it was all he could do to finish. Winning by a comfortable two laps after a three-year absence from Victory Lane was the Olds of the Blond Blizzard, Roanoke's Curtis Turner. Turner's win was the first for his new car owner, Elmer Brooks, and the first for the number 44. Second place went to Hershel McGriff, who inherited Turner's Frank Christian Olds, third to the Pure Sensitized Hudson 3 of Dick Rathmann, fourth to Speedy Thompson's Olds, and fifth was Petty's Chrysler, five laps back. Also competing were Herb Thomas sixth, Eubanks seventh, Baker eighth, Ralph Liguori ninth, Roberts 13th, and Sosebee 18th and last.

On a historical note, the next race of 1954 was the first NASCAR Grand National road race. It had a mixed field of 43 made up of American iron, Jags, MGs, Porsches, an Austin Healy, and a Morgan on the runways of the Linden, NJ, airport. Al Keller's Paul Whiteman Jaguar edged Joe Eubanks' Bud Moore Hudson as the only guys completing the 50-lap grind.

Looking back from the pits towards the homestretch where the grandstands were.

Pole-sitter Buck Baker was third, leading three more Jags of Bob Grossman, Harry LaVois, and Bill Claren.

The bloody racing year of 1955 registered three stops in Columbia and although the Grim Reaper did not harvest the carnage on the stockers that was heaped on the open-wheelers and Le Mans, he did not miss his mark by much. The opener in Columbia was under the lights on March 26, 1955, a Saturday. A field of 22 rolled with the Kiekhaefer Chrysler 300 number 300 of Tim Flock on the pole. The Kiekhaefer assault began on the sand at Daytona a month earlier, and after skipping a 100-miler at Savannah, this was an attempt to go two for two. So far, it was two poles in two tries for Tim and his white monster with Olds, Dodge, Hudson, Packard, Plymouth, Lincoln, Mercury, and a pair of underdog Chevies piloted by veterans Herb Thomas and Fonty Flock. The race unfolded as expected with Tim burying the opposition until lap 132, when the Reaper emerged from the darkness and pointed his bony finger, but missed. Instead of death and destruction, he only spread destruction. Down the homestretch, the speedsters of Joel Million, Billy Myers, Jim McLain, and Gober Sosebee started to ricochet about, with the careening Olds 51 pulverizing the scoring stand into splinters, leaving people, paper, and pencils scattered all over. It was not his or her time to go because nobody was hurt at this horrendous scene of destruction. After that, Tim's Chrysler lost its head and faded into the field while Fonty found his and bulled to the front, edging IMCA star and future USAC Champion Don White for the win. Not just any win, but the first Chevrolet win in Grand National competition. As for White, it was his second second in a row and he was destined to finish third the next day at Hillsborough. Third was Rathmann in the Blue Crown Hudson, Baker fourth, and Tim slid to fifth. At that point, Kiekhaefer realized that he could not win them all. On back came Petty sixth, Junior Johnson seventh, Paschal eighth, Liguori ninth, and Herb Thomas' other Chevy tenth. Dink Widenhouse finished 12th, Eubanks 13th, Sosebee 17th and Billy Myers 19th after their involvement in the big one, and Lewellen 22nd and last. Only a measly 2,900 fans came out to see this historic victory for Chevrolet.

It was July 1955. Gogi Grant's "The Wayward Wind" topped the charts, Elvis sang "Hound Dog" on *The Steve Allen Show*, Dick Clark started *American Bandstand*, Ringling Brothers and Barnum and Bailey Circus folded their tent for the last time, the Bell X-2 topped mach three, the *Andrea Doria* sank, and "In God We Trust" was added to our money. On Saturday night the ninth, the middle 100-miler of the year found only 16 stockers lined up in front of another smallish crowd to see Jim Paschal give car owner Ernest Woods the pole in the Helzafire Olds. An hour and 48 minutes later, Paschal and Jimmy Lewellen gave Ernest Woods his first one-two finish after years of entering pairs of racers in events. It was also, as of this writing, the last time number 78 went to Victory Lane. Odds would have favored Kiekhaefer sweeping, but on this steamy Carolina night, the best the Great White Fleet could do was a third for Tim, a fifth for Buck, and a 15th for Fonty. Billy Carden was fourth, Banjo Matthews sixth, Bob Welborn tenth, Petty 13th, Junior Johnson 14th, and Gwyn Staley 16th and last. The Kiekhaefer sweep was 24 hours away in Weaverville.

The Capital City Triple was finalized on October 15th, as 21 big-timers hit the clay for the last time here in 1955. Junior Johnson put his Olds on the pole with Tim Flock outside and now in such a groove in the Kiekhaefer Chrysler 300 that most races were a battle for second. This time though, Baker, who always runs well here, had him and the others covered until 12 to go when he pitted for a splash of Pure. By the time he got his De Paolo Ford back on the track, all he could do was watch Tim's white monster glisten away under the lights and settle for runner-up. It was Tim Flock's incredible 17th win of the campaign, demolishing all other season records and closing fast on Herb Thomas' career total of 43 wins. Thomas' light blue 92 Smokey Yunick Motoramic Southern 500–winning Chevy was third, Staley fourth, and Massey fifth. Notables on back were Welborn sixth, Johnson seventh, Weatherly flipped his Ford late for eighth, Lewellen ninth, Paschal 11th, Widenhouses Bill and Dink were 16th and 17th, with Petty 19th, and Eubanks 20th. It took just over an hour 49 for Flock to collect the $1,100 and head for Martinsville's 100-miler the next afternoon.

Saturday, May 5, 1956, Needles won the 82nd Kentucky Derby and Perry Como had "Hot Diggity" on the top of Billboard's Hot 100. That night in Columbia, a hefty lineup was set in the Arclite 100 before a decent crowd for a change. They came to see if anybody could put a stop to the victory rampage of Kiekhaefer's Mopars. Kiekhaefer had not lost since March 18th, when Thomas won at Wilson five races before. Commandant Carl did not intend to lose this one as he unloaded three of his gleaming white with red numeraled 500 series Dodges for aces Thompson, Baker, and Thomas. Kiekhaefer also had his three 300 series Chryslers standing by 118 miles to the north in Concord for the same three boys to race the next day. That really must have been the life, with the absolute best equipment in obscene abundance. All they had to do was show up and drive. In addition, being as handsome as Buck Baker was with his thick wavy black hair, well, it was the end of the rainbow. Kiekhaefer was a dictator for sure, but the price a driver paid in clean living was more than offset by constant front running and the piling up of dollars, wins, and points. Tim Flock has the highest winning percentage in history, 20.855, and he owes it to Carl Kiekhaefer, but he finally had to leave the team at the peak of his success three races earlier. At 32, Tim was consumed by ulcers and insomnia, and gave up the ride of a lifetime. Tim won only one more Grand National race. So it was the world against Kiekhaefer, and his Dodges had the front row on the clear nippy night with Buck's 500B fastest and Speedy outside in 500. When the green rag fell, it was Lee Petty, who had been luckless here, leaping out front all the way from seventh on the grid for the opening 59 laps. Ralph Liguori crashed his Dodge on the second lap for 26th and last. Junior Johnson blew a lap later for 25th, Eubanks parked for 24th, and Bobby Johns T-boned Tiny Lund and retired for 23rd while Lund continued. Curtis Turner put famed purple '56 Ford Wild Hog 99 out front for sixty laps until the exhaust broke on the car four months away from winning the Southern 500. That gave the lead to Thompson and it was "so long." Speedy won by a mile over teammate Baker. Thompson's was the first Grand National stock car to carry number 500 to Victory Lane. Third went to Weatherly in the team car to Turner's, fourth was Lund in a brilliant recovery piloting a battered Pontiac, and fifth went to Bob Flock. Others in the show were Herb Thomas sixth in the third Kiekhaefer Dodge, Rex White eighth in his seventh start, Johnny Allen 11th, Paschal 13th, Tim Flock as Bob's Mauri Rose Chevy teammate 15th, Staley 16th, Turner 17th, Petty 19th, Fred Lorenzen in his second career Grand National start 20th, Lewellen 21st, and Billy Myers 22nd.

Bob Flock was 38 and Columbia was his first start of 1956. He had run only once in 1955 as part of a massive seven-car Kiekhaefer effort that involved Chryslers, Fords, and Buicks at Lehi, AR, in a dirt 300-miler. Bob, Fonty, and Tim all had Chryslers under them as Tim edged Bob's number 308 for fourth as Fonty fell out early. That had to be fun as only one other time the three Flock Brothers were on the same team. Bob had only driven seven times since 1951, and was beat up and tired by this night in Columbia. It was his penultimate race, running near the front all night in Mauri Rose's factory Chevrolet number 49. He ended a career of only 36 starts with four wins, 11 top fives, and 18 top tens. *Half the*

Short pilings and a few boards are all that remain of the grandstands.

time Bob finished in the top ten! Bob only won two poles, the first in that inaugural Strictly Stock Car race in Charlotte on June 19, 1949. He was a tired 38, but many said he always had been and still was the best Flock, even in 1956. All three Flocks agreed that he was! The Kiekhaefer Chrysler rampage continued for eleven more races until June 10th. At Concord the next day, it was a one-two-three sweep by the Chryslers with Thompson winning, Baker second, and Thomas third. During the 16-race tear that went from March 18th to June 10th, three Grand National drivers were killed. John McVitty was flipped to death and thrown out in time trials at Langhorne on April 21st. Also during time trials, Clint McHugh went end over end and out of the speedway at Lehi, AR, on June 9th, being ejected before his racer landed upside down in a lake. Then, in the Lehi 300-miler itself on June 10th, Cotton Priddy tangled with Don Carr on the 39th lap and tumbled to his death. Ralph Moody broke the Kiekhaefer streak that day and Bob Flock concluded his career, finishing 11th in Mauri Rose's Chevy, running well, but losing the fuel pump with 13 laps to go. What the Grim Reaper missed with the stockers in bloody '55, he made up for in the spring of '56. Bob Flock lived another eight years, leaving us on May 16, 1964, at only 46 years of age. However, he still comes out to race with his brothers at night. And he is still the best one!

The 1956 curtain-closer in Columbia was Saturday night, September 29th, and radio rocked with "Hound Dog" and "Don't Be Cruel," Elvis' two-sided number-one hits. On Thursday, Milburn Apt flew the Bell X-2 to a manned speed record just under mach 3.2 before he lost it and augured the escape capsule into the sand at Edwards Air Force Base. That same day, the greatest female athlete of all time, Babe Didrickson Zaharias, died of colon cancer at 45. A dozen and a half stockers lined up with Herb Thomas, now an independent, fending off Baker's Kiekhaefer ride. Tim Flock won his 37th and final career pole that night in John Foster's '56 Chevy. Tim shot away and led the first seven circuits until Speedy's Dodge overtook him. As Flock struggled to get back to the front, he crashed for 16th. Speedy's teammate Buck Baker passed him, then Speedy roared back by, and finally Buck edged out front again with 32 to go. Ralph Moody also snuck by to claim second with Thompson third and Fireball fourth, all completing the 200 laps. Fifth was Billy Myers, Billy Carden sixth, Petty seventh, points leader Thomas eighth, Paschal ninth, Allen tenth, and Lund 14th. By the time they returned, Kiekhaefer would be only a memory.

They came on a Thursday night, June 20, 1957, on a hot midsummer night's eve. A good field was on hand and Buck put Bud Moore's Chevy on the pole with teammate and soon-to-be Southern 500 winner Speedy Thompson outside. Tiny Lund was still fishing for his first win and it looked like he had one in his massive hands. Then with eleven to go, a Firestone blew and the Brushy Mountain Motors Pontiac whacked the wall as Fireball had earlier, and it came down to Jack Smith or Baker. It was Smith by about a straightaway over Baker as Californian Marvin Panch brought a Ford in third, all three on the lead lap. Fourth was Paschal, Thompson fifth, Darel Dieringer was sixth in his third Grand National start, Billy Myers seventh, Tiny settled for eighth, Petty 13th, Allen 15th, Fireball 16th, Lewellen 17th, and Neil "Soapy" Castles took 18th in his first Grand National outing.

In September 1957, the country was rockin' to "That'll Be the Day" by Buddy Holly and the Crickets, and Ford introduced the Edsel. *Bachelor Father*, *Wagon Train*, and *Perry Mason* debuted on the tube while *West Side Story* opened on Broadway. Eisenhower sent troops to Arkansas, Scott Crossfield took the X-15 on its first powered flight, and baseball bid farewell to the Polo Grounds and Ebbets Field. On Thursday, September 19th, the first underground nuclear explosion took place near Las Vegas and a 100-mile stock car race was run that night at Columbia. Only 19 cars entered, but there were good pilots with Buck on the pole in Moore's Chevy. It had been only four days since a 300-mile torture test at Langhorne, won by Gwyn Staley, and a couple of weeks since the demo derby at Darlington. That made for some tired iron and even tireder jockeys. The race was uneventful with Buck leading almost all the way, padding his lead toward a second straight championship. Staley was second a lap behind, Bill Amick third, Billy Myers was fourth in his first Grand National start since brother Bobby died in the Southern 500, and Brownie King was fifth. Panch took sixth, Petty eighth, Roy Tyner in his third start 11th, Smith 13th, Paschal 14th, Fireball 15th, Allen 17th, and 500 winner Thompson 19th and last. It took Buck just over an hour 39 to win the $900.

Thursday night was the choice for the Grand Nationals in Columbia, as was the case in April 1958. This was the first of three visits, as in 1955, and Perry Como was topping the charts with "Catch A Falling Star." The Giants and Dodgers were now in California, Arnold Palmer won his first Masters, Castro and his rebels invaded Havana, Sputnik 2 and its dog burned to ashes in space, and *Gunsmoke* won an Emmy. On the 10th, a whopping 33 racecars crammed their way into Columbia Speedway for a 100-miler. In his first and only career pole, Possum Jones put Max Welborn's Chevy out front and the surrounding mob started the mayhem right away. On lap one, eventual Rookie of the Year Shorty Rollins crashed in his second start for last. A couple of laps later, a red flag resulted from second and third starters Panch and Billy Rafter sidelining each other for 31st and 32nd. Then on lap 11, Junior Johnson crumpled his Paul Spaulding Ford for 30th. Junior could be excused for being rusty because he had run only one race in 1957 at North Wilkesboro on October 20th, shortly after his release from the penitentiary in Chillicothe, OH. Pole-sitter Possum petered out on lap 54 for 29th, and on 74, Roy Tyner clobbered Spook Crawford's Plymouth for 28th. There was some racing between the crashes with Smith, Thompson, and Petty as the major combatants. Gene Hege, a Columbian making his first and only Grand National start, crashed on lap 85 for caution number five. The final came when Doug Cox crashed before Thompson out-legged Smith for his first win since taking a Moore Chevy to victory in the Southern 500 the previous Labor Day. Third was Lund, Petty took fourth in his best finish here yet, and fifth came Pagan. Others were Herman Beam 12th in his fourth start, Allen 17th, and usual contender Buck Baker stumbled to 24th. All this racing and crashing was for a winner's purse of $800.

The middle trip of 1958 came on June 5th, only eight weeks after the first. Ten fewer cars entered and the top stars were generally absent. Buck Baker had Bud's '57 Chevy on the pole and led the first 70 laps until Panch crashed and settled for 19th. Jack Smith took over out front and had it in the bag until he lost the fan belt and Junior Johnson put Spaulding's '57 Ford into the lead for the final 22 miles. Second went to unknown George Dunn in his second Grand National ever, driving Manley Britt's '57 Mercury, and third to veteran Fred Harb in his best finish so far. Fourth was Wilbur Rakestraw and fifth came Rollins. Finishing eighth was Columbia's own John Hamby in his first Grand National start, Petty came ninth, Thompson 11th, Pagan 17th, and Baker 18th. Johnson won by a whopping eight laps for his second win of the year.

On Saturday night, July 12, 1958, in a Columbia convertible race, a young man ten days past his 21st birthday, Richard Lee Petty, started the first event of his historic stock car career. Richard started 13th and competently finished sixth, five laps back in Lee's old '57 Oldsmobile 42. While he could not outrun winner Bob Welborn, Fireball Roberts, Larry Frank, Doug Cox, and George Dunn, he did handle the likes of Ken Rush, Castles, Tyner, Allen, Sosebee, Possum, and Glen Wood.

The finale of the season in Columbia occurred on steamy-hot Thursday night, August 7,

A tire once used to cushion a pole shows the ravages of fire and a crowding sapling.

1958. Ricky Nelson's "Poor Little Fool" topped the charts as 21 teams battled the sandy half-mile for 200 laps and it was a Speedy night. The Monroe Motorman was in the midst of the third and last great year of his career. He sat on the pole in Bud Moore's reliable old '57 Chevy Southern 500 winner 46 and led almost all the way with only Welborn also going the 100 miles. Cotton Owens was three laps back in third, fourth was Rollins, and fifth came George Dunn, runner-up here last time. Others were Petty seventh, and Rock Hill's Johnny Gardner 12th. Johnny raced Grand Nationals only in 1958, running all three in Columbia with two other 22nd places. On back came Buck 14th, Lund 16th, Tyner 19th, and Miami's Don Angel opened his five-race career with 21st and last. Speedy did it in a speedy hour 49 for $800 in speedy cash.

The year 1959 was the middle of three in a row when Columbia got a Grand National trifecta. Counting 1955, that is four years with a dozen races and no other venue had that! On April 4th, in the first of three for 1959, a giant event occurred. It was back to Saturday night racing in the Capital City and a giant introduced a giant to the cockpit. This was the evening Buck Baker stuck Buddy behind the wheel of a 1958 Impala for the kid's first Grand National start. It was in a 21-car field and Buck, who used to own this place, qualified seventh in his Thor Chevrolet while Buddy took Dad's old '58 model and timed 18th. The race was a rout as Jack Smith drove Moore's new burgundy Impala 47 to victory in a close one over sportsman ace Ned Jarrett, driving Spaulding's reliable old red 11. Junior Johnson, usually at the controls of Spaulding's cars, was unavailable, and Jarrett jumped at the chance to drive it. Smith and Jarrett finished a whopping nine laps ahead of third placer Lee Petty with Lund fourth and Owens fifth. Further back raced the Turtle in 11th, Speedy 13th, Buddy Baker 14th after retiring with a bum shock, Curtis Turner in a now-rare start

15th, Welborn 18th, Buck 19th, Jimmy Pardue 20th and Rollins 21st and last. Buddy beat Buck their first time out together.

The boys were back on June 18, 1959, good old Thursday night. It was muggy and one day short of the tenth anniversary of the first Strictly Stock race back in 1949. Bob Burdick from Omaha captured his second and last career pole in just his fourth start in a T-Bird. Including his 1961 Atlanta 500 win, that is pretty good for 15 career starts. But it was scarfaced Joe Weatherly from outside row one that jumped away and led the first 43 laps until he and Junior in old 11 roared into the first turn and found G.C. Spencer and Richard Riley tangling. Junior plowed into the rear of Joe's T-Bird and during the caution, the indestructible Joe had to be lifted from the 'Bird as a hastily recruited Jimmy Thompson took over. Thompson's career up to that point sported eight top ten finishes, and the first was in that first Strictly Stock Car race ten years earlier. Buck took over for the next 82 laps until Tommy Irwin battled past in his T-Bird and looked like a winner until 11 to go. That is until Lee Petty, luckless at this place, battled by Irwin with dust flying to take the point. The Old Man rumbled under the checkers by less than a second in his high-finned white '59 Plymouth. Third went to Buck, who blew on the last lap, Benny Rakestraw fourth in the best finish of his 13-race career, and Weatherly copped fifth, relieved by Jimmy T. On back came Burdick sixth, Buddy Baker seventh in his first career top ten, ninth Beam, Tyner 12th, Curtis "Crawfish" Crider 14th, Owens 15th, Junior 16th, Spencer 17th, and Welborn 19th. Legendary South Carolina dirt-tracker Crawfish Crider hit the big time that night, well after he had established himself as a terrific racer. Crawfish, from North Charleston, SC, launched a respectable career and left good memories with a solid reputation of how he charged and how he tried. CCC is one of the best drivers never to win a Grand National race.

August 29, 1959, was eight days after Hawaii became the 50th state, and "The Three Bells" by the Browns was Number 1. The steamy Saturday night found the smallest field that would ever race at Columbia Speedway on hand for its third major race of '59. Of that Buck Baker's dozen, eight were zipper tops, which also ran the convertible circuit. That dinosaur of a tour concluded its fourth and final season the Sunday before with a 100-miler at Southern States Fairgrounds in Charlotte, where Jarrett drove to victory and they crowned Joe Lee Johnson champion. Combined with the fact that the Southern 500 was coming up in nine days, it made sense to convert the old ragtops to hardtops, the zipper tops, and use them instead of their good stuff. Even so, it seems odd that there were so few running that night. The field of 22 for the Charlotte convertible race was much better than this "big time" Columbia lineup. They drew for the pole and Ned's lucky streak continued as he literally grabbed the pole. The attrition on the tired iron took a heavy toll as a variety of mechanical ills depleted the field and Lee with his usual top-notch equipment won handily. Second over a lap behind was Tiny, third came Harb, Tyner was fourth, Wood fifth, and the last man standing was the Ol' Sarge, George Green, sixth. Others that watched the finish from the pits were Spencer seventh, Jarrett eighth, Eubanks ninth, Irwin 11th, and Crawfish 12th. It was more like a benefit race for point leader Petty. L.D. Austin finished tenth and was the only other driver besides Lee that finished in the top ten of the 1959 final standings to appear. Cotton Owens was second to Petty that year by 1,830 and obviously did not try too hard to catch Lee by ignoring this 100-miler. Things were much different in 1959.

The calendar verifies that there was a fourth Grand National race in Columbia in 1959. The second race of the 1960 season ran on a cold, cloudy Thanksgiving Day, Thursday, November 26, 1959. It is also the last chapter in the story of a remarkable car. This Thursday afternoon affair drew 22 entries and for many, it was a last chance. The next race after this was a 100-mile Daytona 500 qualifier on February 12, 1960. By then, all the 1957 model cars would be obsolete. So Turkey Day 1959 was the final chance for these old 1957 models to gobble up some glory and try to add one more race to their history before going to some backwater sportsman or hobby track and race off into oblivion. Of the 22 stockers, ten were 1957 models: one Ford and nine Chevrolets. Oh, but that Ford! Junior Johnson won Dodge's first pole since September 23, 1956, when Royce Hagerty fast-timed a goat in Portland. Junior drove Paul Spaulding's '59 Dodge 11 after their old mount, the 1957 Ford, was sold to Jarrett in the legendary post-dated check episode the previous August. Convertible Champion Joe Lee Johnson qualified outside row one in the Honest Charley '59 Chevy 77 to make it the first and last all–Johnson front row to date in big-time history. Ned started third in that ex–Spaulding Ford, which now sported 38 since 11 was still Spaulding's number. Johnson Junior shot to the early lead, but was dogged by Jarrett, Lee Petty, Jack Smith, and Johnson Joe Lee. Contenders dropped out immediately as Welborn crashed in the opening lap and finished last for 22nd. Then Tiny literally retired his '57 Chevy for 21st, Tiger Tom parked his T-Bird for 20th, and Junior went home with engine trouble for 19th. The second crash occurred on lap 108 and involved Tommy Irwin's T-Bird and the third Johnson on hand, Hubert. Irwin claimed 17th and would race another day, but for Hubert, this was his only day. Hubie drove a '57 Chevy 7 from a respectable tenth on the grid, crashed out after 52.5 miles, and won fifty fish for his first and last Grand National start. Two laps later, motorcycle racer Buck Brigance of Charlotte, a proven winner on two wheels who never quite got the hang of racing on four like his contemporaries Paul Goldsmith and Joe Weatherly, closed out a winless three-year, 16-race career when he blew his '57 Chevy 62 and parked for 16th. Up front, Jarrett was fending off Petty, Smith, and Joe Lee as the laps wound down. G.C. retired next for 15th and Tyner crashed his '57 Chevy on lap 158 for 12th. As the 100-miler drew to a close, it was war between Jarrett and Smith in Bud's hot Impala. And at the line it was Jarrett by just car lengths over "The Red Fox" from Spartanburg with Joe Lee third and Lee fourth, all on the lead lap. Fifth rumbled Bobby Johns in his '57 Chevy, sixth for young Richard, and Shep Langdon took seventh. Shep retired weeks later, after the Daytona 500, completing a 45-race career spanning parts of four seasons. L.D. Austin was eighth, and ninth went to H.T. "Pappy" Crane. Pappy, of Long Beach, MS, got a top ten in this, his first Grand National race, then went to Daytona, flipping his '59 Chevy 58 down the backstretch in the 500 on lap 89 and retiring after a two-race career. Riley was tenth, the Turtle was 11 and Bud Parnell made the second start of his four-race career for 13.

Thanksgiving Day 1959. The number-one song was "Mr. Blue" by the Fleetwoods and a great old race car retired ... Ned Jarrett's 1957 Ford Fairlane 38. However, it used to be shiny and new and number 11. Here is its story. On July 14, 1957, Fireball Roberts drove the brand-new Paul Spaulding Ford number 11 to third on the high dirt banks of the mile and a half Memphis-Arkansas Speedway in Lehi, AR, and it was parked. It reappeared for the last Speedweeks on the sand, February 23, 1958, finishing 17th and driven by Lloyd Ragon. Ragon brought it home eighth at Concord, NC, in the next race. After Junior Johnson got released from stir in Ohio, he took over at Columbia on April 10th in his second race back. He slid into the Spaulding 11 like a fist in a boxing glove and, although he did not win, he had found his ride. Third in Spartanburg, a couple of DNFs, eighth at Manassas, seventh at Old Bridge, thirds at Greenville and Greensboro, and finally on May 18th, victory at North Wilkesboro. Then they had a second on Memorial Day in the Northern 500 on the mile at Trenton, followed by wins in Columbia on June 5th, Bradford, PA, on June 12th, and Reading, PA, on June 15th for back-to-back-to-back triumphs. A last at New Oxford, PA, was followed by second at Hickory, 11th in the Southern 500, and then they cooled off until the weather followed suit, winning the last two races of the year at North Wilkesboro and

"Keep Out" once implored the curious to refrain from approaching the office area.

Lakewood. That is six wins and eighth in points for Junior in the Spaulding Ford for 1958. Number 11 started 1959 with five wins in the first 22 races. The first was at Wilson on March 29th, a second place with Ned up in Columbia on April 4th, Junior first at Reading on April 26th, Junior first again at Hickory on May 2, third at Martinsville the next day, second at Nashville, third at Spartanburg, first at Greenville on June 13th and at Wilson on June 20, fourth at Bowman-Gray, and a third the next day at Weaverville. Junior blew the engine, finished last at the Charlotte Fairgrounds on July 26th, and stepped out of the old war wagon. Enter Ned Jarrett, who knew the car well, had driven it, needed it, and then came the famous yarn of buying number 11 from Spaulding for $2,000 with a post-dated check. All he had to do was win two races in two days to make the check good by Monday morning. No sweat, except for the fact that *he had never won a Grand National race before!* August 1 at Rambi Raceway in Myrtle Beach saw Ned start ninth and win by a lap over Paschal. That was the first $800, now for the rest. The next day at Charlotte's Southern States Fairgrounds, Jarrett found big trouble after starting tenth. Having the steering wheel taped the wrong way by someone sliced and diced Ned's paws until he was losing positions as fast as he was blood. He had to get out and some spectator named Weatherly drove for 50 laps or so. Then, fate hopped in after Junior Johnson's Wood Brothers ride blew and he came to the rescue. Johnson eased into his old easy chair and punched that museum piece to the front once again for the win. Ned got his other $800, robbed a liquor store for the final $400, and made Spaulding's rubber check as good as gold. Actually, Ned probably charmed somebody out of the last $400, and the rest of the storybook finish is true. He needed two wins and got them! Ned changed the number to 38 whenever Spaulding's was in the same race because Paul had 11. Ned had dismal race after race and in the season finale at Concord, he blew for 34 and last. It looked like the old steed was dead at last. As 1960 began, the car was eligible for the first two races and Ned took the worn-out 38 to Southern States Fairgrounds, losing the rear end for 26th. He had a new ride ready and waiting for Speedweek, a red 1960 Courtesy Ford 11. Jarrett hauled old 38 to the last Grand National race it could possibly enter and at Columbia on Thanksgiving Day, November 26, 1959, Jarrett qualified third and won! Research indicates that this car ran 55 Grand National races started by four drivers. It notched 11 wins, 11 top fives, eight top tens, and 25 finishes outside the top ten. That old Ford probably raced off into oblivion, or maybe it languishes covered with dust in some dark corner of a forgotten garage. On the other hand, maybe its original driver, Fireball Roberts, drives it even tonight while it waits for Junior or Ned to come over to the other side. Fireball, Ned, and Junior kind of have a history together. It would not be so strange if they all leaned on old number 11 some midnight at Columbia Speedway and talked old times ... that is, when Junior and Ned come over.

Things were surely different in 1960. Imagine staging a Cup race today on anything but a Saturday or Sunday. April 5, 1960, was a spring Tuesday night in Columbia with a Grand National 100-miler slated at the speedway. Citizens had to choose between Tuesday night on the tube with *The Rifleman, Father Knows Best, The Many Loves of Dobie Gillis, Alfred Hitchcock Presents,* and *The Red Skelton Show,* or Tuesday night at the track with Joe Weatherly, Rex White, Ned Jarrett, Richard Petty, and Buck Baker. The speedway hosted the five mentioned and 16 more in a 200-lapper. The pole was a shocker as unheralded Doug Yates from Chapel Hill drove his red and white '59 Plymouth 23 to the first pole of his career. Outside was Weatherly, subbing for Holman-Moody teammate Johnny Beauchamp in Ford 31 at the other front-row berth as a respectable field lined up behind them. Yates did not roll over when the green fell and was joined up front by the Pettys, Buck, Rex, and Johnsons Junior and Joe Lee. On lap 22, last place starter Joe Eubanks crashed out and finished 21st as his career started heaving its last breaths. Bobby Johns ran out of tires for his borrowed Chevy and quit for 19th as he was actually trying to win the 1960 crown picking up rides where he could. Well past halfway, Weatherly pounded the rail, bringing out caution number two, and parked his teammate's car for 18th. Young Buddy Baker blew for 17th, Crawfish overheated for 16th, and eventual Rookie of the Year David Pearson, in his fifth career start, crashed on lap 140 and took 15th. Up front, Spartanburg's Rex White stretched his lead over fellow Spartan Buck Baker when Jarrett fell out with 23 laps to go for 11th. White went on to win by a lap over Baker with Yates matching his career-best start with his career-best finish, a third. Rex was the eighth different winner in the first nine races. Fourth went to Lee, fifth to Joe Lee, Richard was sixth, Irwin seventh, Junior Johnson in his Daytona 500–winning Daytona Beach Kennel Club Chevy eighth, Spencer ninth, and tenth Bunkie Blackburn, Spook Crawford's new driver, with his first top ten in just his third career start. The last man running 41 laps behind was the 19 of Herman Beam. The action took just under two hours and most people got home in time to see *The Garry Moore Show* at ten.

The schedule in 1960 was brutal: Sunday afternoon at Weaverville, Tuesday night Spartanburg, Thursday night Columbia, Saturday night South Boston, and Tuesday night at Bowman-Gray Stadium. August 18, 1960, was a miserably hot Thursday night and these beat-up cars and tired chauffeurs were wearing out after 30 races with 14 yet to go. As an added bonus for the fans and not the teams, this was the only 150-miler ever staged here. It was 300 grueling, gritty, nasty, bumpy laps. Pole-sitter Tommy Irwin of Inman, SC, in his T-Bird 36 led a solid field of 26 to the green. It was Irwin's second and final pole. Sitting alongside Tommy was his Inman neighbor G.C. Spencer, who had his best qualifying run to date in a miserable old '58 Chevy, a pink 48. However, before they could get to the line, the rear end fell out of Spencer's bomb and he failed to start getting credit for 26th and last. When they got going, Irwin hung around up front with Yates, Rex, the Pettys, Buck, and Cotton. Attrition began as Weatherly's T-Bird broke for 25th, Junior Johnson lost steering for 24th, Pardue crashed the Lowe's Dodge for a caution and 21st, and nearing the halfway point, Bobby Johns' T-Bird broke for 20th. The lead group looked like last time with the matter settling down to a fight between White, Yates, Owens, and Buck Baker. Gremlins got the best of Pearson on lap 134, spoiling his career-best fourth place start (his third) with a 19th, and at halfway, Yates' Plymouth blew for 18th. Down the stretch, it was to be decided between White and Richard Petty as Cotton's Spartanburg winner from two nights earlier lost the rear end with 113 laps to go and Lee Petty's went with 22 remaining. Thinking, no doubt, of Elvis' number-one hit "It's Now or Never," Rex decided to turn it up a notch and pulled away for his second checkers in a row at Columbia and fourth of the year. The team of Rex White and owner/builder Louis Clements were showing their strength as they powered away to a comfortable points lead over the younger Petty, winning the 1960 Championship. Third went to forever young Buck Baker, who was days away from his second Southern 500 victory, fourth to Jarrett, and fifth for pole-sitter Irwin. Others were Possum sixth, Lee seventh, Turtle ninth, Crawfish tenth, Bunkie 12th, and Joe Eubanks 13th in his last race of 1960, his last on the *Silent Speedways of the Carolinas*, and the third from last of his career.

A troubling time was April of 1961. The Bay of Pigs invasion failed miserably, Adolf Eichmann was on trial for war crimes, and General McArthur refused to be Commissioner of Baseball. And most disturbing of all, Jim Bakker married Tammy Faye. On Thursday night, April 20th, 22 stockers lined up to do battle for the winner's purse of $950. Ned Jarrett had his B.G. Holloway Chevy on the pole, flanked by Cotton Owens' reliable old '60 Pontiac.

Blinded now by buckshot, the light fixture may have illuminated Frank Mundy in Victory Lane at the first night race in Grand National history on June 16, 1951.

The race got underway and Jarrett got lost. He roared away in that blue and white Chevy 11 as the competition fell out one at a time. Pardue dumped his old Lowe's '59 Dodge for his new Lowe's '59 Chevy and threw a rod for 22nd and last. Jack Smith was right behind him and blew his Pontiac for 21st. Irwin's T-Bird was next for 20th then on lap 67, George Green crashed his Chevy out for a yellow flag and 19th. Just past halfway, Buck lost the rear end in Buddy's Chrysler 86 for 16th. With legendary fame and enormous popularity still five weeks away, 1960 Rookie of the Year David Pearson busted the A-frame on his '60 Chevrolet 67 and nabbed 14th and $85. The magic was about used up in Doug Yates' old '59 Plymouth when he qualified tenth, only to lose the fuel pump for 12th. At the front, Ned was legging it away as Cotton, the Golden Greek, Petty (since February 24th it was only Richard), and Rex dueled for second. With a mile and a half to go, number 11 sputtered and coughed and rolled dead stick into the pits while old reliable Pontiac number 6 thundered by into the lead. Ned came up three laps short on the Pure and Cotton picked victory from those jaws, zipping home a winner by a lap over Jarrett once Ned got fired up again. Third was Zervakis, fourth Grover Clinton Spencer, and fifth White after winning two in a row. Others were Petty sixth, Harb seventh, Crider eighth, Harry Leake ninth, and tenth, a tight 29 laps behind, Herman the Turtle, with a car so pristine that any rental company in the business would take it back with no question other than "Did you fill it up?" Wendell Scott finished 11th in the fifth start since his debut in Spartanburg on March 4th, equaling his best finish to date with even better results just around the corner. Bradenton Bob Barron was 13th and there was nothing special about it except that he ran one race in 1960 and 31 in 1961 and retired. Lee Reitzel, a.k.a. Dr. L.L. Reitzel, wound up 15th, 78 laps behind, and the last man standing in his first start. The doc operated for 29 more races. The "King of the Modifieds" had done it again: Cotton Owens won this 100-miler going away.

It does not get much hotter than July in Columbia, South Carolina, and on the 20th you could cool off at the movies and see *The Misfits*, *West Side Story*, or *The Pit and the Pendulum*. This was the month Ernest Hemingway and Ty Cobb exited, Roger Maris hit six of his 61 dingers, MLB played two All-Star games as the Nationals won at Candlestick before they tied at Fenway, and the Phillies launched an epic 23-game losing streak. The first commercial airliner was hijacked to Cuba and Gus Grissom blew the hatch too soon, sending Liberty Bell 7 to the bottom of the Atlantic. In the World 600 a few weeks earlier, two men drove black '61 Fords for their last Grand National starts: Joe Eubanks took 13th in 82 and Tim Flock finished 37th in 15. A healthy field of 21 aligned in Columbia including all of the title contenders except Fireball. A third of the field was from Spartanburg or drove a car from there and Cotton Owens, from both categories, took the pole in that wicked, winning white '60 Bonneville 6. Bud Moore's new Pontiac started outside Cotton with Weatherly at the wheel and dashed through the thick, dusty night air to lead the first quarter. During that time, Crawfish's red '61 Mercury broke for 21st and last while Yates' once-potent Plymouth blew for 19th. Jack Smith retired with an oil leak just before halfway for 18th, and after the crossed flags flew, World 600 and Firecracker 250 victor David Pearson flew into the fence for 17th, creating the lone caution. Paschal landed Joe Lee's new Chevy for the night and had 14 cruising to checkers when Cotton locked in on him and thundered by with seven left. Not done yet, Paschal darted high and low as he flailed away at the rear bumper of the widest-wide track Pontiac imaginable. Nevertheless, Owens prevailed for an eyelash victory. It was a 1961 Capital City sweep for the spunky Spartan, mirroring the 1960 version authored by neighbor Rex White. In fact, a Spartanburg driver, or car, or both, had won nine of the last 13 Columbia Grand National races! Third came Jarrett on the lead lap, Junior Johnson fourth in a '60 Pontiac bought from Cotton, and fifth was Weatherly, both two laps back. Rounding out the notables were Zervakis sixth, Petty seventh, Spencer eighth, Greenville's L.D. Austin ninth, Herman the Turtle tenth, Larry Thomas in his third bigtime start 12th, Tiny 13th, fading point leader White 14th, Buck blew for 15th, and Pardue was 16th. As for the cigar-chomping Cotton Owens, he was at the top of his game and a contender no matter where he raced.

Friday, April 13, 1962, and surprisingly, super-superstitious Joe Weatherly raced in the Arclite 200 that night and sat on the pole in Bud Moore's '61 Pontiac. With Jack Smith lined up outside row one and Rex White, Cotton Owens, Buck Baker, and G. C. Spencer also in the field, it looked like a safe bet a Spartanburg entity would win its fifth in a row in Columbia. It was looking even more likely as Weatherly jumped out front followed by Smith, White, and shocking Jim Bennett, who started third in his fifth Grand National start. But Bennett, from Jonesboro, GA, was the first to retire with engine problems for 19th. He was a blip on racing's radar screen as he finished fifth at Greenville six days later and 15th at Myrtle Beach two days after that, never to race with the big boys again. He died in 1990. Cotton's old reliable '60 Pontiac that won both races here last year overheated on lap 33, claiming 18th. Up front, Joe still led and Ned was the only one challenging for the lead, which he got for good with a handful of laps left. About that time, the only caution flew as Wendell Scott, running in the top ten, crashed his '61 Chevy for 16th and still managed to beat Darlington's Frank Sessoms making his first of five career Grand National starts in Gene Stokes' '61 Studebaker 31. Frank did not quite have what the other Studebaker-driving Frank had here back in the inaugural of 1951. When the 200 dusty laps were done, it was Jarrett edging Weatherly for the win with Smith two laps back in third, Paschal fourth, and Spencer fifth. Other chauffeurs were White sixth, Petty seventh, Buck eighth, Ralph Earnhardt ninth, Crawfish 11th, Buddy 13th right where he started on the 13th, and the Turtle still running 14th. Ned took an hour and three-quarters to win the whopping $1,200 prize.

July 7, 1962, was a typically hot, lazy, southern Saturday night and a good crowd arrived for the race after Fireball Roberts won the Firecracker 250 the previous Wednesday, Independence Day morning at Daytona. Twenty entries arrived, some no doubt on their way back up the eastern seaboard to their shops and garages in the Carolinas and Virginia. Jack Smith put his black and red-roofed Pontiac on the pole with Petty outside. Weatherly lined up third, Rex fourth, and so on until 18th where '61 Chrysler number 87 sat, but Buck was not in it. For the first time since the opener in 1951, Buck Baker missed the lineup at Columbia, a streak of 24 straight races and four wins. For whatever reason, Buddy got the call. The green fell and Smith, Weatherly, Petty, White, Jarrett, and Owens jockeyed for the lead. At 20 laps, Petty blew and at 60, Larry Thomas demolished his Dodge. The race settled down to a battle between five Spartanburg cars and Jarrett. After touring the 200 gritty laps, it was Rex White back in Victory Lane for the third time at Columbia and the sixth of the season. Close behind was Weatherly in Bud Moore's "Dirt Dauber," trailed by Smith, Owens, and Jarrett all a lap back. Sixth went to Irwin, ninth to Wendell despite parking because he ran out of tires after 186 laps, 11th to the Turtle, 13th to the Crawfish, 14th was Buddy, 15th came Cayce, SC's Joe Penland in his first career Grand National start, driving for Floyd Powell, and 16th to Paschal. Rex got his $1,000 in a record speed of 96 minutes and 12 seconds. He out-stripped the field on the night of the day "The Stripper" rose to number one on the charts, by David Rose.

Perspective. Thursday night, May 2, 1963, they ran 100 miles at Columbia Speedway and kicked off an interesting month in history. Sandy Koufax no-hit the Mets and Don Nottebart did the same to the Phillies. Early Wynn struck out number 300 and Mantle slapped

A pine tree has blasted its way through the asphalt of Turn One.

one off the façade at Yankee Stadium. Bob Dylan walked off *The Ed Sullivan Show* while Peter, Paul, and Mary won a Grammy for "If I Had a Hammer" about the same time their "Puff the Magic Dragon" hit number two. Parnelli took Indy. Gordo Cooper became the last man to go into space alone in the final Mercury mission and race riots wracked Birmingham. In Hollywood, Dick Van Dyke, E.G. Marshall, and Shirley Booth took home Emmys. A few things really stand out about this race that will be evident soon. They lined up with Richard on the pole and Buck barely missing quick time in second. Baker won his last pole in Greenville on October 28, 1961, and he never got this close again. Honestly, it was a weak field as some drivers on the way up did not have good rides and those on the way down did not either. A lot of never-will-bes filled in the grid. When the green waved, it was Richard, Buck, and Ned distancing themselves from the pack. Cautions marred the event as Bobby Isaac crashed out for 21st, Maurice Petty did the same for 20th, and Weatherly in a borrowed ride followed suit for 19th. Charlotte's Jerome Warren had his best finish in the last of five 1963 career starts in a Ford for 18th, 87 laps behind. Next was hometown Sammy Fogle in a Mercury in his last of eight career starts, also in 1963, for 17th. Jimmy Massey crashed out for 16th on lap 137. At the front, Petty led, but Jarrett and Baker would not go away. Staying with the leaders at the three-quarter mark was Jack Smith in his last full year of Grand National competition, although he ran only 29 of 55. Frequent cautions kept Buddy Baker in the hunt, too, in Buck's old '62 Chrysler 7. All five thundering around the old oval was a most memorable display. In fact, Buck and Buddy had never finished on the lead lap together in their entire careers. The cautions ended after 13 and it was a sprint to the finish with Richard Petty finally winning in Columbia. But he did it with Buck Baker beating away at his back bumper. Buck made up for missing the last race here by whipping a younger Ned Jarrett in third, Buddy fourth, and Smith fifth in a Plymouth. All five of these current and future great drivers finished on the lead lap. Sixth was Castles in yet a third Baker entry, '62 Chrysler 86, which was a respectable two laps back. Seventh was Wendell, tenth LeeRoy Yarbrough, the Turtle 11th, Pardue 13th, and the Crawfish still running in 15th. A throng of 5,000 left after a little less than two hours of action, having seen a great close race between Hall of Famers whose careers would span from the first Strictly Stock race on June 19, 1949, until Buddy's last race 29 years and one day later on May 3, 1992. This 100-miler represents a passing of eras. Young newcomers Richard Petty, Buddy Baker, Bobby Isaac, and LeeRoy Yarbrough battled old timers Buck Baker, Jack Smith, Joe Weatherly, and Ned Jarrett. It is all perspective.

As usual, the return match for 1963 was on a Thursday, August 8th. It was the month Craig Breedlove jetted to a land speed record of 407 miles per hour in *The Spirit of America*, the X-15 rocketed 67 miles up, and the Great Train Robbery took place in England. The Kingsmen released "Louie, Louie" and Reverend Martin Luther King made his famous "I have a dream..." speech at the Lincoln Memorial in Washington. In Columbia, 22 stockers waited under the lights before almost 9,000 for the Sandlapper 200. Petty had the pole with Moore's burgundy and black Bonneville 8 of Weatherly outside. Bobby Isaac had Bondy Long's black 99 Fastback inside row two, flanked by Junior Johnson in the famous Ray Fox Impala 3. The field was dotted with some pretty good boys and a real unusual story. The Sandlapper 200 also had a very interesting first. The '63 Petty Plymouth scooted to a comfortable lead with challengers Jarrett, Johnson, Isaac, Buck Baker, Smith, Weatherly, and Cotton's Dodges of Pearson and Rookie of the Year candidate Billy Wade. Ed Livingston crashed early to bring out a caution on lap ten for 21st. On lap 102, Johnson was making a charge to the front when he lost control passing for third and launched himself over the rail at the end of the backstretch. Junior crashed down an embankment, coming to rest on his lid in the bushes, perilously close to some parked cars. Johnson was shaken, not stirred, in his hair-raising ride out of the park, getting credit for 17th. On the restart, Joel Davis smacked the wall and the third and final caution flew. It was not until lap 104 when Pearson took over the point from Petty and settled in for healthy period. As David paced the field, Buck parked his Pontiac for 15th with suspension ills. Newcomer J.D. McDuffie retired for 14th after starting sixth. Then Petty started reeling Pearson in, deftly banging his way by on lap 166, and holding on to beat Pearson by half a straightaway. Third went Isaac and fourth Jarrett, both on the lead lap. Fifth two back was Spencer, sixth Wade, seventh Smith, eighth Cale, ninth Wendell, 11th Weatherly, who broke with 15 laps to go, Crawfish 12th, and Augusta's Frank Warren, in his second career start, the last man running in a '61 Pontiac number X.

Now the unusual story of 18th place finisher Billy Oswald. Billy was from New York City and made a total of two career Grand National starts. His first showed some promise as he purred home ninth ten years earlier on June 21, 1953, in the International 200 at Langhorne. Oswald started 38th and last on the oily one-mile circle that killed Frank Arford in time trials. He brought his Porsche home ahead of guys named Baker, Keller, Flock, Eubanks, Schneider, Rexford and 22 others. The fascination is why he waited over ten years to try again, why at Columbia instead of up north, and why in a junk '61 Mercury. Billy Oswald started last twice, never out-qualifying anybody in his whole Grand National career.

Now for that very interesting first. In the battle of arguably the two greatest stock car careers in NASCAR history, Richard Petty and David Pearson went head-to-head 550 times between the first qualifier for the Daytona 500 on February 12, 1960, and the Champion Spark Plug 400 on August 17, 1986, in Michigan. In between, Petty won 200 races and Pearson 105. They finished one-two 63 times. The first time they went one-two was in this Sandlapper 200. The final time and score? The last Petty-Pearson one-two finish was on June 12, 1977, when Petty edged Pearson in the NAPA 400 at Riverside. They raced head-to-head for nine more years and never did it again. The final score in Petty-Pearson one-two finishes was Pearson first 33 times and Petty 30.

In April 1964, Douglas McArthur died and the Polo Grounds came down as the Mets opened at Shea Stadium. Arnold Palmer won the Masters, Sandy Koufax tossed his ninth complete game without a walk and became the first major leaguer to strike out the side on nine pitches. Sidney Poitier was the first African-American to win the Best Actor Oscar and the Chesapeake Bay Bridge-Tunnel opened. The Grand Nationals arrived for the Columbia 200 in the midst of an absolutely tortuous five races in nine days. How could that be possible? A 62-race season helps! They ran Saturday, April 11th at Weaverville, where Panch won; Sunday, April 12th at Hillsborough, where Pearson won; Tuesday, April 14th at Spartanburg, where Jarrett won; then here on Thursday, April 16th, and North Wilkesboro on Sunday, April 19th. A *wicked* schedule, but 22 teams hauled down from Spartanburg, and Pearson took the pole with Jarrett outside. Petty, Wade, Yarbrough, Panch, Lund, and Hutcherson lined up next. Just about the time the lights kicked in, the packed house saw Pearson jump out front for the first 18 laps until Tiny Lund slipped by for 13. Jarrett brought the caution flag when he spun down the front stretch and tagged the pit rail. He repaired it and found himself behind everybody, luckily never losing a lap. Jimmy Helms' third career start ended on the grid as his ancient Buck Baker Chrysler would not start for 22nd and last, right where he started. Buddy only made it a lap before he broke the shifter for 21st, right where he started. Tiny relinquished the lead when his Graham Shaw Ford overheated and parked for 19th. Overheating also took out Larry Frank on lap 35 for 18th and Baker's other old '62 Chrysler lost its brakes with Castles aboard, retiring for 17th on lap 48. LeeRoy Yarbrough put his yellow '63 Plymouth number 45 in the lead for 23 tours until he gave it up to Pearson. All the while, Jarrett was dissecting the field in his royal blue '64 Courtesy Ford, passing cars as he got to them, while the crowd sensed they were watching an almost impossible charge to the front. Wade took the lead from Pearson on lap 75 and seemed to have things going his way for over 60 laps. Petty lost the rear end on the Plymouth to claim 15th after 129 laps. Jarrett drew closer and closer until he caught Wade in traffic and swiped the lead on lap 137 and was untouchable. Ned eventually lapped the field turning an early disaster into an absolute rout. Second was Panch, third went to Yarbrough, fourth Wade, and finishing fifth rumbled Dick Hutcherson. After this, Hutch loaded up and went back to Iowa, his three-week foray into the Grand National ranks over with two poles and two top fives in four dirt track starts. He would return in January 1965 driving a Holman-Moody Ford and stay in one capacity or another until his untimely death while driving through Columbia on November 6, 2005, returning from vacation. Sixth was Pearson, seventh Elmo Henderson, eighth Pardue, ninth the Crawfish, 11th Ralph Earnhardt, and Wendell Scott 14th, the last man running. It took just over an hour and 33 minutes for Jarrett to pull off the amazing comeback despite six cautions, the first of which he caused.

The oppressive heat across America in August of 1964 was due to more than just the weather. North Vietnam fired on the U.S.S. *Maddox* in the Gulf of Tonkin and three days later, the U.S. started bombing back. Three missing civil rights activists were found buried in an earthen dam in Mississippi and race riots exploded in Jersey City, Paterson, and Elizabeth, NJ, as well as Philadelphia and Dixmoor, IL. At the Democratic Convention in Atlantic City, LBJ was nominated. *Mary Poppins* opened at the box office and the Beatles were on top with a song that should have been the race winner's theme on Friday night,

Strange barrier transition from railroad track to wood takes place at the end of the homestretch.

August 21, 1964. The Sandlapper 200 field of 21 lined up that hot August night like the one Neil Diamond sang about years later. Jarrett had the pole, Petty was outside with not-so surprising Doug Yates and Junior Johnson in row two. The race got off with Petty leaping out front with Pearson, Yates, and Johnson in tow. But a flat tire early on Pearson's Dodge nearly put him down a lap. Like Jarrett in the spring race, David found himself in a huge hole with everybody to pass, but almost all race to do it. His first break came on lap 17 when Petty retired with hemi problems for 17th. The next fortuitous occurrence took place at the halfway point when Johnson, who inherited the lead when Petty retired, blew his yellow Ford and was out for 14th. Then Buddy Arrington spun his Dodge into the infield, backed into traffic, and got creamed by E.J. Trivette and Bobby Isaac. Arrington and Isaac made up row four at the start and two more major Pearson rivals were history. Billy Wade put Bud's big Bristol Lincoln-Mercury 1 on the point until lap 145 when the rear end roasted itself and he took tenth. Ned had the lead and could surely hang on as tough as he was. With ten to go, blue smoke started trailing from the blue Ford and after a few more rounds, Pearson was sitting with a two-lap lead over Doug Yates and Jarrett was climbing out. Pearson did not exactly back into the win, but it was close. Chapel Hill's Doug Yates never came closer to a win in an 86-race career dating from 1952 to 1965. Third was Jimmy Pardue, who had a month and a day to live, fourth was Jarrett not running, and fifth eased Doug Cooper. Other notables were Doug Moore from Chattanooga in the best finish of his 29-race career in sixth, Wendell seventh, eighth came Gastonia's Jim Dimeo in the best finish of a three-race career spanning from August 9th to the next night at Winston-Salem, and Buck's two beat-up '62 Chryslers finishing 15th with Neil Castles and 21st with Steve Young, completing only a lap. In two races, Buck's two Chryslers ran a total of 107 laps. The last two finishers ran their entire careers in 1964 as Charlotte's Young had nine starts and Charleston's Don Branson eight. And that Beatles song for winner Pearson's theme? "A Hard Day's Night," because it was.

For the first time since the Grand Nationals started coming here, they decided to race on Wednesday night. The balmy spring day turned into a threatening spring evening. Nevertheless, over seven thousand came to see a slim field of 18 without the top Mopar boys do it in the dirt for the Sandlapper 200. The date was April 28th and it was the day after Edward R. Murrow died and Pampers were invented. It was the day that U.S. Marines invaded the Dominican Republic and the day before an earthquake rocked Seattle, killing five. With Jarrett on the pole in one of two factory rides, the ne'er-do-wells were foaming at the mouth for a chance to score big. This happened a lot in 1965 without Chrysler around. Outside Ned was Inman's G.C. Spencer in a '64 Ford and row two had Paul "Little Bud" Moore inside. People used "Little Bud" because some confused him with Bud Moore, the car owner. It was very easy to keep them straight. One was a legendary car builder and owner from Spartanburg with a decade and a half in the big time standing about six feet six inches tall. The other was an excellent up-and-coming sportsman short-track driver from Charleston standing about a foot shorter. It was impossible to confuse the two if one just half-listened to the context of what was being said. Outside Paul was Tiny Lund of Cross in his familiar wrinkled orange and white Hallmark Homes '64 Ford 55. It was an all–South Carolina first four since Ned was residing in Camden at the time. Uncharacteristically, back in 11th lurked the factory Ford of Dick Hutcherson. At the green, Jarrett assumed the lead and felt he could outlast, if not outrun, these guys. His plan was right on as Moore crashed his Louis Weathersby Plymouth while running with the leaders on lap five for 18th and last. On lap 22, Tiny forged ahead and ten laps later G.C. steamed into the pits overcooked for 17. At 25 miles, another '64 Ford of Cale Yarborough led for three laps before Hutch slipped by for a pair. Lund roared to the front on lap 55 and was still there just past halfway when Buddy Baker wracked up Buck's old '64 Dodge 88, which was actually an ex–Cotton Owens machine and still a good car. He started fifth in the Old Goat, as it was called, and was hanging around the leaders when he crashed out for 14th. Jarrett grabbed the lead back, but the ensuing restart triggered another melee. Cayce, SC's Joe Penland had a shunt that ended his four-year, seven-race career with a best-ever 12th after a best-ever seventh place start. Penland's caution allowed a reluctant skyward glance, revealing raindrops spitting down. A different thunder than had been heard all evening followed, brief pitchforks of lightning piercing the blackness behind the lights. The green fell on lap 110 with a sense of urgency and by the time they roared back around, the Big Fisherman powered past Jarrett and took the lead. Shortly thereafter on lap 123, the sky opened up, NASCAR threw the red and checkers, and a happy, wet, midweek crowd scurried to the parking lots and home. Tiny Lund had his first win since the 1963 Daytona 500 and a hard-fought one that was well deserved, making up for a few others that got away. Jarrett was second and Neil Castles third in a big '65 Plymouth Fury 86 of Buck Baker's stable. It is a car that had a fine life until the end of the season, as it and Buddy took second to A.J. Foyt in the Firecracker 400 at Daytona and Buck and Buddy co-drove it to second 14 laps behind Jarrett in the Southern 500. Fourth was Dieringer and fifth went to Hutcherson who made his move too late to beat the rain. On back came Tyner sixth, Wendell ninth, Cale tenth, and 12th was Greenville's Jeff Hawkins in the third of a nine-race career spanning four years. The 32-lap career of David Warren from Cleveland, NC, started and ended in a '63 Ford, starting 16th and overheating for 17th, retiring to the back pages of Grand National history after 16 miles.

Although rain-shortened, the one hour, six minutes, and 55-second race counted the same as the Daytona 500 for Tiny in the win column.

Of course, it was Thursday night and miserably hot and sticky on August 19, 1965. The world seemed to be coming apart at the seams. The month saw Morley Safer report on CBS that we were losing the war in Vietnam. Watts rioted and burned for six days. West Chicago burned, too. The Beatles' movie *Help* opened in New York to coincide with their famous Shea Stadium concert and an Ed Sullivan appearance. Joe Engle took the X-15 to 82 miles up and Cooper and Conrad lapped the globe 120 times in Gemini 5. The Reds' Jim Maloney hurled his second no-hitter of the year, the Giants' Juan Marichal whacked Dodger John Roseboro on the coconut with a bat, and Casey Stengel retired. At Columbia Speedway, the first of the final 13 Grand National races held there was staged and only three different guys will win that baker's dozen. The Mopar boys were back and the place was jammed, with no threat of rain. Many came out to see if Curtis Turner would make his long-awaited return, and he did, but to watch. He tried at Spartanburg five days earlier and crashed in time trials. A terrific field of 23 entries was on hand and the heavies were there. Dick Hutcherson had the pole with Junior Johnson outside. Row two included Jarrett and Lund. Three had Petty and Pearson. And some more good shoes were on back, like Cale and LeeRoy, Paul Moore and Darel, Tiger Tom and Wendell, and Buck and Buddy brought up the rear. Ford had the top four spots, but Chrysler was back and hungry. Junior put the yellow Holly Farms 26 out front at the onset and stayed there as the weeding-out process got underway. On lap two, Bob Derrington, Tiger Tom, and J.T. Putney had a grinding crash at the head of the homestretch for the first caution. Paul Moore, driving for Elmo Langley, parked for 18th and leader Johnson snapped the throttle linkage and loaded up for 17th. That gave the lead to Hutcherson, who kept that gold and white 29 on the point, only slowed by a couple more cautions. On lap 56, Buddy Baker was doing a good job of keeping up in the Old Goat until he cracked the rail and retired for 15th. The career of Union, SC's Sam Smith ended at 108 laps when he bounced Sam Fogle's yellow '63 Ford 31 off a dirt bank and his Grand National dream evaporated in 13th place. That is about when Cotton made a wedge adjustment to get more traction coming off the turns and Pearson's Dodge went from O.K. to great. On lap 116, the Dodge passed the gold Ford and except for a few laps during pit stops, Pearson was gone. With the finish in sight, Ned crashed out, costing him points as Hutcherson closed the gap on him in the title chase. It was a Pearson-over-Petty finish this time by about a second, with Hutch third on the lead lap. Fourth came Lund, fifth Yarborough, sixth Yarbrough, seventh Jarrett, eighth Scott, ninth Castles, tenth Buck, and in 12th shot Dieringer. It was an outstanding race, taking Pearson almost an hour and three quarters to gain his 12th career win.

The world had cooled off a bit by April 1966, but not enough. Staff Sgt. Barry Sadler's "The Ballad of the Green Berets" was number one on the airwaves as B-52s started pounding North Vietnam. Another B-52 lost an atomic bomb, which was found in the Mediterranean. The USSR's Luna 10 was the first satellite to orbit the moon, and brand-new Atlanta–Fulton County Stadium opened with the Braves winning their 18th game in a row (the first 17 in Milwaukee). Jack Nicklaus won his second Masters in a row, the Celtics won the NBA title with Red Auerbach retiring as their coach, and Lee Marvin won an Oscar as Kid Shelleen/Tim Strawn in *Cat Ballou*. At Columbia Speedway on Thursday the 7th, a surprising crowd of 11,000 came to see the Grand Nationals race, 24 hours after Ford withdrew from the series. This time it was a tiff over Ford's overhead cam engine that NASCAR had restricted so much it was impractical. Chances are it would not have been used on the short tracks anyway. Did it mean that the public embraced the circuit more without the

Fords (Jarrett, Hutcherson, Turner, Johnson, Isaac, Lorenzen, Panch) than it did without the Chryslers (Petty, Pearson, Paschal, Goldsmith)? Could be that Petty-Pearson was just that big to NASCAR? Maybe the fans had already bought their tickets before the boycott was announced. Whatever the reason, it was an overflow crowd under the Thursday-night lights. Maybe they just were not that wild about staying home and watching *Batman, Daniel Boone, F Troop, Star Trek, Bewitched, My Three Sons,* and *That Girl*. Two dozen cars lined up with Tom Pistone on the pole in a two-year-old Ford, with J.T. Putney outside in Louis Clements' Chevy 19. Row two saw Buddy in Buck's '65 Chevy 88 and John Sears in another two-year-old Ford. So where were the Mopar stars? Pearson in a two-year-old Cotton Owens Dodge was outside Stick Elliott's Chevy in row three and Petty was outside Clyde Lynn in row nine after hopping the rail and leaving the track in time trials. He at least got it raceable. The last time the independents were licking their chops this much in Columbia, Tiny Lund won an abbreviated 100-miler. The green waved and Pistone waved bye-bye in his blue Shoney's 59. However, Tiny would not be as lucky as before, overheating quickly and parking on lap 13 for 24th and last. Three laps later the Old Pro Buck Baker lost the water pump in his '66 Olds 87 for 23rd. Pearson struggled past Pistone on lap 54 and led for 30 rounds until Putney led for one and Goldsmith in a borrowed Bob Cooper '65 Plymouth 02 assumed real command. The racing was furious and it was every man for himself! On lap 95, Buddy Baker joined Dad on the sidelines as for the second Columbia race in a row he pounded the wall for 19th. A few laps later, Pearson reclaimed first with Goldy glued to his bumper. Pistone tried to keep up, but faded, as did Putney and Sears. Petty, on the other hand, was doing all he could to race a wreck into contention and was moving up. With a lap to go, Goldsmith was darting, feinting, and beating away at Pearson's museum piece, but could not outfox the Silver Fox-to-be. David sped to his second win in a row at Columbia, his second win in a row in 1966, and was going to add the next two races at Greenville and Bowman-Gray to make it four straight in a two-year-old car. As for Paul Goldsmith, he was a close second, having finished fifth in the same 02 four days earlier when Pearson won at Hickory and the Fords were still racing. (Turner was second, Isaac third, and Jarrett fourth.) An interesting fact about Goldy was that although he already had two wins in 1966, until Hickory, *he had not even run on Grand National dirt since he won the last beach race at Daytona in 1958!* Paul Goldsmith was a racer ... two wheels or four, dirt or asphalt. Third was a game pole-sitter Tom Pistone, two laps back, with front row mate Putney fourth, also two down, and Sears fifth. Adding to the scenery was Petty sixth, the Wild Injun seventh, and Toy Bolton eighth. Gastonia's Bolton ran his fourth and last Grand National race that night, matching an eighth place at Hickory with this one, departing the tour having nothing to be ashamed of in his big-league career. On back came Scott ninth and Ringgold, GA's Wayne Woodward 11th, matching his Hickory best-ever career finish in the third of a seven-race 1966 career. Buck's third miserable entry was that beat-up '65 Fury 86 driven by Soapy Castles to 15th, with the last man running, Jim Tatum of Jacksonville, FL, 17th in the second of an uneventful five-race career. Spartanburg's Pearson won the 1000 fish in just over an hour and a half.

The simmering summer of '66 peaked in August and historic events dotted its passing, a mixture of the horrible, memorable, and wonderful. It started horribly as Charles Whitman gunned down more than a dozen innocent citizens from the University of Texas Tower. Lenny Bruce OD'd two days later and Martin Luther King, Jr., was stoned in Chicago. The Beatles released *Revolver* here and *Yellow Submarine* across the pond, beginning their last U.S. tour. Race riots exploded in Lansing and Waukeegan. A daytime meteor entered and exited the Earth's atmosphere in the only known occurrence of that sort and was seen from Utah to Canada. Francis Chichester launched the first solo sailing voyage around the world, the first U.S. lunar orbiter lapped the moon, and on the 29th, the Beatles played their last U.S. concert at Candlestick Park. In the middle of all of that, the wonderful happened at Columbia Speedway on the sultry, sticky Thursday night of August 18, 1966. This one gets discussed when the legendary races of yore come up as something that *cannot* happen again. A bulging crowd of nearly ten thousand watched a big lineup of 26 take the grid. The Fords were given the green light to return to the Grand National fold during the week and would be in full force soon. The race prior to Columbia was the Dixie 400 in Atlanta 11 days earlier and was consumed with controversy. Junior Johnson had Fred Lorenzen driving the infamous "Banana Boat" Ford and Curtis Turner drove Smokey Yunick's Chevelle that NASCAR Chief Technical Inspector Norris Friel said had a list of violations that ultimately numbered 175. Nevertheless, it sat on the pole and both Turner and Lorenzen, who started third, led a lot before Curtis blew and Fred crashed within nine laps of each other mid-race. Others at Atlanta were not allowed to run for much less grievous infractions, like Cotton's Dodge with David Pearson, which were streaking to the championship. LeeRoy Yarbrough's Jon Thorne Dodge and Ned Jarrett driving Bernie Alvarez's Ford were both sent home. It was a black eye for NASCAR and there were plenty of hard feelings to go around. Turner felt everyone should lighten up and had a one-race deal to drive Junior's more conventional dirt track Holly Farms Ford at Columbia. A banana boat configuration would not do much good in a dirt track setting. Holly Farms wanted Curtis to look good and told him for the race he had to wear a suit. And he did ... *a business suit!* "I dipped this one in that fireproof stuff this morning," Turner exclaimed to the throng of onlookers glued to his every move. He loosened the tie a bit, hiked up the long sleeves some, and sans jacket, stuck that baby on the front row much to everyone's delight. Regardless of what other horrors were going on in the world, everything was fine under this umbrella of light in the South Carolina Capital City. Another crowd-pleasing occurrence was the appearance of Bobby Allison in his J.D. Bracken '65 Chevelle that he had been in since June 15th. Bobby made 11 starts in it, notching two poles and two wins. He got pole three this night at the expense of the "new" Curtis Turner and the track record. He sailed that little red and white 2 around that dirty half-mile at a scorching 73.469 miles per hour. Row two had Petty and Pearson. Row three saw Langley and Hylton. The fourth row was made up of Hutcherson and Michigan rookie Johnny Wynn in Spartanburg builder John McCarthy's ex–Bud Moore '64 Mercury 06. Row five found Buddy Baker and John Sears with Spartanburg sportsman ace Buster Sexton 12th in his first-ever Grand National start, Wendell 13th, Friday Hassler 16th, and Clyde Lynn 18th in a '64 Ford he flipped spectacularly in time trials. Tiny Lund lined up 19th in that same exhausted orange and white '64 Ford 55 in their 55th start together, Larry Hess was 20th in a Rambler, and Tom Pistone started 26th and last after arriving at the track with barely enough time to line up, let alone make a time trial. The stage was set for war!

Looking at the bare stats, this 100-miler might even appear dull. When the big field roared off, Turner bulled his way past the little Chevelle and took the lead. It was very tentative, but he held it for 134 laps with Allison, Pearson, Petty, Hylton, Hutcherson, and Baker beating and banging away behind him. Other fun took place on lap 17 when a furiously-racing Tom Pistone was passing them as he got to them and lost it entering turn one. The Tiger struck the railing at the perfect angle to launch the two-tone blue '64 Ford 59 over it and into the lighted sky, then into darkness. It nosed harmlessly down, settling among the small trees and shrubs fringing the backside of the first turn embankment. Doug Cooper fell out on lap 41 for 25th in the '65 Plymouth 02 that Goldsmith drove so well in the spring. After experiencing his best start in eighth, Johnny Wynn lost the engine in McCarthy's old

Merc, and Wynn's 21-race Grand National career ended. It all happened in 1966 for Johnny in the same car as he had two sixths in his first three starts and two sevenths later. Clyde Lynn parked his old 20 due to the ill effects of his time trial tumble for 22nd. A routine pit stop was not so routine when Turner brought his race-leading Ford to the attention of the Junior Johnson crew under the green on lap 134 for the only planned stop. It was not supposed to last long enough for Curtis to be eligible to vote there. He could have been a candidate! When he finally got out of stir, everyone else pitted and they set no records either. Curtis was behind, though, and really punched that 26 around the oval like he had so many other 26s. Petty was out front for a couple until pesky and popular number 2 scooted under and Allison had the lead. The Hueytown Hustler held the point for 30 laps until his 327 cubic inches started wilting. On lap 167, unstoppable David Pearson powered past Petty and ambushed Allison for the lead. Contenders Hylton, Hutcherson, and Baker had enough adversity to render themselves afterthoughts. With Turner screaming past a rapidly fading Allison and closing on the others, a three-car Armageddon was at hand. With less than five to go, McDuffie got crossed up and ditched his '64 Ford along the backstretch for 12th, bringing a caution flag that doused a surely explosive finish. Under the yellow, Spartanburg's David Gene Pearson rolled to the checkered flag with Petty and Turner lined up right behind. Even though nearly 10,000 enthusiasts did not get to see the incredible race to the wire that was inevitable, no one felt cheated. They saw blazing speed, spectacular crashes, and Grand National racing at its historic best. Fourth was Hylton in his mustard-yellow '65 Dodge 48 and fifth cruised Hutcherson's Ford, both two laps behind. Sixth went to Langley's old '64 Ford, seventh to Hassler, eighth Buddy, ninth Sears, and tenth Bob Cooper. Pole-sitter Bobby Allison was 11th, ten laps back, Wendell 13th, Buster Sexton 14th, Tyner 16th, Larry Hess Rambered to 17th in the yellow 44 Ambassador, Tiny idled around for 18th, Canadian Don Biederman was 19th, and Joel Davis was the last man in 21st, 43 laps behind. For Pearson, it was an even dozen wins for what was to be his first championship year. For Curtis Turner, he had a couple of poles at Daytona in 1967 driving Yunick's newest Chevelle number 13, but this night was "suited" for his highest dirt track start and finish his until his twin-engine Aero Commander burrowed into the Pennsylvania countryside. Do not see this as a race with one guy leading the first 134 laps, two cautions, and a caution-flag finish. See this as one of 63 Pearson-Petty one-two finishes, six racers fighting almost all the way to the wire, cars flipping and leaving the track, and one of the most legendary figures in NASCAR history in his last/best race. This was a gem. *A diamond!*

The tour stopped in Columbia for another Thursday nighter on April 6, 1967, for the Sandlapper 200. The night before, Wilt the Stilt hauled down a record 41 rebounds for the 76ers. Later, U.S. bombers targeted Haiphong for the first time, Surveyor 3 soft-landed on the moon, Gay Brewer won the Masters, Muhammad Ali refused induction into the army and was stripped of his boxing title, and the Beatles signed a contract to stay together for ten more years. A slim field of 19 was on hand with no factory boycotts for an excuse. However, the winds of change were blowing. Curtis Turner barrel-rolled Smokey's Chevelle practicing at Atlanta the week before and the two long-time on-again, off-again partners parted ways. Smokey said he did not want to build the car that killed Curtis Turner. At Columbia, Pearson was there to defend his and Cotton's three wins in a row there, but for some reason Owens and number 6 did not show. They ran one more race together ten days later at North Wilkesboro and called it quits afterwards because of a tiff over who was supposed to have ridden with whom to the Columbia race. The number one song on the *Billboard Hot 100* was the Turtles' "Happy Together." The Yunick-Turner and Owens-Pearson teams were not. Hutcherson put his Bondy Long Ford on the pole with Petty outside. Behind them

Turn Two and its bleached banking had a median of weeds.

came Paschal and Sears, Langley and Hylton, Lund and Dick Johnson, and Scott and Bobby Allison in that exhausted '65 Chevelle number 2. Early dueling saw the lead swapped back and fourth between Petty and Paschal six times by lap 80. Allison blew on lap 11 for 19th and last. When Petty passed Paschal for the lead, Richard was gone. Paschal slipped back and finished a lap behind in second, followed by Hutcherson, Hylton, and Castles in Buck's old Oldsmobile. Further back came Scott sixth, Joel Davis in his last "silent speedways" race seventh, Elmo eighth, Lund 12th, and Sears 16th. Over 6,000 fans witnessed Petty win $1,000 in just over an hour and a half.

The dog days of summer 1967 simmered on. Twins pitcher Dean Chance pitched a perfect game *and within two weeks* a no-hitter. Dodger Al Downing struck out the side on nine pitches and the Doors' "Light My Fire" reached number one on the charts. Amanda Randolph, Paul Muni, and Brian Epstein died, and the final episode of *The Fugitive* aired. On Thursday the 17th, 24 stockers competed in a 100-miler on the dirty sand at Columbia Speedway. Sprinkled among the two dozen participants were about six with a chance to win. Pole-sitter Richard Petty with 19 checkers already under his belt was the favorite, flanked by Buddy Baker, now driving Cotton Owens' Dodge. Also on hand were Lund, Hutcherson, Paschal, Hylton, and Bobby Allison's ancient but fast Bracken '65 Chevelle again. About 7,000 sweaty spectators were ready to see if anybody could stop Petty. For the first two laps, nobody could until Allison roared up from fifth to grab the point for 34 laps. Hutcherson blew the Ford after a mile and a half for 24th and last while seventh starter Dick Johnson parked hard against the wall for 22nd and a caution flag on lap 12. Petty got back out front and the crowd roared its approval as Allison reclaimed it for the next 135 laps. Meanwhile, Paschal crashed Bill Friedkin's Plymouth 14 on lap 55 and loaded up for 20th, Buddy kept up for a while before parking Cotton's Dodge with a broken axle on lap 69 and 17th, and Tiny blew 28 laps later for 15th. With less than 10 miles to go, Petty started reeling Allison back in and rattled by on lap 189. Giving it his all, Bobby pushed a little too hard and slapped the rail in turn four, losing even more ground. Richard romped away from there and became the first, *and last*, person to win 19 races in a season, doing it in *37 races*. And Petty still had 13 more chances in the 1967 season! The win broke Tim Flock's 1955 record of 18 wins that seemed unreachable. Second was Sears a lap back with Elmo third, Allison a fading fourth, and Hylton fifth. Also of note followed Wendell tenth, and 11th, in his finest race 50 laps back, roared Franklin, NC's Harold Stockton in an ex–Buck Baker Oldsmobile 35. This was the best, and last, finish in Harry's six-race 1967 career. Roy Tyner was 12th, Castles 14th, Tom Raley 19th, also in the midst of a nine-race 1967 career, and Jackie Fox 24th. This Fox from Asheville drove in his first Grand National this night and wound it up three weeks later at Hickory in a 57-lap career. At this stage of Richard Lee Petty's career, it did not matter if you were the Asheville Fox or the Silver Fox, nobody could beat the Man Who Would Be King.

Anyone old enough to remember 1968 will recall April and what they were doing when informed that Reverend Martin Luther King, Jr., had been assassinated in Memphis. Three days later in Hockenheim, Germany, the Flying Scot became airborne into a stand of trees in a Formula Two race and Jimmy Clark, the greatest Grand Prix driver of the day, was gone. It was the same as if Richard Petty lost his life in a sportsman race. Frankie Lymon overdosed six years after leaving his teens, HemisFair opened in San Antonio, and Rod Steiger and Katharine Hepburn hefted Oscars. Roberto De Vicenzo signed an incorrect scorecard, losing the Masters to Bob Goalby, and President Johnson signed the Civil Rights Act. Jimmy Ellis beat Jerry Quarry for Ali's vacated heavyweight crown and college kids gone wild took

A burned section of the Second Turn fence is wedged in the limbs of a mature tree.

over the administration buildings at Columbia and Ohio State Universities. Meanwhile, 23 Grand Nationals lined up in the dirt in Columbia. It was a decent field before a little less than 7,000 fans on a spring Thursday night, the 18th. Petty had the pole, surprising John Sears was outside and you just knew he would sneak into Victory Lane someday. He never did. Row two had Hylton's yellow Dodge 48 and Pearson's blue and gold Holman-Moody Ford 17. The third pairing consisted of Yarborough in Lyle Stelter's Mercury 56 and Isaac in K & K Insurance Dodge 37. Also on hand were Buddy Baker in Ray Fox's white Dodge 3, Chargin' Charlie Glotzbach in Cotton's burgundy and black Dodge 6, and Buck Baker in his own new red and white Oldsmobile 88. With a fine cast of characters like that, you would think they could have a better race. At the drop of the green, Petty jumped out front and stayed there for 14 laps until Catawba's Bobby Isaac came barreling by and took the lead ... for good. Bobby had not won a Grand National race since the second qualifier at Daytona on February 21, 1964, but when it is your night, it is. The last 186 circuits were all his for his second career victory and only Glotzbach and Hylton stayed within shouting distance, completing all 200 laps. Fourth was Buddy, Petty fifth, Sears sixth, Pearson seventh, Langley eighth, Yarbrough ninth, and Castles tenth. On back finished Buck 12th, Wendell 13th, and nobody else that mattered. Isaac would not wait 50 months to win again, pulling off another 15 days later in Augusta. In fact, this might have been the springboard leading to 28 more wins and a Grand National Championship over the next two years. But this should have been a better race.

The second trip of 1968 to Columbia occurred on Thursday night as usual, August 8th. That sultry summer night was hot and deadly in Miami as riots burned Liberty City. Elsewhere, 100,000 music lovers met at the Newport Pop Festival, the whole world watched as violence punctuated the Democratic National Convention in Chicago, the Beatles' "Hey Jude" was the first song released on the Apple label, and William Talman, who played loser Hamilton Burger to Perry Mason, died of cancer. In the Palmetto State's capital, two dozen stockers were poised for 200 laps in the Sandlapper 200. The main participants were Buddy Baker on the pole in Ray Fox's Dodge with Petty outside. Behind them rode Paul Moore in Bondy Long's Ford 29, flanked by Isaac in the orange Dodge 71. Peppering the pack were such luminaries as Yarbrough sixth, Glotzbach seventh, Bobby Allison eighth, determined Sears ninth, Pearson tenth, and Tiny 16th. Ten men with a solid shot at the $1,000 top prize. The green silk waved and Buddy Baker led for a mile until Moore nosed the gold Ford out front for 26 laps. Buddy swiped it back and the pop of a blowout sent Moore skidding into the rail and onto the trailer for 24th and last. On lap 72, Isaac emerged to take the point and hold it for 26 miles as Petty parked the Plymouth with a bum oil pan for 21st. Allison retired the reskinned Bracken '66 Chevelle 2 for 17th with a sick mill and Buddy followed shortly thereafter with a turn two shunt for 16th. With 75 laps left, Pearson made his move on Isaac and shot to the front with Isaac, Glotzbach, and Yarbrough dogging him all the way. A scary moment occurred on lap 178 when Big John Sears, one of the best drivers never to win a race, lost the handle in slippery turn three and vaulted L.G. DeWitt's Ford over the rail, bounding end over end into the surrounding trees and darkness. Sears was O.K. and settled for an uncharacteristic 13th. It was the only career non–top ten finish here for John. A few laps later, Isaac popped a tire, the rail, and finally the hemi, going to the trailer for 11th. But wait, here came Chargin' Charlie in Cotton's Dodge ... and he would cotton to steal one from his Spartanburg neighbor and ex-partner Pearson. The laps wound down and with one to go, Glotzbach nosed the Dodge ahead of Pearson as they slammed away at each other for the advantage. Real racing! Off of four and down the stretch they came banging and rubbing and smoking and it was Pearson's Ford under the checkers first with the

Weeds clearly mark the lanes in the Fourth Turn.

nose of Charlie's 6 covering the 17 on David's door. A lap back in third and praying for a Pearson/Glotzbach crash was LeeRoy Yarbrough, again in Lyle Stelter's Mercury 56. The transplanted Floridian living in Columbia was fresh off winning two of the past three races in his newly acquired ride in Junior Johnson's white Ford 98. The star was rising quickly for LeeRoy. Fourth was Elmo and fifth was Soapy. Adding to the scenery were Tiny sixth, Wendell eighth, and in his first of two career top tens was Laurinburg, NC's Walston Gardner in a black and yellow '67 Ford 93. This win was the first of four for Pearson over the next 16 days as he streaked towards 16 wins and the 1968 championship.

The Grand National tour made its first appearance of 1969 on the spring Thursday night of April 3rd. The world was pretty quiet, too, because it was the "Spring of Love." The first artificial heart was implanted, Bill Singer of the Dodgers got the first save officially recorded by MLB, and the first MLB game was played outside the U.S. The Concorde had its maiden flight, George Archer won the Masters, and Smokin' Joe Frazier took the heavyweight crown. Cliff Robertson and Katharine Hepburn took home Oscars, Sirhan Sirhan was convicted and sentenced to death for assassinating Robert Kennedy, Charles de Gaulle resigned, and Paul McCartney confirmed he was not dead. For the Columbia 200, a sizable field entered, but only four had an honest chance to win: the Fords of David Pearson and Richard Petty, and the Dodges of Bobby Isaac and James Hylton. Isaac took the pole with Pearson outside. Pretending to be a contender was Jabe Thomas, who put his '68 Plymouth on the grid third with Petty outside in fourth. When they got the go, Isaac jumped out front and stayed there for 48 laps. A two-car crash on lap seven brought out the first yellow when Tyner and Jack Etheridge tangled. Jack was an old-timer with three previous starts, the first being in Strictly Stock race number two on the Beach in 1949, where he finished tenth. This was the farewell for the 53-year-old Jacksonville, FL, native who never did better than that first race on the sand 20 years earlier. Etheridge got 24th. Up front, the lead swapped furiously as Pearson took it for a lap, then Sears for 14, Hylton for five, until Petty settled in for 82. With a quarter of the 100-miler left, Isaac put Harry Hyde's 71 out front after having lost a lap earlier when he stalled on his first pit stop. The gutsy comeback looked like it might fall short as Petty zipped by to lead for a mile with 16 to go. However, the Catawba veteran was not to be denied and bullied back past Petty, winning by about half a lap over Pearson, who had also rattled past Richard's Ford. Fourth went to Hylton, fifth Sears, sixth Langley, Soapy seventh, Earl Brooks finished where he started in eighth, Dick Johnson ninth, and Jabe claimed tenth. Worth mentioning were Wendell 12th and Dave Marcis 21st as Isaac won in just over 87 minutes before a sizable 8,200 fans.

The 1969 finale in Columbia was naturally on Thursday, but for the first time in seven years, it was not in August. This one was in the dying days of summer on September 18th. About 30 members of the Professional Drivers Association (PDA) boycotted the inaugural Talladega 500 four days earlier for fear that the tires could not handle the speeds nearing 200 miles per hour. However, on the Capital City dirt, 23 Grand National touring pros gridded their stockers for 100 miles of thrills, PDA or no PDA. The leader of the Talladega revolt was PDA President Richard Petty, who sat on the pole this warm evening. He lined up with Bobby Isaac, who defied the PDA and finished fourth at Talladega, sitting outside of him. The nearly 7,000 onlookers signaled their approval of Isaac's stance in the matter by cheering him heartily as often as possible. Always a contender but never a winner was John Sears in third with Cecil "Flash" Gordon alongside. Frank Warren timed an old Chevelle in row three with Pearson. There really was not anyone else with any chance to win unless Isaac, Pearson, or ninth place starter James Hylton fell out, even though James had yet to win. Isaac jumped out front for the first three laps until Petty grabbed the point for the next 131. In the meantime, nobody that mattered retired until a wild ride experienced by Pearson on lap 82 jolted the crowd. A tire failed on the blue and gold 17, sending the point leader over the second turn guardrail near the head of the backstretch, splintering the typical fairgrounds-type board fence upon touchdown. Pearson was unhurt and he returned that night to Spartanburg, never to lap the Columbia oval again. In 14 starts there going back to his 1960 Rookie of the Year season, he won five times (four in a row and five of six in one stretch), had a pair of seconds, a sixth, and a seventh. His first four Columbia starts were in his '59 Chevy and he never cracked the top ten. His only other non–top ten result was this high-flying, fence-busting episode that was his spectacular farewell. The orange Harry Hyde–prepped Dodge of Isaac stormed by Petty on lap 135 and to the deafening approval of the fans, edged away for a half-lap victory over PDA President Petty. Third went to Hylton two miles back, fourth to Sears, and fifth came Eldon Yarbrough. Yarbrough was from Jacksonville, FL, the same as LeeRoy Yarbrough. Eldon raced in three Grand National races, one in 1966, one in '67 and this one in 1969. The first two were dismal, but he ended his career with a top five in Stelter's '67 Ford that LeeRoy drove to third here a year ago. Sixth was Elmo, seventh J.D., eighth Wendell, ninth Flash, tenth old Bill Champion, and no one else very interesting. No one except Spartanburg sportsman terror Johnny Halford, making his first start in an ex–Cotton Owens Dodge 57, the last man running in 17th, 34 laps behind. However, this race was about Bobby Isaac, who ran against the PDA, won the race, and won the appreciation of the fans.

Ah, the '70s! In April, the world was taking some strange and memorable twists. The next 33 years of NASCAR were influenced by President Richard Milhous Nixon signing a bill to limit cigarette advertising on television effective New Year's Day, 1971. *Midnight Cow-*

boy and John Wayne won Oscars, Paul McCartney announced that the Beatles had split up, and "Let It Be" was number one for two weeks. Apollo 13 radioed, "Houston, we have a problem!" Billy Casper won the Masters, Earth Day was launched, and on race day in Columbia, U.S. troops invaded Cambodia. Thursday night, April 30, 1970, was the spot on the timeline for the Columbia 200. It was an evening with Petty and a couple of other top wheelers, but the independents rose up to try to steal the show again. Troy, MI's Larry Baumel timed quickest in a black Ford 68 for his first career pole in 11 starts. Just as surprising was Halford's barely missing it and having his career best start in an old ex–Owens Dodge 57. Row two consisted of Frank Warren and Flash Gordon. Three was Bobby Allison in his red and gold Dodge 22 and Ron Keselowski in an orange Dodge 62. Mired back in seventh was Petty, ninth sat Isaac's Dodge, 11th Hylton, 16th Dave Marcis, and 23rd came Benny Parsons' Ford. There were 27 in all and the ne'er-do-wells were poised for victory. At the start, Halford put the Ervin Pruitt Dodge out front for a mile or so before Ron Kaye, as Keselowski billed himself, led for nine. Kaye tangled with Baumel and sailed into a ditch along the backstretch between the rail and a wooden plank fence, vanishing from view. Ron reappeared in the final rundown in 25th. It was Kaye's seventh of 68 starts and after hitting that gully, he never led again. On the restart, Halford led until Warren replaced him on lap 26. Johnny Halford never led a Grand National race again, either. On lap 30, a bone-jarring crash occurred when Tyner, Dick May, and Ed Negre mixed it up at the head of the main straightaway. Then four rear ends, a brake line, and a radiator parked contenders Marcis in 17th, Parsons 16th, Halford 15th, Warren 14th, and Langley in 13th places. For Frank Warren, his Grand National career spanned 396 races from 1963 to 1980. After leading 71 laps that night, he only led one more in his whole career, during a caution in the 1977 Daytona 500. With the pretenders dropping like flies by halfway, Richard Petty took over and checked out. Allison had a Mario Rossi Dodge from Spartanburg in the runner-up spot a lap back with Isaac three back in third. Castles was fourth on the lap with Isaac and fifth finished Hylton. Seventh rumbled James Sears, younger brother of John Sears, in what was the best finish of his six-race, five-year career. Tragically, James burned to death in a sportsman race on August 3, 1973, on the main straightaway at one of the one-shot wonders of the *Silent Speedways of the Carolinas*, Starlite Speedway in Monroe. Wendell was 11th to round out the names in the race. Petty's victory was in a car he drove for owner Don Robertson, who also fielded the Plymouths of Jabe Thomas. It was Robertson's first career win. Petty would be back in his family car for the next race on May 9th at Darlington and thrill a national television audience live on ABC with his infamous pit wall–blasting, barrel-rolling, upside down–landing, shoulder-breaking, main straightway demolition. Nevertheless, on this spring night in Columbia, it was $1,500 and the trophy for Richard Petty.

On Thursday, August 6, 1970, Columbia Speedway's Grand National life had 55 weeks left. This was the last big-time dirt track race held there and the *penultimate* NASCAR Grand National dirt-track race run ever! Fifty-five days later, in Raleigh on September 30th, the dirt curtain came sadly down. Columbia Speedway was not dead yet, though, and on this sultry evening there were 25 stock jockeys there to prove it. Too bad Buck, David, Cale, LeeRoy, Tiny, and even Curtis Turner, who still had two months to live, did not race that night, or at Raleigh either. Maybe they did not realize that they were stuck on asphalt from now on. NASCAR doesn't dwell too much on tradition. The dirt tracks had to go, but the suits could have marked the passing of a fabulous era in some fashion. Richard Petty nabbed the pole and pesky Ron Keselowski put Dodge 62 outside, having repaired it after its ditching here in April. Warren and Castles were in row two with Champion and Hylton lined up behind. Others with a shot were Isaac in seventh, Big John Sears eighth, Elmo ninth,

Top: Ken Meisenhelder's Chevelle sits in the pits before Columbia's final dirt race on August 6, 1970. The scorers are beneath the STP sign in front of the scoreboard. *Bottom:* Petty's pole-sitter waits the start on August 6, 1970. Beyond it is Daytona 500 victor Pete Hamilton in the brown shirt talking to eventual race winner Bobby Isaac in a white uniform.

Sitting on the pit rail that last Columbia dirt track dusk on August 6, 1970, are, from left to right, James Hylton, Frank Warren, Bill Champion, and Richard Petty.

Bobby Allison 11th, Parsons 12th, Marcis 15th, and Dick Brooks 17th. When the green waved, it was good-bye Richard. He sped away and sent that blue 43 drifting through the turns like the master he was. It was some of the last laps ever run on dirt by Petty, Allison, and Isaac, Elmo, Wendell, and the Wild Injun Roy Tyner. In fact, Tyner was the grand old man that night, having run the third race of his 31 career starts on this dirty mix of sand and clay on September 19, 1957. On lap 21, front-runner Frank Warren popped the rail in turn three and collected an aspiring 28-year-old from Elloree, SC, in his first start, Lee Roy Carrigg in Ford 87. Winning number and name, but his nine-race 1970 career was a bust. While Petty paced the pack, a three-car melee occurred on the leader's 72nd lap in turns one and two as Parsons, Marcis, and Keselowski, all on different laps, clobbered each other, calling it a night. As the cross flags approached, the unlikely took place when Petty's worn Goodyears lost traction and around he went. Luckily, Isaac drove a Dodge because that is what he had to do to avoid the spinning Plymouth. On lap 96, Isaac assumed the lead for good, nipping Petty by about a straightaway for the win, his ninth of the year and 30th overall. Third went to Allison's Dodge a lap back, with Sears fourth in his usual fine effort, and Soapy fifth. Other notables that last dirty night in the Capital City were Elmo sixth, Hylton ninth, Tyner tenth, Wendell 12th, Kesolowski 14th, Marcis 15th, Parsons 16th, Brooks 17th, Warren 21st, and Bill Champion, who the records show "Quit" after a lap for 25th and last.

As the old saying goes, you don't appreciate what you had till you don't have it anymore and that was Grand Nationals on dirt. Anyone who saw them on the clay at Spartanburg, Columbia, or Concord must surely miss them. The Automobile Racing Club of

Top: Dignitaries cut the ribbon over the new asphalt for a sportsman race on March 11, 1971. *Bottom, left:* Ex–Grand National star Johnny Allen's sportsman was up front that first asphalt night. *Bottom, right:* "The Iron Man" Jack Ingram was also on hand and later became the first Busch Series Champion in 1982, repeating in 1985.

America (ARCA) still runs on one-mile clay ovals in Illinois at the romantic-sounding State Fairgrounds in Springfield and DuQuoin. On September 1, 2003, Tony Stewart beat Ken Schrader in a dirt-slinging, broad-sliding demolition derby that saw a field of 37 battle through a dozen cautions for 57 laps and one red flag before Stewart's own Home Depot Pontiac 18 drifted home the winner. They are fantastic races and NASCAR could do that occasionally, too, if they wanted it. Stewart and Schrader are two of the few that could have held their ground in the early days when drivers were uncommonly tough and pure, unlike the polished, media-groomed bunch today. Ah, ... for the good old days!

April 8, 1971, was the night of the first Grand National race since the Columbia Speedway's paving. One racecar unloaded that morning from its trailer hooked to the truck with

Top: Richard Petty's Plymouth was there early on Thursday, April 8, 1971, to test the new surface. *Above:* Petty calmly prepares to limber up his Plymouth. *Right:* The author skipped class that Thursday morning to watch practice and meet a king, Richard Petty.

a big silver box and blue cab. Written in blue on the sides of that silver box were the words "Plymouth by Petty." Richard was there hours before other teams, getting extra practice indicative of why he was to be The King. He had won four of ten races already in '71 including the Daytona 500 and Carolina 500 at Rockingham. As the sun rose higher, the sounds of rattling chains and clanging and squeaking haulers and trailers coming in over the hump

Neil Castles makes a political statement with his Free Lt. Calley Dodge Charger at the April 8, 1971, race at Columbia.

at the entrance to turn one filled the air. Twenty-seven racers eventually arrived trying for 26 spots on the grid. One of the next to arrive was Soapy Castles and a white and red '69 Dodge Charger 06 with "Free Lt. Calley" adorning the rear quarter panels. Lt. William Calley was convicted on March 29, 1971, and court-martialed for murdering 22 women and children in the infamous My Lai Massacre in 1968. President Nixon sentenced him to house arrest at Ft. Benning, GA. John McCarthy, a young racecar builder from Spartanburg, brought a plain white 1970 Dodge Super Bee with black and gray 38s on it for Chargin' Charlie Glotzbach. It had noted car owner H.B. Ranier's name in tiny letters on the sail panels. They finished seventh in their first start four days earlier in the Atlanta 500. Time trials began and in a minor surprise, James Hylton put his yellow Ford 48 on the pole obviously with a new track record of 84.229 miles per hour, almost 12 miles per hour faster than the dirt record. Outside row one was Spartanburg's Dick Brooks in Mario Rossi's red and gold '70 Charger 22. Behind them were Parsons in a yellow Ford 72 and Petty. Row three held Bobby Allison in his own red and gold 1971 Charger and Langley in Ford 20 bummed from Clyde Lynn. Seventh came Castles flanked by Brooks' protégé Marv Acton, a transplant to Spartanburg from Porterville, CA, driving Dick's old *old* Plymouth 32. Ninth was Glotzbach with Rookie of the Year-to-be Walter Ballard alongside. Just as the sun set, the green fell and Hylton took off, leading the opening 37 laps before Parsons swiped it. Ron Keselowski, having seen some success here, "Quit" after seven laps for 26th and last. On lap ten, E.J. Trivette from Deep Gap, NC, lost his brakes and parked his orange and white '71 Chevelle 56 for 23rd. After 177 races dating to 1959 and no top fives, E. J. raced again a week later in Maryville, TN, and called it a career. Benny had his L.G. DeWitt Ford out front as Petty, Brooks, Allison, Hylton and Glotzbach hung close, swapping positions just behind. On lap 119, Marvelous Marv Acton, running four laps back, pounded the steel in turn one for the evening's lone crash, getting credit for 16th. During that caution, everyone pitted in a poorly lit opening between the scoring stand and haulers across the railroad rails on the inside of the homestretch. When a racer stopped, crew members just walked up to it and did their thing, adding a can of gas, changing tires, and making the windshield sparkle with a towel and bottle of Windex. Then they stepped back and the cars stormed out on the speedway again. With 81 laps to go, Petty passed Parsons and led for a few laps until Brooks slipped by for two. Petty got it back and held on for 74 rounds when Benny edged alongside with three laps to go. But Richard was not about to give the ex–Detroit cabbie from Ellerbe his first big league win and slammed back past him on the penultimate lap, holding off Parsons for the $1,700 prize. Benny was runner-up a second behind with Brooks a few car lengths back for third. Two laps in arrears came Hylton, Langley, and Chargin' Charlie sixth. Allison was another lap back in seventh, Champion eighth, Soapy ninth, and Warren tenth. Other notables were Flash Gordon 11th, Scott 14th, McDuffie 15th, and Sears an uncharacteristic, non-competitive 21st. It was a memorable day and night for the last Thursday Grand National run here.

It was a final hot summer night, a Friday this time, August 27, 1971, and the swan song for this tough old oval where 30 racers, 22 Grand Nationals, and eight Grand Americans poised for battle one last time. It was the third of six "mixed" races that season and looked silly with big stockers and little pony cars. It did not count as a Grand National win if a pony car finished first, as Bobby Allison discovered at Bowman-Gray on August 6th. That

Legendary Wendell Scott unloads his Ford Torino, April 8, 1971. Note the mismatched trailer tires.

Bobby Allison prepares to board his own '71 Charger for the April 8, 1971, race as Cousin Eddie looks on.

was the first of six such match-ups, and even though Allison won in a Mustang, he does not get credit for the victory, forever stuck at 84 wins, tied for third all-time with Darrell Waltrip, and one ahead of Cale's 83. There was a great animosity between the two groups. Nevertheless, this was Columbia Speedway's goodbye in its final race. Time trials were completed with Petty on the pole and H.B. Bailey of Houston outside in a red Pontiac Firebird 36. In H.B.'s 31-year career of just 85 big-time races, he never won a pole, but this was next best. Row two in this wacky field found old-timers Tiny Lund in a blue Pepsi Camaro 55 and Jim Paschal in factory-backed red, white, and blue AMC Javelin 14. Behind them were Siler City's Wayne Andrews in black Mustang 15 in his third career start and Hylton's Grand National Ford. Lined up in row four were Bill Shirey in an aged orange Plymouth 74 and The Old Pro Buck Baker in his white and blue Firebird 87 Jr., making his 28th start here. He won his first anywhere here in 1952 and was still qualifying top-eight 20 years later. Flash Gordon rounded out the top ten in a big yellow Mercury 24 ninth alongside veteran Elmo Langley in a green Torino 64. There were 20 others behind these, but not a one had a prayer of a chance. The first half mile went to Petty, but Keselowski crashed out for last, 30th, just like last time here. In four Columbia starts, he crashed thrice, quit once, and completed a miserable 91 of a possible 800 laps. Racing back to the caution flag, Bailey stormed past Petty to lead the next 11 rounds, a few of which were behind the pace car. In his 26 Grand National starts prior to this, Bailey never led a lap. After the restart, he still led the likes of Richard Petty, who was not rolling over. H.B. found himself on top of the sport for five and half miles until Richard out-muscled his way past. About that time, Acton parked Brooks' ancient reskinned Plymouth on lap 11 for 29th. A guy who would eventually find his niche in another facet of auto racing, Richard Childress, ended his 11th career start by overheating on lap 17 for 26th. On the 55 circuit and still badgering leader Petty every lap, H.B. got the Firebird crossed up entering the first turn and pulverized the rail, nearly leaping off into the night. He got credit for 24th.

H.B. Bailey went on to three more glorious heights in his lengthy career. He led for six laps in the blazing 1972 Southern 500, bringing home a beautiful '71 Pontiac 66 in a career-tying best finish of fifth. The other was in a 1965 Daytona qualifier. Not bad. He led another lap in the 1986 Southern 500, but his next honor came in his final qualifying attempt ever. By luck of the draw, he was the first man out to make an official time trial for the inaugural Brickyard 400 in 1994. H.B. timed his Alameda Auto Parts Pontiac 36 and had that first pole in his hands with the quickest lap of the day until the next driver went out. He failed to make the field and the 58-year-old Bailey towed back to Texas, never trying to race with the big boys again. (Fellow Houstonian A.J. Foyt barely made it, starting 40th of 43 in his final career stock car start.) Herring Burl Bailey reached the final and ultimate glorious height when he left this dimension on April 17, 2003, at 66 years of age.

James Hylton scorched the new asphalt at a record speed of 84.229 miles per hour.

On lap 52, old-timer Paschal, a winner here back in 1955, pushed his Javelin to the front for 15 laps. But Richard would have none of that, regaining the point on the 67th circuit and battling off the little pony cars until the 124th, when another Grand American defector, Tiny Lund, put the Pepsi Camaro around Petty and settled in for the longest period out front of the night, 64 laps. During Tiny's tenure up front, McDuffie demolished his '69 Mercury against the second turn railing on lap 162 for 19th and everyone made the only pit stops necessary. From the green flag to the checkers, it boiled down to a war between Petty and Grand American superstars Lund and Paschal with over 8,000 spectators going wild. Hylton was fading and Buck Baker was just marking time with a sick Firebird under him. With 13 laps to go, Petty made a daring move under those infield lights as he outhorsepowered the Camaro and Javelin down the backstretch, passing Tiny just as they braked for turn three. From there, no amount of snuffing, snorting, beating, and banging could keep Richard Petty from his second straight victory in a row here and seven for 24 overall. Tiny dropped back the last few laps and came home runner-up by about half a homestretch. Third a little further back was the AMC ace, the Tattooed One, Jim Paschal.

This was Jim Paschal's last race on the *Silent Speedways of the Carolinas*. He was the only leader of the first race in Columbia other than winner Frank Mundy. Jim also led in the last race 20 years later. For the whole Grand National life of Columbia Speedway, Paschal bookends the venue as not only a competitor, but also as a favorite to win! He ran the Javelin twice more in 1971 and drove a Junior Johnson–built, Richard Howard–owned Chevrolet 27 in the 1972 World 600, blowing the engine with 62 laps left for 16th place, ruining a sure top ten or better result. And that was it. This last Columbia race was his fourth from

Spartanburg duo of Dick Brooks in Mario Rossi's Charger took third on the asphalt, April 8, 1971.

last start. He was 45 years old and had 25 Grand National wins in 421 tries when he retired. Jim finished in the top five over a quarter of the time and in the top ten over half the time, won two World 600s, ranked in the top ten in points ten times, and finished 23rd in the first Strictly Stock Car race ever held on June 19, 1949. Yet the astute panel of experts choosing NASCAR's 50 Greatest Drivers left him off that list in favor of less-deserving drivers. It is more unthinkable than it is with Jack Smith's ridiculous omission. Jim Paschal raced long and hard, winning races in 11 of his 25 seasons. The Navy man with the tattoos to prove it and eternal buzz cut is in everyone's Top 50 that have a memory beyond "The Modern Era."

Fourth that final evening went to James Hylton and fifth to Jabe Thomas in the last of his three career top fives. Others were Langley seventh, Wendell Scott 12th, and Buck Baker 17th. At Columbia Speedway, Buck had four wins in 28 starts, 15 top fives, 18 top tens, and six poles. He was fifth in the first Grand National race ever run under the lights in 1951 here and the last man running in the final here. Like his old pal Jim Paschal, Buck also competed in the first Strictly Stock Car race ever run, finishing 11th.

Columbia Speedway lived from June 16, 1951, to August 27, 1971, in Grand National and Winston Cup years. It hosted Studebaker's first win, Frank Mundy's first win, Buck Baker's first win, the first Grand National night race, the first Chevrolet win, Richard Petty's first race (in a convertible), Buddy Baker's first race, the first of 63 Pearson-Petty one-two finishes, and numerous other firsts of lesser importance. The Capital City oval also saw the next to last dirt-track race in Grand National history and the next to last race, period, on the *Silent Speedways of the Carolinas*.

3. Columbia Speedway

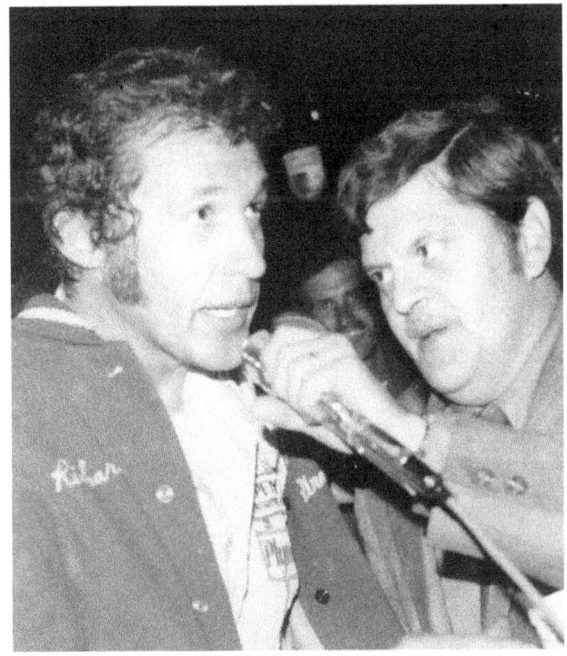

They are racing bicycles and tricycles there now as those original lights have long since gone out, blinded by the shattering blasts of local marksmen, and their poles felled by weather, vandals, and those in need of firewood. But the thunder of the dead racers and the roar of the departed souls cheering them on live forever. Perry Smith is standing in the dusty pits, leaning on that Studebaker waiting for the Rebel, who is not yet eligible for these netherworld dashes. The Three Flocks are there, Fonty and Tim winning with Bob always close. Fireball's ready to drive that unstoppable Paul Spaulding '57 Ford number 11. The ghostly gathering of past winners Curtis Turner, Jim Paschal, Lee Petty, Buck Baker, Speedy Thompson, Jack Smith, Tiny Lund, and Bobby Isaac joke around with those that came close, such as Herb Thomas, Marshall Teague, Joe Weatherly, Joe Eubanks, LeeRoy Yarbrough, Bob Welborn, Bill Blair, Red Byron, Gober Sosebee, Dick Hutcherson, and H.B. Bailey. The lights shone first

Top: Sunset washes through the stands as E.J. Trivette and his Chevelle await the start of the April 8, 1971, race. *Above:* Track Announcer Jim Seay interviews 1971 Sandlapper 200 winner Richard Petty.

Now cracked and faded, the Start/Finish has probably not been repainted since the track's original paving before the 1971 Winston Cup season.

here, but are unnecessary now to the mists and vapors and things that race in the Columbian night.

Track History by the Numbers

RACES:	43
YEARS OF RACES:	1951 (2), 1952, 1953, 1954, 1955 (3), 1956 (2), 1957(2), 1958 (3), 1959, (4—2nd race of '60), 1960 (2), 1961 (2), 1962 (2), 1963 (2), 1964 (2), 1965 (2), 1966 (2), 1967 (2), 1968 (2), 1969 (2), 1970 (2), 1971 (2)
WINNERS:	R. Petty (7), Pearson (5), Buck Baker (4), Isaac (4), Jarrett (3), S. Thompson (3), White (3), T. Flock (2), Owens (2), L. Petty (2), J. Smith (2), F. Flock, Junior Johnson, Lund, Mundy, Paschal, Turner
MOST POLES:	7—Richard Petty
RACE RECORD:	76.514 mph—Richard, 1971 Plymouth (4/8/71)
QUALIFYING RECORD:	85.137 mph—Richard Petty, 1970 Plymouth (8/27/71)
WINS BY MAKE:	Chevrolet (10), Dodge (10), Plymouth (9), Ford (5), Oldsmobile (4), Pontiac (2), Chrysler, Hudson, Studebaker
MOST STARTS:	28—Buck Baker
MOST LAPS LED:	972—Richard Petty
MOST TOP FIVES:	15—Buck Baker
BEST AVERAGE START:	6.9—Buck Baker, 4.4—Richard Petty (24 starts)
BEST AVERAGE FINISH:	8.5—Buck Baker, 5.7—Richard Petty (24 starts)

4
Hartsville Speedway, Hartsville, South Carolina

There is not much left near the corner of Racetrack Road and Fifth Street in Hartsville, SC. This is a track where imagination plays the biggest part in seeing the past. It is in old Mr. Skinner's backyard. The concession stand was still there until a year or two before. And, yes, he remembers the filming of *Thunder in Carolina*, meeting Rory Calhoun, Alan Hale, Jr., and John Hines. A junkyard covers most of what remains, with wrecks and derelicts lined up on turns one and two. It is overgrown so badly that it is almost impossible to see the speedway. There is no reason to believe the third-mile oval was once the center of the stock car world for one day back in 1961. The first and second turns on the south end are cleaved by a road built to bring the heaps into the infield, leaving a cross section that had the skull of some large junkyard rat adorning the rim of the banking. Infield fences of wire,

Street signs provided a clue in finding the fading remains of the Hartsville Speedway.

posts, and cable are so overgrown that they are barely visible at all. An infield pond used for watering the track is green and all but dried up. There is a faded white post marking the start/finish line competing for space with a huge oak tree. A like new-looking cable still hangs from post to post marking off the infield. North turns three and four are completely gone, probably leveled in some grandiose notion that cleared land meant an instant Wal-Mart or something. It has not happened yet. There is a very tall, crooked pole inside turn one, nearly obscured by trees now, that survived all these years. That pole is clearly visible in the movie *Thunder in Carolina*. Also in the movie, Rory Calhoun's character Mitch Cooper limps on crutches to his car in the muddy Hartsville infield, a result of his opening-scene third turn rollover. Hartsville is never once mentioned, but the Hartsville Rescue Squad rushes to the scene of Cooper's flip. In the background behind Mitch are the neighboring houses and they are still there. Later in the film, Cooper is still on crutches while his foot heals. He brings young Les York, played by John Hines, to this Hartsville venue to drive the rebuilt '57 Chevy 8. It is the same track used in Les York's mid–movie racing debut. Hartsville went Hollywood as only Darlington and Indianapolis had. What was the one and only Hartsville Grand National like? Thunder back to the steamy South Carolina summer of '61.

It was the first full day of summer, Friday, June 23, 1961, and "Travelin' Man" by Ricky Nelson was the #1 song. In Hartsville, The Old Pro Buck Baker was the travelin' man. The Spartanburg chauffeur gave Chrysler its first win since he capped off his championship year behind the wheel of a big, white Kiekhaefer Chrysler 300 on November 18, 1956, in Wilson, NC. Kiekhaefer never entered another race and most people thought Buck mad to build the heavy-finned monsters for himself and Buddy in 1961 after being a solid Chevy pilot since his '56 title. Eighteen stock jockeys arrived for 150 hot, sandy laps around the one-

Today, jungle-like vegetation all but obscures the infield spectator fence.

Junkyard wrecks and derelicts now rust away where the First Turn used to be.

third mile speedway with the Golden Greek, Emanuel Zervakis, garnering his second and final career pole. It was a small, but very respectable cast co-starring Richard Petty, Rex White, David Pearson, Junior Johnson, Ned Jarrett, Jack Smith, Wendell Scott, Curtis "Crawfish" Crider, and Herman the Turtle Beam. Buck drove Buddy's 86, averaging just over 46 miles per hour to edge Smith's Pontiac, the only other car on the lead lap at the checkers. It was a very good day for Spartanburg drivers as all four entered grabbed the top four spots with 1960 defending champ White third and 1960 Rookie of the Year Pearson fourth. Pearson would cop the Firecracker 250 at Daytona 11 days later for his second, shocking major win in a row. He had won the World 600 only three weeks earlier. By the way, the Greek crashed out mid-race.

Hartsville Speedway has a Hollywood history unlike most speedways. In what is a reasonably accurate portrayal of stock car racing in the 1950s, Hartsville Speedway is a star! Made in 1959 and released in 1960, the opening credits of *Thunder in Carolina* are placed over action on Hartsville's dirt. A camera mounted to the left front bumper facing the front wheel and side shows Buck in his '59 Thor Chevrolet slinging it around the oval. The engine's roar and dusty footage from another camera mounted on the rear bumper captures Baker being dogged by Spartanburg's Joe Eubanks' 82 1958 Ford. That red and white racer with Elmo Henderson's name on the roof is also shown during a pit stop that says as much about the era as anything. Tee-shirted guys putting in gas, not changing tires, and pitting on the infield grass in front of a meager afternoon crowd. Rory Calhoun, a dead ringer for Curtis Turner, plays the movie's hero Mitch Cooper. Hartsville Speedway is located very near Darlington, the focal point of *Thunder in Carolina*. The ghost of Mitch Cooper probably stops by both on hot midsummer nights when the spirit world is most active, when the third and fourth turns reappear, and when the ghost stands are half-full again. For a one-shot wonder, Hartsville not only has a ghost story to tell, it has a Hollywood story to tell. None of the other *Silent Speedways of the Carolinas* can do that. Few tracks anywhere can!

Track History by the Numbers

RACES:	1 (6/23/61)
YEARS OF RACES:	1961
WINNERS:	Buck Baker
MOST POLES:	Emanuel Zervakis
RACE RECORD:	46.234 mph—Buck Baker, 1961 Chrysler
QUALIFYING RECORD:	54.970—Emanuel Zervakis, 1960 Chevrolet
WINS BY MAKE:	Chrysler
MOST STARTS:	Tied by 18 drivers
MOST LAPS LED:	At least 1—Buck Baker
MOST TOP FIVES:	Buck Baker, J. Smith, White, Pearson, Junior Johnson
BEST AVERAGE START:	1st—Emanuel Zervakis
BEST AVERAGE FINISH:	1st—Buck Baker

5

Cleveland County Fairgrounds Speedway, Shelby, North Carolina

There is nothing to finding this old track. Go south from Charlotte on I-85 and take Highway 74 toward Shelby, then Business 74 into Shelby and it is on the right. The old clay half-mile is still there and looks as if it could be readied in a few days. A little grading, some rails here and there, and it would be right for racing. In turn one, the kudzu wrapped itself around the guardrail, thriving in the scorching Carolina heat. Over in turn two at the head of the backstretch is where one of the most significant incidents on all of the *Silent Speedways of the Carolinas* occurred. The hell that broke loose on that unholy patch of Shelby real estate is a horror yarn that is no less unbelievable today. The third turn looks raceworthy and imagining Buck Baker cocking that big white Chrysler through there is no problem. A wire fence blocks turn four altogether, making what little is left of the main straightaway tough to negotiate. Down at the grandstand, a serious barricade of barrels and wood makes a lap of the clay half-mile impossible. The Grand National circuit stopped here six times between 1956 and 1965 when strange things happened and controversy reigned over this venue just off Business 74 east of Shelby. The bizarre happened early on in the track's history.

The Cleveland County Fairgrounds grandstand still waits for the long-gone racing crowds.

5. Cleveland County Fairgrounds Speedway

It started on sweaty Friday night, July 27, 1956, with a field of 17 including all the big names in the middle of the run for the '56 title, which Carl Kiekhaefer was determined to win. Since Daytona in February, he bombarded almost every race with at least two of his cars, but they were not always Chryslers in '56. This event had Thompson and Baker in Dodges. Herb Thomas deserted Kiekhaefer 20 days earlier after the Spartanburg race and had his own Chevrolet. Moody and Roberts brought De Paolo factory Fords, Billy Myers and Paschal had Stroppe and Frank Hayworth Mercurys, Petty was in his Olds, Rex rode Max Welborn's Chevy "X," Staley had one from Hubert Westmoreland, and Allen had Spook Crawford's Plymouth. Harold Kite, 1950 Daytona Beach winner, drove for the eighth and next to last time in a new Ford. Carden's Merc and Eubank's Ford spiced up the grid. The strange occurred midway through this one when NASCAR scoring lost count of the laps. Therefore, they just ran an extra one. Kiekhaefer got his win, the first in over a month, and Thompson nabbed his seventh trophy of the season. Moody, Myers, Roberts, and Baker followed. The boys were not scheduled back until next year.

However, they came back on Tuesday night, October 23, 1956. They came back because Carl Kiekhaefer wielded power and influence with Bill France, rented the Shelby oval, and weaseled a 100-miler into the schedule where ten days earlier there was none. He needed an extra race so his white Mopars, mainly Buck Baker's, could catch Herb Thomas, who was thumbing his nose at Mr. K., having left him months earlier in the torrid title chase. It was the 53rd race in what then became a *56-event* tour. Twenty-seven cars and most of the big names were there. Pete De Paolo brought five, count 'em, five factory Fords. Yet Doug Cox shocked the cold crowd, taking the pole in an unheralded Ford, and then tried to warm the fans up with an early engine fire. Just past halfway in the 200-lap bonus race, Baker was sailing along out front, well ahead of the second-place war, when tragedy struck as that pack exited turn two. Speedy Thompson, Baker's Kiekhaefer Dodge mate, was battling ferociously with Thomas' familiar Chevrolet 92 for second. With Herb inching by on his left, Thompson's dark side surfaced as he pulled one of the *dirtiest* tricks in stock car racing by nosing left into the Chevy's right rear fender just as it was about to clear. The Dodge sent 92 careening hard right, across the backstretch, and head-on into the outside rail. After bouncing off, Herb was blasted by the next several racers, including Smith, who flipped, Myers, Moody, Carden, Lund, and Petty. Thompson never missed a beat and continued on, finishing fourth. Carden and Lund continued, too, but Thomas was mangled for the second time in two years. They hauled Herb Thomas away to the hospital with massive internal injuries and a fractured skull. Herb's surviving until morning was wishful thinking, but he pulled through somehow. He was done for the year, though, and the 1956 Grand National crown was Kiekhaefer's and Baker's. It actually took *another* race before Baker passed Thomas for the points lead, but he had the title as soon as Thompson struck. Herb Thomas still finished second in the standings, but was never, ever the same. Buck, Speedy, and Kiekhaefer were booed unmercifully for the rest of the year. The fans and the press exonerated Baker because he was nowhere near the crash and not considered a dirty driver. Did Thompson act on his own? Was he following Kiekhaefer's orders? Did he do it to gain favor with Mr. K without direct orders? Or was it an accident, as Thompson and Kiekhaefer always maintained?

Herb Thomas was on top of the sport where he had been for years until the very moment Thompson ambushed him exiting turn two in Shelby that chilly autumn night. Herb most probably would have won his third championship if not for the crash. He *would* have won it if an extra race had not been added. Prior to the crash, he was victorious six times in '56 and at one point on a western swing, captured three out of four driving for

Kudzu thrives in the scorching summer sun, devouring the First Turn guardrail.

Kiekhaefer. His final and 48th career victory came on June 3, 1956, in Merced, CA, in Kiekhaefer's Chrysler. Over eight months after the crash, he came back unspectacularly on July 4, 1957, in Raleigh, again in Pennsylvania, and then in Darlington. That tragedy is recounted in detail elsewhere. Herb drove once more in North Wilkesboro in 1962 and will get his tribute in that chapter.

On Saturday night, May 4, 1957, the next race was held with a top-notch field taking the green. Roberts, Goldsmith, Panch, Paschal, Smith, Baker, Owens, Petty, Thompson, Billy Myers, Allen, and Lund had factory rides and were at or near the front all night. However, pole-sitter Lund dominated the evening, leading the opening 115 laps and again late before the axle snapped on his Pontiac. He finished tenth as the Fords of Roberts, Goldsmith, and Panch swept the Dearborn marque to the win by three laps over Paschal's Merc, the Black Widows of Smith and Baker, Owens' Pontiac, Petty's Olds, Speedy's Black Widow, and Tiny's idle Pontiac. Less than 4,000 saw two cautions and an hour 49 minutes of top-notch action.

They returned on another Saturday night, September 21, 1957, only 19 days after the Flock-Myers-Goldsmith disaster in the Southern 500, and Herb Thomas came to announce his retirement. Buck Baker took Bud's Bel Air wire-to-wire on the way to his second straight title, beating another solid field. The factories were gone, but stiff challenges were offered by Panch, Amick, Staley, Petty, Allen, Goldsmith, Weatherly, Roberts (who crashed while leading), Paschal, and Thompson. Speedy won the tragic Southern 500 on Labor Day, but was in a rag of a '56 Ford owned and usually driven by Dick Beaty.

It took eight years, but in 1965, the cars and stars of the Grand National circuit came

5. Cleveland County Fairgrounds Speedway   93

Top: The Patch of Hell at the head of the backstretch where on October 23, 1956, the infamous Speedy Thompson–Herb Thomas crash occurred. *Bottom:* Turn Three looks smooth and ready for thundering, broadsliding stock cars.

Turn Four and the homestretch are now fenced off for all except those midnight movers.

back for the last two times. The first was Thursday night, May 27th, just four days after the World 600. It was also the first of three races in four nights on silent speedways at New Asheville Speedway on Saturday, and the finale for Harris Speedway on Sunday. In the penultimate 100-mile dash in Shelby, a small field of 20 started with Hutcherson on the pole. He led for 175 laps until his gold and white Ford's axle snapped and Jarrett inherited a huge lead, winning by 22 laps over Paul Moore's yellow Plymouth. Hutcherson still finished third, 25 laps behind.

They returned for the swan song exactly ten weeks later on the stormy night of August 5th. Six less starters took the green for this one than last time, but it was a much better field even with only 14. This was the third race since Chrysler returned to competition from the hemi boycott and the Thursday night, weather-braving crowd of over 6,000 was evidence of that. The results were the same as before, but Jarrett won by only four laps instead of 22. As in May, he inherited the lead, this time when Pearson had a bad pit stop after leading the first 126 laps. Richard Petty was second, Hutcherson third, Castles in Buck's Oldsmobile fourth, and Pearson salvaged fifth. Thus ended the major-league career of the Cleveland County Fairgrounds dirt.

Six races were run, but one monumental event shook the credibility of a driver, his owner, his team, the sanctioning body, and virtually extinguished the career of a driver who at 33 years of age had many winning miles yet to go. Now the track is used for motocross, rodeos, and rabbit shows. The spirits get a kick out of those. Nevertheless, you can bet this silent speedway has ghosts and is lousy with them. Pick a night in late October and go out there when the leaves are rustling and a chilly wind is blowing down from the Blue Ridge.

Maybe Herb clobbers Speedy coming out of two, runs down Baker, and gets that 1956 crown and the last laugh over Mr. K. Only the ghosts know.

Track History by the Numbers

RACES:	6
YEARS OF RACES:	1956 (2), 1957 (2), 1965 (2)
WINNERS:	Buck Baker (2), Jarrett (2), Roberts, Thompson
MOST POLES:	1—Buck Baker, Cox, Hutcherson, Lund, Moody, Pearson
RACE RECORD:	64.748 mph—Ned Jarrett, 1965 Ford (8/5/65)
QUALIFYING RECORD:	67.797 mph—David Pearson, 1965 Dodge (8/5/65)
WINS BY MAKE:	Ford (3), Chevrolet, Chrysler, Dodge
MOST STARTS:	5—Buck Baker
MOST LAPS LED:	175—Dick Hutcherson
MOST TOP FIVES:	3—Buck Baker, Marvin Panch
BEST AVERAGE START:	3.2—Speedy Thompson (4)
BEST AVERAGE FINISH:	6.4—Buck Baker (5)

6
Harris Speedway, Harris, North Carolina

This track is so confusing, even the ghosts are mixed up on where to haunt. Back in the early sixties, Harris Speedway was a raucous quarter-mile dirt track where every Sunday afternoon, the local boys, some really fine drivers like Preston Humphries and Paul Ghost, whacked each other around until somebody else won. It is the last place, even in the 62-race season of 1964, that one would imagine the Grand National tour running. Actually, it was the next to the next to the last place. The teams came dragging in for the incredible 60th race of the season. The longest season ever had been the 56 in '56, helped by the extra race Kiekhaefer, et al., staged in Shelby to stomp Herb Thomas and steal the title, which they did. However, no such shenanigans were afoot here. It was just NASCAR's utter disregard for the physical and mental well-being of the speed addicts that raced, the exhausted

The track was paved when the Grand Nationals raced there, but now the locals run on dirt that was beneath.

crews, and their own officials. With the loss of Weatherly, Haberling, Roberts, and Pardue in stockers, added to Sachs and McDonald at Indy, with Marshman yet to die in December testing at Phoenix, *everybody* was tired. Yet unbelievably, there were still a pair of races to go and a whole week to rest up until 1965!

The confusion is that there was the quarter-mile dirt track at Harris, but they built a new paved one-third mile facility west of it. That is where the Grand Nationals ran. Years later, they ripped off the asphalt and it is the dirt track raced on regularly now. The Grand Nationals ran on the asphalt, which is gone, so the dirt is left. The trees growing up through the concrete grandstand of the old original quarter-mile dirt Harris Speedway is an image impossible to ignore. Even though those seats never overlooked a Grand National race, that view is one of the eeriest. The dirt track there now was underneath the paved oval that hosted a pair of Grand Nationals in 1964 and 1965. So what happened at Harris anyway?

It was Sunday, October 25, 1964, in the Blue Ridge Mountain foothills and the colors were spectacular. CBS had the National Football League, NBC had the American, and Billy Wade had Bud Moore's Marauder on the pole at just under 65 miles per hour. Competition was stiff after a rare week off following the National 400 in Charlotte. Cotton brought two Dodges up the hill from Spartanburg, Pearson's 6 and Isaac's 5. Jarrett, Petty, Crider's two Mercs, Larry Thomas, and Wendell also lined up on the chilly Sunday afternoon. Wade led the first 100 laps and fell out, finishing 18th. Then Pearson led for 59 more before retiring to 15th. The last 40 were Richard Petty's and he copped his 36th career win. Ned was a lap back in second, Crawfish had a career-best third, Isaac fourth, and Thomas fifth in an independent Dodge.

Billy Wade, originally from Houston, moved to Spartanburg. He won Rookie of the Year in 1963 as Pearson's teammate, chauffeuring a Dodge from Cotton Owens' garage across town. During a stretch of nine days back in the steamy New England July of 1964, Billy pulled off a feat never before accomplished. Not performed by Herb Thomas, Tim Flock, Buck Baker, Lee or Richard Petty, or by any of the greats of the sport's first 15 and half seasons. *Billy Wade won four races in a row, wheeling the red and black Bud Moore Mercury Marauder 1.* Young Billy ran one more race after Harris, finishing fourth a week later in Augusta. He died horribly against the first turn wall in Daytona, riding the banks all by himself while running over spikes for Goodyear to test the development of the inner-liner on January 5, 1965. Darel Dieringer, Wade's teammate, moved to Moore's first chair.

Larry Thomas also ran that next week in Augusta and finished just ahead of Wade in third. Then, a week later, he finished fifth in his last race at Jacksonville, NC. He was driving for the factory-backed Burton-Robinson Racing Team Plymouth formally driven by Jimmy Pardue. On September 22, 1964, a blowout sent Jimmy shattering through the rail at Charlotte as he was testing tires for Goodyear, too.

Dieringer, Wade, and Thomas pulled Pardue bleeding and dying from Car 54. Thomas got the ride, changed the number to his familiar 36, and had all the promise in the world. The promise was broken in the pre-dawn hours of January 19, 1965, on I-75 in Georgia, when Larry died two weeks after Billy.

What is the biggest race on Memorial Day? Why, it is the 100-mile classic at Harris Speedway, of course. They raced the Grand Nationals at Harris a final time on May 30, 1965, the same day Jimmy Clark won the Indianapolis 500. The reason Harris went head-to-head with Indy was that nobody in NASCAR-land really cared what happened at Indianapolis. Stocker Bobby Johns did claim seventh as teammate to Clark in a Lotus pitted by the Wood Brothers that day. Johns would have been Rookie of the Year up there if not for some guy named Andretti. In the week since the World 600 on May 23rd, Grand National

Top: An eerie grandstand populated now by trees and ferns overlooks the original track. *Bottom:* From the midpoint of the backstretch into Turn Three, the stockers roared.

races were run at Shelby and New Asheville, *Silent Speedways of the Carolinas* both, and won by Jarrett and Junior respectively. On Memorial Day, 22 men, 20 of which were independents, went after the $1,000 first place purse. Incidentally, $1,000 goes to the leader of each lap at Indy. Paul Lewis took the pole, but G.C. Spencer stole the show. He started outside front row, led early, lost the lead to Jarrett, won a torrid battle with the other factory FoMoCo of Dick Hutcherson, ran out of gas with the end in sight, and still beat Dick Dixon by four laps for second.

Slim fields with few top cars, one-sided finishes, and thin crowds combined for a sad finale at a track that probably never should have even held a Grand National race. The grandstand where the trees have pushed through the concrete, the light fixtures grown into the pines, and a bony arm sticks out of the collapsed ticket booth for the $2 admission are all part of the nightly action. You can bet Billy Wade and Larry Thomas are in the show when the cold mountain winds of October rattle the dead leaves of summer at Harris Speedway, and they are still running up front.

Track History by the Numbers

RACES:	2
YEARS OF RACES:	1964, 1965
WINNERS:	Richard Petty, Ned Jarrett
MOST POLES:	1—Billy Wade, Paul Lewis
RACE RECORD:	59.009 mph—Richard Petty, 1964 Plymouth (10/25/64)
QUALIFYING RECORD:	Billy Wade—1964 Mercury, 64.787 (10/25/64)
WINS BY MAKE:	Plymouth, Ford
MOST STARTS:	2—Arrington, Castles, D. Cooper, Jarrett, Manning, Putney, Scott, Tyner
MOST LAPS LED:	311—Ned Jarrett
MOST TOP FIVES:	2—Ned Jarrett
BEST AVERAGE START:	4th—Ned Jarrett
BEST AVERAGE FINISH:	1.5—Ned Jarrett

7
Occoneechee Speedway, Hillsborough, North Carolina

Perhaps the most fascinating of all *Silent Speedways of the Carolinas* is Occoneechee Speedway. It looks the part of a lost, haunted racetrack speeding headlong into oblivion with nature taking a firmer grip every minute of every hour of every day. It is coursed now by a nature trail, but is still fantastic! From downtown Hillsborough, cross the Eno River south on Church St., turn left onto Route 70A and make another left onto Elizabeth Brady Road. A dirt path leads into the woods off to the right, winding its way to the longest of the silent speedways. Through the thick cover of pine trees and up on the side of an indistinguishable hill is an enormous concrete grandstand. Trees, bushes, and vines have been pushing towards the sky through the crumbling concrete for nearly 40 years since mortals

"Haunting" aptly describes the crumbling concrete stands at Occoneechee Speedway.

last sat there. Emerald-green moss provides satiny seat cushions for tonight's after-hours guests, filling the stands nightly as they did fifty years before. Now the thick undergrowth, the fallen offices and restrooms, and a lone light pole staring blindly on the start/finish line remain to recall the days of glory. It creates an eerie atmosphere in broad daylight, let alone at midnight. Imagine voluptuous, fading 30-year-old Hollywood has-been Jayne Mansfield traipsing around among sportswriters, waiting to plant one on the victor of that March 10, 1963, 148.5-miler. She returns repeatedly since that messy mayhem in the blackness of a foggy Louisiana highway on June 29, 1967. And she still has a good head on her shoulders.

Moving clockwise towards turn four, a high dirt bank with a flimsy wire fence on top protected the fans in the stands from the thundering stockers a few feet away. This is a big dirt speedway, blazing fast, nine-tenths of a mile in length, with long straightaways and wide, sweeping, slightly banked turns. Two parallel ruts around the track are much too far to the inside in the turns as the slope of the banking is where the racing took place. Summertime trees and vines hang low over the track, a jungle-like scene in every way. In each direction, it was all green up the backstretch. The canopy of trees makes it like a hothouse without the house. A clearing near the end of the backstretch looks down a steep bank at the mighty Eno River, only feet away. The river is a pale greenish-brown, making it hard to distinguish from the summertime emerald environment through which it meanders. One wonders about the racecars that must have splash-landed down there during the wild decades of sportsman and modified racing before. Across the track from the Eno is another wire fence protecting the infield patrons. The long backstretch eases into the arc of the second turn and right back to turn one. That homestretch recalls old photos of racers streaking by with that big grandstand packed with fans watching where all the trees stand so tall now. Another trail leads up the hill behind the grandstand where a dilapidated fence runs the border. A restroom is folding down and the track office, half collapsed, holds a blue-trimmed ticket window, sofa, refrigerator, and the remnants of what was the busiest spot around on race day. Occoneechee may be the epitome of the *Silent Speedways of the Carolinas*. Built on a plain, the track is two-thirds surrounded by the Eno River. It rests in a crook of that mighty creek, which is reachable by careening racecar at any point from the middle of the first and second turns all the way to the third turn. It would take quite a launch to make it from the third, but backstretch to river is only a few feet. And all downhill! It is inconceivable that dozens of racers did not land in the Eno with dire results between 1949 and 1968. Thirty-two big-league races and only speedster Louise Smith is rumored to have made it to a watery conclusion. Occoneechee Speedway is the fourth most prolific silent speedway, the second largest, second fastest, and jam-packed with a glorious history.

On Sunday afternoon, August 7, 1949, Occoneechee Speedway in Hillsborough, NC, played host to the third Strictly Stock Car race ever. Jim Roper won the first at Charlotte in June, Red Byron the second on the Beach in July, and next they challenged the then-mile of dirt on the banks of the winding Eno for 200 fast miles. Twenty-eight actual stock cars were on hand guided by 26 men and two brave women. Many big names started, like the Flock Brothers, Gober Sosebee, Herb Thomas, Curtis Turner, Glenn Dunnaway, Lee Petty, Jimmy Lewellen, Bill Blair, Red Byron, and Charlotte winner Jim Roper in the same Lincoln number 34. And those gutsy gals, Atlanta's Sara Christian and Greenville's Louise Smith, had a pair of '47 Fords in the field. One source says that Curtis Turner was fastest qualifier, but most do not say. The fact is that record keeping, and in this case reporting, was scarce and inaccurate. Nevertheless, Flocks Bob and Tim dueled much of the steamy Sunday afternoon, punctuated by a grinding three-car crash. Future Hall of Famers Louise Smith and Herb Thomas retired early along with Lewellen. Then on lap 38, Sara Christian in her third straight start tried to three-wheel it to the pits after a mechanical failure and spin in turn four cost her a right front wheel. Since it was impossible to execute a left turn into the pits with all that weight gouging into the dirt, her Ford 71 was nailed by Felix Wilkes' Lincoln 5. With nowhere to go, point leader Red Byron in Raymond Parks' Daytona-winning Olds 22 joined the scrap heap. Moments later on the restart, Bob Smith promptly went over the first turn banking. There were no retaining barriers except a dirt bank with a wire fence on top in front of the grandstand. Alleged pole-sitter Curtis Turner's three-year-old Buick fell out next for 20th. The sibling rivalry boiling over at the front ended with ten miles left when little brother Tim's Olds 90 broke a spindle, one of the weakest parts on a truly stock car, and Bob cruised his Olds 7 to victory over Gober Sosebee's Cherokee Garage Olds 50. Dunnaway, piloting his third different stocker in three races, took third in Olds 55, having finished last in the first two. Fourth went to Fonty Flock in a Buick and fifth to Bill Snowden in a Ford. Also in the rundown were Bill Blair sixth, Tim Flock seventh, bib-overalled Otis Martin eighth, Lee Petty in his second career start had wisely switched to the lighter Plymouth marque for ninth, and Buddy Helms tenth in a Hudson. Bob Flock pocketed $2,000 for averaging almost 77 miles per hour before nearly 18,000 fans. Incredibly, Richard Petty would win the final Occoneechee race 19 years later for $400 less in front of 11,000 fewer fans at half 1949's distance. Jim Roper, after skipping The Beach, finished 15th, won $50, and went back to Great Bend, KS, where he raised horses and raced horsepower, becoming "Alfalfa Jim."

The return took place on Sunday afternoon, August 13, 1950. Dick Linder led 26 others in time trials, which saw Lloyd Moore roll a Mercury, injuring his back. Outside row one starter Curtis Turner jumped out front and paced the field for 45 laps. Coming off

Emerald green moss cushions the cement for the ghostly twilight gatherings.

back-to-back wins at Rochester, NY, and Charlotte, where he had led all 200 laps of each, a flat cost him two miles and Pee Wee Martin took over for a dozen rounds. Sterling Long flipped a Hudson, but was OK. Coming up quickly from 15th, 21-year-old Fireball Roberts took the lead on the 58th circuit, slipping home the winner over a fast-closing Turner. It was Roberts' first win after only two previous outings. Linder took third, young Bill Rexford fourth, and Clyde Minter fifth. Further back came Petty seventh, Herb Thomas eighth, Johnny Mantz tenth, Martin faded to 12th, future USAC great Don White 15th, Marshall Teague 17th, Jimmy Florian (who won shirtless in Ford's first-ever win at Dayton on June 25) was 19th, Lewellen 21st, Dunnaway 24th, and Blair 27th and last. Fireball was hot, but would not win another Grand National race for six years!

The second Hillsborough visit of 1950 occurred on the cool autumn afternoon of October 29th. It was the 19th and last race of the season and packed with drama. Bill Rexford had a slippery grip on the first Grand National points title because if he faltered and Fireball Roberts recorded a strong finish, the young Floridian would steal the championship. Time trials saw Fonty Flock sizzle with a speed of nearly 86 miles per hour for the pole. Fireball took second and Rexford was a dismal 29th, *dead last!* Needless to say, things looked good for Roberts. Louise Smith almost ended her day before it started during time trials when she launched her Nash off the first turn, touching down among the underbrush with the wheels pointing skyward. Remarkably, the car was repaired well enough to start 25th. The 200-lap grind started with Flock leading the first third and Roberts hot on his heels. Turner and Paschal fell out right away with point leader Rexford joining them, saddling him with 26th. Bill Rexford had done everything in his power to gift-wrap the title for Roberts. However, they did not call him Fireball for nothing. Yes, it is a baseball moniker, but he refused to stroke his way to the title, unlike the "big picture" racers in the modern era. Roberts put his Olds 11 out front on the 72nd circuit for six laps until Fonty in Bob Flock's Olds took it back. Then Roberts led, then Flock, then on lap 126, fully aware of the stakes, Fireball blew the engine in Sam Rice's Rocket and the race and *title* were gone. Only six laps later, Flock fell out with mechanical trouble, with Ms. Smith and Herb Thomas parking, too. With no lights and the sun setting behind the hills, the chilly day ended 25 laps early with Plymouth-pushing Lee Petty claiming his second career win, the first in over a year. Second was Buck Baker still looking for those first checkers, still over a year away. Third was Weldon Adams, fourth Tim Flock in the Plymouth that won the first Southern 500, and fifth came Bill Blair in Olds number 41.5. Bill Rexford became the youngest Grand National Champion at 23, a distinction he still holds as of this writing. Fireball Roberts was never nearly this close to a title again ... and neither was Rexford.

It was Sunday afternoon, April 15, 1951, and at Hillsborough, nasty weather disappointed over 11,000 fans. The second straight race, this one a 150-miler, was called after 95 laps with Fonty Flock leading them all from the pole to beat Frank "The Rebel" Mundy's Studebaker. Third was Blair, Tim Flock fourth, and Neil Cole fifth. A whopping 33 cars started, with other notables being Herb Thomas seventh, Paschal eighth, Petty ninth, Dunnaway tenth, Roberts 14th, Rexford 19th, Turner 27th, Frank Luptow 30th, and 1949 Indianapolis 500 winner Bill Holland 31st in that long-running 1950 Southern 500–winning Plymouth 98 Jr. For Frank Luptow, it was his last of five Grand National starts. He lost his life in an AAA stock car race on September 21, 1952, at deadly Lakewood Speedway in Atlanta when a broken axle sent his Olds into endless flips.

October 7, 1951, an autumn Sunday afternoon, found 24 stockers at Occoneechee for the second visit of the season. Four days earlier, Bobby Thomson hit the shot heard 'round the world. Three days later, Joltin' Joe hung up the pinstripes for good. Five days after that,

A towering light pole still stands, enduring the elements for nearly 40 years.

I Love Lucy premiered on CBS. Except for Fonty Flock leading the first 86 laps, Herb Thomas' Yunick Hudson went wire-to-wire in the 150-miler. Leonard Tippett had a career-best finish a lap back in second, Eubanks was third, Paschal fourth, and Petty fifth. Further behind came Donald Thomas sixth, Blair ninth, Billy Myers 12th, Lewellen 13th, Fonty blew for 15th, Baker 19th, and Sosebee 21st out of 24. Herb and Smokey won $1,000 for just over two hours of work.

June 8, 1952, a Sunday afternoon, found a slim field of 19 challenging Occoneechee for 100 miles, the shortest distance raced there yet. The Flock Brothers dominated with Fonty on the pole at a blazing nearly 92 miles per hour and Tim outside. They finished just the reverse. Dick Rathmann was third, Blair fourth, and Lewellen fifth. On back came Petty sixth, Eubanks seventh, Thomases Donald tenth and Herb 16th, and Buddy Shuman 17th. In just under one and a quarter hours, Tim gained his second win in a row, tying Herb Thomas for the career lead with 11.

Twenty-nine cars arrived for the second Hillsborough event of 1952, a 150-miler on Sunday, October 12th. Bill Blair took the pole at nearly 76 miles per hour and led for the first six laps until Fonty dominated for the last 143 in the Southern 500–winning Air Lift Special Olds 14. Donald Thomas with relief from brother Herb was second in the Yunick Hudson 9, Blair was third, Tim Flock fourth, and Petty fifth. Others were Paschal 17th, Lewellen 20th, Eubanks 21st, Rathmann 25th, Herb Thomas 27th, and Cotton Owens 29th and last. Flock took $1,200 back to Atlanta for the win.

For the first time since 1949, Occoneechee got only one date in 1953, August 9th. A field of 19 arrived for the 100-mile test and may as well have stayed home as Curtis Turner ended a two-year win drought by taking the pole and leading all 100 laps in Frank Christian's Olds. Even Herb Thomas and his Hornet could not mount a challenge as he trailed the Blond Blizzard across the finish line second, with Petty third, Eubanks fourth, and Blair fifth. Other top shoes were Paschal sixth, Lewellen ninth, Turner's teammate Fonty Flock 12th, Tim 16th, Buck 18th, and Rathmann 19th after a lap-three crash. A measly crowd of around 4,000 watched another Hillsborough sleeper.

This week the Baltimore Orioles and Milwaukee's Hank Aaron played their first games. Bill Haley and the Comets recorded "Rock Around the Clock" and the lone visit of 1954 took place on the Sunday afternoon, April 18th. This one had a lot more spectators, a lot more entries, and a lot more excitement than seen here in a few years. Buck Baker took the pole in an Olds and was flanked by Gober Sosebee. Buck led the first 12 laps until passed by "the other" Thomas, Donald, in the Pure Hudson 31. Donald kept it there until Baker's teammate Emory Lewis rolled his Olds on lap 65 and Don slowed to avoid the trouble, allowing Herb to scoot past. Herb led the remainder with Donald on his back bumper all the way. Herb Thomas got his 32nd win while Donald was denied his second. Baker was third, Rathmann fourth, and Turner fifth. On back came Eubanks seventh, Liguori 11th, Paschal 24th, Lewellen 25th, Sosebee 26th, and newcomer Bob Welborn 27th. Over 5,700 saw Herb take the $1,000 in just over an hour and a quarter.

Over 8,000 fans braved the cold, windy Sunday afternoon of March 27, 1955. The stands at Occoneechee were dotted with boys wearing coonskin caps as "The Ballad of Davey Crockett" by Bill Hayes was number one in the country that day. A field of 21 lined up with Kiekhaefer's Chrysler fleet represented by only Tim Flock's 300 on the pole. After John Capps tossed a five-year-old Lincoln early, Tim started to stink up the show until lap 48 when a spindle broke, leaving the second half to the Helzafire Olds 78 of Jim Paschal. Olds took the next three spots with Baker, Don White, and Joel Million. Fifth was the Columbia winner the night before, Fonty Flock, with Petty sixth, Liguori seventh, Junior Johnson 12th, Donald Thomas 13th, Rathmann 14th, Herb T. 16th, Tim 17th, and Lewellen 20th. The fans shivered the whole hour and 13 minutes.

The 45th and final race of 1955 was Sunday afternoon, October 30th. This was the month with premiers of *The Honeymooners*, *Alfred Hitchcock Presents*, *Captain Kangaroo*, *The Mickey Mouse Club*, and Dem Bums finally won their only World Series. Nineteen fifty-five was also the year of the most phenomenal season ever by a race driver on a major circuit. Tim Flock in the big white Kiekhaefer Chrysler 300 sponsored by Mercury Outboards won 15 races, over a third of them all, *and ten times won the pole and led every lap!* With his second Grand National Championship in his pocket, Tim had little to prove because he was the best, driving the best, and racing for the best. He humiliated 24 competitors by, you guessed it, capturing the pole and leading every lap for the win. Add one to the stats noted earlier. Also add $1,100 to his winnings for the year, which grew to a record of nearly 38,000 1955 dollars. The 6,000 fans saw the next five finishers Turner, Baker, Herb T., Dave Terrell, and Joe Weatherly complete all of the 100 laps. Further back came Dink Widenhouse seventh, Staley eighth, Massey ninth, Welborn tenth, Panch 11th, Lewellen 15th, Paschal 19th, Liguori 20th, Thompson 21st, D. Thomas 22nd, and Petty 23rd. It was a great field and to dominate it as he did this race and all season is a feat never to be equaled.

It was an eight-race Kiekhaefer winning streak since March 25th that the competition had to deal with for a Sunday 100-lapper on May 13, 1956, at what was now billed as a .9 mile oval. A field of 31 included top drivers paced in time trials by red-hot teammates Buck Baker in Chrysler 300 and Speedy Thompson alongside in 300C. They had each won three of the last six races. Row two saw a pair of factory Fords for Turner and Roberts and row three had Eubanks in a Ford and Herb in Chrysler 300B. The fourth row held Billy Myers

"Two on the aisle, please."

in a Mercury and Petty in a Dodge, then row five with Owens in a Pontiac and Moody in a Ford. There were other great drivers further back. It was Earth versus Kiekhaefer, and 7,500 came on a glorious Mother's Day to watch. The green silk waved and Thompson went to the front for the first 57 laps with challenges from Baker, Petty, and Roberts. Baker passed and led lap 58 with a trio breathing down his neck. It was anybody's race when Petty lost it coming off the second turn and then there were two. Banging away at each other, they drifted full bore out of four and thundered to the checkers with Buck nipping Speedy by a fender with Petty and Roberts feet behind. Earth lost again as Kiekhaefer not only won, but also had a two-car sweep. Fifth was Owens a lap back, sixth came Staley, seventh Weatherly, eighth Moody, ninth Massey, and tenth Myers. Others were Thomas 11th, Eubanks 12th, White 13th, Johns 15th, Allen 18th, Turner 26th, Paschal 28th, and Blair 30th. The competition included the Ford, Dodge, Chevrolet, Pontiac, Mercury, and Plymouth factory teams and no one, no one, could have dreamed that Kiekhaefer's winning streak was only *HALF* over! Petty, Turner, Roberts, Flock, Weatherly, Staley, Paschal, Moody, Owens, Thomas, Goldsmith, Smith, and Johnson were all past winners, future Hall of Famers, and helpless for eight more races to stop this steamroller. Not until Ralph Moody won in De Paolo's Ford at Lehi, AR, on June 10th did the nightmare end. These big-dollar Detroit factories with their top-notch drivers afforded stiff competition to Kiekhaefer and lost race after race. It was total and complete domination never seen before and never to be witnessed again.

Always on Sunday afternoon they came, this time September 30, 1956, for 99 miles. The day before, Buck sliced into Herb's point lead with a win at Columbia. Now with five races left (Shelby's 100-mile fiasco had not been added to the schedule yet), every point was crucial for Baker and Thomas. Twenty-three stockers arrived, many after the tedious, wind-

A mature hardwood first broke through the stands decades ago.

ing, pre–Interstate overnight trek from Columbia to Hillsborough. It was a competent field led by the big white Chryslers of Baker and Thompson, Thomas' point-leading Chevy, the De Paolo Fords of Roberts and Moody, Petty's Dodge, Paschal and Myers in Mercurys, and Allen's Plymouth. Thompson had the pole, but the main attractions were Baker and Thomas starting bumper-to-bumper in third and fifth respectively. Thompson jumped out front for a couple of laps until Baker took over. Billy Myers torched his Mercury, running near the front on lap 27. Baker gave way to Roberts for a lap after they restarted, then Buck took it back. Brownie King rolled a new Chevy on lap 49 while Buck led until the 69th when Fireball grabbed it back for a round. Just as before, Baker powered 300B past Roberts' 22 and figured to bring it on home. Only this time, Fireball found a way. On lap 84, Fireball matted the gas, slammed past Buck for first, and it stuck. At the checkers, he had a comfortable lead and De Paolo could call the suits in Detroit and announce a win. Third, two laps back, was Thompson, and fourth Herb, giving up points to Baker again, but still with a comfortable lead. Fifth was Bunk Moore, sixth Harvey Henderson, seventh Bobby Keck, eighth Ed Cole, ninth Moody, and tenth was Lund. Others were Petty 12th, Paschal 19th, Myers 20th, and Allen 23rd and last. It took almost an hour and 22 minutes for the 7,200 onlookers to see Roberts take the $950 top prize. A week later, he beat Baker again at Newport, TN, for two in a row. Kiekhaefer *was* beatable!

On Sunday afternoon, March 24, 1957, there was one topic on the lips of the crowd attending the 99-mile battle at Occoneechee and it was not racing. The day before, Frank McGuire's University of North Carolina Tar Heels defeated Wilt Chamberlain's University of Kansas Jayhawks 54 to 53 in triple overtime for the NCAA Championship. A slim, but good, field assembled for the only visit of the season on a blustery day that had the factories out in force including the brass from Chevrolet. *And did they deliver!* The front row went to two De Paolo Fords piloted by Roberts and Panch. Baker led the first three laps from his third starting spot, while another De Paolo Ford of Ralph Moody crashed on the first lap. Fireball led for 38, but broke a wheel and it was Buck again. Around halfway, Panch edged out front until 21 to go when Buck passed Marvin's fading FoMoCo and breezed home almost a lap ahead of teammate Thompson. Third went to a third teammate in another Hugh Babb–owned '57 Chevrolet Black Widow Bel Air driven by Jack Smith. Detroit was pleased. Factory finishers were fourth Goldsmith in Yunick's Ford, fifth Petty in an Olds, ninth Allen in Spook Crawford's Plymouth, 11th Panch, 12th Paschal in Bill Stroppe's Mercury, Lund 13th in a Petty Olds, Billy Myers 16th for Stroppe, and Roberts and Moody 17th and 19th in the 19-car field. Some 8,000 turned out for an embarrassing $650 to win.

Race six of the 1958 season was on March 23rd, Sunday afternoon. Only 18 racers showed up for 99 laps and Buck in his Moore '57 Chevy almost carbon copied his 1957 triumph. The National Champion led early, gave way to Panch's Ford, then reclaimed the money spot with 14 laps to go, cruising to his 37th career win, one behind Tim Flock in the all-time totals. Panch finished second, third was Thompson, fourth Petty, and fifth Curtis Turner in an original Holman-Moody Ford. Others were Allen sixth, Smith 12th, Californian Eddie Pagan 13th, and Herman Beam 16th. Eight thousand fans watched the 76-minute show.

Sometimes people finally get their due and it happened on September 28, 1958, as most of the South settled down to digest their after-church chicken and an afternoon of the NFL and napping. A field of 33 showed in Hillsborough for the chance at an $800 first prize in 110 laps, 99 miles around the sweeping dirt oval on the banks of the Eno. Tiny Lund shocked the onlookers by snatching the pole, driving the '58 Chevy 86. Cotton Owens started outside Tiny in a Pontiac, old-time moonrunner Gober Sosebee was third in a Chevy, and rookie Shorty Rollins fourth in a '58 Ford. Some interesting drivers were Joe Eubanks, driving on a team with his Spartanburg neighbor Owens, early career starts for Tommy Irwin and a kid in Olds number 2, Richard Petty. A couple of other graybeards besides Sosebee were Ted Chamberlain, who had been away for about four years, and Blair, who started race number one in 1949, as did Lewellen, Baker, and Petty. When they got the green, Owens hopped out front and stayed there for 32 laps. Richard Petty blew an engine and convertible ace Larry Frank broke a tie rod. Lund shot past Owens, holding the point until lap 46, when the A-frame snapped and the pole-sitter/race-leader was done. That gave the lead to Johnson in his rugged Paul Spaulding '57 Ford 11 and he looked like a sure winner. Then with 12 laps left, a steering failure sent the Ronda Roadrunner crashing and in his 133rd start, Spartanburg's Joe Eubanks got a long-awaited, much-deserved victory by half a mile over Doug Cox. Baker was third and Irwin fourth, both a lap behind, with Lee Petty fifth, two back. Others were Rollins sixth, Roy Tyner seventh, Sosebee eighth, Blair 11th, Chamberlain 12th, Johnson 15th, the Turtle 16th, Speedy 19th, Massey 20th, Owens 22nd, Lund 25th, Frank 28th, and young Petty 31st.

For Joe Eubanks, it was his first and only win in the big time, where he recorded three poles. Eubanks' Grand National career began with a 19th, driving fellow Spartan Bud Moore's Mercury 4 in the first Southern 500. Joe hung up his goggles after a 13th place in John Dunbar's Ford 82 in the 1961 World 600. In between, Eubanks had good runs driving for Moore in Hudsons and Oldsmobiles from 1950 to 1955. He timed in the middle of the front row for the Southern 500 in 1952 and came home seventh. Joe finished in the top ten in points from 1951 through 1954, when he was fifth. *He was in the top five over 25% of the time and in the top 10 nearly 75% of the time!* How had a guy run that well without winning? He had never gotten over the hump of being a winner, but came close in one of the biggest stock car races ever, the 1951 Motor City 250, on the flat mile dirt at the Michigan State Fairgrounds in Detroit. Bill France talked virtually every American auto manufacturer into entering the August 12th marathon. This epic had 59 entries, 15 different makes, drivers from all NASCAR divisions, AAA stock and big car divisions, IMCA stars, west coasters, outlaws, five cautions involving thundering multiple-car crashes, and a record 14 lead changes among six drivers. It was four hours, 20 minutes, and 28 seconds of spine-tingling, edge-of-the-seat-racing in front of 16,352 fans for $5,000, a new Packard convertible, and all the publicity the winner and his manufacturer could stand. It had everything except a woman and Fireball Roberts. Marshall Teague was on the pole, led a lap, and Fonty took over. Then Tommy Thompson led, then Flock, then Thompson, Flock, Thompson, Flock, Sosebee, Flock, and Curtis Turner for 81 laps. During a titanic fight for first with 25 laps remaining, Thompson and Turner bombed away at each other, sliding into the wall as Joe Eubanks' Olds 82 cruised by. That was the good news for Joe. The bad news was that he did not know he had taken first. Turner parked in a steamy, smoking heap, but Thompson was just smoking, got the Chrysler going, and set off after Eubanks. As Joe continued to breeze along oblivious to the history in his grasp, a smoldering Thompson dashed past Eubanks with 18 circuits remaining and won by a whopping 37 seconds. The next closest finisher was Johnny Mantz's Nash, six laps behind. The loudest noise heard that day was the door of opportunity slamming closed before Joe could race through it. He drove his own Ford 82 in 1956 to 15th in points, finishing half of his 26 starts in the top ten. In 1957, he finished ninth in the second race of the season at Concord and sat out the next 52. He should have had other chances, but the call never came. Only one man thought he could win and he was right in Joe's backyard. When Eubanks won at Hillsborough, he had been cajoled into returning by Cotton Owens, who talked him out of retirement and into the seat of the num-

Ruins at the top of the stands may be the press box from which Jayne Mansfield and her daughter watched Junior Johnson win on March 10, 1963.

ber 6 Pontiac for the '58 Southern 500, which Joe led for 25 laps. He finished out the season with Cotton, running seven races in all for 34th in the standings. Eubanks drove a baby blue '58 Ford 82 sponsored by What-A-Burger for most of 1959, finishing 32nd in points. He is mentioned along with footage in the screen classic *Thunder in Carolina*. In '60, he sat out again, and in '61 drove two races, calling it a career with a final 50th in points. Joe passed away on June 21, 1971, just short of his 46th birthday. Joe Eubanks was an outstanding driver during his dozen off-and-on years on the Grand National circuit, finally hitting the jackpot he deserved on an autumn Sunday in Hillsborough.

March 1, 1959, was the Sunday after the Lee Petty–Johnny Beauchamp Daytona 500 controversy, which was finally decided on Wednesday. Twenty-two stockers were on hand for the 99-miler worth $800 to the winner. The entries were not the big names, but the race turned out to be about the best. Curtis Turner had one of ten $5,500 Holman-Moody–built T-Birds from their Power Products Division, which were very impressive at the Beach, with Beauchamp second, Pistone eighth, Tim Flock ninth, Raul Cilloniz 12th, Eduardo Dibos 48th, and Fritz Wilson 56th buying and racing seven of them. Turner's claimed 13th at Daytona, but had the pole here, flanked by Pistone in another one. Curtis led the first lap and swapped spots with Pistone regularly. Tommy Irwin and Larry Frank both ramped off into the wild blue, but failed to find the smooth-flowing waters of the Eno. A new player emerged with four to go when Bob Welborn put his '59 Chevy past leader Pistone with Turner nipping at his fins. They took the white flag and Welborn felt the sickening skip of a fuel-starved racer. Curtis slipped by Bob, but still had to deal with Tiger Tom. They drifted out of turn four and Turner stretched his T-Bird over the stripe to edge Pistone by feet for his 15th career win. Welborn coasted to third, fourth to Petty, and Buck fifth. On back were Wood sixth,

Eubanks eighth, Owens ninth, Speedy 13th, Lund 14th, Junior 19th, and Lewellen 21st. Turner and Pistone started and finished first and second with Turner completing the job in about 73 minutes before 7,500 witnesses.

The second visit of 1959 was September 20th, the day after Khrushchev was barred from Disneyland. Twenty-two speed merchants appeared at Fantasyland on the Eno for 110 laps, with Jack Smith putting a Chevy on the pole. He rocketed away for the first 50 laps until an axle snapped and Tiger Tom put his tired, but twice-victorious T-Bird 59 on the point. Junior Johnson, driving a new Spaulding Dodge, was late arriving, starting at the rear. However, he screamed through the field from 22nd, last, and was challenging for first when he was taken out in a crash with Sgt. George Green. Johnson got the goat going again and soldiered on. With 21 left, Pistone broke a spindle and Papa Lee got his 38th career win by a lap over Cotton's 1959 T-Bird "Thunder Chicken" 6. Third was Richard Petty despite retiring with a broken axle. Fourth came Greenville's Larry Frank, fifth Tyner, the Turtle sixth, G.C. seventh, Buck 12th, Smith 16th, Rex 17th, Speedy 18th, Ned 19th, and Junior "Illegal Rear End" Johnson was disqualified for last. Lee averaged 77.868 before about 7,000 spectators.

Memorial Day weekend, May 29, 1960, and 23 lined up the day after Jarrett and Massey teamed to win at Spartanburg. Boring would be a kind way to describe this as Lee Petty took the pole, then led all 110 laps for his 51st win. He had started with son Richard flanking him on the front row for the first time, but youth faded fast. It took less than 73 minutes for Papa Lee to cop the $900 in his Petty-blue 42. Second was "Gentleman Ned" Jarrett, third Jack "The Red Fox" Smith, fourth Tommy Irwin, fifth "The Old Pro" Buck Baker, sixth Richard "Squirrel" Petty, seventh "The Golden Greek" Zervakis, eighth Joe Eubanks, ninth Junior "The Ronda Roadrunner" Johnson, and tenth was Gerald Duke. Rex took 11th, 12th was Everett "Cotton" Owens, 14th David Gene Pearson, 15th Herman "The Turtle" Beam, 16th A. M. "Spook" Crawford, 17th Curtis "The Blond Blizzard" Turner, 19th Joe "The Clown Prince" Weatherly, 20th Roy "The Wild Injun" Tyner, and 22nd Ronald "Bunkie" Blackburn. This sleeper should have been the "Nickname 99." The only caution was for Turner's flight off the turn into the shrubs, but short of the drink.

The late summer Sunday afternoon of September 18, 1960, found a dozen and a half entries with less than 50% of those having a shot to win. As it turned out, 17 of them were racing for second. As did his father in the spring, Richard Petty put his blue 1960 Fury on the pole and led all 110 laps for $800 winner's share. He was challenged by front row mate Junior Johnson until lap 75, when Junior's Ray Fox–tuned, Daytona 500–winning '59 Chevy 27 skidded over the banking and into the pines. Richard was home free with Jarrett finishing second a lap behind. Third on his way to the Grand National Championship raced Rex White in a Chevy. Finishing fourth and destroying his legend and nickname rumbled Herman "The Turtle" Beam in his best career finish until then. He was seven laps back in his 1960 Ford 19 and beat some stout competitors, like fifth placer Pardue, Irwin sixth, eighth Buck, Papa Lee 11th, Johnson 13th, Pearson 15th, and Frank last. It was Richard's second pole and third victory. Only 197 to go.

Back to the Schedule from Hell, 1961 style, as three races were slated for three days in a row with Occoneechee getting the Easter Sunday slot in the middle. It was a make-up date for a rainout in March. April Fool's Saturday saw "The Golden Greek" Emanuel Zervakis win his first in Greenville, so the drive up to Hillsborough was not a bad hop for him. Twenty stockers showed for the April 2nd 99-mile dash on a miserably cold day. Jarrett cracked the record with a pole speed of nearly 92 miles per hour in a Chevrolet. Junior's Holly Farms Poultry '60 Pontiac flanked him. Ned jumped out to lead this Easter Parade, but it was curtailed way short as he fried the rear end after only nine circuits. That gave the point to Owens for a couple rounds until Johnson settled in for a long stint driving a car he bought from the little Spartan. With victory in his palm Sunday, Junior's 333 horses turned rotten with 19 laps to go. Reminiscent of Eubanks' Motor City Madness of '51, Cotton high-tailed it and hopped out front without knowing it, while Johnson, with egg on his face, jumped back on the dirt after a lengthy stop and ran like a wild hare. When the checkers fell over the bunny-white Pony, Cotton was a basket case. He could not believe that he had risen to the lead and won. Richard Petty and Buck Baker were in the lead lap second and third. A little cross was Junior in fourth a lap back and Rex White, the Easter Monday winner at Bowman-Gray, found fifth. Other notables were Pardue sixth, Irwin seventh, Spencer ninth, the Turtle 12th, Wendell 13th, Zervakis 14th, Maurice Petty trying to resurrect his driving career with Papa Lee still hospitalized 15th, Ned 19th, and Crawfish 20th and last. Forty-nine hundred fans sacrificed themselves on this blustery day, but it was a Happy Easter for a guy named Cotton, which just seems right.

October 1961 was a month of memorable events. Maris asterisked Ruth's home-run record and the Yankees won another World Series. *Ben Casey*, *The Dick Van Dyke Show*, and *Mr. Ed* premiered on the tube. The X-15 broke two altitude records, Outer Mongolia was admitted to the UN, and Ned Jarrett wrapped up his first Grand National Championship at Bristol on the 22nd. Two races later, October 29th on the autumnal banks of the Eno, 20 jockeys assembled for a little pre–Halloween party with lots of tricks and treats for the participants and fans. It was the 52nd and final event of the season. First was a trick on the fans paying to see a 150-miler, but got a 148.5 instead because the race was 165 laps instead of a correct 167. Weatherly was tricked out of a sure win the night before at Greenville when a flat with eight to go foiled the Bud Moore Pontiac. However, the Clown Prince, piloting the same maroon and black Pontiac 8, bagged the pole and led every lap at Hillsborough save one that was paced by Johnson. Nobody had a ghost of a chance against Joe as front row Rex finished a lap back in second, new Champion Jarrett third, and Maurice Petty still subbing off and on for Papa fourth. It was spooky that Johnson's Holly Farms teammate Fireball Roberts made his last appearance at the track where he refused to stroke exactly 11 years to the day earlier, costing him the 1950 championship. Roberts scared up fifth place even though he blew an engine late. Further back raced drivers costumed the Turtle seventh, King-to-be Richard tenth, Crawfish 11th, the Ronda Roadrunner 12th, Great Scott 15th, Buck 17th, Doc Reitzel 18th, and Tattooed Jim 20th and last. Weatherly made no bones about the fact that he won nine times, but was fourth in the standings due to first-year car owner Bud Moore not chasing points. Joe won eight more than Champ Jarrett while racing in 21 less events. But never fear that Halloween Eve's Eve because the 1962 season was only a week away and Weatherly would get his title times two.

Occoneechee made the schedule once out of 53 in 1962, getting the big hangover date of March 18th, the day after St. Patrick's. It was the month the first K-Mart opened, the Beatles performed pre–Ringo on the BBC, Wilt scored 100, and Jack Paar quit. A healthy crowd of over nine thousand saw a bunch of tired warriors that had trucked up from Savannah overnight where Jack Smith won. This Sunday, Weatherly paced 20 others from the pole in Bud Moore's "Dirt Dauber," the year-old Pontiac reserved for the clay. He swapped the lead with Richard Petty four times in the first 102 of the 110-lap chase when with an unlucky eight to go, the old warhorse's transmission failed. Rex White found himself leading and nipped Richard by half a tick for his second checkers of the year. The trio of White, owner/chief mechanic Louis Clements, and a gold and white 1961 Impala 4 took the $1,000 first prize. Paschal was third and Smith, who started last, came in fourth in the lead lap.

7. *Occoneechee Speedway*   113

Looking up the slope of the Third Turn banking that drops off steeply on the back.

Buddy Baker was fifth, a lap back in Buck's Chrysler, with Maurice sixth, Ralph Earnhardt seventh, Buck ninth in Buddy's Chrysler, Jarrett tenth, Weatherly 11th, Scott 12th, the Turtle 15th just ahead of Crawfish 16th, and Owens escaped with $50 for 20th. Last was Tommy Irwin, who interestingly crashed with Buck on the opening lap due to a solid wall of red dust, which precipitated a lengthy red flag so the water wagon could spread some of the Eno's bounty on the parched surface.

March 10, 1963, was a Sunday to remember at Occoneechee Speedway for the drivers, spectators, and special guests. However, five days earlier, Patsy Cline, Cowboy Copas, and Hawkshaw Hawkins perished in a plane crash in the piney hills near Camden, TN. On race day, Pete Rose started spring training as a Cincinnati Red while a stellar field in Hillsborough found Weatherly on the pole for the third straight time in a new Bud Moore Pontiac, befitting the defending Grand National Champion. Outside was Paschal in a '62 Petty Plymouth. Row two had Petty and Junior Johnson in his white Holly Farms Poultry '63 Chevy 3. The next six were Isaac, Jarrett, surprise entrant Nelson Stacy, Pardue, and Buck Baker. Weatherly led a lap, then he and Johnson swapped it back and forth until halfway of the 148.5 miler when Joe's fuel pump quit. Petty led a little until Junior remembered the special guest waiting to plant a big one on his mountain-man mug in Victory Lane. None other than Jayne Mansfield, with daughter in tow, graced the press box getting as much attention as the dirt slingers forty rows below. Meanwhile, Johnson paced the pack for the last 78 circuits, edging Paschal by a couple of ticks at the wire. Junior parked the Fox Chevy in the Winner's Circle and got cheek-smooched from the fading star to the roaring delight of the fans. Petty was third in the lead lap followed by Jarrett fourth, Pardue fifth, Floyd Powell

The rim of the Third Turn with the racing surface to the right and the backside drop-off to the left.

seventh, the Turtle in his 84th consecutive finish ninth, Buck 11th, Crawfish 14th, Weatherly 15th, Stacy 17th, Pearson 19th, Isaac after a flight into the trees 20th, and Wendell 23rd and last. Junior's win gained him the attention of glamorous Jayne, maybe filling him with lust and desire, but bets are that she could not make biscuits like Flossie. No matter, in the words of the Four Seasons' number one hit of the day, Junior could surely "Walk Like A Man."

It was not his last race, but it was his last win. On Sunday, October 27, 1963, Joe Weatherly won his fourth consecutive Hillsborough pole, 19th career-wise, and led most of the way for his 25th Grand National victory enroute to his second straight Grand National Championship. Joe drove a maroon and black Bud Moore 1963 Pontiac 8 even though they had officially shifted to Mercury before the Southern 500. It would be the 1981 Daytona 500 before Pontiac won another pole position. In the 150-miler (two laps were finally added to make it so), Joe led the first 84, then Junior put that '63 Chevy out front for awhile, as did Richard. Then with 42 left, Weatherly retook the lead and streaked home by over a lap on Petty Plymouth pilot Bob Welborn in one of his last starts. Bob Montgomery did the honors over the airwaves on the Universal Racing Network and their post-race interview photo together was widely circulated. Surprising Doug Cooper was third, Buck fourth, and Crawfish fifth in a fine run. On back were Petty sixth, Massey seventh, up and coming Larry Thomas eighth, graybeard Bill Widenhouse tenth, Wendell 11th, Junior 13th, Pearson 15th, Pardue 16th, Jarrett 20th, Wade 21st, and Lund 23rd.

Bud Moore and Joe Weatherly had a new shop, a new marque, and a second straight Grand National Championship, although that one needs explanation. Bud refused to go through the rigors of the full schedule. Therefore, he gave Joe the best equipment most of the time, but Weatherly had to scrounge for rides occasionally. Over his two title years, he drove for 10 different owners. In fact, the Wood Brothers won the 1962 car owner points title even though the champion driver was Weatherly. In 1963, however, they shared the championship honors. The 1964 season started and three straight titles for them appeared probable. Second place came hard at Concord in the opener in the famous instance of Bud rocking the side of Lund's lapped Ford for not moving over for leader Joe. Weatherly finished fourth for west coast Mercury boss Bill Stroppe in the only event at the Augusta International Speedway road course. He started last, finishing 14th in Bill Morton's '62 Ford at Jacksonville in the famous race won by Wendell Scott. Joe followed that with tenth at Savannah in a '63 Ford number 92, which was also the great Spartanburg-transplanted Georgia moonshiner Jack Smith's last race. Four starts and four different rides to begin the double title defense and Joe had the point lead! Then off to Riverside, a now-abandoned California track, where Weatherly had finished seventh in Moore's Mercury in the '63 season finale. He started 16th, but early into the 500-mile marathon, lost the transmission and parked in the garage. Driven by an unprecedented third consecutive Grand National Championship, Weatherly pleaded for Bud to slip another tranny under that ill-fated Marauder and they did. Though many laps down, a decent finish and lots of championship points were within reach with over half the race left. Joe stormed back on course, turning laps as fast as leader Dan Gurney, when he drifted into the uphill right-hander at the end of the esses. Clear color footage shows it all as Joe roars by and a telltale wisp of blue smoke mists from under the rear end as he heads up the rise. Was it the experimental brakes failing that were installed at Bill Stroppe's shop earlier? At that time, the unseen, unfilmed Lord of the Underworld swiftly swung his scythe at "The Clown Prince" and got him *and* his brakes. Number 8 thundered into the turn six grandstand wall so hard that the left front was smashed all the way to the middle of the grill and the center of the roof bowed. An 8 outlined in red was stamped on the wall as if to signify the spot where 41-year-old Joseph Herbert Weatherly left us. It is easy to see Joe's head and shoulders lurched powerfully into the wall with his car. Weatherly did not like shoulder harnesses, but it would not have mattered. There was *no* safety device then that would have saved him. Besides, the scythe had already swung. The mortally wounded Mercury ricocheted back across the track and onto the slope of a dirt bank where it very nearly tipped over on the driver's side. They rushed to save him, but found horror and heard the whisper *"Don't bother, he's mine."* It was January 19, 1964, when Bob Montgomery's baritone came through radio speakers across the South with the dreadful announcement, the nature of which had only been heard one other time, six and a half years earlier with Bobby Myers. The Voice of Stock Car Racing did his job, reluctantly announcing that Weatherly had been killed. The three-hour time difference made it a dark, cold winter Sunday night in the Southeast, and this revelation made it considerably darker and much, much colder. Unfortunately, it was just a warm-up to similar news in the following 53 weeks as the Grim Reaper harvested Eddie Sachs, Dave McDonald, Fireball Roberts, Jimmy Pardue, Bobby Marshman, and Billy Wade in racers, plus Larry Thomas in his personal car. Eddie was known on the Indy circuit as "The Clown Prince of Racing." The shocking *Life* magazine photo of firefighters spraying chemicals on Sachs' corpse, still strapped into his smoldering American Red Ball Special, is unforgettable. How many Clown Princes can be lost in one year?

In addition, 1964 was the backbreaking, calendar-cramming, mind-numbing Schedule from Hell when the madness finally peaked at a dizzying 62 races from November 10, 1963, back around to November 8, 1964. That is a race every 5.85 days. So do not whine about today's slate. These men raced and died in front of mostly small crowds, mostly on dirt, for pocket change. Network television contracts? Maybe, just maybe, ABC's *Wide World of Sports* would slip it in between curling and track a few weeks after the fact. The only way to see a stock car race in color was on a promotional film for a half hour on TV or at the auto show, usually the previous year's Southern or Indianapolis 500.

What a week in 1964! Ford introduced the Mustang, Sidney Poitier won the first Best Actor Oscar by an African-American, Shea Stadium opened as did the Chesapeake Bay Bridge-Tunnel, and on race day, Arnold Palmer won the Masters. April 12th on the banks of the Eno saw the first annual Joe Weatherly Memorial 150, the second in a string of four races in five days. Panch won at Weaverville the day before with Spartanburg and Columbia looming. A field of 27 was on hand in Hillsborough, but Bud Moore and Weatherly's replacement Billy Wade went home after finishing third at Weaverville. There were 26 others that wished Cotton Owens and David Pearson had followed Bud back to Spartanburg. Pearson put Cotton's factory Dodge on the pole and except for 50 laps led early by Petty, they trounced the field by three laps. Dick Hutcherson in his second Grand National start finished second, Larry Thomas tied his best career finish yet for third, Ralph Earnhardt came from next-to-last to fourth in an old Ford, and Bobby Keck fifth. Others were Crawfish sixth, Wendell seventh, Junior ninth, Richard 12th, LeeRoy 14th, Marvin 17th, Tiny 18th, Ned 20th, Maurice 22nd, Buddy Baker 23rd, Pardue 24th, and Frank started and finished 27th and last in the Turtlemobile. It was David's sixth career win, for which he netted $1,400.

Sunday, September 20, 1964, was the second trip to Hillsborough for the touring pros and 28 of them entered. Cotton Owens made his second start of the year "just for fun." He won at Richmond six days earlier as he and David ran one-two. So why not try it again? However, it was Jarrett's turn and the Newton native hustled his blue 11 home first a lap ahead of the game Cotton. Larry Thomas was third again, Wendell had a super fourth, and

Summertime's dense green forest all but covers the narrow backstretch path viewed from Turn Three towards Turn Two.

Wintertime's view of almost the exact same look up the backstretch.

Buddy Arrington fifth. Also competing were Crider sixth, Pardue 13th, Pearson 14th, Petty 16th, Buck (13 days after his historic third Southern 500) win got a hundred bills for 20th, and Cale was 22nd. Somewhere in the shadows that Sabbath on his pale horse was Death, sizing up his prey, buzzards circling overhead, sickle gleaming. He found his prey, but decided to wait a few hours. He wanted more speed. He wanted it grisly. He wanted to do it when the young man would not have those pesky rescuers on the ready to try to foil his bloody scheme. The Reaper usually wins, and on September 22nd, late in the day, he unleashed a precise swing and a blood-red 1964 Plymouth, Car 54, exploded through the steel and wood of the third turn at the Charlotte Motor Speedway making near 150 miles per hour. James Mansfield Pardue of North Wilkesboro was in flight. The racer was already breaking up as it augured into the steep red embankment on the backside of the turn, flipping and cartwheeling hundreds of feet downhill until it came to rest in a tangle of chain-link fence with poor Jimmy skewered on a pole. Ironically, Billy Wade was one of the first on the scene with Bud Moore teammate Darel Dieringer. All three had been testing the Goodyear safety inner liner by running over spikes, causing blowouts. Billy himself would buy it shortly on January 5, 1965, at Daytona, doing exactly the same thing with another death scene as gruesome as the worst nightmare could conjure. Since Death had already put his ice-cold embrace around Fireball Roberts there in May, but not without a fight, maybe Charlotte is where Death took shines to the youthful Pardue and Wade. However, nobody said a last good-bye to Jimmy at Hillsborough because he would be in Martinsville the next Sunday for sure. But instead, James Mansfield Pardue went home from Charlotte to North Wilkesboro ... in a box.

The first of two races at Occoneechee for 1965 took place on Sunday, March 14th, as

23 stockers arrived amid the Chrysler hemi ban. With no Petty and no Pearson, more than 7,500 still showed up for the Ford battle. Junior took the pole at over 98.5 miles per hour and ran away at the drop of the green. Ned Jarrett tried to stay close, as did Junior's front row buddy Hutcherson. The image always remembered is Gene Hobby bouncing off the grandstand dirt barricade in a '64 Dodge and flipping down the front stretch. It happened on lap 41 and he was unhurt, but it totaled that baby-blue 99. Surprising third place starter Doug Yates in a new Plymouth lost oil pressure after only 23 laps and retired. Hutcherson dropped out of contention with a long stop to repair his brakes. With 30 to go, Johnson's Holly Farms 26 Ford lost a Goodyear and two laps having it changed, putting Jarrett into the lead the rest of the way. Junior salvaged second, Paul Moore was third in his pesky Plymouth, Langley was fourth, and Buddy Arrington nipped Buck for fifth. Further back were Crawfish eighth, Hutch 12th, Dieringer 15th, Yarborough 21st, and Wendell 23rd and last. Ned's win put him one ahead of Johnson, 40 to 39, in the career wins tally.

October's winds cut through the cloudy Sunday afternoon gathering on the 24th. Even though Chrysler was back, only about 4,500 fans bothered to come out to watch 20 stockers challenge the nine-tenths on the Eno for a hundred miles. Hutcherson took the pole at almost 99 miles per hour, but Pearson took the lead from fifth on the grid. Junior Johnson started beside Hutcherson in row one and stayed there, pulling one of the oldest tricks in the stock car book. Junior fendered Hutch's right front tire, causing the Iowan to take an early unscheduled pit stop. Luckily, Hutcherson had plenty of time to catch up, which he did, and then some. Meanwhile, Johnson had a suspension failure while leading and Pearson's Dodge went on the bum. When the checkers waved after 112 rounds, Dick had a comfortable three-lap lead over Tom Pistone's Shoney's '64 Ford. Third was Paschal driving for an absent Richard Petty, fourth found Cale Yarborough in 06, and Paul Lewis was fifth. Trailing came Pearson sixth, Dieringer seventh, Buddy Baker 11th, Wendell 14th, Junior 15th, Ned 16th, and Jimmy Helms 20th and last.

A week earlier, Helms was the unfortunate soul who had to deal with the Reaper. Jimmy had the Grim One take the wheel from him for a few seconds so his '63 Ford 53 could be zeroed into the driver's door of a sparkling white 1965 Plymouth 01 carrying a very, very infrequent participant named Harold Kite. An air of gloom permeated the grounds because the specter in the black shroud had struck again at his favorite new haunt, the Charlotte Motor Speedway, and put his frigid arms around Kite on lap two of the National 500 the previous Sunday. Kite won the 11th race in Grand National history, the first of the 1950 season, on the sands at Daytona in a Lincoln. That day he beat the world and everybody was there. Maybe it was an even better field than the 1951 Motor City 250. Kite also drove for Bud Moore in the first Southern 500 and finished 38th, but raced only a few times in Grand National during the 15 years that followed. He was only 43 when his number came up.

The month saw the debuts on the tube of *The Monkees*, *That Girl*, and *Star Trek* as the Beatles released *Revolver*. Meanwhile, NASCAR's revolvers arrived in Hillsborough as the Joe Weatherly Memorial 150 was back on Sunday, September 18, 1966. Chrysler and Ford were duking it out again and by this time in the season, with only four races left, Pearson looked like a champ, having already won 15 times. All David had to do was not have a complete collapse and he would beat fellow Spartanburg (Inman) driver and Rookie-of-the-Year shoo-in James Hylton for his and Cotton's first Grand National Championship. Both were at Hillsborough along with 21 others for 167 dirty laps. It was déjà vu all over again as Hutcherson took the pole and Johnson, recently unretired, started outside as in the 1965 edition of the Weatherly. Instead of those two banging it out and letting Pearson slip by, Hutch led

The wintertime affords a much clearer view of the Eno River flowing just feet down the hill off the backstretch.

the first ten laps, and then Junior took it for ten, until the Keokuk Comet dominated for the last 146 for his second straight win on the Eno. Junior had front-end problems and fell out shortly after losing the lead. However, Pearson charged on, doing what got him the points lead in the first place, and finished second by the length of the homestretch. Paul Lewis was a solid third, rookie Hylton fourth, and John Sears fifth. Others were two-time 1966 victor Elmo Langley sixth, Castles seventh, Wendell eighth, Buddy Baker 17th, Pistone 18th, and Johnson 20th. Only about 6,500 racing enthusiasts stopped by that afternoon, probably not knowing that they were watching the last gasps of a once-mighty stock car giant. Hillsborough's death rattle was getting louder and louder as was that of big time dirt track racing in NASCAR.

For the penultimate major race at Occoneechee Speedway on Sunday, September 17, 1967, the memorial to Joe Weatherly was removed from the name. The crowd shrank even more, by about a thousand, and the number of top-notch entries diminished. The old track was alive, but barely, with only 5,500 people there. It was a large field compared to recent races, matching the 28 in this race in 1964. Richard Petty sat on the pole and led all but ten laps when Tiny Lund shoved a year-old Ford out front. A pair of thundering crashes early on punctuated the chase as two men were carted off for some sheet time. On lap 12, tenth place starter Jack Harden, an Alabama NASA engineer, launched himself into suborbital flight and missed a splashdown by nosing into the pines in a cloud of dust and splinters. Shortly after Harden was hauled away with back injuries, Paul Dean of Sweetwater, TN, suffered a neck injury when he mixed it up on the main stretch like Gene Hobby a couple of years earlier by rolling and flipping his new Ford until it was reduced to junk. Both he and Harden recovered during the off-season. Except for Hutcherson keeping it close, Petty won an incredible eighth in a row dating back to August 12th and was not done yet. Buddy Baker drove a Cotton Owens Dodge to third in a prelude to their successes together a couple of years hence. Hylton finished fourth and G.C. Spencer fifth. The final rundown had Langley sixth, Bobby Allison seventh, Lund 16th, and Wendell Scott 27th. There was one last, sad visit to go.

Nineteen years, one month, and eight days after that first 200-mile thrill show around the new Occoneechee Speedway, the 32nd and final Grand National race, a 150-miler, was held on the muggy Indian summer Sunday of September 15, 1968. It was the day after Denny McLain won his 30th for the Tigers and the day before Nixon appeared on *Laugh-in*. Although nothing was said officially, rumor had it that this would be the final big race at Hillsborough. The popular line was that the new super speedway in Talladega, AL, would get the mid–September date. That was a cop-out! Although there were many Occoneechee races staged in September, several were also held in October over the years. In addition, with the wacky schedules that NASCAR came up with, it could have found plenty of other dates if the powers-that-were wanted a race there. All 32 races were held on Sunday, too. What was wrong with Saturday? Anybody believing Talladega took Hillsborough's race date is sadly mistaken. Truth is, it was time for Hillsborough and its ilk to go. Bye-bye dirt, hello asphalt, television, and eventually big dollars. The end was at hand and stock car racing's roots started taking it on the chin big time when Occoneechee was dropped after 1968.

The final lineup consisted of 24 led by pole-sitter Richard Petty with David Pearson's blue and gold Holman-Moody Ford 17 outside. It was a great front row for a historic final race. Third was veteran G.C. Spencer in Plymouth 49 flanked by Bobby Isaac in Harry Hyde's orange 71 K & K Insurance Special Charger. Fifth was Buddy Baker in Ray Fox

Turn Two with the top rim visible through the trees.

Dodge 3 and the master of the dirt, Curtis Turner in Friedkin Enterprises Plymouth 15 alongside in sixth. Except for Bobby Allison and James Hylton, the rest were mostly also-rans and back-markers. When the green sent the boys on that last journey, Petty led Pearson and the others for 74 laps. With some spine-tingling, door-to-door banging, Pearson led for 11 laps before they swapped it a couple of more times. In the meantime, Baker made only five laps before losing the drive shaft and on lap 116, Curtis Turner rolled into the dusty pits with a blown engine. Four laps later, Pearson parked it and after 11 more, Isaac hung it up. Even Spencer conked out and Petty coasted to a yawner of a seven-lap victory over Hylton and of 15 rounds over Soapy Castles. Fourth went to Sears, fifth Worth McMillion, sixth Allison, seventh Tyner, eighth Earl Brooks, ninth Elmo, and tenth Spencer. Then the big show loaded up, went over the hump at turn one, out onto Elizabeth Brady Road, and another gate closed on auto racing history.

There was great progress made over the years between the third Strictly Stock Car race ever held here in 1949 and the 1968 curtain dropper. Let us see ... the size of the field was bigger in ... 1949, 28 cars to 24! Well, the crowd was probably larger in ... 1949, 17,500 to 6,700! O.K., at least the money was bigger in ... 1949, $2,000 to $1,600! Whether it was NASCAR, the fans, or just the times, Occoneechee was dying on the vine and its demise inevitable. Too bad!

Curtis Morton Turner was 25 years old in 1949, running in the first three Strictly Stock Car races ever at Charlotte, Daytona, and Hillsborough with little or no success. The fourth race at Langhorne he won. Back then, the cars were stock and he *was* the Blond Blizzard. In 1950, Fireball got win number one, edging Turner on the banks of the Eno. Then Curtis won the pole for the first Southern 500, but in the second Hillsborough race of 1950, Turner was last. After a bad finish in 1951, he came back to win at Occoneechee in 1953. He finished fifth in his only Hillsborough appearance in '54 and second in '55. Of course, Curtis Turner won the Southern 500 in 1956 and did not go to Hillsborough that year, or '57 either, because he concentrated on the ragtops. Turner was at the peak of his skill and performance. In '56 he teamed in twin factory Fords with bosom buddy Joe Weatherly and won 22 of 42 races on the convertible circuit, but amazingly lost the title to Bob Welborn, who won only three. He won both at Hillsborough from the pole and at Weaverville as the *only* finisher! In 1957, he copped 11 to Welborn's six, but Bob was ragtop champ again and Turner was ... sixth. In 1958, he was fifth in the standings, winning the first Rebel 300 at Darlington, a convertible race, and four of five. In 1959, back in Grand Nationals, he won the pole and led every lap of the race at Hillsborough. In 1960, he finished way back on the Eno, but by then was involved in the building of the Charlotte Motor Speedway and organizing a driver's union. Everybody knows those stories. Bill France kicked Curtis Turner out of NASCAR for life or until Labor Day 1965, whichever came first, for trying to unionize the drivers. So Turner raced with USAC and ARCA and won some. He won the stock car division of the Pike's Peak Hill Climb in 1962 and was second in '61 and '63. Also in '63, he limbered up Smokey Yunick's new Fiberglas Special Offenhauser at Indianapolis and wiped it out before time trials. However, by mid–1965, stock car racing needed a shot in the arm so France let Turner back in if he promised never to be bad again. Ford thought him washed up, so he hopped in Petty's Plymouth in Spartanburg and crashed in time trials. He finally drove in the Southern 500 in a non-competitive Plymouth, *and then* Ford caved in and got him a backup Wood Brothers ride for the inaugural American 500 at Rockingham. The "washed up" 41-year-old started fourth and ran up front all the livelong day, beating Cale Yarborough for the win, Turner's first Grand National in over six years. He was so washed up that he won the Permatex 300 at Daytona the next February. The exploits

Collapsing like a house of cards, the speedway office is almost at ground level.

in rental cars and airplanes, the boozing, the women, the wild parties, pal Joey Weatherly, the wacky gags, have been told and retold. Why? Because they're true. In 1967, Turner was the first person to qualify at over 180 miles per hour, winning the pole for the Daytona 500 in Smokey's Chevelle, but had an incredibly violent crash practicing in Atlanta, racing infrequently after that. Yunick all but quit! Then in 1968, Turner landed the Friedkin Plymouth ride for Labor Day, finishing a very respectable sixth in the Southern 500. Curtis Turner had lackluster runs after that, including a 13th in the swan song of the great Occoneechee Speedway. Curtis Turner never announced his retirement, he just did not race after that. Occoneechee did not announce its retirement either, also not racing after that. So on September 15, 1968, two of the classic, all-time great careers in the history of stock car racing ended. On October 4, 1970, Curtis Turner may have been playing one last practical joke, or maybe he just fell asleep, became ill, or was stinking drunk. Nevertheless, on that day, as one of the last *Silent Speedways of the Carolinas* races was run in North Wilkesboro, Turner's Aero Commander 500 augured into the rich Pennsylvania landscape near Punxsutawney with golf pro Clarence King aboard. Curtis Turner was a rough, headstrong, handsome race driver of extraordinary skills, who made millions and squandered millions. How good was Curtis Turner? Nobody was better. How good was Occoneechee Speedway? No track was better.

So that is Hillsborough's Occoneechee Speedway. The great thing is that it is still there and a group named Classical American Homes Preservation Trust (CAHPT), who bought Ayr Mount, located across the Eno from the backstretch, provided the funds for Preservation North Carolina (PNC) to buy Occoneechee's 60 acres from the estates of William H.G. France, Sr., and Enoch Staley in 1997. PNC created a nature trail that winds through the grounds of this fading stock car giant, which is actually a good thing. But will it be trashed, littered with McDonald's cups, cigarette butts, and Styrofoam? No matter how careful the preservationists are, the haunting nature of its decaying majesty is in jeopardy, although a tract of cookie-cutter houses would be infinitely worse. Regardless, the huge, ghostly grandstand populated by pines and the hard concrete padded by satiny-green moss await the nightly throngs. When the hoot owls sing to the croaking toads and the silvery moonlight filters through the canopy, you can see those misty figures clinging to the wire fence. You can see Bob, Fonty, and Tim still winning. There is Sara Christian being blasted in turn four and Fireball still pushing as hard as he can, the points be damned. Smokey and Herb's big Hudsons jousting with Kiekhaefer and Baker's bigger Chryslers. Luckless Joe Eubanks finally winning his only big-time checkers over and over again. Curtis Turner leading every lap in that T-Bird as Papa Lee knocks folks out of the way in his Olds. Little Joe Weatherly capturing those Pontiac poles and coming home first, only now he gets to kiss Jayne Mansfield, who heads there often, never missing a race. Back in the golden days of stock car racing, it was the biggest dirt track they ran. Today ... *it still is!*

Track History by the Numbers

RACES: 32
YEARS OF RACES: 1949, 1950 (2), 1951 (2), 1953 (2), 1953, 1954, 1955 (2), 1956 (2), 1957, 1958 (2), 1959 (2), 1960 (2), 1961 (2), 1962, 1963 (2), 1964 (2), 1965 (2), 1966, 1967, 1968
WINNERS: Buck Baker (3), L. Petty (3), R. Petty (3), F. Flock (2), T. Flock (2), Hutcherson (2), Jarrett (2), Roberts (2), Thomas (2), Turner (2), Weatherly (2), Eubanks, B. Flock, Junior Johnson, Owens, Paschal, Pearson, White
MOST POLES: 4—R. Petty, Joe Weatherly
RACE RECORD: 90.663 mph—Ned Jarrett, 1965 Ford (3/14/65)
QUALIFYING RECORD: 99.784 mph—David Pearson, 1964 Dodge (4/12/64)
WINS BY MAKE: Oldsmobile (6), Plymouth (6), Ford (5), Chevrolet (4), Pontiac (4), Hudson (3), Chrysler (2), Dodge, T-Bird
MOST STARTS: 22—Buck Baker
MOST LAPS LED: 486—Richard Petty
MOST TOP FIVES: 13—Buck Baker
BEST AVERAGE START: 9th—Buck Baker, 9th—Lee Petty (20)
BEST AVERAGE FINISH: 7.1—Buck Baker, 6.3—Lee Petty (20)

8

Newberry Speedway, Newberry, South Carolina

Newberry Speedway held one Grand National race. *A one-shot wonder!* That overgrown grandstand held only 900 people the night the big boys came to town in 1957. Light poles still hold the shiny silver receptacles that once illuminated the red Carolina clay. A dilapidated concession stand and office decay atop the stands that sit silently as weeds and wild flowers pour through the cracks in the crumbling concrete. The protective wire fence that once held the hurtling stockers from the spectators is so choked with vines that one cannot see through it. The peeling yellow gate in that fence rests ajar where fans once streamed onto the track to the pits to meet their heroes. The skeletal remains of the scoring stand looms in the infield behind the pit wall with its rusty stairs, the blue tarp cover long gone save a few tatters. The pit wall remains in place although the pines have pushed some of

On October 12, 1957, the smallest Grand National crowd ever, 900 fans, sparsely populated this grandstand to see the great Fireball Roberts beat a fine field.

A crumbling aisle is choked with weeds and wildflowers.

Blue tatters hang from the once-busy infield scoring stand.

the sections askew. Completely overgrown with high weeds, the infield hums with all manner of creeping, buzzing creatures seen and unseen on searingly hot summer days. There are numerous undamaged light poles all around, indicating one of three things: the area really is secure from trespassers, the citizens of Newberry do not own shotguns and rifles, or the fine people who live here are terrible shots. This is the only one of the *Silent Speedways of the Carolinas* where the illumination system looked ready to light up with the throwing of a switch. Yet only history remains to shed light on that Saturday night and the big crowd that stayed away.

Nine hundred people. It is a lot of folks to invite to a wedding. It is a lot for a Christmas card list. It is a whole lot of people even to know. However, it is not a lot to attend a Grand National stock car race. Pretty sad, in fact! Nevertheless, that is how many souls showed up on Saturday, October 12, 1957, at the Newberry Speedway. There must have been some very good football games in the area that night because nobody came out to the track. With 23 cars on hand, there were probably about half as many people in the pits as in the stands. The infield must have *really* been empty. But the drivers that competed for the $900 first prize were first class. Of the top ten finishers in the 1957 points standings, the top nine were at Newberry for race 50 of 53. They were big stars, too. Spartanburg's Jack Smith put his Chevy 47 on the pole with Greenville's Johnny Allen outside in Spook Crawford's Plymouth. Bud Moore's recent Southern 500–winning Bel Air piloted by Speedy Thompson was in row two with Staley. The third row had Buck driving another route to the 1957 championship alongside Whitey Norman. Brownie King was inside Californian Bill Amick and his Holman-Moody Ford for the fourth row with Ken Rush and Fireball behind them. Scattered on back were Petty, Panch, and Pagan. It was an excellent field racing for a dollar a

Fans went down to meet their heroes through a yellow grandstand fence, still ajar.

Today the top row offers this view toward the First Turn.

spectator! Smith led early and then gave way to Thompson. Baker passed Speedy until Fireball took over for the final 117 to beat Buck by a lap. The track was in horrendous condition and broke up badly as huge holes developed. Oddly enough, there were no crashes, not many DNFs, and they got the job done in less than a minute under two hours. The other top finishers that night were Smith third, Panch fourth, Staley fifth, Thompson sixth, Allen seventh, Rush eighth, Norman ninth, and King tenth. Other notables were Bill Amick 14th, Greenvillle's L.D. Austin 15th, Pagan 16th, Jack Marsh in the first start of a three-race career 17th, and last-place Lee took 23rd.

Now only relics and fading memories remain of the night the top stock car drivers in the world stopped off in Newberry. *They risked their necks before the smallest crowd in Grand National history!* Now the stands are packed and the lights make the red clay glow as Fireball, Buck, Lee, Jack, Gwyn, Speedy, Eddie, and the others come back in the night to battle through the potholes of Newberry.

Track History by the Numbers

RACES:	1 (10/12/57)
YEARS OF RACES:	1957
WINNERS:	Fireball Roberts
MOST POLES:	1—Jack Smith
RACE RECORD:	50.398 mph—Fireball Roberts, 1957 Ford
QUALIFYING RECORD:	56.514 mph—Jack Smith, 1957 Chevrolet
WINS BY MAKE:	1—Ford
MOST STARTS:	1—Tied by 22 drivers

MOST LAPS LED: 118—Fireball Roberts
MOST TOP FIVES: 1—Roberts, Baker, Panch, J. Smith, Staley
BEST AVERAGE START: 1st—Jack Smith
BEST AVERAGE FINISH: 1st—Fireball Roberts

9
Salisbury Super Speedway, Salisbury, North Carolina

If you thought the term "superspeedway" came about with Talladega or Daytona in the '70s, then you are wrong! Charlotte-based promoter Bruton Smith used it to tout his .625-mile dirt track on U.S. 29 at Airport Road about three miles east of the beautiful city of Salisbury, NC. Now there are trees, small buildings, and a very bland manufacturing plant on the site, and even it is vacant—a shuttered factory decaying on a silent superspeedway. One cannot imagine what made the track so "super" that the big time never came back after one race, especially with Bruton Smith behind it all. It is a one-race wonder and there is not the faintest trace of it left. But in the early fall Sunday afternoon of October 5, 1958, thirty of "Some of The Nation's Best Drivers," as Bruton's newspaper ad promised, hauled into this new venue to contest for a whopping "$4,600," also noted in the ad. Smith listed 14 of Grand National's best, adding "and many others." Eight of those listed actually started that day and he *could* have mentioned a youngster with five races under his belt named Richard Petty. The King-to-be was not much of a draw yet and it cost three bucks to get in.

No trace is left of Salisbury Super Speedway at U.S. 29 and Airport Road.

Across U.S. 29 are tracks of another kind, where thousands of doomed U.S. soldiers traveled their final miles to the Confederate prison camp in Salisbury.

In the 68th start of a solid 71-race career, Atlanta's old 'shine-runner Gober Sosebee put his black Cherokee Garage 1957 Chevy 50 on the pole, the fourth of his nine-year career. His first was in Strictly Stock Car race number 2 at the Beach on July 10, 1949. Others in Bruton Smith's "Nation's Best Drivers" that day were brothers Speedy and Jimmy Thompson, Tiny Lund, Cotton Owens and teammate Joe Eubanks, fresh off his only career win a week earlier in Hillsborough, soon-to-be Rookie of the Year Shorty Rollins, Buck Baker, Herman Beam, and Tommy Irwin. The green fell on Sosebee and 29 others around 3:30 that afternoon and almost one hour and 43 minutes later, Lee Petty completed the scheduled 160 circuits first in a '57 Oldsmobile with Buck Baker the only man on the same lap. It clinched the 1958 Grand National Championship for Petty over Baker, the Randleman veteran's second of three, while ending Buck's string of titles at two. Third was Owens, fourth George Dunn, and fifth Tyner. Further back came Doug Cox sixth, pole-sitter Sosebee seventh, Eubanks eighth, Ken Rush ninth, Lund tenth, Irwin 13th, and 52-year-old Ted Chamberlain 19th in the 62nd of 63 career starts dating back to Strictly Stock event number 5 in Hamburg, NY. Shorty Rollins rolled to 21st and Richard Petty made fifty fish for swimming home in 22nd place, only 23 laps behind in his father's '57 Olds 2. He had used two other numbers so far, but had not hit on 43 yet. Herman Beam beat five other speedsters including Speedy for 25th.

Only a hundred yards away from Bruton's site on the south side of U.S. 29 is *another* type of track. This one is for trains and the route likely carried thousands of the doomed

Yankee souls heading to the old station in Salisbury and on to the Confederate prison nearby where *11,700* United States Army soldiers died. They rest in 18 trenches beneath the sod of the Salisbury National Cemetery. Surely, the air around Salisbury is swirling with restless spirits, the ghosts of fighting men all. So there is no doubt that Lee, Buck, Gober, Speedy, Joe, Tiny, and the others fading into the shadows of memory are in good company out at the corner of Airport and U.S. 29. This most unholy of towns is the site of the Salisbury Supernatural Speedway, where military personnel are always welcome.

Track History by the Numbers

RACES:	1 (10/5/58)
YEARS OF RACES:	1958
WINNERS:	Lee Petty
MOST POLES:	1—Gober Sosebee
RACE RECORD:	58.271 mph—Lee Petty, 1957 Olds
QUALIFYING RECORD:	72.162 mph—Gober Sosebee, 1957 Chevy
WINS BY MAKE:	1—Oldsmobile
MOST STARTS:	1—Tied by 30 drivers
MOST LAPS LED:	1 at least—Lee Petty
MOST TOP FIVES:	1—Lee Petty, Buck Baker, Owens, Dunn, Tyner
BEST AVERAGE START:	1st—Gober Sosebee
BEST AVERAGE FINISH:	1st—Lee Petty

10

Starlite Speedway, Monroe, North Carolina

There is no speedway in sight. The old fairground is an area of business parks and warehouses now. However, there are acres in the midst of it all in a low land where one of the *Silent Speedways of the Carolinas* stood. On the opposite side of the valley sits a gorgeous farmhouse with a barn and stable, a corral with horses, cows, and even a bull. Near the entrance to the mini-ranch, Starlite Speedway filled the grassy spaces now covered with soccer fields in front of the farm. It is the farmhouse of Nelda Jean Davis, whose granddaddy Jim Williams bought the land in 1922. Her dad Parks Williams added a drag strip in 1957, then built the speedway and there were races on it every Friday night. The public address announcer for a while was a fellow named Humpy Wheeler. Racing had long since ended when Ms. Davis sold some of the land and had the track, 8,000-seat grandstand and all, bulldozed in 1985. Nelda Jean Davis owned the racetrack where a unique race in Grand National history took place. In fact, it turned out to be an interesting rout.

Now soccer players run, pass, and kick where on that rainy spring night, May 13, 1966, the independents had their way. Because the Chrysler factory teams stayed away and Ford's double OHC engine had been banned by NASCAR months earlier, it was one of the most

Nothing remains of Starlite Speedway except the view of Davis Ranch, homestead of the family that built the track in their front yard in 1957.

Soccer fields punctuate the acres where the speedway was razed in 1985.

wide-open races ever run in Grand National history. Although Petty and Pearson could have entered their Mopars, they stayed home and there was not a factory-backed stock car closer than Charlotte. It was an all-independents' show with 125 miles, 250 laps, to get it done. Twenty-five speedsters qualified and it was not a bunch of bums, either. Inman's James Hylton was on his way to Rookie of the Year and took his first of four career poles in Bud Hartje's yellow, white, and red 1965 Dodge. Outside was thirteen-year veteran Elmo Langley in the fastest of the 13, count 'em, *thirteen* 1964 Ford Galaxies that made up over half the field. It should have been the called "The 1964 Ford 250." Elmo was about three weeks away from his first career win at Spartanburg in his orange 64. Inside row two in another orange 1964 Ford was Joan Petre's 73 with Buddy Baker, who was about a year and a half short of his first victory. To Buddy's right was Charles Triplett from North Wilkesboro in a '65 Dodge 40 in his first, and last, Grand National. Fifth was John Sears in his 1964 Ford and sixth timed J.D. McDuffie in a 1964 Ford he owned. The fourth row found a pair of new Chevrolets with Putney's 19, wrenched by Louis Clements, and Tyner in Truett Rodgers' 9. Behind them came Castles in Buck's big '65 Plymouth Fury 86 and Clyde Lynn in his '64 Ford. There were other crowd favorites further back, like previous series winners Wendell Scott in a '65 Ford 14th, Buck Baker 17th in a new Oldsmobile, Dieringer starting Reid Shaw's 1964 Ford 20th, Pistone's Shoney's '64 Ford 24th, and Lund 25th and last in a, you guessed it, 1964 Ford owned by Lyle Stelter.

Threatening skies hurried the start and when the green flapped, the lead swapped around early and often between Hylton, Langley, and Sears. Finally, Dieringer put 0 first and motored away to an *eight-lap* win over Lynn. Twelve back in third was Scott and fourth Castles in Buck's Fury that had finished second the year before with Buddy in the Firecracker 400 and second with Buck and Buddy in the Southern 500. Fifth was Henley Gray, Ernest Eury sixth in his second start, seventh Gene Black, Joel Davis eighth in a '65 Plymouth 77, Elmo ninth, and Derrington tenth. McDuffie had the only crash for 11th and Johnny Wynn was 13th in an ex–Bud Moore '64 Mercury 06 tuned by John McCarthy. Indian Trail, NC's Bunk Moore ended a 24-race career spanning 11 years with 14th, Buck broke for 16th, one-timer Charles Triplett got 17th, Pistone 18th, Sears 19th, Lund 20th, Hylton 22nd, Buddy Baker 24th, and the Wild Injun Roy Tyner 25th and last. The winner that Friday night, Darel Dieringer, was literally moonlighting from his day job as driver of Bud Moore's Mercury Comet 16. By the way, that Comet won the Southern 500 in September, and another at North Wilkesboro before that, with Dieringer up. Only about 2,500 attended that night at a track that seated 8,000, probably afraid of a rainout.

Ten years later, the track died, but not before the front-stretch incineration of James Sears, little brother of Big John Sears. The horror occurred on the night of August 3, 1973, in a sportsman race. In 1985, property owner Nelda Jean Davis had the grandstand razed, the speedway bulldozed, and a business park built on some of it. Later, music concerts were held on the grassy slopes of another part, Woodstock-style, with the likes of Tanya Tucker, Marie Osmond, Tracy Byrd, and Garth Brooks entertaining. Exactly where the track was, though, are soccer fields now. Darel comes back in the dark to haunt the site of his third career victory with his old pals Wendell, Elmo, J.D., Buck, Tiny, and Roy. Maybe the cows get a little spooked when the men return to race across the way. Are there ghost concerts, too? Maybe Marty Robbins puts on a show by starlight after the race. Starlite was the name of the place, you know, so imagine ex-racer Robbins hanging with his old pals. Ms. Davis may have a front yard filled with all kinds of spirits just racin' and singin' the night away.

Track History by the Numbers

RACES:	1 (5/13/66)
YEARS OF RACES:	1966
WINNERS:	Darel Dieringer
MOST POLES:	1—James Hylton
RACE RECORD:	60.140 mph—Darel Dieringer, 1964 Ford
QUALIFYING RECORD:	65.099 mph—James Hylton, 1965 Dodge
WINS BY MAKE:	1—Ford
MOST STARTS:	1—Tied by 25
MOST LAPS LED:	178—Darel Dieringer
MOST TOP FIVES:	1—Dieringer, Lynn, Scott, Castles, Gray
BEST AVERAGE START:	1st—James Hylton
BEST AVERAGE FINISH:	1st—Darel Dieringer

11
Harris Speedway, Concord, North Carolina

This *Silent Speedway of the Carolinas* had at least three different identities. According to Vicki Harris Proctor, her father Roy Harris owned, operated, and promoted the half-mile clay oval, beginning as Harris Speedway, from 1949 until 1964. It was a busy place, holding a dozen Grand Nationals between 1956 and 1964, with three in 1957. Finding it is tough. Speedway Place from the Poplar Tent Road side dead-ends in the general area of the track, but it is reachable more easily going north from Charlotte on I-85 to Route 73 South or Davidson Highway. Execute a right onto Hanover Drive and by following Channing Circle, you will actually circumnavigate the well-disguised remains. A turn is in a clearing of a beautiful neighborhood and was revealed only by shadows on the snow-patched landscape. The unmelted snow accented the topography because the low winter sun hit the banking's slope

Fence and large gateposts mark the track's entrance at the end of Speedway Place.

at an angle, keeping it in the shade longer and outlining the turn clearly. Near the end of the banking are pine trees spoiling the turn's sweep as the slope levels off smoothly. Even without the snowy covering, the land mass is shaped exactly as a grass-covered banked turn.

A sports article in the *Concord Tribune* of May 5, 1956, bills it as "the first late model, strictly stock race ever held in Cabarrus County." So much for accuracy in reporting, as the strictly stock races only ran in 1949. It also names the venue as "Concord Speedway (formerly Harris Speedway), off the Poplar Tent Rd." A large advertisement elsewhere trumpets "BIGGEST RACE EVER FOR CONCORD!," "GRAND NATIONAL CHAMPIONSHIP," "(NEW CARS ONLY)," "OVER $30,000 IN IMPROVEMENTS," "All Nationally Famous drivers," and "New Concrete Grandstand & All Other New Facilities Making The New Concord Speedway The Finest in the Nation." The center of the spread has an aerial photograph of the track with "NEW CONCORD SPEEDWAY" pasted in the center. The ad includes an accurate list of 26 drivers and cars all competing for the reasonable admission price of $3.00, "Children under 12 admitted free with paid escort." The ad closes "A BRUTON SMITH Promotion." If all of that were not enough, the article points out "Beauteous Sue Evans, Cadillac Records singing star, and Ann Reeder, former Charlotte Carousel Queen, will ride in the pace car starting the race." Their glamour shots are included along with those of Dashing Dink Widenhouse, Handsome Herb Thomas, Tempting Tim Flock, and Becoming Buck Baker.

On Sunday afternoon, May 6, 1956, an outstanding field of 30 cars showed up with a large factory representation. Kiekhaefer had his three white Chryslers wheeled by Baker in 300, Thomas in 300B, and Thompson in 300C. Other entries and weird numbers were De Paolo's Fords with Carden and the hometown Concord Comet Dink Widenhouse in B-29. Brother Bill was in a Buick, while Tim Flock drove 285, Owens 295, and Lund drove Pontiacs. Mauri Rose's Chevy had Paschal up, and other Chevies carried Rex White in X, Johns in 7A and Staley. Mercurys were on hand with Billy Myers and Liguori in 271, Petty and Blair in Dodges, Panch's Ford, Allen in Spook Crawford's Plymouth 264, and a rookie named Fred Lorenzen in Chevrolet 150. There was an Olds in the field so about all makes were represented, *but the race was a bust*. Thompson took the lead on lap six and stayed there for the next 195. Baker was second and Thomas third to make it a Chrysler sweep with Flock fourth and White fifth. The main action was a rollover by Panch during time trials, but he got it repaired in time to wreck it again later. Johns crashed early with Paschal, who thrilled the crowd by circling once in reverse. The Kiekhaefer win was the sixth in a string reaching 16 straight. Speedy won the day before at Columbia in Mr. K's Dodge.

Renamed Concord Speedway and still promoted by Bruton Smith, the tour ran the half-mile for two of the first five races of 1957 and came back at the end of the year for more. The first of the Concord Trifecta was Sunday afternoon, December 2, 1956, after a one-week postponement due to cold weather. Kiekhaefer's Chryslers and Dodges were gone with no more 16-race winning streaks ... ever! On this frigid day, Panch made up for his one-man crash fest of last May by leading all but the first two laps in a De Paolo Ford, edging Goldsmith's Yunick Chevy for the trophy. Bill Amick was third, Lund fourth, and Petty fifth. There were many other great drivers there such as Paschal, Turner, Weatherly, Eubanks, Myers, Carden, Smith, and Moody. Ralph Earnhardt subbed for Fireball again as at Hickory earlier, and Johnny Allen warmed up for his three famous spectacular crashes of the early '60s by whacking a pole with Spook's Plymouth, depositing it in the grandstand. Nobody was hurt, but a young man ran from the scene singing Sam Cooke's number-one hit of the day, "You Send Me."

Two months and a day later they returned, on Sunday, March 3, 1957, to a crowd of around 11,000. There were only 20 cars, but the factories were at war and the field was outstanding. Californian Bill Stroppe had Mercurys for Paschal and Billy Myers. Petty had Oldsmobiles for himself and Tiny. Hugh Babb brought Bud Moore–tuned, fuel-injected Black Widow Chevrolets for Smith, Thompson, and Baker. De Paolo had factory Fords for Roberts, Panch, Weatherly, and Turner. Add Allen's Plymouth, the Wood Brothers Ford for Glen, Cotton in Eubanks' Ford, and ex–Sportsman champion Jarrett's own Ford and that was an extremely talented grid. To put the factories in their place, Mel Larson wandered in from Vegas and stole the pole in a year-old Ford. It was tight early, but after Wood went bottoms-up on lap 78, Jack Smith dominated and took the checkers over Baker, Thompson, Roberts, and Larson. The 1–2–3 sweep for the Black Widows was reminiscent of the Kiekhaefer sweep in the first Concord race in 1956. Oddly enough, Baker and Thompson were involved in that one, too.

On Sunday, October 13, 1957, the third visit took place the day after a bone-jarring, 100-mile torture test over the washboard at Newberry. The larger field of 26 played before a crowd a third the size attending the last 100-miler here. Billed as New Concord Speedway, it was the venue's third name in four races. The factories were gone, but the race was just as exciting as Roberts beat Petty by almost a lap. Petty slowed, taking time to knock Baker into a rollover to the extent that Buck needed relief from Jimmy Thompson. Buck Baker and Bud Moore had the last laugh, though, as they clinched the 1957 Grand National Championship with a ninth. Ken Rush was third, Panch fourth, Smith fifth, and Thompson in Moore's Southern 500–winning Chevy sixth.

The one appearance of 1958 was on Sunday afternoon, March 2nd, for 200 laps. It was one week after the final race on the sand in Daytona, which was definitely the end of an era in stock car racing. This race was the first of the period post-sand and pre-high banks for Daytona Beach and NASCAR. It was a doozy with a good field, an unbeknownst farewell, and a four-day finish. First, a field including Daytona runner-up Turner, Petty, Staley, Thompsons Speedy and Jimmy, Pagan, Smith, Owens, Baker, Paschal, and Allen. Turner led from the outside of the front row and pulled away every lap. Only after a late caution did Petty "unlap" himself uncontested by Turner. Speedy was third followed by Staley and Pagan. *But not so fast.* Petty protested and NASCAR's Chief Scorer Joe Epton poured over the cards until announcing the winner as Lee Petty on Thursday, March 6th. The other finishers stood as they were. Looking back, it is somewhat reminiscent of the 1948 Indianapolis 500, the '62 Southern 500, or Wendell Scott's win in '63. There have been scoring snafus since racing began and this one lasted four days.

Solidly calling the winners through all major NASCAR races from its inception in 1947 until 1985 was Joe Epton from Cherokee Springs in Spartanburg County, SC. Epton moved to Daytona to help construct the new speedway in 1958 and remained in the employment of Bill France, Sr., until 1988. Joe Epton was the Father of Scoring for NASCAR, even punching the clocks on Buddy Baker's historic 200.447 mile per hour dash at Talladega on March 24, 1970. Scoring debacles and innovations notwithstanding, Joe Epton was steadfast and rock-solid until drawing his final breath on August 29, 2005, in Green Cove Spring, FL, at the age of 85. That day, the *Silent Speedways of the Carolinas* got a new Chief Scorer ... for eternity.

The farewell to Grand National racing that day was by Billy Myers, who lost his brother Bobby the previous Labor Day at Darlington. Billy had a lackluster day in his *Silent Speedways of the Carolinas* finale, finishing 25th. He won a convertible race two weeks later at North Wilkesboro, raced at Richmond in a ragtop when Staley died, and finished third in an open-air Merc at Bowman-Gray on Easter Monday, April 7th. On Saturday night, April 12th, back

The sweep of the banking is unmistakable with a row of pines growing along the rim.

at Bowman-Gray, he was leading a modified race with five laps to go when he suffered a fatal heart attack. The powerful Myers Brothers were gone in seven months. Both top-notch drivers still ply their trade in the netherworld starting grids of today.

Race five of 1959 was held on Sunday, March 8th, the same day Harpo, Chico, and Groucho last appeared together on live television. A huge crowd witnessed Curtis Turner make no mistake about it this time. He took the lead from Tiger Tom's T-Bird and never looked back for his 16th career win. Interestingly, Turner picked up his eighth win in the 39th Grand National race ever on June 24, 1951. It only took eight years and 346 races to amass the next eight. Second was Owens, Petty third, Johnson fourth, and Thompson fifth. It was Turner's intention to "Stagger Lee" this time, as Lloyd Price's top tune suggested.

The curtain fell on the season, Sunday, October 25, 1959, a beautiful autumn afternoon. Last races usually mean big fields and that was the case this time, as 34 teams packed in one more before the 1960 season started in two weeks. The Spartanburg team of Bud Moore's '59 Chevy and Jack Smith came from 18th on the grid to win by a lap over newly-crowned, three-time champ Lee Petty. Bakers Buck and Buddy, also racing '59 Chevies out of Spartanburg, were third and fourth, the younger's best finish up to that time. Glen Wood was fifth.

The Grand Nationals stayed away for three years until another trifecta in 1962. The opener took place on Monday, November 11, 1961, a cold night that saw empty seats by the hundreds. Those that braved the weather saw a sweep of major proportions. With a good field of 26, Spartanburg cars took the front row to start and the first four finishing spots, all but Virginian Joe Weatherly from the 'Burg. Smith booted leader Weatherly's Dirt Dauber 8 in turn one after they took the white flag and zipped home the winner. It was Jack's second win in a row here going back to the closer of 1959. Cotton ran third, Rex fourth and Ned fifth. Smith and Weatherly squared off afterwards and a lot of jawing took place, but no punches were thrown. There were vows on both sides that it was not over yet.

The 1962 Daytona 500 was an extraordinary display of the Pontiac power of Smokey Yunick and the domination of the great Fireball Roberts. Roberts proceeded to be fastest with a track record of over 158 miles per hour in the first qualifier, which he won easily. Then Fireball romped home leading 144 laps of the big race from the pole, completing a dramatic sweep of the Speedweeks. A week later, a damp, dreary Sunday, February 25, 1962, found a Fireball-less field of chasers from Daytona assembled on the cold clay of Concord. Only two drivers came close to Roberts seven days earlier. Joe Weatherly won the second Daytona qualifier, finished third a lap back in the race, and had the Concord pole. Richard Petty masterfully drafted Roberts all day finishing second as the only man on the lead lap in the 500, led the second most with 32 circuits, and lined up in Concord with Weatherly. Other top ten finishers from Daytona gridded on the dirt were Jack Smith, Fred Lorenzen, Rex White, and Ned Jarrett. Buck Baker was not on hand as he tore out a large section of the flimsy single strand of guardrailing at Daytona sustaining the most serious injury of his career, some broken ribs. Son Buddy was in the field in Dad's Chrysler.

The 8,000 fans that braved the cold saw Jarrett fall out first after only 17 laps for 20th and last place. Early excitement found a big crash eliminating Stick Elliott for 17th and Lorenzen for 16th. White was left with 15th. After Cotton Owens' swift number 6 blew on lap 69 for 13th, only nine more circuits were run before the weather gave Weatherly the win. After just 78 laps, 39 miles, Joe was first trailed by Petty, again the only one on the lead lap. One behind came Ralph Earnhardt in Robert Smith's 1961 Pontiac 75 in third, Jack Smith fourth, and Buddy Baker brought the Chrysler 87 in a solid fifth. Other wet notables were Paschal sixth, G.C. seventh, Wendell eighth, Irwin ninth, Tom Cox tenth, and fittingly in the muck and mire, Crawfish 11th and The Turtle 12th. Joe appropriately piloted Bud's 1961 Pontiac Dirt Dauber taking the 500 clams for winning the race at less than half the scheduled distance.

Sunday afternoon, May 6, 1962, the teams drug themselves into Concord for a 100-mile duel. Drug themselves because they ran Friday night in Richmond, Saturday night in Hickory, and now Sunday afternoon down the road in Concord. *Three consecutive nights!* How could a schedule so brutal come about to begin with? The toughest of the tough ran all three: Weatherly, White, Smith, Jarrett, Petty, Paschal, Allen, Scott, and pair of real animals, Crawfish and Turtle. There was a slight break, though, as time trials were cancelled due to poor track conditions. *Oh great!* The track's not good enough for one at a time, so just put all 20 of them out there at once. Twenty mostly tired cars guided by worn-out drivers took the green on a track in horrendous shape. Ned had enough and parked after a single circuit. Rex also went only one lap because of a car fire. Paschal, Allen, and Crider also withdrew. Interestingly, the Wood Brothers came with Panch, but fell out, as did Earnhardt and Welborn. Moore's Dirt Dauber ran a limited dirt schedule with Joe Weatherly at the wheel. When it got a little beat up, they just straightened out the dents and ran it again. It was a great number 8 and this time it got a little temperamental for the last quarter of the race. The accelerator jammed and Little Joe would rocket down the straights. When he got to the turns, he cut the car off with the ignition key and clicked it back on just in time to gun it down the stretch. *A true man at work!* It was good enough to fend off Cotton, who came in second, followed by Wendell Scott's outstanding showing in third, Smith fourth, and Maurice Petty fifth. It was a fitting end for three days on the road.

One week after the 1963 season ended in Riverside, 1964 kicked off at the newly renamed Concord *International* Speedway. Maybe searching for redemption from the dusty, pot-holed race two years earlier, the "International" was added. The advertisement in the *Concord Tribune* stated that the race was "AN INTERNATIONAL SPEEDWAY PROMOTION." There was no sign of other countries on the grid although a good field of 26 showed. The date was Sunday, November 10, 1963, and the race was the Textile 250. There was an extra 50 laps added and a whopping $1,350 to win. Jack Smith made his last *Silent Speedways of the Carolinas* start here, but ran the next three races. Jack ran Augusta's one-shot, three-mile road course; Jacksonville, FL, where Wendell Scott won his only race; and Savannah, where he was second. His old rival Joe Weatherly was killed at Riverside in the next race, but Jack was not there and never was anywhere again. And speaking of Weatherly, this was the last *Silent Speedways of the Carolinas* appearance for the great Clown Prince of Racing and two-time champion. He got his due with his last win in the Hillsborough chapter.

Jarrett won this first test in Grand National's most horrific year and should have given the money to Lund. Tiny, running hopelessly behind, blocked leader Weatherly's charge towards the checkers in the waning laps as Ned narrowed the gap. When Ned passed Joe, Weatherly spun Lund and took off after the new leader. Tiny was not through yet and went back after the newly crowned champ. Tiny rammed the Pontiac 8 again in turn four and when they sped past the pits, Bud hurled a rock in what appeared to be a perfect strike, nailing the Big Fisherman's Ford right between the 3 and the 2. If complimented about the pitch, Bud would have pointed out that he was aiming at Tiny's head. Naturally, there was a lot of pointing and shouting, but one thing is for sure: Bud Moore versus Tiny Lund would have made an interesting heavyweight fight. Joe did manage second, followed by Richard, David, and Maurice Petty. Tiny and Bud were destined to team up in Grand American Cougars and Mercury Montegos numbered 16 in 1968.

The final chapter in the big-time history of Concord International Speedway played out on the hot Thursday night of June 11, 1964. Since the last visit, we lost President Kennedy and Joe Weatherly, and Fireball Roberts lay charred in Charlotte Hospital fighting for his life. Twenty cars arrived, but only 19 started because Buck stuffed Ray Fox's Dodge in warm-ups. Richard took the pole and won the race. In between, Pearson and Cale Yarborough led, the latter giving the Turtlemobile a fine drive before it overheated. Petty beat Pearson, Jarrett, Scott, and Crider and that was it on the Concord clay.

Robert Edelstein's Curtis Turner biography *Full Throttle* details a scene that unfolded at this storied oval. It was 13 months after the last NASCAR Grand National event there.

GARA, the Grand American Racing Association, scheduled the fledgling circuit's opener at Concord with main draw Curtis Turner standing by. It was a stormy Saturday, July 31, 1965, and Curtis sat in the soggy infield of the cancelled event. He was preparing to split when the Lincoln's phone rang. It was Darlington's Bob Colvin calling from Atlanta, where he and others had just browbeat big Bill France into reinstating Turner. NASCAR cemented Curtis' return in the infield of Concord Speedway.

Beautiful houses now sit at the end of the dirt road the maps list as Speedway Drive. Nothing is left except some gate posts to remind Vicki Harris Proctor where her daddy and Bill France made a contract in 1949, just days before NASCAR was founded at the Streamline Hotel. But wonder if the residents of those beautiful houses ever have restless nights as the underworld speed demons of another dimension chase each other through their yards and gardens and garages and breakfast nooks. Imagine Buck Baker and Billy Myers there, Curtis and Lee still feuding, and Joe and Tiny pounding away at each other. Do not be surprised if those homeowners peek from behind their bedroom curtains on moonlit

11. Harris Speedway

Snow accents the slope of the banking where the sun's angle kept it from melting.

nights with hounds baying and owls screeching to see three translucent white Chryslers out front, speeding towards eternity.

Track History by the Numbers

RACES:	12
YEARS OF RACES:	1956 (2—1 was 1st of '57), 1957 (2), 1958, 1959 (2), 1961 (1st of '62), 1962 (2), 1963 (1st of 64), 1964
WINNERS:	J. Smith (3), Weatherly (2), Jarrett, Panch, L. Petty, R. Petty, Roberts, Thompson, Turner
MOST POLES:	2—S. Thompson, Weatherly
RACE RECORD:	66.352 mph—Richard Petty, 1964 Plymouth (6/11/64)
QUALIFYING RECORD:	69.257 mph—David Pearson, 1963 Dodge (11/10/63)
WINS BY MAKE:	Ford (3), Pontiac (3), Chevrolet (2), Chrysler, Oldsmobile, T-Bird, Plymouth
MOST STARTS:	9—Cotton Owens, Jack Smith
MOST LAPS LED:	384—Curtis Turner
MOST TOP FIVES:	6—Jack Smith
BEST AVERAGE START:	5.3—Cotton Owens
BEST AVERAGE FINISH:	7th—Jack Smith

12

Spindle Center Fairgrounds Speedway, Gastonia, North Carolina

The ad reads, "See the daredevil touring pros in a long-distance grind—A test of nerve, skill, and steel for $4,200 in prize money." How could a body stay away with a come-on like that? However, they must have on Friday night, September 12, 1958, because the daredevil touring pros never returned. On the other hand, maybe they do ... as usual on the *Silent Speedways of the Carolinas*.

Off U.S. 29 in Lowell, NC, at Fair and Ledwell Streets, a sign in a field announces the future site of the Gaston Christian School. Past the sign are piles of uprooted, guardrail-quality posts and gate poles. In the high weeds and briars, and with towering evergreens galore lined about, the hidden Spindle Center Fairgrounds Speedway lies dormant. The rusty-brown beams of the old grandstand loom in plain view high behind those trees where they have been corroding away for nearly 50 years. The metal-framed stands that once held thousands of screaming fans has most of its boards rotted away and a capacity crowd of oaks

Summertime line of tall, leafy trees and evergreens at Spindle Center Fairgrounds.

12. Spindle Center Fairgrounds Speedway

Wintertime line of same tall, bare trees and evergreens now revealing the metal framework of the Spindle Center Fairgrounds Speedway grandstand.

and pines straining skyward in their places. Oaks and evergreens thrive where the greats raced in '58. The lights that shone brightly through the red dust that Indian-summer night rest bullet-riddled and blind in a bed of weeds. In front of those stands, a set of steps lead down to the start/finish line across from the pits. There the undercarriage of a large modular home that was probably the scoring stand, concession stand, track office, rest rooms, or maybe all four, decays. The homestretch is a one-groover now as evidenced by ATV and deer tracks left in the mud. The slope of the turn one banking is obvious even though covered by brush. A racer going over the rim of turn two with its 40-foot drop-off would most certainly have landed some serious sheet time. The backstretch was straight in '58, but now sports a serious dogleg left. Down in turns three and four, the track gets even more interesting as a relic of the past reappears with the dilapidated board fence. The high wooden fairgrounds dirt track–type planks are all but gone and will soon disappear completely as the ravages of time and vandals have their way. The nearly boardless barrier has fueled countless and frequent bonfires indicated by mounds of cinders nearby. The crossover gate to the infield where Baker and Petty, et al., entered nearly half a century ago is still agape as if to let their Netherworld comrades in to line up for battle beneath the stars. The remaining lights still in place show the way for no mortals as the trees and vines slowly choke them to death. Through the fourth turn and into the home stretch lies the Spindle Center Fairgrounds Speedway racing with time ... and this old track is losing very badly. However, on September 12, 1958, it was the place to be when those "daredevil touring pros" were in town to thrill and excite.

It was the *fourth* event after the especially car-killing Southern 500 only *eleven* days earlier. Although two of those four races were on the same day (one in California), most of

Facing the grandstand with its capacity crowd of saplings, brush, and vines.

the touring pros were tired. There was a 100-mile event two days after the 500 in Birmingham and most of big names made that show. However, they could not get up for Spindle Center's 200 laps on a third-mile of clay. Of the 19 that did compete, some contenders were on the grid, like Buck Baker starting second and Speedy Thompson 12th, both in Bud Moore '57 Chevies. Point leader Petty had a '57 Olds seventh, but son Richard declined to make what would have been his sixth career start. Soon-to-be Grand National Rookie of the Year Shorty Rollins from Corpus Christi, TX, lined up fourth in a new black Ford 98 while Julian Petty also brought a pair of powerful '57 Chevies for Welborn starting fifth and polesitter Lund. Spook Crawford's two-car team, led this night by Tyner's Dodge, gridded third. A dozen others were on their marks and set to go that muggy evening. It was not just a once-in-a-lifetime chance to see big-time stock car racing in Gastonia, *it was the only time!* If the race started at 8:30 P.M. as the ads declared, then Tiny was parking the pole-sitter at 8:31. The 250-pound Harlan, IA, giant took only a lap to snap the Bel Air's A-frame for that infamous trip from first to last. However, even more downright amazing is the story of Vernon West in Spook Crawford's other entry, a new Plymouth 66. Vern put his foot to the mat and clocked that Fury outside row eight for 16th in the first start of a promising career. The green waved and when they came back around to complete lap one, the hemi in Vern's mount died and that promising career was in the books. Vernon West got $50 for a third of a mile of racing and never strapped himself into a Grand National stocker again. Was it shortest, most insignificant career in big-time racing history? *Try to find one shorter!*

Speaking of short, you would think an event of this magnitude in 1958 Gastonia would have been awarded more than a dozen short lines in the *Gastonia Gazette*, but that is all it got. They squeezed it in betwixt much more in-depth coverage of the Mt. Holly Hawks' big win over the Stanley Blue Devils, the Belmont Raiders' squeaker over the Mecklenburg

12. Spindle Center Fairgrounds Speedway

Top: A dilapidated fence and skewed gate are a magnificent example of a silent speedway. *Right:* Two different types of light fixtures once lit the way for fans and heroes alike.

Rebels, and the Chicago Bears' exhibition victory over the Cleveland Browns. High school football definitely ruled Gaston County that Friday night as reflected in the Saturday morning sports section. It did report that Spartanburg ace Buck Baker's victory helped him continue to chop away at runner-up Lee Petty's point lead, with Welborn third on the lead lap, Whitey Norman fourth, and Speedy fifth. Other finishers were Harb sixth, Keck seventh, rookie Rollins eighth, Harvey Hege ninth, and High Point's Bob Walden tenth in his fifth of six straight top tens. The whole affair took 83 and a half minutes at a sizzling 47.856 miles per hour on the Spindle Center clay as Buck captured his third win of the 1958 campaign.

The daredevil touring pros never came back in the flesh after that hot night in '58. However, if you look at the place 50 years

For one night only, on September 12, 1958, nineteen Grand National stars lined up on this homestretch for 200 laps.

later, it does not take long before you can imagine the light poles back up and straining to illuminate through the red dust, the excited spectators in the festive stands, and 19 shiny stock cars at the ready. On second thought, specters and those shiny cars of yesterday do not need lights. The moon and stars work just fine on the *Silent Speedways of the Carolinas*.

Track History by the Numbers

RACES:	1 (9/12/58)
YEARS OF RACES:	1958
WINNERS:	Buck Baker
MOST POLES:	1—Tiny Lund, 1957 Chevrolet
RACE RECORD:	47.856 mph—Buck Baker, 1957 Chevrolet
QUALIFYING RECORD:	51.650—Tiny Lund, 1957 Chevrolet
WINS BY MAKE:	1—Chevrolet
MOST STARTS:	1—Tied by 19
MOST LAPS LED:	1 at least—Buck Baker
MOST TOP FIVES:	1—Buck Baker, L. Petty, Welborn, Norman, S. Thompson
BEST AVERAGE START:	1st—Tiny Lund
BEST AVERAGE FINISH:	1st—Buck Baker

13
North Carolina State Fairgrounds Speedway, Raleigh, North Carolina

Within sight of the football home of the North Carolina State Wolfpack, Carter-Finley Stadium, is the North Carolina State Fairgrounds. Blue Ridge Road, Trinity Road, Youth Center Drive, and Chapel Hill Road in Raleigh bound it. Just motor right up, park behind the main grandstand, and walk on in. A bulldozer may be hard at work creating a mountain in the infield for a motocross or off-road race of some sort, but the speedway is mostly intact. That dude on the dozer could have the track race ready in a day or so. The grandstand looks out at motocross, tractor pulls, and concerts, and is clean and ready for use. The first turn finds the original track surface buried beneath tons of dirt used for other forms of racing. The whole backstretch from the exit of turn two to the entrance of turn

The last dirt track looks ready to race again from in front of the main grandstand.

three is practically ready for stockers. The sweep of the turns is still very impressive and is actually banked a lot more than it appears. It is easy to imagine Petty chasing Pearson, cars cocked sideways, a plume of beige dirt and dust spraying from the tires as they fight the track for grip. The surface is not the red clay, but a tan, gritty, pebbly texture that a thousand rains could have left behind from the original smooth cover. Then out of four and down the main straightaway to the finish line that comes alive in the nightly Netherworld shows. Shows like those 50 years ago when drivers opened the doors, strapped themselves in, and most Grand National races were on Carolina dirt.

It began on Saturday, May 28, 1955, a cloudy day in the capital of the Old North State, with spring showers predicted. A big crowd was on hand and a fine field of 27 set to go in a 200-lap grind around the neatly groomed half-mile oval. Tim Flock had Kiekhaefer's Mercury Outboards Chrysler on the pole with Welborn's Chevy outside. Junior's Olds and Speedy's Chevy made up row two. Row three saw Buck's Olds and Fonty in Mr. K's other white Chrysler. Through the field were Paschal, Petty, Dink Widenhouse, Rathmann, Staley, Blair, and subbing for his injured brother Herb was Donald Thomas in Smokey Yunick's Hudson. Tim jumped out front early, but by lap ten, Junior Johnson roared past and was gone. Nothing could stop him ... except the weather. When the skies opened up on lap 172, the Ronda Roadrunner had a lap lead over Fonty Flock. Baker, Petty, and Staley rounded out the top five. The fans would have to wait to see a full 100 miles. A long wait. *Fourteen years!*

There were seven Grand National races at deadly Raleigh Speedway across town before they ran on the Capital City dirt again. Fourteen years is a long time between races and not a single driver from that first race was still in the big time for the return engagement on Thursday night, June 26, 1969, race 27 of 54. Relatively speaking, the North State 200 did not have the star power of the 1955 model. In fact, there were three or maybe four top-shelf chauffeurs in the field of 24. Bobby Isaac had the orange 71 Harry Hyde–wrenched K & K Insurance Dodge on the pole with Pearson's blue and gold Holman-Moody Ford 17 outside. Soapy slipped his Dodge in third on the grid with Petty outside. That other maybe, kinda-sorta, top-notch guy, James Hylton, was fifth. Hylton was coming off 1965 Rookie of the Year honors, second in the final standings in 1966, another runner-up in '67, and a slip to seventh in '68. This race was the halfway point of the '69 season and Hylton was right in the hunt for the championship, in which he eventually finished a close third. Did that make James Harvey Hylton of Inman, SC, taking on the big bad Ford and Chrysler factories, top-drawer in '69? You bet it did! In fact, he started winning races a year later. The balance of the field held some old hands and good guys with only Scott and Langley with previous wins on their resumes. The race itself had some wacky goings-on as Pearson led early and held a comfy lead over Petty late. In his haste, Petty uncharacteristically got sloppy and ditched 43 outside turn one. That is all David needed and he was home free by three laps over his long-time rival. Hylton was third 11 laps behind, followed by Sears, Langley, and Scott. The old fairgrounds dirt would have one more chance to be special.

Instead of hats and horns and some sort of fanfare worthy of a truly landmark event, NASCAR let the era of the dirt track slip away for good on Wednesday night, September 30, 1970. About 6,000 race fans witnessed that last battle on the dirt and what a shame it was. It seems that instead of a Sunday afternoon with Bill France hosting bands and guests and flags and media hype and ABC's *Wide World of Sports*, the powers-that-were chose to let the truly greatest era of stock car racing die unnoticed. It is hard to believe that everybody and his brother did not try to run that last scheduled dirt race. It is a *real* shame Curtis Turner, probably the greatest dirt track driver in Grand National history, did not suit up

13. North Carolina State Fairgrounds Speedway

Turn Four is banked slightly more than it appears, with a nice view of the stands and the famed Dorton Arena behind it.

for the first time in two years and 15 days. His last race had not been that long ago when appropriately he drove in the finale at Hillsborough in 1968. Curtis never really retired, he just stopped racing. The sad part of it is that "The Babe Ruth of Stock Car Racing" had less than four days to live that Wednesday night. Just think of it. He drove in the first Strictly Stock Car race, June 19, 1949, on the dirt in Charlotte. The Pettys, Holman-Moody, the Wood Brothers, Cotton Owens, or some team could have given him a ride that autumn night in Raleigh. What a perfect pair of bookends that would have been for his career and that of dirt. He could have announced his retirement with the last dirt race! There could have been a big celebration on Sunday in Raleigh. "The End of Two Eras," the ads could have trumpeted. Instead, Raleigh was run in obscurity on a Wednesday night, and while his buddies raced at North Wilkesboro on Sunday, Curtis Turner plowed up the Pennsylvania countryside with the nose of his Aero Commander. Even unbilled, it was truly the end of two eras. NASCAR is awful in honoring its traditions, often chloroforming them altogether. Obviously, 55 Southern 500s were enough.

The Home State 200 itself was an anticlimax to 21 years of great dirt track history. Big John Sears took the pole and led early. Then Benny Parsons paced the pack over the next 89 laps until Petty got out front and it was all over. Not even in a Petty Plymouth, but a borrowed one, Richard won easily over Soapy Castles by two laps, with Isaac third, Hylton fourth, and Cecil Gordon fifth. Notables in that field were Bobby Allison sixth, Marcis seventh, Langley 18th, and Scott 20th. Then they loaded up the trucks and trailers and literally left NASCAR's heritage in the dust.

The track is still in pretty good shape. It is in *great* shape for the annual state fair tractor pulls, demo derbies, and the Southern Home Show. However, when the midway rides

The back half of the speedway is seen in the photograph taken from the Second Turn.

close at midnight and the families go home, check over at the last dirt track. There you will find it to be a ride that never closes. And just maybe old Curtis shows up after all.

Track History by the Numbers

RACES:	3
YEARS OF RACES:	1955, 1969, 1970
WINNERS:	Junior Johnson, David Pearson, Richard Petty
MOST POLES:	1—Tim Flock, Bobby Isaac, John Sears
RACE RECORD:	68.376 mph—Richard Petty, 1969 Plymouth (9/30/70)
QUALIFYING RECORD:	72.942 mph—Bobby Isaac, 1969 Dodge (6/26/69)
WINS BY MAKE:	Oldsmobile, Ford, Plymouth
MOST STARTS:	2—Tied by 14 drivers
MOST LAPS LED:	182—David Pearson
MOST TOP FIVES:	2—James Hylton, Richard Petty
BEST AVERAGE START:	2nd—Bobby Isaac
BEST AVERAGE FINISH:	1.5—Richard Petty

14

Raleigh Speedway, Raleigh, North Carolina

There is not a trace left to find of Raleigh Speedway, once located two miles north of Raleigh off Race Track Road, according to 50-year-old maps. Raleigh Speedway lay north of the I-440, east of Old Wake Forest Road, and west of the railroad tracks alongside Atlantic Avenue. Race Track Road is gone and there are a few new roads in that area now known as North Raleigh Industrial Park. Many railroad tracks were added and abandoned since the speedway disappeared leaving mostly wooded areas behind and not many clues. Any trace is covered by half a century of pine needles. A comparison of those old maps and ones of today include things that appear on both, especially Pinecrest Drive, Apache Drive, and the main rail line. The current intersection of Wolfpack Lane and Tarheel Drive would be exactly at the head of the backstretch, an area in the densest darkness of racing history. In that location, the land to the east is a downhill slope. Considering the present topography and the fact that developers could have moved tremendous amounts of dirt and even rerouted the train tracks, the Wolfpack/Tarheel spot is the focal point of the old layout. Moreover, it is the largest level area out there. One can imagine where the rest of the big, one-mile, high-banked paperclip was situated from that spot. This venue drips with auto racing history, from the most hilarious to the most horrendous events of the *Silent Speedways of the Carolinas*, and they each happened 112 days apart in 1953.

This place was wild! For seven events, this was regarded as the *other* super speedway on the tour besides Darlington. It was, at a paved mile, the longest

Nothing remains of Raleigh Speedway, but Tarheel Drive and Wolfpack Lane should be at the head backstretch where unimaginable horror claimed two young men.

of the *Silent Speedways of the Carolinas*. It was fast and it killed. If *any* plot of land *anywhere* once raced upon is visited after hours, this one is. The inaugural event was a challenge to the AAA and the Indianapolis 500. Of course, it did not have the worldwide acclaim of its northern cousin, but 49 teams ran and it was the fourth super speedway event in NASCAR history. The men that opened the doors to drive were all there on Sunday, May 30, 1953. Brutal heat swept everything east of the Mississippi and veteran Carl Scarborough died from it at Indianapolis while chasing Bill Vukovich, who drove oblivious to the temperature, winning his first 500. In the the Old North State, it was searingly hot that Saturday, too. Asphalt was rare on the tour back then and a mile of it for 300 revolutions was a test only surpassed by the 364 they suffered on Labor Day in Darlington. It was broiling hot! Slick Smith sat on the pole of 16 rows of three in Frank Christian's Olds 4 with Bud Moore's Hudson 82 of Joe Eubanks in the middle and Bill Blair's Olds 2 outside. Through the line-up were all the greats: the Fabulous Flocks, the Thomas Brothers, Petty, Baker, Roberts, Lewellen, Speedy, Paschal, Turner, Welborn, McGriff, Wood, Owens, soon-to-die Frank Arford, and big car pilots Liguori, Winfree, and Rathmann. Makes represented were Hudson, Oldsmobile, Dodge, Plymouth, Nash, Ford, Lincoln, Studebaker, and Mercury. Where were Chevy and Pontiac? As it turned out, it did not matter where, or *if*, you qualified, for this four-and-a-quarter-hour torture test. Lead changes were plentiful, scoring went afoul as was common in those days, and the Flocks stole the show. First there was the Ted Chester Hudson 91 of Brother Tim, defending Grand National Champion. Tim was going fine until his riding mechanic, er, *monkey*, pulled open the right front inspection door used to check tire wear and took a stone right between his beady little peepers. *He went bananas!* Imagine storming down the backstretch at over 100 miles per hour with a berserk simian in a matching driver's suit flailing around your cockpit and Herb Thomas banging away at your back bumper. The pit stop to expel Jocko Flocko cost Tim 600 coconuts, the difference between second and third places. Jocko Flocko rode shotgun in eight Grand National events, co-winning at Hickory on May 16th. Meanwhile, Brother Fonty took command with just over one hundred left and, without the luxury of qualifying or trousers, won the $3,500 and his second super speedway victory. From 43rd on the grid because he missed time trials, Fontello Truman Flock, sporting his now two-race winning "Bermooda" shorts, matched his Southern 500 title of 1952, this time beating Speedy Thompson by a lap. Jocko-less Tim was third, Herb Thomas fourth, and Dick Passwater fifth. It was a superb race and epitomizes the zany, freewheeling era that the *Silent Speedways of the Carolinas* represent. It gets no wackier than this!

The aforementioned Frank Arford was a wealthy Hoosier sportsman not unlike his Indianapolis pal Tony Hulman. He owned the car driven by the red-hot points-leading Dick Passwater, who in twelve 1953 starts, followed a sixth at Daytona with his first career win at Charlotte, six top fives, and nine top tens. Arford knew his place was not behind the wheel, but life was good and he ran four races, too, much like Rick Hendrick used to do. Arford completed this one 47 laps behind in 28th out of 49, got $50, and smiled all the way. *He had 22 days to live.* On the Pensacola half-mile June 14th, Frank was 12th with his star sixth. On June 21st, he let his zeal for the sport get the best of him when he tackled one of the deadliest speedways in the country ... the oily, nasty Langhorne Mile. The Reaper was waiting. When Frank met his end that miserable afternoon, he did it in front of thousands of spectators in the grandstand. Frank flew from his flipping Olds like the car's other parts and they carted him off the track before the horrified throng. And what of his driver Dick Passwater? He lost his owner, benefactor, teammate, and friend. Dick went from top of the heap to running with the big boys just one more time *in his life*; a splendid ninth place in the '53 Southern 500.

Saturday, May 29, 1954, the boys returned, but 15 less for this renewal. Another great field was present as Smokey's Hudson 92, wheeled by Herb Thomas, whipped Rathmann by two laps in this caution-free 250-miler. McGriff was third, Petty fourth, and Lewellen fifth. Others were Keller sixth, Baker ninth, Blair tenth, Fireball 20th, Turner who led awhile 22nd, Speedy 27th, Paschal 28th, Donald Thomas 29th, and Eubanks 33rd. This time they pulled it off in just under four hours.

The only year they ran twice at the long black mile was in 1955. The fields continued to dwindle when they returned on August 20, 1955, the day man first went 1,800 miles per hour in an airplane. Only 29 speedsters showed for this Friday night show. Kiekhaefer's white monsters were reigning supreme on the Grand National tour, but somebody forgot to tell Herb Thomas. He put Smokey's '55 Buick in the Winner's Circle, trailed by Tim Flock's Chrysler 300 second, Welborn's Chevy third, Lewellen's Olds fourth, and Staley's Chevy fifth. Further back were Baker sixth, Junior Johnson seventh, Fonty in 301 eighth, Massey tenth, Speedy 11th, Jim Reed 13th, Eubanks 17th, Carden 18th, Petty 22nd, Langley 23rd, and Paschal 26th. Nearly 10,000 watched the proceedings.

Friday, September 30, 1955, is a date that will live in infamy as the day James Dean's silver Porsche Spyder "Little Bastard" 130 crashed head-on into the black and white 1950 Ford of student Donald Turnipseed on Route 46 near Chalome, CA. Three thousand miles away under the lights in Raleigh, the gentlemen went 100 miles in as many laps, and Mr. K's Mopars copped first and third. Brother Fonty nabbed the hardware and Tim showed, sandwiching Herb Thomas' Southern 500–winning Chevy of 25 days earlier second. Donald Thomas was fourth and Bill Widenhouse fifth. Thirty-six cars got the green and the outstanding field raced less than 90 minutes to complete the assignment. Others such as Welborn, Baker, Petty, Staley, Thompson, Johnson, Lewellen, Eubanks, Paschal, Jarrett, and Turner failed to make a difference.

Baking heat met the entrants on the afternoon of Wednesday, July 4, 1956. A 36-car lineup was paced by pole-sitter Lee Petty, who led no laps and was out first. The lead swapped around between Mundy, Thompson, and Baker in Kiekhaefer Mopars, and Roberts in De Paolo's Ford. Unbelievably, it was Fireball winning for the first time since Hillsborough *in August of 1950!* Thompson was second two laps back and had the results protested on his behalf by the wily Mr. K, but NASCAR denied it. Mundy was third, Herb Thomas, on the verge of a split with Kiekhaefer, was fourth in his own Chevrolet, and Tim Flock, who left the old man himself a few months earlier, was fifth in Mauri Rose's Chevrolet. Others were Goldsmith sixth, Panch seventh, White ninth, Smith tenth, Baker 11th, Paschal 12th, Carden 14th, Allen 22nd, Staley 23rd, Eubanks 25th, Billy Myers 26th, Moody 28th, and Petty 36th. It was the first super speedway win for Roberts.

The penultimate race at the paperclip oval was again run on Independence Day, 1957, a scorching Thursday afternoon with a tremendous field of 53 lined up for 250 miles. The reason for the big field was that this was a sweepstakes race, meaning the NASCAR convertible drivers were also allowed to participate. The factories may have been gone, but everybody was there. The Garden State's Frankie Schneider sat on the pole in a Chevy with Welborn outside in another. Buck had Bud's 87 third and the highest-starting ragtop was the Welborn Chevy of Possum Jones. Scattered through the pack were Owens, Goldsmith, a topless Turner, Herb Thomas making his first start since the bone-smashing mugging at Shelby the previous October, Weatherly in a ragtop, Thompson in another Moore Chevy, Wood in an open-air Ford, Petty in an Olds, and Billy Myers and Paschal in Stroppe Mercurys. Staley, Roberts, Panch, Lewellen, Smith, Allen, Frank, Zervakis in Donleavy's convertible Ford, Dieringer in a ragtop Ford, Amick, and Lund, the slowest qualifier, also made the show. A star-studded roster rivaling Daytona or Darlington. Near tragedy struck on lap 78 when also-rans Bobby Keck and Roger Baldwin, in a pair of ragtop rags, tangled, smashing into Paschal's Mercury in his pit stall. Two crewmembers were seriously injured, but recovered. Herb Thomas fell out with mechanical trouble and settled for 46th place. During a race-long battle, the lead changed hands often between Welborn, Schneider, and Goldsmith. And the winner was ... Smokey Yunick's black and gold beauty of Paul Goldsmith. Frankie Schneider ran a great race, nabbing second, Weatherly's convertible was the first of that ilk at third, Thompson fourth, and Welborn fifth. On back were Wood sixth, Baker seventh, Panch eighth, Staley 12th, Roberts 13th, Turner 14th, Petty 15th, Lewellen 16th, Smith 17th, Allen 18th, Dieringer 35th, Amick 43rd, Paschal 48th, Owens 50th, Lund 51st, and Billy Myers 52nd. The great Herb Thomas was about done as a driver. He entered the Southern 500 on Labor Day with the intention of racing, but Fonty Flock talked his way into the car, and the carnage that followed is well known and recounted elsewhere. Herb had qualified ninth at Raleigh, though, and in every way, this was his last legitimate race as a contender. As it turned out, he was a pretender and left after 100 laps with brake trouble, never to contend again. Except for the pit crash, it was a great race and they would do it one last time.

A sweepstakes took place on another hot Fourth of July, a Friday afternoon in 1958. However, this would be the last Independence Day spent by big-time stock car racing in the Capital City of the Old North State because in 1959, the high banks of Daytona took it for good. The curtain closer here had two more cars than 1957 with much the same cast. Only this time subtract Herb Thomas, who had all but retired, Billy Myers, who died at Bowman-Gray, Frankie Schneider, and Goldsmith, now driving an Indianapolis roadster. Add talented rookie Shorty Rollins, Miami's Bobby Johns, Eddie Pagan, Herman Beam, and Junior Johnson to the Class of '58. Cotton Owens took the pole in Yunick's Daytona-winning Pontiac 3, leading 30 laps before Welborn, Wood, and Baker took turns up front. Then Roberts, Rollins, and Baker waged a real war until Fireball put Frank Strickland's 1957 Chevy in Victory Lane, but not without some last-minute drama. Half of 1957's pit crash, Bobby Keck, blew an engine and became a rolling chicane for Welborn and Roberts with 15 laps remaining. The two greats locked bumpers in the melee and stayed glued until separating in time for Fireball to beat Buck by a lap. Two months later, these two Hall of Famers would finish the same one-two in the Southern 500. The Raleigh Finale saw Rex third, rookie Rollins fourth, and Speedy fifth. The highest finishing ragtop was Welborn's in seventh. Others were Petty sixth, Pagan ninth, Paschal tenth, Johns 11th, Wood 13th, Beam 17th, Turner 19th, Weatherly 27th, Smith 32nd, Owens 45th, Allen 46th, Lund 49th, and Johnson 54th. It was Fireball Roberts' fourth super speedway checkers, tying him with Herb Thomas, and he would break the tie in his next opportunity.

No tale of the Raleigh Speedway would be complete without mention of the horrible events of Saturday night, September 19, 1953. Due to the success of the Memorial Day Grand National, NASCAR scheduled a 220-mile modified-sportsman race under the lights and the 60 fastest qualifiers attempted to cheat death for $15,000. They billed it as the first major racing event ever scheduled under the lights. On the pace lap, Bill Blevins' racer stalled on the backstretch and sat squarely in the fast groove as 59 other speedsters came around the big oval, took the green, and pounded towards the helpless Blevins. A police officer witness said that car number 50 had pulled up behind the stalled Blevins to give him a push on the pace lap. Whether or not that was the car of Jesse Midkiff was not reported. Pole-sitter Glen Wood and a dozen or so swerving daredevils passed. Then the inevitable happened as racer after racer piled into the two stopped speedsters and each other. The

Compare a map of today with one from 1955 and this view north up Tarheel Drive cannot be off more than inches from the deadly backstretch.

impacts were incredible as the car-rending disaster took place before the terror-stricken eyes of 10,000 unbelieving fans. There were two separate explosions and flames reportedly shot 70 feet into the night sky. A woman watching through a crack in the fence on the backstretch saw the entire accident unfold and collapsed in shock. She became one of many petrified onlookers and injured drivers carted off to local hospitals. When the fires were extinguished, Blevins was still seated behind the wheel of his smoldering, totally destroyed racecar. Midkiff was still aboard his torched machine, too, with his head crushed. After an 80-minute delay, the race continued and Fireball Roberts led until engine failure sidelined him. The red-flag cleanup took so long that the race was shortened by 50 laps and Buddy Shuman took the win over Bill Widenhouse. There were many stock car drivers in that nightmare, like fifth placer Bobby Johns, Cotton Owens, Joe Eubanks, Buck Baker, Joe Weatherly, and Curtis Turner. The Angel of Death took a pair of young men that September night, the only driver double-fatality at a major race in NASCAR history. Cheat death? Not that night, as two young men, Bill Blevins and Jesse Midkiff, were incinerated in the most gruesome of ways imaginable, and into the blackness they race.

Now the old speed plant lies restlessly beneath the rails, streets, warehouses, offices, and pine needles with memories of the old-timers. *Ghosts?* The old race grounds of the Raleigh Speedway are as hallowed and haunted as any. Many of our departed stars still contest the blistering fourth dimension asphalt there. Roberts, Rathmann, the Thomases, the Myers, the Flocks, Turner, Frank Arford, Lee Petty, Paschal, Smith, Baker, Beam, Lund, and the list goes on. You will also find Bill Blevins and Jesse Midkiff racing their powerful modifieds through the void, screaming north up the backstretch where Tarheel meets Wolfpack. And Jocko Flocko suits up again to wave at the drivers as he roars by.

Track History by the Numbers

RACES:	7
YEARS OF RACES:	1953, 1954, 1955 (2), 1956, 1957, 1958
WINNERS:	F. Flock (2), H. Thomas (2), Roberts (2), Goldsmith
MOST POLES:	1—F. Flock, T. Flock, Owens, L. Petty, Schneider, Slick Smith, H. Thomas
RACE RECORD:	79.822 mph—Fireball Roberts, 1956 Ford (7/4/56)
QUALIFYING RECORD:	83.896 mph—Cotton Owens, 1958 Pontiac (7/3/58)
WINS BY MAKE:	Ford (2), Hudson (2), Buick, Chevrolet, Chrysler
MOST STARTS:	7—Buck Baker, Paschal, L. Petty, Thompson
MOST LAPS LED:	334—Fireball Roberts
MOST TOP FIVES:	5—Herb Thomas
BEST AVERAGE START:	9.4—Jim Paschal, 4th—Herb Thomas (6 starts)
BEST AVERAGE FINISH:	7.9—Buck Baker

15

Wilson County Fairgrounds Speedway, Wilson, North Carolina

Of all of the *Silent Speedways of the Carolinas*, this may be the easiest to find. Wilson County Fairgrounds Speedway is right on Route 301 in Wilson, NC, at the well-established Wilson County American Legion Fair Grounds. Just turn in off 301, go through the main gate, pass through another to the speedway area, and that is it! *No weeds, no briars, no critters to fight.* The track's outline is a one-lane groove of sand mixed with red clay as the foundation of the track, which has a distinct berm indicating the inside edge. The faint slope of the first turn banking is evident in the last few yards against the grandstand, where it was abruptly whacked off by a grader's leveling blade at the wall's end. The backstretch is lined with the light poles from turn two to the third turn. Into turn three against that inside berm, the angle of banking is slight, but visible. The beginning of the homestretch wall off turn four is ragged and reveals an excavated, fire-damaged post. Perhaps it was scorched in the fire of 1959. Further down the stretch the wall joins the freshly painted grandstand. However, a new gray coat cannot hide the scars from the cars that it repelled in metal-bending defiance. Twelve times from 1951 until 1960 they came, entertained, and added to the rich legend of this sport. Grand National men held sway here for the last time 46 years ago

A fresh coat of gray paint had the Wilson Speedway grandstand race ready again.

and the crowds were treated to some of the most improbable happenings in stock car history.

It started on Sunday, September 30, 1951, when 17 Grand National cars and stars arrived at the sandy fairgrounds for the start of a nine-year, 12-race run. Fonty Flock sat on the pole in his Red Devil '51 Olds, coming home first over Brother Bob's Gray Ghost '51 Olds for the $1,000 prize. Lewellen was third, Paschal fourth, and Bill Snowden fifth. The win tied Fonty with hard-partying Curtis Turner for the career lead in victories at eight. Further back was Baker sixth, Donald Thomas tenth, Blair 11th, and Donald's brother Herb 14th. Over 7,000 fans paid to see the action and wanted more.

They got it on Sunday, September 28, 1952, and the car count was 22. There were big names combining for most definitely an *unbreakable* record. The track literally went to pieces and the cars followed. Incredibly, there was only one crash, but 11 others fell out with mechanical troubles, nine related directly to a rough surface. When the sands of the hour glass were about to be flipped for the third time, this one mercifully ended with the Hudson of Herb Thomas leading all the way, crossing the finish line a lap ahead of Petty, Blair, Paschal, and Rathmann. Shuman was sixth, Tim Flock seventh, Lewellen ninth, Fireball 16th, Southern 500 winner Fonty Flock 18th, and Baker 21st. That record, not unexpectedly, is for the *slowest Strictly Stock, Grand National, Winston Cup, or Nextel Cup race ever run.* An *ice-cold* 35.398 mile per hour average for 100 miles is all they could muster as parts and potholes were dodged for two hours 49 minutes and 30 seconds. It was all in a day's work for Herb's 13th career win.

It was a hot Sunday, June 28, 1953, and for the second time in three days, Rathmann rolled into the pits second, this time to Fonty Flock, the winner of the inaugural 100-miler here. There were 22 entries, but no car-killing track as it took less than two hours at almost 54 miles per hour. Early on, Pop McGinnis heaved his big Hudson 13 over on its side and carved out a trench in turn three for 21st. Third was Herb, fourth Eubanks, fifth Baker, Speedy sixth, Tim seventh, Petty ninth, Lewellen tenth, Blair 14th, Welborn 16th, brother-of-the-winner Donald Thomas 22nd and last in Yunick's number 9.

A small but quality field was on hand Saturday night, October 4, 1953. Olivia, NC's Herb Thomas had won a 100-miler the night before in Bloomsburg, PA, and many of those men made the long trip down to Wilson. It was another romp for Herb Thomas in the Hornet from the pole, leading all 200 laps in the one hour 47 minute laugher. Second was Speedy, third Fonty, fourth Petty, fifth Ralph Liguori, Rathmann sixth, Baker seventh, Lewellen ninth, Sosebee tenth, Turner 11th, and Eubanks 15th in the 17-car field. A whopping throng numbering 10,000 saw it all.

An even smaller field of 16 came on May 9, 1954, a spring Sunday afternoon. Paschal had the pole, but Buck led early before giving it up to Herb Thomas. Then Buck took it back until Rathmann swiped it. On lap 170, Dick stuffed the powerful Pure '54 Hudson into the fence and Baker cruised to Victory Lane. Second for the second straight race was "The Dirty Indian" Al Keller a lap back in a Hudson, third was Ralph Liguori in a career-best finish for the Tampa open-wheeler, fourth Petty, fifth Paschal, Blair sixth, Weatherly seventh, Herb Thomas tenth, Rathmann 13th, Donald Thomas 14th, and Eubanks 15th of 16. It took 115 minutes in the only appearance of the season in Wilson.

After Wilson's omission from the schedule 1955, the Grand National circus returned on March 18, 1956. A large field entered in front of a small crowd of 5,000 on a rainy Sunday afternoon. Herb Thomas paced the 32 entrants in his Yunick '56 Chevy 92. It was a battle royal on the gritty half-mile with Thomas versus the big white Kiekhaefers of Tim Flock, Baker, and Thompson. Just six laps past the halfway point, the skies opened up and

15. Wilson County Fairgrounds Speedway 161

Scars from the cars of yore remain reminders of past crashes and heroic dashes.

Thomas' Chevy had a narrow win over Baker and Flock. A lap back in fourth was Paschal, fifth Bill Widenhouse, Liguori sixth, Bobby Myers seventh, Rex White eighth, Thompson tenth, Lund 11th, Petty 13th, Smith 14th, Allen 15th, Johnson 24th, Billy Myers 26th, Eubanks 29th, Staley 30th, and Lewellen 32nd.

Race 56 in '56 was held at Wilson November 18th and it was curtains for the deadly and controversial Grand National season. Buck Baker had the points title jammed into his mitts after Kiekhaefer henchman Speedy Thompson took out point leader Herb Thomas less than a month earlier at Shelby on October 23rd. As Thomas' badly battered body still lay in Charlotte Hospital, a field of 24 put the season out of its misery. After all, the 1957 campaign had already started *a week earlier* in Lancaster, CA, with a Marvin Panch victory! It was also uncertain whether Kiekhaefer could stand the verbal abuse he and Thompson were deservedly receiving every time they had shown their mugs in public since Carl's Cleveland County carnage. So on a Sunday afternoon, the Great White Fleet with Baker, Thompson, and Jack Smith were up against a stellar field. Wily old Ford boss Pete De Paolo was determined to keep the Commandant from going out a winner. Pete brought five, count 'em, *five* 1956 Fords to Wilson to challenge for the $950 top prize. He employed Fireball Roberts, Joe Weatherly, Ralph Moody, Bill Amick, and Billy Carden. Last races of the year used to, and to a degree still do, bring out extra entrants racing for old times' sake, testing the waters for the future, or auditioning. Back in these days, there were also extra seats and old cars 100 miles from obsolescence for use one last time before banishment to some backwater oval. But there were factory stars like Petty in a '56 Dodge; Mel Larson from Vegas in a Ford; Staley, Zervakis, and Lund in Chevrolets; Allen and Blackie Pitt in Plymouths; Paschal and Billy Myers in Mercurys, and other field-fillers. But scratch the statement about the old cars 100 miles from obsolescence to be used one last time because every single car in the race was a 1956 model. Any way you sliced it, this was the universe against the Kiekhaefer Outboard Chryslers, winner of the past four.

Round one went to the Boat Motor Madman as Baker put a Chrysler on the pole with Moody outside. The green waved and Thompson roared away from third to lead and stayed there for 185 laps before the gas-guzzling Chrysler pitted for Pure. Baker led for the next 12 before he had to get a splash, too. As he slipped down the sandy backstretch half a lap from the checkers, new leader and gas-gambler Joe Weatherly's Ford coughed and by turn three was dead stick. De Paolo left Joe out trying to go the distance without a pit stop. Baker was closing furiously on the silent, snail-like Ford. With the overflow crowd delirious, down the stretch they came and at the wire it was Weatherly's white Ford 12 by inches over crusty Carl Kiekhaefer's screaming 300B. The stands erupted as the win was very popular indeed. When Joe crossed the finish line, he turned left off the track while Buck continued around, passing the scoring stand at the end of the straightaway. Unbelievably, Kiekhaefer protested, saying that Baker passed the official timing clock located in the scoring stand first and should be the declared the winner instead of Weatherly. Where De Paolo was and why he was not defending his position, which was first, is unknown. He probably never believed the victory could ever be taken from his Ford. Hours later, in the worst ruling in NASCAR history, Chief Scorer Joe Epton gave the win to Baker and Mr. K. The reversal defies all logic.

The scoring stand was typically located somewhere around the start/finish line and contained an electric clock that started at 00000 and flipped one number every second. Each car had at least one scorer there with a clipboard with the car's number affixed to the back. The scorer wrote down the number appearing on the clock in a corresponding box when his or her car passed the scoring stand, not the start/finish line. In a 200-lap race, there were 200 little boxes to fill. Each scorer held up the back of his or her clipboard every time his or her car completed a ten-lap interval. The Chief Scorer and his assistants recorded the cars' numbers as the boards were held up just to keep a rough, but fairly accurate running score. It was *never, ever* meant to determine the outcome of a close finish! Eyeballs and cameras were and are for that. Scoring stands are now normally located before the start/finish line, preventing a similar travesty.

Thompson finished third in the lead lap with Buck and Joe. Others were Roberts fourth, Amick fifth, Panch sixth, Carden seventh, Moody eighth, Petty ninth, Staley 12th, Allen 13th, Smith 14th, Myers 16th, Paschal 18th, Lund 19th, and Zervakis 20th. Commandant Carl got his win, the fifth in a row, to end the season. His cars won 30 of 56 races and had a two-year total of 52 wins out of 90 starts, including 16 in a row in the spring, and *stole* the '56 Grand National Championship. Kiekhaefer had his top drivers quit him mid-season, mechanics, too, and was generally despised. He was booed and jeered unmercifully and liquidated his racing assets before the start of the 1957 season. No team has ever dominated stock car racing as Kiekhaefer. With the absolute best equipment, best personnel, best luck, and bottomless pockets, Carl Kiekhaefer wrote a two-year chapter in stock car history that will not be equaled. He did not beat a bunch of bums either. They were high-dollar Detroit factory teams with big names. Moreover, there were some top-quality independents, too. Hated or not, Carl Kiekhaefer set the standard by which all racing teams before or since should be measured.

St. Patrick's Sunday afternoon, March 17, 1957, saw a field of 21 sprinkled with top-drawer pilots for 100 miles in the midst of the factory wars. De Paolo's Fords had Roberts, Moody, and Panch. Chevrolet had Hugh Babb–owned, Bud Moore–tuned fuel injected Black Widows for Baker, Thompson, and Smith, a trio still intact from the Kiekhaefer days.

15. Wilson County Fairgrounds Speedway

Turn Three still reflects an inside berm with a dirt path out wide in the racing groove.

Bill Stroppe had Mercurys for Billy Myers and Paschal. Olds was repped by Petty Engineering with Lee and Lund. And to be reckoned with were Yunick's Goldsmith Chevrolet and Spook Crawford's factory Plymouth of Johnny Allen. Nine others filled out the field including Emanuel Zervakis. Time trials went to Ford with Fireball and Panch in row one and the first half of the race went to Fireball, too. Then Roberts handed off to teammate Moody, who led the second half. End of story, next race. Baker was second two laps back, followed by Speedy, Lee, Tiny, Paul, Brownie King, Charlie Cregar, Fireball, and Smith tenth. The only crash was Billy Myers on lap 40 netting him last. A capacity crowd of over 10,000 jammed into the neatly kept fairgrounds.

Sunday, March 16, 1958, dawned and the Grand Nationals went at it for the second time in 24 hours. The day before, Turner won a 150-lapper at Fayetteville. This time Turner found himself on the outside of the front row next to Panch. Turner jumped out front for a lap before Pancho took over for the following 72. The Roanoke Rumrunner retook the point until lap 160 when a sickening snap signified his drive shaft was shot and his day was done. Lee Petty soft-pedaled his Olds to an easy four-lap win over Baker's Chevy. Even further back were Panch third, Smith fourth, Reds Kagle fifth, Turner 13th, Allen 16th, and Thompson 20th. A slim crowd of only 3,400 saw the Petty romp.

Maybe it was because "Smoke Gets in Your Eyes" had graced the Billboard Hot 100 for months. Possibly, because *Some Like It Hot* opened that day in theatres across the land. For whatever reason, this was also the day the grandstand burned to the ground at Wilson County Fairgrounds. It happened on Sunday, March 29, 1959. A pair of Virginians, Paul Sawyer and Joe Weatherly, put on the race while the Wilson Fire Department put out the stands. The nearly 9,000 folks that showed up learned what standing room only was all about.

Panic and disaster were avoided due to the calm, authoritative voice of another Virginian and retired Marine. Announcer Ray Melton deftly marched the fans from the stands and added to his considerable legend as the premier public address announcer in stock car racing. Time trials were cancelled, but Weatherly did not give himself the pole, just outside front row. He led the first four laps before Welborn took over for five. Weatherly's old pal Turner raced away in his '59 T-Bird for the 165 laps and seemed to be in control until the two-year-old Paul Spalding Ford of Junior Johnson zipped by and led the final 24, winning by a dozen car lengths over Turner. Racing to his first top five was Richard Petty third, Papa Lee fourth, and Pistone fifth. Others were Eubanks seventh, Weatherly ninth, Owens 11th, Baker 15th, Lund 17th, '58 Rookie of the Year Shorty Rollins 19th, Welborn 20th, Thompson 21st, Panch 22nd, and pole-sitter Ken Rush 24th and last. It was a very memorable *and hot* day in every way.

The penultimate visit to Wilson was on Saturday, June 20, 1959. This was the meat in a three-races-in-four-days sandwich. Lee won two nights earlier in Columbia, where Weatherly was injured in a crash. As in the previous "grandstand fire" race, there were no time trials for the field of 24. Jarrett won the pole drawing, but never contended. Only Tiger Tom's yellow T-Bird 59 could finish on the lead lap with Junior, who won his second Wilson 100 in a row in that same old Paul Spaulding '57 Ford number 11 as before. Further back came Wood third, Lee Petty fourth, Buck fifth, Lund sixth, Buddy took his second seventh in a row which were also his first two top tens, Owens 11th, Beam 13th, Eubanks 19th, Jarrett 20th, Irwin 21st, Weatherly 23rd, and Thompson 24th. It was Johnson's fifth win of the year and seventh in 24 races. He did it all in that tired Ford 11 that was a winner to the end.

The big-time book closed on this neat, convenient, well-kept venue for racing on Sunday, April 17, 1960. Again, it was the middle of three races, this time in *three days!* Weatherly took the honors the day before at Hickory and Bowman-Gray was hosting a Monday night race. Fortunately, this time the tracks were fairly close together and the travel was not killer as usual. Wilson paid $1,275 to win, $475 more than Hickory and a whopping $675 more than the Stadium. Four less cars came to Wilson than Hickory, but four more than showed at Tobaccotown. In his first career pole position, "The Golden Greek" Emanuel Zervakis and his white Monroe Shook 1960 Chevrolet 85 gave Weatherly, the Pettys, the Bakers, White, Welborn, Jarrett, Pistone, and Johnsons Joe Lee and Junior someone else to consider. The last 100 miles got underway and it was Zervakis, Weatherly, Petty, and Pistone swapping the top spots. But wackiness was just around the corner ... *again.* It would have behooved the Greek to take on a splash of Pure because he won handily *without* a pit stop. So the tech inspectors opted to take a peek at the gas tank on 85 and found it slightly smaller than the *Exxon Valdez.* Instead of going wire-to-wire for the win in an hour and 49 minutes, he went from Victory Lane to last *in an instant!* They let him keep his pole, but not his first win. Joe Weatherly, who had one career win on April 15th, had three by sundown on the 17th with his second in a row. In 22 days, he would take home the trophy in the Rebel 300 at Darlington in a Holman-Moody ragtop. Maybe in some strange way, though, this race evened things out for the Kiekhaefer scoring stand fiasco at the 1956 season-ender when they robbed Joe of the win. Third went to Pistone, fourth White, and fifth Baker, Sr. Others were Joe Lee Johnson sixth only 63 days from winning the first World 600, Richard Petty seventh, Welborn eighth, Junior in the Daytona-winning Chevy tenth, Jarrett 13th, and 19th the Greek, who was sadder than a souvlakis without tzatziki.

Richmond's Emanuel Zevakis ran his first Grand National on the Beach in 1956, piloting his own Chevrolet, lining up 76th and finishing there. *Started and finished dead last!* If nothing else, he was consistent. It took 17 races over three years, driving for himself and Richmond neighbor Junie Donleavy, skipping 1959 altogether, before Zervakis finally cracked the top ten in a race. He hooked with Shook and came back in 1960 with an eighth in his Daytona qualifier and tenth in the 500. Two races later, he won his first pole in the finale in Wilson, became a regular front runner notching eight top tens in 14 tries, and took eighth in the final standings. Then came 1961 and the Golden Greek arrived! In 38 starts in Shook's Chevies, Emanuel recorded two wins, 19 top fives, and 28 top tens, resulting in third for the national title. That '61 Grand National Point Standings top ten was a Hall of Fame Who's Who of Jarrett, White, Zervakis, Weatherly, Roberts, Junior Johnson, Jack Smith, Petty, Paschal, and Buck Baker. Needless to say, Zervakis could race with anyone. He won at Greenville and Norwood, MA, finishing in the top ten 16 of his last 17 races. In 1962, he drove his own Mercury only 11 times with two top tens. Then in 1963, he entered his own car three times, did nothing, and hung it up after a lap for last in the Southern 500. He finished last in his first race and last

Wire fence, cement wall, and burned post meet at the start of the homestretch.

in his last race. But in between, Emanuel Zervakis proved he could drive, no question about it. On June 23, 2003, the Golden Greek crossed over at 73.

The Wilson County Fairgrounds Speedway was a very good half-mile of sandy clay that had its share of legendary moments. Drivers and fans endured fire and rain, a snail's pace record-setting race, and the strangest scoring reversal in racing history. The ghosts must be having a ball there on a nightly basis.

Track History by the Numbers

RACES:	12
YEARS OF RACES:	1951, 1952, 1953(2), 1954, 1956 (2), 1957, 1958, 1959 (2), 1960
WINNERS:	H. Thomas (3), Buck Baker (2), F. Flock (2), Junior Johnson (2), Moody, L. Petty, Weatherly
MOST POLES:	3—Herb Thomas
RACE RECORD:	58.065 mph—Junior Johnson, 1957 Ford (6/20/59)
SLOWEST RACE IN HISTORY:	35.398 mph—Herb Thomas, 1952 Hudson (9/28/52)
QUALIFYING RECORD:	60.500 mph—Emanuel Zervakis, 1960 Chevrolet (4/17/60)
WINS BY MAKE:	Ford (4), Hudson (3), Oldsmobile (3), Chevrolet, Chrysler

Most Starts: 12—Buck Baker
Most Laps Led: 254—Curtis Turner
Most Top Fives: 8—Buck Baker, L. Petty
Best Average Start: 5.5—Buck Baker
Best Average Finish: 6th—Buck Baker, 5.1—L. Petty (11 races)

16

Dog Track Speedway, Moyock, North Carolina

Moyock, NC, is tucked away in Currituck County, in extreme northeastern North Carolina, where a good four wood would land in Virginia on the fly. The remains of this northern and easternmost of the *Silent Speedways of the Carolinas* would be typical if not for the fact that it is a dump, too. This is a swampy, sandy, tidewater area where seven nights of big-league stock car racing in the sixties occurred. Between 1963 and 1964, Dog Track Speedway went from a quarter-mile dirt to a third-mile paved, but there is no evidence of the paved version. All the facilities are next to a dirt track that could be either a quarter or a third of a mile long. Since Harris (NC) Speedway morphed back to dirt from asphalt, maybe that is what happened. On the other hand, maybe the dogs came back and pavement hurt their little paws. Entering the grounds off NC 168, the road bisects two huge fields once used for ample parking, as evidenced by towering light poles still standing. A dirt path to

Dog Track Speedway's spectator area is an unsightly, litter-strewn dump.

the north skirts the dump and comes out between the first and second turns. Across from the pits is a confusing combination of a low chain-link fence, a filthy, stagnant moat, and the big concrete slab where evidently the grandstand, concessions, betting windows, and offices were located. Dog Track Speedway has a very unusual arrangement and is most unkempt. It was hard to imagine Lorenzen and Johnson slugging it out around this place, but in 1963, they and other greats did, too. Time has been very unkind to this track and local citizens have done little to help. You might say Dog Track Speedway has literally gone to the dogs. However, here is a taste of the happenings and its place in stock car history.

What could be more exciting than a Tuesday night in Moyock? Probably a lot of things compared to the action out at Dog Track Speedway on September 11, 1962. This was the first of seven times that the touring pros went to the dogs on the quarter-mile sand in Moyock. The inaugural show, sandwiched two days after Weatherly won Richmond and two days before Lorenzen won Augusta, was a dud with only 15 entries and Jarrett going wire-to-wire by a lap over Weatherly. This venue was practically Joe's home track as he lived about 30 miles away in Norfolk. Only six cars finished as Crawfish Crider's Mercury was third, Mel Bradley fourth, and George Green fifth, although he did not finish. Herman the Turtle had one of his career-best finishes with sixth and Wendell Scott was the last man standing seventh. There were other notables in the slim field with Buck tenth, Petty 11th, Welborn 12th, and Larry Frank fresh off his Southern 500 win eight days earlier 13th. It is surprising that the big time ever returned.

Nevertheless, they did, twice in 1963. Since Tuesday night did not work so well, they tried Thursday this time. The date was July 11, 1963, and only 14 teams showed this time, a loss of one from 1962. Wonder why? The night before, they raced in Savannah for $1,000 to win (Jarrett did) and had to trek almost 500 pre–Interstate 95 miles to vie for $550 in Moyock. However, the field was a little better than 1962 and controversy reigned as NASCAR did not know who won until hours after the race. Ned thought he had a sweep of back-to-back races, but a scoring recheck proved that a long pit stop for a flat tire cost him his big advantage. Copping his second Grand National victory was North Wilkesboro's Jimmy Pardue in Pete Stewart's Ford. Buck was third, Mark Hurley fourth, and Soapy Castles fifth. Langley, the Turtle, and Crawfish made the top ten, as did pole-sitter Junior Johnson in the storied 1963 Holly Farms Chevy 3. In his second career start and getting his second 12th place driving a 1961 Ford X was J.D. McDuffie. Petty, Weatherly, and Scott all failed to finish. Two days later, they raced at Bowman-Gray Stadium, and the night after that at New Asheville. That was four races in five nights! It was brutal back then.

Back to Tuesday night at Dog Track on September 24, 1963, for 300 laps, and controversy returned with them. With another slim car count there was real quality. It was a two-car slugfest between Jarrett in Bondy Long's Ford and Weatherly in Bud Moore's Mercury. Ned got the checkers, but Joe claimed he won. NASCAR took their sweet time with the recheck and Chief Scorer Joe Epton let Jarrett keep the win. *Nine* laps back was Pearson third and Petty fourth. Fred Lorenzen must have been lost in the area and decided to race claiming fifth. On back were Cale, Buck, and Pardue. Daytona 500 winner Tiny Lund took 14th out of 15.

When the big dogs, uh boys, returned, they ran the one and only 24 Hours of Moyock. Has a nice ring to it. In addition, for the first time they raced on asphalt. The locals must have decided the dogs were not coming back. It started on another summer Thursday night, August 13, 1964, with Pearson out front in his Cotton Owens Dodge when the skies opened up. Thank goodness there was no race elsewhere the next night so they returned for the finish. In a big gamble on Friday, August 14th, Jarrett risked his neck on worn tires

16. Dog Track Speedway

Peering back down the homestretch and pit area from soggy Turn One.

and a dry fuel tank to swipe the win from David by the lap Pearson lost for a late service stop. Richard was third, Bunkie Blackburn fourth, and his teammate Bill McMahon fifth in a pair of gold 1964 and 1963 Pontiacs.

Fayetteville, NC–born Bunkie Blackburn's fourth here equaled his best career big-time finish, which he accomplished three times in 71 starts between 1960 and 1970. The next one was in his fifth from last race during the 1966 Rebel 400 in Ray Fox's Dodge 3. In 1967, he raced to numerous speed records on the Bonneville Salt Flats in a Smokey Yunick Camaro. He topped it all off with a wire-to-wire win in the 1968 Permatex 300 during Speed Weeks, proving that it was not smart to monkey with Bunkie. He crossed over on February 28, 2006, in Cleveland, TN, at 69 years old.

Unable to nail down a weekend date, but still on the schedule, Dog Track came back on Tuesday, August 24, 1965, and Hutcherson made it look easy. The Keokuk Comet came from third to lead the final 268 laps and nip Jarrett and Petty for his seventh win of the season. Big names were Lund fourth, sportsman ace Sonny Hutchins fifth, Bakers Buddy and Buck next, Dieringer ninth, Wendell 14th, Cale 16th, and Pistone started and finished last. Maybe "The Dog" will someday get a race date on a weekend.

It did on Sunday, November 7, 1965, and it was notable for a couple of reasons. Moyock had the privilege of dropping the curtain on the 1965 season where Ned Jarrett secured his second Grand National crown, his 13th win of the season, and the *final* win of his career. Ned would give it one more season, but go winless and finish a dismal 13th in the standings. Those who called him "Gentleman Ned" were talking only about his off-track demeanor because he would knock your tail in the wall as quick as Lee Petty, as often as Buck Baker, and as hard as Curtis Turner. He tied Junior Johnson for wins that Sunday at 50, but Junior

The backstretch is better suited now for a swamp buggy.

must have had a voodoo doll to keep Ned from winning any races at all in 1966. The Tidewater 300 was held on a blustery, windy, sand-swept day, even for extreme northeastern North Carolina. The biggest field ever assembled there put on a memorable show and Ned took 'em by a lap. Isaac sat on the pole in Junior's yellow Ford 26 and finished a lap off the pace. Buddy gave Buck's '65 Chevy its best run for third. Paschal was fourth as Petty's teammate, and Pistone was fifth. Others were up-and-coming Sam McQuagg eighth, Tyner 15th, and a long, long way from home, Miamian Bobby Johns 16th. A lady even made her one and only start, the pretty Goldie Parsons, who drove Buck's Olds 89 to a 14th after starting 21st. It would be over a decade before a woman started another Grand National. The 1965 race had plenty for which to be remembered.

Sunday, May 29, 1966, saw a swan song for a dog track. The slim Memorial Day weekend crowd got a one-lap bonus as NASCAR scoring screwed up again and added one to the scheduled 300, but it did not matter. Spartanburg's David Pearson drove Cotton's 1964 Dodge 6 home first by a lap over Lund with Hylton third, Sears fourth, and Scott fifth. Richard Petty competed in his sixth race at the remotest of the *Silent Speedways of the Carolinas* and never left a winner, something quite unexpected. He had the pole and led this one for the first 84 circuits before his ignition failed. Buck brought three cars and did not drive, and Buddy drove for someone else. Dieringer, Pistone, Langley, Castles, and Tyner were there as fillers.

The Dog Track Speedway had some memorable races and the sandy little oval is well on its way back to the tidewater from which it came less than 50 miles from the Kitty Hawk-Kill Devil Hill area. Moyock was hard to find for mortals, but the ghosts have it much easier: fan ghosts, crew ghosts, driver ghosts, and dog ghosts. Wonder if Orville and Wilbur prefer cars or dogs.

16. Dog Track Speedway

Track History by the Numbers

RACES:	7
YEARS OF RACES:	1962 (1), 1963 (2), 1964 (1), 1965 (2), 1966 (1)
WINNERS:	Jarrett (4), Pardue (1), Hutcherson (1) Pearson (1)
MOST POLES:	2—Ned Jarrett, Richard Petty
RACE RECORD:	63.965 mph—Ned Jarrett, 1964 Ford (8/13/64)
QUALIFYING RECORD:	69.164 mph—Richard Petty, 1965 Plymouth (5/29/66)
WINS BY MAKE:	Ford (5), Chevrolet (1), Dodge (1)
MOST STARTS:	7—Wendell Scott
MOST LAPS LED:	739—Ned Jarrett
MOST TOP FIVES:	6—Ned Jarrett
BEST AVERAGE START:	1.7—Ned Jarrett (6)
BEST AVERAGE FINISH:	1.3—Ned Jarrett (6)

17

Harnett County Speedway, Spring Lake, North Carolina

Go north of Fayetteville through Fort Bragg a few miles on Route 210 to Bethel Church Road and turn right. There is no sign for Race Track Road, but it is a dusty trail to the right, meeting another dirt road also intersecting from the right. Walk down that road, up some hills, past a lake and a couple of merging paths, until the telltale signs of a racetrack appear, i.e., garbage. Upon closer examination, the trail ends just behind the crumbling remains of the large concrete grandstand. Huge, mature pines reach cloudward in the very spot where fans cheered that Sunday fifty-plus years earlier at the only Grand National held there. Down in front of the stands is a wide trail that was once the main straightaway, now cluttered with pines and shrubs. The sandy soil of Harnett County has surged downhill and the once formidable front stretch wall has surrendered to the pressure, partially collapsing,

Dormant for decades, Spring Lake's grandstand is the epitome of a silent speedway.

17. Harnett County Speedway

Looking from the top reveals moss-covered cinder blocks and dozens of trees.

allowing the earth to swallow it up over decades of erosion. The first turn is still quite visible and one could easily imagine Herb Thomas barreling around the corner in that big Hudson with the sand flying. The top rim, the gradual banking, and the sweep of turns one and two are plainly recognizable. The backstretch is wide open for roaring stockers to kick up the sand until entering the third and fourth turns, which are not in nearly in the same condition as those at the other end. There are not as many pine trees at this end as these turns are the victims of years of erosion. Sadly, that erosion is obscuring the memories of what happened on that one and only day when Harnett Speedway was the center of the stock car racing world.

It happened on Sunday, March 8, 1953, and a chilly wind blew across the sand hills of Harnett County, NC. A large field assembled on the new circuit to see the big guns of NASCAR. Quite a few in that crowd of 7,000-plus were soldiers from Ft. Bragg, only a few miles away. All the top jockeys were there, too, including Herb Thomas in Smokey Yunick's Fabulous Hudson Hornet, Tim Flock's blue Blackburn Auto Service Hudson, former AAA Indianapolis 500 pilot Dick Rathmann in a Walt Chapman Hudson, Lee Petty in his Dodge, the Spartanburg team of Bud Moore and Joe Eubanks in the Oates Motors Hudson, and Fonty Flock in the fast Frank Christian Olds. Other drivers and makes taking part were Herschel Buchanan's Nash, Don Oldenburg's Packard, Ray Duhigg in a Plymouth, Herb's brother Donald Thomas in a Ford, and Weldon Adams in a Studebaker. What, no Chevy? Curtis Turner and Bill Blair started, too. Eight makes, 32 drivers, $1,000 to win in 200 laps of war on a virgin half-mile of sandy dirt.

New track, large field, and top drivers, a cannot-miss combination. Right? WRONG! It was a *lousy* race. Herb Thomas sat on the pole, took the lead immediately, and never looked back. End of story. Two hours and eight minutes later, this yawner was over. Rathmann was

Top: The main straightaway is wide and ready for a field of huge 1953 stock cars. *Bottom:* The hill is slowly swallowing up the homestretch retaining wall.

17. Harnett County Speedway

Turn Three has lost some of its size due to the wind and rain, but it is clearly there.

three laps back in second, Petty third, Dick Passwater fourth, and Buchanan fifth. Except for the infield crowd helping right Johnny Patterson's overturned Olds, the race was a stinker.

The old place off Race Track Road is fading fast, where all the right ingredients failed and the big boys never came back. Or do they? When the neighbors hear that distant rumble and roar, is it the cannon fire from Fort Bragg, or is it the racers of '53? The sand swirls around after dark, a chill wind blows, and plumes of dust are kicked up by Smokey and Herb's Hudson breezing to victory again in a rout.

Track History by the Numbers

RACES:	1 (3/8/53)
YEARS OF RACES:	1953
WINNERS:	Herb Thomas
MOST POLES:	1—Herb Thomas
RACE RECORD:	48.826 mph—Herb Thomas, 1953 Hudson
QUALIFYING RECORD:	51.918—Herb Thomas, 1953 Hudson
WINS BY MAKE:	1—Hudson
MOST STARTS:	1—Tied by 32 drivers
MOST LAPS LED:	200—Herb Thomas
MOST TOP FIVES:	1—H. Thomas, Rathmann, L. Petty, Passwater, Buchanan
BEST AVERAGE START:	1st—Herb Thomas
BEST AVERAGE FINISH:	1st—Herb Thomas

18

Forsyth County Fairgrounds, Winston-Salem, North Carolina

It is now the Dixie Classic Fairgrounds and filled with modern exhibition halls, buildings, concessions, a barn, and a 4,500-seat grandstand. That grandstand is all that is left of the half-mile dirt track at the former Forsyth County Fairgrounds Speedway in Winston-Salem, NC. The stands face the paved midway, where the Grand Nationals sent up their plumes of red dust over 50 years ago. The track disappeared in 1985 and a line of out-of-service Winston-Salem squad cars rest in what was the first turn. Not much imagination is needed to see the outline of a racing surface in places. The dirt track backstretch lies right beneath the asphalt ribbon now disguising it as the fairgrounds midway. Through the third turn and into the fourth, long-necked geese waddle around where Hudsons and big white Chryslers used to drift onto the main straight and head for those 4,500 seats.

May 29, 1955, was a spring Sunday and 23 Grand Nationals lined up for the first of two scheduled there for the season. As it turned out, it was to be the *only* two as Bowman-Gray Stadium was the venue of choice in Tobaccotown. The mighty Kiekhaefer Chrysler 300 of Fonty Flock took the pole and brother Tim timed sixth. There was an outbreak of yellow fever that day as the slowdown silk flew eight times. Fonty fell out early. Smokey's Hudson had Herb's brother Donald in the saddle, but crashed on lap 142. Junior Johnson started up front, but succumbed to mechanical woes. Tim fell out in the other Kiekhaefer, Buck's axle broke, Staley lost his rear, and Volney Schultz's 69 had the coolest name and number in the race. Just under two hours after the start, Petty beat the only other driver to

In 1955, the Forsyth County Fairgrounds hosted its only two Grand National races.

complete 200 laps, Jim Paschal. Fred Dove nested in third followed by Rathmann and Johnny Dodd, Jr.

The angels of good fortune smiled lovingly that Sabbath in Winston-Salem even though crashes ruled the day. However, this caution-filled afternoon was timid compared to what was taking place all over racing's global landscape. Three days before Petty won at Winston-Salem, Grand Prix great Alberto Ascari was dashed to the pavement while testing in Monza, Italy. He was released from the hospital after suffering a broken nose four days earlier as the only Grand Prix driver to vault into the azure Mediterranean in Monte Carlo. Twenty-four hours after Petty's win, the 38th Annual International Sweepstakes took place on Decoration Day at the Indianapolis Motor Speedway. Bill Vukovich crashed with several others, including two-time 1954 Grand National winner Al Keller. The Mad Russian hit Johnny Boyd, who was trying to avoid the crashing big cars of Keller and Rodger Ward. Vuky's Fuel Injection Special careened over a short wooden fence, flipped under the backstretch bridge, bounced off several parked autos, and cartwheeled endlessly high into the air with the winner of the two previous 500s strapped inside. *Life* published a photo of Vuky's charred hand protruding grotesquely skyward from underneath the smoking, overturned roadster. The only other drivers that were the absolute icons of their discipline to die on the track racing are Dale Earnhardt and Ayrton Senna. Each was the undisputed leader of his sport and perished at full speed in front of thousands of fans, Vukovich and Earnhardt in their premier events, Earnhardt and Senna on worldwide television, and Senna and Vukovich while leading the race. The carnage of 1955 peaked on June 11th as Pierre Levegh's Mercedes exploded on top of a dirt embankment on the 34th lap of the 24 Hours of Le Mans in front of the main grandstand and the Grim Reaper swung his giant sickle through the doomed crowd. Screams filled the air, as did body parts and a rainstorm of blood, when the engine and front suspension mowed through the crowd, instantly killing 83 spectators before stopping in the seats short of other lucky souls. A headless corpse hung from a telegraph pole for hours as the 24-hour race ticked on. The horror of '55 actually began with big car pilot

Geese waddle around Turns Three and Four where stockers roared 50 years earlier.

"Please rise for the playing of our National Anthem."

Larry Crockett dying in a colorful locale called Puke Hollow at Langhorne in March. April's death showers brought May's death flowers as Mike Nazaruk followed Larry in Puke Hollow a month later, then Manny Ayulo bought it at Indianapolis while practicing before the 500. July saw Indianapolis 500 pole-sitter Jerry Hoyt's slaughter in a sprinter in Oklahoma City, and Indy front row pal Jack McGrath cashed it in at Phoenix in November. It was unspeakably horrible everywhere except in stock car racing. The AAA quit. The Pope said, "Basta!" Congress formed a committee. Maybe the Rider on the Pale Horse was working too hard elsewhere to visit the stock car crowd. Later, he would find the time and visit frequently.

A wilting Winston-Salem Sunday, August 7, 1955, thankfully rode well on the safe side of the ill winds that owned auto racing. The field included 22 top shoes such as Tim Flock's Chrysler 301 on the pole with teammate/brother Fonty outside in 300. Petty completed the Forsyth County sweep for 1955 and history in a new Dodge. Paschal was runner-up in the

Helzafire Olds, Baker took third in his Buick, Carden copped fourth in an Olds, and Eddie Skinner finished fifth in a Dodge. Welborn was sixth, Tim seventh, Bill Bowman brought a Nash eighth, Billy Myers ninth, Staley 13th, Fonty 16th, Arden Mounts rolled a Hudson on the main straight for 18th, Junior blew for 19th, Herb lost a clutch for 21st, and George Parrish was 22nd and last in a Studebaker. Herb Thomas was returning after a vicious flip in Charlotte two months earlier, but his Yunick Hudson failed. Then, after 122 Hudson starts, 38 wins, and a Grand National title in that marque, *Herb never raced a Hudson again.* Mr. Hudson went Chevy and within a month, Herb and Smokey won their third Southern 500. At the Forsyth County Fairgrounds, the gods of racing smiled twice during the roughest summer racing had ever known.

Where life and death decisions were once made at breakneck speeds under blue skies and sunshine, children scream and lovers steal kisses at breakneck speeds under the bright lights of the midway. This patch of unreal estate in front of 4,500 empty seats has seen more than its share of emotion. The seats are not as empty as one might think as those ghostly-white Chryslers go for the win here they never got and Herb takes that last Hudson ride again and again.

Track History by the Numbers

RACES:	2
YEARS OF RACES:	1955 (2)
WINNERS:	Lee Petty (2)
MOST POLES:	1—Fonty Flock, Tim Flock
RACE RECORD:	50.583 mph—Lee Petty, 1954 Chrysler (5/29/55)
QUALIFYING RECORD:	59.016 mph—Tim Flock, 1955 Chrysler (8/7/55)
WINS BY MAKE:	Chrysler, Dodge
MOST STARTS:	2—Tied by 13 drivers
MOST LAPS LED:	126—Buck Baker
MOST TOP FIVES:	2—Lee Petty, Jim Paschal
BEST AVERAGE START:	1.5—Fonty Flock
BEST AVERAGE FINISH:	1st—Lee Petty

19

Coastal Speedway, Myrtle Beach, South Carolina

Kelly Lee Brosky, Supervisor of the Horry County Public Information Office, with her staff and friends, pinpointed the exact location of this all but forgotten member of the *Silent Speedways of the Carolinas* beside and under the Myrtle Square Mall. It is two blocks off the beach in the middle of town on a litter-strewn, ant mound–covered eyesore. The track is in a horseshoe configuration as the north turns and the last few yards of the straights were lopped off to construct Myrtle Place (a street) and the mall parking lot. Due to the position of the sun, the main straight runs south directly at what is now a Wachovia bank, and then curves left through the corner of its parking lot to form the first turn. There begins an unmistakable and still slightly banked turn with the very definite semi-circle of trees lining closely the inside, probably along the infield berm. The crest of the entire sweep of the turn is visible and with a slight drop-off on the backside. Nowhere on the property is there even the vaguest hint of a light pole, guardrail, or post. No other clues at all except the topography

Unmistakable is the curving inside tree line and slight slope of the banking.

19. Coastal Speedway

An auto path from 21st Street leads to the infield as it probably did 50 years ago.

of the turn. There is an auto path coming from 21st Avenue that runs perpendicular across the middle of the second turn and through an opening in the trees having all the earmarks of the entrance to the infield. The parking lot of one of the numerous goofy golf courses that litter the landscape in Myrtle Beach cuts into the straightaway off turn two. The backstretch, which was to the oceanside, is a wide flat path, tree-lined on the inside, that leads straight back to the lopped-off end at Myrtle Place. Litter can be pretty because whoever maintains the plants and flowers in the neighboring buildings dumped the old ones here. Only an old telephone pole in the debris field might have served some electrical purpose in the lot's racing days. Nevertheless, here is the ghost on the coast and the stories it has to tell.

Saturday night at the beach! What could be better? A Grand National stock car race Saturday night at the beach! And how about just over a block from the ocean! Grand Nationals on the Grand Strand! That is what they had on August 25, 1956, when the daredevil speedsters invaded Coastal Speedway for the first of two visits. They started racing at Rambi Raceway out on Route 501 towards Conway in 1958, but it began for the City of Myrtle Beach right downtown. The warm sea breeze welcomed 20 stock car aces led by the formidable Kiekhaefer team of white Chryslers with points leader Buck Baker and stablemate Speedy Thompson. There to battle them were the De Paolo Engineering Fords of Roberts and Moody. Petty showed along with Yunick's Herb Thomas Chevy, Billy Myers and Paschal in Mercurys, Eubanks in a Ford, and Allen in a Plymouth. Moody had the pole, but was taken out in a lap 61 crackup. Thomas was in the running until pitting under the caution on lap 76 and promptly disqualified *for adding fuel during a yellow flag period*. Nice 1956 rule! After that, a guy quite used to beaches, Daytona's Fireball Roberts, out-legged Billy Myers

Beware of danger that lurks in the bushes when searching for traces of races.

to the wire for the winner's share of 950 clams. Paschal's Merc was third, then Buck and Speedy rounded out the top five. In order to run down Baker in their championship duel, 13th placer Thomas ran the next day, the only Myrtle Beach racer to do so, in a 123-miler on the half-mile asphalt *in Portland, Oregon!* Try that in 1956. He won $200 for seventh.

The second visit was a year and a day later on Monday, August 26, 1957, and it was a slim, but quality field. Only 15 teams entered this last tune-up for the Southern 500 one Monday away. It had been days since the last race at Old Bridge, NJ, which ended the annual Northern Tour. Johnny Allen won his first career pole in a Plymouth, but finished dead last with a fan problem under the hood, not in the stands. Other top stars on hand were Panch, Thompson in Bobby Keck's Chevy, Smith, and Petty, none of which contended. The first-time winner was Gwyn Staley in his Julian Petty Chevy by a lap over Eddie Pagan, who switched coasts to warm up for the Southern 500, placing second. Roberts was third, Buck fourth, and Greenville's L.D. Austin fifth. Staley drove a zipper-top, a convertible quickly converted to a hardtop. Problem is: no rear window, no points. However, Staley obviously did not care because he failed to make the top 50 in the point standings anyway. One week later in the 500, he fell out on lap 22, five laps before the tragic crash that claimed Bobby Myers. He went on to win two more races by September 15th, notching wins at historic Syracuse and deadly Langhorne in a ragtop against a fantastic field of mostly hardtops. That was three wins in 20 days, the only Grand National wins of his career. Gwyn Staley stopped winning *and* breathing on March 23, 1958, on the clay of Richmond in a convertible.

It is easy to find Coastal Speedway when visiting the Grand Strand. Go there at night and hear the roar of the crowd, but is it the folks playing goofy golf, or the unliving in the Grand Strand's grandstands? BEWARE! We know Staley's there slinging sand and whipping the field over and over. And watch out for that last-place finisher from 1956. He is still on the track, too, in his ghostly Fury 64. His name is *Spook* Crawford!

Track History by the Numbers

RACES:	2
YEARS OF RACES:	1957, 1958
WINNERS:	Fireball Roberts (1), Gwyn Staley (1)
MOST POLES:	Ralph Moody (1), Johnny Allen (1)
RACE RECORD:	50.782 mph—Gwyn Staley, 1957 Chevrolet (8/26/57)
QUALIFYING RECORD:	58.886 mph—Ralph Moody, 1956 Ford
WINS BY MAKE:	Ford, Chevrolet
MOST STARTS:	2—Allen, Buck Baker, L. Petty, Roberts, S. Thompson
MOST LAPS LED:	1 (at least) Roberts, Staley
MOST TOP FIVES:	Buck Baker (2), Fireball Roberts (2)
BEST AVERAGE START:	2.5—Fireball Roberts
BEST AVERAGE FINISH:	2nd—Fireball Roberts

20

Jacksonville Speedway, Jacksonville, North Carolina

Just motor north on U.S. 17 from Jacksonville, take a right on Piney Green Road, left on Old 30, and it is a mile or so on the left. This example of the *Silent Speedways of the Carolinas* is buried in thick woods behind a mobile home less than a half mile off on Old 30. It is a muddy, rutted, and heavily overgrown trail with vegetation devouring everything. The most visible remains of Jacksonville Speedway consist of two-by-six boards ten or twelve feet long, set staggered and backed up by a dirt embankment. It is the backstretch retaining wall and to pound it in a stocker also meant pounding the good earth of Onslow County behind it. The grandstand and pits were on the other straightaway, and high on the outside of turns one and two stands a rusty old wire fence atop the high dirt bank that held the cars inside the track. The main straightaway is only a clearing where the pits were. There is no trace of

The backstretch retaining wall is gradually returning to the decaying forest floor.

Mature hardwoods are moving the boards and retaking the track.

the stands or the caboose that allegedly once stood at the start/finish line serving as the offices and concessions. There is a crossover to the infield leading right to the clearing of the pit area. Turns three and four are barely visible with the wire fence looming over the retaining bank as at the other end. The groove is quite swampy most of the way around with an inside barrier still easily seen made up of short telephone-type poles connected by a steel cable. Years of uncontrolled growth have allowed saplings to sprout from the rotted tops of the posts. Then the silence is pierced by the creaking of trucks and trailers and the rattling of dogs and chains of the phantom haulers that are unloaded nightly by those crews arriving from the other side just as in the steamy, sultry summer of 1957.

The heat was visible as it caused the surrounding soybean and tobacco fields to appear to waver under a scorching summer Sabbath sun in Jacksonville, NC. It was June 30, 1957, and there were a bunch of tired teams that rolled into the sandy half-mile oval. The day before, Petty won a rain-shortened 93.5-miler in Spartanburg a grueling 350 non-interstate miles away. So for the teams that did both races, you must admire men and women that would make that trek for a thousand clams to win. Quite a few did, like Baker, Thompson, Petty, Roberts, Paschal, Lund, Smith, Allen, Billy Myers, and a few determined also-rans. The field of 19 roared away with Petty leading from the pole. It was not long before the rough, sandy surface started taking its toll and Petty fell from contention. Baker legged away from the crowd and took this one in Bud Moore's Chevy in a rout. Paschal was second three back, Lund third nine behind, George Green fourth, and Jack Smith, a cool 21 laps off the pace, fifth. It made a pretty dull day for nearly 4,000 sandblasted fans. On back came Huck Spaulding seventh in his second start, Petty eighth, Dieringer 11th, Roberts a Herman Beamish 12th 92 laps behind, Thompson 13th, Myers 15th, and Allen blew an engine on the 12th lap for 19th and last, pocketing $50. Let us see ... 350 miles from Spartanburg to win $50 ... that's 14 cents a mile. *Not a good deal!*

That first race was so great it took the Grand Nationals seven years to return. The week they did, LBJ clobbered Barry Goldwater in the presidential race and Paula Murphy blistered the sand at the Bonneville Salt Flats to become the fastest woman on Earth at 226.37. On Sunday, November 8, 1964, the tragic 62-race season came to a merciful end at Jacksonville Speedway with Petty holding a 5,000-plus points advantage over Jarrett.

Stock car veterans Joe Weatherly, Fireball Roberts, Jimmy Pardue, and part-timer Dave McDonald had each died a horrible death. Others were erased in sprints and Indy cars. This month would end with the death of part-time stocker Bobby Marshman at Phoenix, testing his Pure Firebird Lotus Ford Special. Nineteen sixty-four was a season everyone wanted finished, and thank goodness that for the first time since the 1953 season closed, the next campaign did not start within just a week or so. The 1965 tour started January 17th at Riverside, a continent away.

So on this cold, gray, blustery day, 25 stockers were gridded on the gritty oval. Doug Yates captured his second and final career pole in the '63 Plymouth 72 with Jarrett alongside. Row two saw Lund's familiar orange 55 Ford and soon to be officially crowned champion for the first time Richard Petty outside. Behind them were Spencer and Paul Moore, Isaac and Buck Baker, and in row five Scott and Pearson. Back in the ninth row outside of Elmo Langley was a young man in the Burton-Robinson '64 Plymouth 36 destined for stardom, Larry Thomas. The freezing crowd of about 3,500 roared as the race got underway and Yates jumped out front for nine laps. The first car out brought to a close the two-race career of Hardeeville, SC's sportsman ace Bubba Into in an old '62 Dodge 91. Bubba opened his big-time career a week earlier at Augusta. On lap ten, Jarrett passed Yates for first and held it for 29 laps until Petty took over for 26. Meanwhile, Bakers Buck and Buddy fell out for 23rd and 22nd respectively with rear end troubles and Paul Moore's familiar yellow '63 Plymouth 45, with the big red light burning on the dash, parked forever in 20th place. Lap 65 saw Pearson shove Cotton's Dodge 6 out front for 39 circuits as an oil leak sidelined Tampa, FL's Lewis "Possum" Jones for 19th. Jones was a more than competent driver whose 47-race Grand National career went all the way back to the 1952 Southern 500. In 1957, he won two convertible races, in '58 captured a Grand National pole in Columbia, and in 1960 had three runner-ups that with a few breaks could have easily been wins. He was only 32 years old, but he had seen enough. With a 23rd in his next and last race, the 1965 Daytona 500, a really good driver named Possum retired. About the same time Pearson lost the lead to Jarrett on lap 104, Isaac parked Cotton's Dodge 5 for 17th with suspension woes. Ned started padding his lead while the other contenders struggled and faded. Larry Manning crashed an antique '62 Chevy on the 150 lap for a brief caution, but it was not enough to keep Jarrett from roaring away in the last quarter for a one-lap win over runner up Petty, Spencer third, Doug Cooper fourth, and Larry Thomas fifth. Further back came Soapy sixth, Crawfish seventh, Tiny ninth, Pearson tenth, Wendell 11th, and Frank Graham of Charleston Heights, SC, shut down an eight-race, four-year career with a 12th.

After Pardue crashed through the rail and plunged down a 300-foot embankment to his death at Charlotte on September 22nd, the Burton-Robinson factory Plymouth team went after the most promising young driver they could find. They found Thomasville, GA's Larry Thomas, a 29-year-old veteran of 122 races. When hired in time for the National 400 at Charlotte where Pardue died, Larry was on a streak of 12 top tens in the last 14 races. He was hot and ready to win. Burton-Robinson changed the number on the Plymouths from Pardue's popular Car 54 to 36, the number Thomas had used in the overwhelming majority of those 122 events. In fact, Pardue was a lot like Thomas in 1964 with top fives, top tens, and everything except a win. So Larry Thomas finished the '64 season with a 20th at Char-

20. Jacksonville Speedway

A rusty wire fence is still atop the dirt-retaining bank in Turn Two.

A young sapling sprouts from the rotted top of a fence post, making it a perfect planter.

lotte, fifth in his old ride at Harris, third at Augusta, and a fifth here at Jacksonville. Bring on 1965 'cause Larry Thomas is *ready!* In truth, 1965 was not a vast improvement over bloody, fiery '64. The Grim Reaper started earlier with Billy Wade on January 5th, killing him in Bud Moore's Mercury while testing tires at Daytona. At Riverside in the opener on January 17th, a fan was erased while watching the 500 from a fork lift when the Grim One's bony hand nudged it down a hill. On January 22nd, Larry Thomas took delivery of a new 1965 Plymouth and probably a hot one. Up and on the road in it early on January 25th, Larry lit out from Atlanta to Daytona on I-75 south, probably for some sort of preparation for the 500 only a few weeks away. In the cold pre-dawn darkness near Tifton at about 5:20, Thomas' Plymouth rammed at high speed the rear end of just-off-duty security officer George Hollis' car, hurdled the guardrail, flipped down a 35-foot embankment, and crashed upside down by the side of a railroad track. George Hollis was unhurt, but Thomas' feet were horribly protruding from beneath the hissing, smoking hulk when the rescuers arrived. However, this situation was beyond help. Everyone said he was asleep at the wheel and his seatbelts were obviously unused. The brightest new light in stock car racing was extinguished in the icy, misty darkness of a Georgia Interstate.

What happens in Jacksonville, NC, after hours on that overgrown tract of unreal estate when the breeze rustles the pines is known only to the dead. It is a good roll call for a track that only hosted big-league racing twice. Buck and Tiny are the only men that ran both. Speedy, Fireball, Lee, Jack, Darel, Wendell, Elmo, Billy Myers, and Isaac are also on that ghostly grid. However, one ghost is starving. Starving for that first win that everyone said was sure to come. Everyone also said he was asleep at the wheel. The ghost running the hardest in that frigid void is still-up-and-coming Larry Thomas.

Track History by the Numbers

RACES:	2
YEARS OF RACES:	1957, 1964
WINNERS:	Buck Baker, Ned Jarrett
MOST POLES:	Lee Petty, Doug Yates
RACE RECORD:	57.535 mph—Ned Jarrett, 1964 Ford (11/8/64)
QUALIFYING RECORD:	64.285 mph—Doug Yates, 1963 Plymouth (11/8/64)
WINS BY MAKE:	Chevrolet, Ford
MOST STARTS:	2—Buck Baker, Tiny Lund
MOST LAPS LED:	126—Ned Jarrett
MOST TOP FIVES:	1—Ten drivers
BEST AVERAGE START:	2.5—Tiny Lund
BEST AVERAGE FINISH:	6th—Tiny Lund

21

Champion Speedway, Fayetteville, North Carolina

In Fayetteville, NC, on Highway 301 South, there is a big lot filled with modular homes, scrap metal, old army vehicles, and cranes, the steel kind without feathers. It is Fayetteville Steel Erectors and Metal Buildings, Inc., 3469 Gillespie St., in South Business Park. Ray Weaver is the owner and he bought the site in 1986 and plowed the Champ under. Champion Speedway was still in good shape when razed and all he saved was the walk-through gate. It is old and rusty and still has a few ominous strands of barbed wire dangling helplessly from their guides that point away from each other at the top. Ah, but who through that ghostly portal walked those years ago? There is also a pile of broken concrete and steel rebars that secured the barriers in the ground so that a speeding '59 Chevy could not knock it down. That pile was the outside retaining wall circling the entire third-mile track. Not much of that remains because the rest was used as fill. An ordinary chain-link fence survives from those race days of yore.

All that Ray Weaver saved in 1986 from Champion Speedway is a pedestrian gate.

What about the nights in that scrap yard with those T-Birds, Chevies, and '58 Fords rumbling around in the dark? The drivers can see that the track is in great shape still and Mr. Weaver and his bulldozers have not changed a thing to those men who race from twilight to twilight. He did not move that gate either as Turner, Weatherly, Baker, Smith, Staley, and Petty laugh their way through the haunted passage just as they have since 1958 when it started. This track has a very strange history as far as the spacing of its racing goes. In the 1958 Grand National season, three of the first seven races were at Champion Speedway. They came back to raise the curtain on the 1959 season and never returned. Or do they?

After the 1957 season ended in Greensboro on Sunday, October 27, 1957, everybody had time to go trick or treating on Thursday and be back to start the 1958 season the following chilly Sunday, November 3rd. A field of 22 came with newly crowned, two-time champion Buck Baker in Bud Moore's Chevy with Petty's Olds, Smith, Thompson, Staley, White, Possum Jones, and Lund in Chevies, Yunick's Goldsmith-piloted Ford, Massey's Wood Brothers Ford, and Spook Crawford's Plymouth with Johnny Allen. And all for $630 to win. *Unbelievable!* Jack Smith had it in the bag until mechanical failure put him in the wall with five left and a star on the rise and champion-to-be Rex White notched his first big-time win. Petty was second, Lund third, Staley fourth, and Massey fifth. It was not all bad for tough-luck Jack ... he pocketed $195 for seventh.

After Daytona and Concord, the touring pros came back to Champion for race number four for '58. Beware the Ides of March! A larger, better field appeared for this Saturday night shootout paying 600 bucks to win! Perhaps considering that Turner won the 50-miler in just over 53 minutes, it was not a bad night's work. Six hundred dollars an hour is good pay now, but of course, it was longer than that with travel, practice, and qualifying. Turner had Staley pounding away at him when the checkers fell with Baker third, Frankie Schneider fourth, and Harb fifth. Rex White, winner here in November, was sixth, with Welborn, pole-sitter Petty, Weatherly, Thompson, Allen, Pagan, and Smith (who only won $50 this trip) faring worse.

This was Gwyn Staley's last Grand National race. Staley did not run the next day at Wilson, NC, like most of the others, including Turner. He waited until eight days later, when he was booted by Fayetteville fourth-placer Frankie Schneider going into the first turn on the first lap of a 100-mile convertible race in Richmond. Gwyn's familiar 1957 Chevy 38 ragtop barrel-rolled into the tall wooden fairgrounds fence and back onto the track, coming to rest upside down on the red clay. Rescuers righted the car and the lifeless body of the popular 31-year-old Burlington, NC, veteran was hauled away. Between August 26th and September 15, 1957, Staley put that 38 in Victory Lane three times with the big boys, the final time at deadly, oily, treacherous Langhorne. Not that there is any doubt about his talent, but Staley beat the best that day, starting 25th in a 48-car field and winning by two laps in good old 38, that same Julian Petty '57 Chevy. Gwyn Staley was not good, *he was great!*

After events at Hillsborough and Wilson, they returned 21 days later on Saturday night, April 5, 1958. Race seven paid another whopping $600 for less than an hour's work. This third visit of the young season to Champion saw 29 speed demons take the green with Bob Welborn, the replacement for the recently departed Staley, climb into Julian Petty's Chevy 38 and take second on the grid. As if weird things do not happen often enough, in this, the first race since Staley's death, Welborn won in Staley's old car. And guess who was flailing away at his back bumper? Frankie Schneider, the man that punched Staley's ticket to the hereafter at Richmond a fortnight earlier! Thompson was third followed by Turner, Baker, Petty, White, and Smith. This was an *eerie* night.

One would think NASCAR was going to schedule this track forever the way it had taken a liking to it. However, after a respite of a full two weeks since the 1958 season closed at Atlanta's Lakewood Speedway, the opening curtain for '59 went up again at Champion Speedway. It was the cold Sunday afternoon of November 9, 1957, and "It's Only Make Believe" by Conway Twitty was the number-one song in the land. Some familiar, some new, and some old faces showed up to race before the big, new asphalt monster at Daytona was christened in another three and a half months. The familiar faces were Welborn, Wood, defending Grand National Champ Lee Petty, Baker, Johnson, Lund, and White. The new mugs included Tommy Irwin, soon-to-be convertible champ Joe Lee Johnson, Jimmy Pardue, Charley Griffith, and a kid who had nine starts under his belt from 1958, Richard Lee Petty. Some old-timers eased in, including Jimmy Thompson, who had not run in years, and

A pile of concrete is the wall that once enclosed the track. The rest became landfill.

Jimmy Lewellen, who finished 16th in Strictly Stock race number one. For an astounding winner's share of $600, again, Welborn, again, took it back to Greensboro. He drove Julian Petty's '57 Chevy, again, only 46s adorned the doors where 38s used to be. Wood and Baker followed on the lead lap with Tyner fourth and Junior Johnson fifth. Young Dick Petty finished where he started in 13th and Charley Griffith finished where he started, 25th and last, completing no laps at all. His luck was about to change with a third in the inaugural Daytona 500.

They never came back in this life and all that is left are old army trucks, piles of concrete, mud holes, and cranes without feathers. But after dark, Gwyn Staley comes back to the scene of his last race and walks through that rusty gate with Turner, Weatherly, Old Man Petty, Buck, Speedy, Jack, Tiny ... and "It's Only Make Believe" plays on the PA system.

Track History by the Numbers

RACES:	4
YEARS OF RACES:	1957 (1st of '58), 1958 (3–1 was 1st of '59)
WINNERS:	Welborn (2), Turner (1), White (1)
MOST POLES:	2—Lee Petty
RACE RECORD:	59.170 mph—Rex White, 1957 Chevrolet (11/3/57)
QUALIFYING RECORD:	62.665 mph—Jack Smith, 1957 Chevrolet (11/3/57)
WINS BY MAKE:	Chevrolet (3), Ford (1)

21. Champion Speedway

MOST STARTS:	4—Austin, Buck Baker, DeZalia, Harb, King, L. Petty, White
MOST LAPS LED:	191—Bob Welborn
MOST TOP FIVES:	2—Buck Baker, Schneider, Staley, Turner, Welborn
BEST AVERAGE START:	2.8—Lee Petty
BEST AVERAGE FINISH:	5.2—Buck Baker

22

Southern States Fairgrounds, Charlotte, North Carolina

At the southeast corner of Sugar Creek Road and U.S. 29 in Charlotte stands a shopping center with lots of Asian and empty stores anchored by a Park 'n' Shop that is as much eyesore as it is supermarket. It stands on the site of the Southern States Fairgrounds that held 17 100-mile Grand National races from 1954 to 1961. It actually lasted two seasons after the opening of the Charlotte Motor Speedway. However, there is no trace of it left to stir the imagination; no rusting guardrails, no pine trees popping through the concrete grandstand, no wooden fairgrounds fence, not even a bullet-riddled light pole. There is no magic in a dirty asphalt parking lot 45 years after the show closed. Postcards of the old fairgrounds show a lovely lake in the infield that today has been reduced to a miserable little litter-strewn rivulet surrounded by scrub brush and all that nasty pavement.

It started on Friday the 13th, 1954, a muggy August night. For Chrysler's Lee Petty it was not unlucky at all as he passed pole-sitter Buck Baker and was never headed. A good field of 22 partook of the action, with Dick Rathmann's Pure Sensitized Hudson two laps back in second, Bob Welborn third, the Concord Comet Dink Widenhouse fourth, and Baker fifth. Others were Eubanks seventh, Blair eighth, Owens ninth, crashing Gober Sosebee tenth, Herb Thomas 14th, McGriff 15th, Lewellen 18th, and Paschal 20th.

Back the boys were six weeks later on Friday night, September 24th. Oregon's Hershel

Another great track gone without a trace, with an ugly Park 'n' Shop anchoring the site.

McGriff had the fast time in an Olds, leading every mile to beat Petty by a lap. Baker was third, Rathmann fourth, Eubanks fifth, Herb sixth, Dink seventh, Lewellen eighth, Tim ninth, Bill Widenhouse 11th, Bill Amick 21st, Panch 22nd, and Paschal 23rd. It was McGriff's second straight win and Tim Flock's second straight race back driving Buck Baker's Olds. He quit altogether after winning the big one in Daytona in February, but a disqualification for a soldered carburetor butterfly reduced him to 62nd. Many spectators went home that might and tuned their televisions to NBC at 11:30 for the debut of *The Tonight Show Starring Steve Allen*.

Friday night, June 24, 1955, was another stinker as Tim Flock won the time trials in his Kiekhaefer Chrysler and never looked back. He led every lap for the fourth time in '55. Baker ran second, Staley third, Welborn fourth, Junior Johnson fifth, Dink sixth, Paschal seventh, Eubanks eighth, Petty ninth, and Speedy 15th. Twenty cars were no match on dirt for Tim Flock at the peak of his career.

With Hurricane Connie churning towards South Carolina, the hot, humid Friday night of August 5, 1955, had the circuit pros back at Southern States. However, the track was in awful shape and only 15 racecars came. When it was over, eight of those could not take the beating on the rutted, pockmarked surface. High Point's Jim Paschal in the Helzafire Olds passed the unpassable Tim Flock and romped the final 147 laps to win. Staley took second, Baker third, Welborn fourth, Tim fifth, Shuman sixth, Junior Johnson eighth, Petty tenth, Lewellen 12th, Carden 13th, and Dink the Concord Comet last.

Sixth place finisher Buddy Shuman started 11th in Buck Baker's '54 Oldsmobile 87 and never led, never contended, and never ran another Grand National race. Buddy tragically burned himself alive smoking in bed in a Hickory hotel room on November 13th. He was on the eve of heading up Ford's Stock Car Racing Division, a position ultimately going to 1925 Indianapolis 500 winner Pete De Paolo. At 40, Buddy Shuman left this side with hundreds of modified wins and one Grand National victory on July 1, 1952, in Niagara Falls, Ontario. He also won the double fatality modified inferno in Raleigh on September 19, 1953. Anxious to drive Shuman's Fords, Curtis Turner was heartbroken at the loss of his good friend and predicted he would win the Southern 500 for Shuman. On Labor Day, September 3, 1956, he did so convincingly.

Friday night, June 15, 1956, and a threat of showers could not keep almost 8,000 fans from the half-mile oval at Sugar Creek and U.S. 29. A quality field was there, but the race was not as hot as the temperature since only four of 19 finished. Mechanical problems sent car after car to the trailers as Ralph Moody crashed out late and still managed eighth. Fireball led from the pole, then Speedy Thompson of Monroe put his Kiekhaefer Chrysler out front for the final 173 laps. Turner was second five laps behind, trailed by Petty, Roberts, and Baker fifth. Others were Herb sixth, Tim seventh, Paschal 11th, Billy Myers 13th, Junior Johnson 14th, Weatherly 15th, Eubanks 16th, and Carden 18th.

Junior Johnson's 14th-place finish in the Brushy Mountain Motor Pontiac 55 was the other story that night. Robert Glenn Johnson, Jr., got another number on June 2, 1956: number 2348. He was pinched while watching the family still in the Brushy Mountains of Wilkes County, "The Bootlegging Capital of the World." The first race he ran post-arrest was this one. He raced next on July 1st at Asheville-Weaverville, seizing 20th. On August 12th at the Elkhart Lake Road Course, he copped a 26th and last in a De Paolo Ford. Finally, on November 11th at Hickory, he escaped with 15th. Then it was vacation time and the Ronda Rumrunner went away for the next 11 months to the luxurious confines of the Chillicothe Federal Reformatory in Ohio. They sprung him on December 27, 1957, and he was ready to win.

Remember Elvis on *The Ed Sullivan Show* the first time? That was September 9, 1956. It was still on everybody's lips and hips on hump day, September 12th, when the stock cars returned to Southern States for the '56 finale. Twenty-six speedsters ran it and the best Kiekhaefer could do was seventh, which was news. On paper, it looks more lopsided than it was. Ralph Moody went to the point on lap 79 and brought his De Paolo Ford home a winner. He was half a lap ahead of Billy Myers and pole-sitter Joe Eubanks with Panch fourth, Thomas fifth, Lund sixth, Thompson seventh, White eighth, Paschal ninth, and Petty tenth. Fireball, Buck, and Glen Wood had forgettable nights.

Three trips to Southern States punctuated the 1957 Grand National campaign. A spring Friday night, April 19th, saw Roberts going after his third win in a row. *And he got it!* After Buck Baker dominated the first 165 laps in his Black Widow Chevy, Panch took over, and then gave it up to the flying Fireball, who fetched his fourth win of the year. Panch and Baker also finished on the lead lap. Petty, Paschal, Earnhardt, Allen, Smith, Myers, Goldsmith, Lund, and Thompson did not figure in the outcome.

On a summer Friday night, July 12, 1957, about 8,000 dust-eaters saw 21 stockers contend for the generous $700 first prize. Some big names ran that night and Panch, Baker, and Petty crossed the line within a couple seconds of each other in a race that saw six lead changes. Thompson was fourth, Roberts fifth, Billy Myers sixth, and Paschal seventh in the final rundown. Others were Smith, Allen, Bobby Myers, Amick, and pole-sitter/last-finisher Lund, who broke a gas line in the Brushy Mountain Motors Pontiac normally driven by vacationing Johnson.

Bobby Myers started eighth and finished 19th in Whitey Norman's '56 Ford 1A, completing only 26 laps before the engine blew. He was not a Grand National tour regular, but a holy terror on the Carolina and Tennessee dirt tracks in a sportsman car. Myers reigned as North Carolina State Champion in 1952 and Tennessee State Champ in 1954. He was 30 years old and one of the most promising drivers racing. Lee Petty handpicked him to drive a second Olds in the big one, the Southern 500. Petty had been putting Lund or Earnhardt in his second entry, but decided to see what young Myers could do in top-flight equipment. When 500 time trials were over, Bobby Myers had the Petty Engineering 4 planted in the middle of the front row between Cotton Owens and Curtis Turner. Myers' boss was two rows back in the middle of the third row between Bud Moore's '57 Chevies of eventual winner Speedy Thompson and Buck Baker. In the first 27 laps, the lead swapped furiously with six changes as Owens led first, then Turner, then Goldsmith, Myers for one, Turner again, and Owens again. Then disaster struck! Fonty Flock was struggling around the blistering-hot asphalt in Herb Thomas' ill-handling Pontiac 92 and already nine laps behind. Fonty, the 38-year-old 1952 "Burmooda" shorts winner, lost control on the backstretch when he said he "was nudged out of passing space" and the car began "swaying." He scraped to a stop against the guardrail rear end first, just a couple of feet past the end of the grandstand wall, facing downhill, angled toward the traffic. A dozen cars, including leader Owens, passed the sitting duck black Pontiac of Flock before the arrival of the 13th car, Bobby Myers. With Goldsmith right behind, Myers smashed headlong into Flock. Goldsmith, in Smokey Yunick's black and gold Ford 3, was riding half a car width to the outside of Myers and blasted his way through the already demolished and spinning 92 of Flock. Myers' disintegrating Olds rolled side-over-side four times, never getting airborne, and spewing parts and the engine through the third turn. It came to rest on its right side facing out. Goldsmith's Ford barrel-rolled, then leapt into the air for a series of high-altitude nose-down pirouettes, landing upright with the roof nearly flattened. Flock's Pontiac overturned, also stopping on its right side facing out. The right front wheel was smashed under the right side door and the left front wheel was set squarely in the center of the front where the grill was. Paul described the crash in the promotional film produced by Pedrick Piston Rings. He said he was following a car length behind *Billy*, not Bobby, and could "see that his windshield was a little bit fogged up and I couldn't see through the car ahead." Paul continued that he moved to the outside and saw a car in the groove and then there was an explosion. He explained, "Billy's car just disappears" and relates flipping and stopping upright. A stunned Paul Goldsmith surveyed the damage. Then he leaned forward, put his hands on the smashed hood, and lowered his head between his outstretched arms. With Bobby Myers' twisted, motorless, smoking hulk of scrap resting on the passenger side, the fatally wounded Bobby was hanging down across the interior toward the track. The front end was gone, and the roof had to be peeled open from back to front for the 30-year-old's removal. It took a few minutes before he was placed limply on the stretcher for the trip to McLeod Hospital in Florence. Myers was pronounced dead, but that was corrected and legendary public address announcer Ray Melton put out a desperate call for blood at the raceway. As over a hundred fans either arrived at or were en route to the hospital, Bobby Myers left this Earth. Brother Billy Myers climbed out of his '57 Ford during his first pit stop after the crash and was relieved by Pee Wee Jones, who did a great job finishing seventh. From the Eye in the Sky, Dave Rodgers relayed the terrible news to millions listening worldwide, including Bobby's nine-year-old son, known today as Dale Earnhardt's famed gasman Chocolate Myers. Flags at the raceway were lowered to half-staff.

Fonty rumbled home third at Daytona in Bill Stroppe's factory Mercury back in February. He inexplicably did not race again until talking washed-up Herb Thomas out of his Labor Day ride. After the crash, Fonty was a battered mess, allegedly having last rites performed over him at the track. He was reportedly in a coma with little or no chance to survive. His shocking picture was splashed across the front page of the *Spartanburg Herald* the morning after the crash. Lying in a hospital bed, there stared hairy-chested Fonty, face cut up, nose bloodied and bruised, and arms positioned above his head with his left one in a cast. The front-page AP story about Fonty Flock said that he was retiring. He recalled promising his wife that he would not race that day. Fonty officially had a broken left arm, eight stitches in his nose, and neck and head bruises. With the incredible doubleheader impacts he absorbed and lack of safety equipment that '57 Pontiacs had, it is miraculous that Fonty took another breath after Labor Day morning 1957. He never gripped a steering wheel professionally again and was the color commentator on the radio broadcast of the 1964 World 600 when Fireball Roberts crashed on lap seven. Truman Fontello Flock joined his departed pals due to natural causes on July 15, 1972, at the age of 52. Actually, Bobby Myers is the one who died of natural causes because he died racing. Fonty Flock just died.

Paul Goldsmith finished out the year with Yunick, winning four races and finishing 13th in points. He went to USAC stocks and Indy roadsters. Goldy bravely raced on for 11 more winning years, rejoining NASCAR in 1964, then retiring mid-season after the 1969 Yankee 600 at Michigan on August 18th.

It is all a long way from reporting a 1957 race at Southern States Fairgrounds to the history just covered, but all racing is connected in some way. One story leads to another. It is hard to tell of Bobby Myers' last complete Grand National race at Southern States without noting his next outing that killed him. That makes it impossible to leave out Fonty Flock, a major factor in stock car history from before World War II until Labor Day 1957, after which he never raced again either. And although Paul Goldsmith raced on for years, his description of the crash on film is absolute first, hand knowledge and he may not be willing to discuss it now. However, on July 12, 1957, Charlotte was fortunate to experience Bobby

Myers complete his last Grand National race. The fans never know when good-bye is for good.

The third visit for 1957 came on Saturday, October 5th, the day after the Russians launched Sputnik and two days before Dick Clark launched *American Bandstand*. Lee Petty took the pole and led most of the way in an Olds, edging Fireball Roberts' Ford. Pagan was third, Baker fourth, and Lund fifth. Others competing were Smith ninth, Bobby Myers 12th only 33 days after Bobby's demise, Speedy in that Southern 500–winning Chevy 17th, Panch crashed for 18th, Allen 20th, and Weatherly 26th. Petty won the $900 first prize in just under two hours. The next afternoon, there was a sweepstakes race in Martinsville, VA, for 250 miles. What a schedule!

Friday night, April 18, 1958, saw one of the all-time snoozers. Turner's Holman-Moody Ford 26 won the pole and led every lap for his second straight win, as he had copped first at Lakewood in Atlanta five days earlier. Smith was a lap back in second, Allen third, Petty fourth, with Turner's teammate on and off the track, Joe Weatherly, fifth. Further back was Baker sixth, Owens seventh, Pagan 12th, Dieringer 14th, Carden 16th, and Panch 17th.

The boys returned Friday night, September 5, 1958, four days after the car-killing Southern 500. Therefore, the 25 starters did not include many stars. There were four lead changes between Petty, Johnson, Welborn, and Baker, who led the last 97 laps for only his second win of the year. Thompson was a lap back in second, soon-to-be Rookie of the Year Shorty Rollins third, Bob Walden fourth, and Bill Poor fifth. Others were Petty tenth, Massey 14th, Owens 15th, Welborn 17th, Johnson 19th, Matthews 23rd, and Lund last.

May 22, 1959, Friday night, was the first of three trips to town and this one was close. Twenty-five took the flag and 109 minutes later, Lee Petty in a two-year-old Oldsmobile fought his way past Weatherly, Welborn, and Baker to nip Lund at the stripe by a second. Cotton was third in Eubanks' Ford, Thompson fourth, and Baker fifth. Others were Welborn eighth, Smith tenth, Jarrett 11th, Weatherly 16th, Junior Johnson 18th, and Richard Petty 19th.

It was a Sunday afternoon on hot, dusty July 26, 1959, when a huge field of 35 took the green led by pole-sitter Buck Baker in his '59 Thor Chevy. With yellow silk flying about every 11 laps, the pack never got spread out and five drivers finished on the lead lap. Heading that parade in Bud Moore's '59 Chevrolet was Jack Smith of Spartanburg. Greensboro's Welborn was second, Spartanburg took third with Baker and Owens fourth, and Greenville, SC's Larry Frank finished fifth. Nine cautions waved as Ralph Moody made an increasingly rarer appearance for sixth, Buddy Baker was eighth, Wood ninth, Lee Petty tenth, Lund 11th, young Richard 12th, Thompson 24th, Banjo in a third Baker Chevy 25th, Weatherly 26th, and Junior last. But wait, we'll be right back.

In what has to be the quickest turnaround on record, they returned to Southern States the next Sunday afternoon, August 2, 1959, after a race the night before in Myrtle Beach. That was the race Jarrett *had* to win because he had purchased Spaulding's '57 Ford with a check post-dated Monday, August 3, 1959. Ned pulled off step one by taking the car to Victory Lane, but the tape on the steering wheel was wrapped badly and sliced Ned's hands to ribbons. So at Southern States, Ned qualified tenth, but his mitts were oozing life and he had to give it up to Weatherly for a few laps. Then, after Junior Johnson's car retired, he took over for Weatherly and went the distance. Of course, it did not matter *much* that Johnson had raced and won in the Spaulding car for two seasons and was totally familiar with it. Junior brought 11 home first, Ned got credit for the win, and Monday morning the $2,000 check morphed from rubber to paper. Paschal was second, Welborn third, Irwin fourth, and Frank fifth. Further back were Eubanks ninth, Buck 13th, Lund 14th, Lee 18th, Richard 20th, Buddy 21st, Junior 25th, and last Owens 29th. The handwriting was on the wall for this and any other track near I-85 and U.S. 29 in Concord because a superspeedway was rising there and Southern States had three races left.

The 1960 season opened on cold Sunday afternoon, November 8, 1959. A field of 28 lined up with most of the big names on hand. Buck took the pole again in his Thor Chevy and led twice. Panch held the point awhile, too, but crashed before halfway for 22nd. Westcoaster Scotty Cain torched his T-Bird on the backstretch while Buck and Richard Petty engaged in a spirited game of bumper tag. It cost Buck the race due to a lengthy stop for repairs. Richard fared worse with a DNF for 12th. The duo of Jack Smith and Bud Moore again took top prize by a lap over Welborn, with Buck third, Tyner in a great run fourth, and Thompson fifth. Further back was Lee seventh, Tiny ninth, Pistone tenth, Spencer 11th, Joe Lee 13th, White 14th, Paschal 19th, Irwin 21st, Jarrett 26th, Buddy Baker 27th, and Junior last.

The sixth of '60 was back at Southern States two weeks after Junior Johnson won the Daytona 500. Two significant events occurred in the sports world this Sunday afternoon, February 28, 1960, although one was not so apparent. The first occurred in Lake Placid, NY, where the U.S. stunned the world by beating the USSR the day before in Olympic ice hockey, then clobbered the Czechs 9 to 4 for the gold. In Charlotte, a field of 21 showed for a wintry 100-mile chase. Only a third of the starters finished on the rapidly deteriorating surface. Lee Petty started first, but retired after 38 laps for 20th. Joe Lee blew for 17th. Johnny Beauchamp got his Holman-Moody Ford stuck in the mud for 16th. Eventual Rookie of the Year David Pearson in his third start overheated for 15th. Youngster Cale Yarborough lost his rear end for 14th. Buck blew for 13th. Jarrett DNF'd for 11th. The Turtle finished 59 laps behind in tenth. Pistone's distributor quit distributing for ninth. Eubanks drove home fifth with Junior in a Wood Brothers Ford fourth. Lee relieved Plymouth pal Doug Yates and finished a lap back in third, but won the race. He won the race for son Richard by banging at Rex White in the last 20 laps so Rex could not mount a charge. And that is the other big story of the day: Richard Petty's first victory. It was important for the Petty clan, but who could have guessed that Richard had 199 more to go? It started here on one of the *Silent Speedways of the Carolinas*.

It was Sunday afternoon, frigid November 6, 1960, and surprising that after 1100 miles of Grand National racing had been run at nearby Charlotte Motor Speedway, the tour would still return to decrepit old Southern States Fairgrounds. It was three weeks since Speedy put the Wood Brothers Ford in Victory Lane in the inaugural National 400 at CMS, and seven days since Johns won the initial Atlanta 500 in Owens' Pontiac, that the 1961 season started. As in 1960, this tired old oval got the privilege of hosting the season opener. Unlike 1960, this was also the final one for Southern States Fairgrounds Speedway. It was an eventful early November as Ward Bond joined that ghost wagon train in the sky the day before, JFK debated Nixon two days later, the Senate passed the Civil Rights Bill two days after that, and Clark Gable didn't give a damn for the last time on the 16th. It was a time of beginnings and endings. This race was both as around 4,000 fans braved the weather to see 20 stockers bring an end to big-time dirt track racing in the Queen City, where it had held events since the start on June 19, 1949. Lee Petty took his final pole and led the first 17 circuits. Then one-week newly crowned Grand National Champion Rex White, driving the gorgeous gold and white Louis Clements Chevy 4, took the point for 31. As in the previous race here, Old Man Petty and the diminutive White dueled fiercely as Lee took over again for the next 90, then Rex for 19. Out of nowhere, Joe Weatherly, in a '58 Wood Brothers Ford zipper-top with no rear glass and as obsolete as the track, snuck in to lead the final 39 laps. The old oval did not go down without a fight, as the surface broke up badly, exacting

Appearing in old photographs as a nice infield lake, it is reduced now to a littered stream.

a toll on the competitors. Junior Johnson started last and broke three axles in his Pontiac during time trials and the race, the last one borrowed from a fan in the infield. Rex finished second, Lee Petty third, Buck fourth, and 1960 Rookie of the Year David Pearson fifth. The other prominent finishers were Beam sixth, Richard Petty 11th, Elmo 12th, Pardue 13th, Irwin 15th, Jarrett 16th, Buddy Baker 17th, Junior 18th, Crider 19th, and Pistone last.

Lee Petty was the story here, but nobody knew it yet. Not a real popular guy, the taciturn, all-business Petty is undoubtedly one of the very greatest drivers of all time. Maybe better than his famous son. Lee took his 18th and final pole that day in Charlotte. Two Sundays later in the next race and the last before Speedweeks, 46-year-old Lee got the final win of his amazing career, number 54, in a 100-miler on the half-mile in Jacksonville, FL. In the thirteen-year existence of NASCAR's premier division, the Petty Patriarch won a race in *every single season he competed.* In 1949, he waited until the penultimate race at Heidelberg, PA. In 1950, he dramatically held off until the very *last* race at Hillsborough gaining his second-career checkers. After that, he never waited so long again, winning the season openers in 1953 and '55. On October 18, 1959, Lee won a 100-miler at North Wilkesboro for win 48 and tied Herb Thomas for most. Thomas had his last win on June 3, 1956. The next time North Wilkesboro rolled around, on March 27, 1960, Lee got win 49, becoming the winningest driver in Grand National history. Lee Petty took the career wins lead on March 27, 1960, at 49, upped it to 54, and held it for seven years, a month, and 16 days until Richard took it forever. However, Lee never added another win after race two of 1961. He was a 46-year-old veteran with no retirement in sight on February 24, 1961, as he drove in the second 100-mile qualifying race at Daytona. With three laps left, he locked bumpers with old chum Johnny Beauchamp. They vaulted over the flimsy single strip of guardrail in turn three and flew like arrows with Petty's '61 Fury 42 attached to the back bumper of Beauchamp's '61 Impala 73. They crash-landed on Earth against a chain-link fence near the entrance to the tunnel under turn four. That either survived is absolutely astounding. Petty still edged Beauchamp like in the 1959 Daytona 500, only this time it was for 15th. Lee was in bad shape, survival iffy at best, with a punctured lung and other severe internal injuries, a crushed chest, broken thigh and collarbone, and countless lacerations and bruises. He was laid up four months, but amazingly returned on July 13, 1963, finishing fourth at Bowman-Gray. Four races later, he retired on July 19, 1964, after nine laps at Watkins Glen for 22nd place. Richard crashed on the next lap for 21st. Buck Baker got close to Petty's record at 46 wins when he won the 1964 Southern 500, but never won again. In 1965, Jarrett and Johnson started with 37 apiece. They raced neck and neck, racking up victories, and at season's end, they both had 50. Richard Petty was closing fast with 40. Nearing the peak of his career in 1966, Richard won eight more and ended with 48. Johnson drove seven times and never won again. Jarrett retired the same day as Johnson, but did not win again either. Junior and Ned are tied forever at 50. Then came 1967 and Richard went on a tear that will *never* be equaled. At Richmond on April 30, 1967, he tied his father for wins at 54. Next was the Rebel 400 at Darlington on May 13, 1967, and win 55 put Richard on top of the all-time victories column for good. *Twenty-seven wins for the year* secured two titles for Richard: The 1967 Grand National title and The King. Four hundred and twenty-seven races after he tossed the family Buick at the Charlotte Speedway in Strictly Stock Car Race Number One, exactly 15 years and a month later, Lee hung up his helmet. He started overseeing the Petty operation until deciding to leave and pick up the clubs. Fifty-four wins (13% of the time), 231 top fives, 332 top tens, and the all-time best average finishing position of 7.6 place. He left the planet again on April 5, 2000, at the age of 86, but with all the action he saw at the two dirt ovals in Charlotte, you can bet he still comes around and around and...

Track History by the Numbers

RACES: 17
YEARS OF RACES: 1954 (2), 1955 (2), 1956 (2), 1957 (3), 1958 (2), 1959 (3), 1960 (2—1 was 1st of '61), 1961

WINNERS:	L. Petty (3), J. Smith (2), Buck Baker, T. Flock, Jarrett, McGriff, Moody, Panch, Paschal, R. Petty, Roberts, S. Thompson, Turner, Weatherly
MOST POLES:	4—Lee Petty
RACE RECORD:	59.439 mph—Joe Weatherly, 1958 Ford (11/6/60)
QUALIFYING RECORD:	64.103 mph—Buck Baker, 1959 Chevrolet (11/8/59)
WINS BY MAKE:	Ford (6), Oldsmobile (4), Chevrolet (3), Chrysler (3), Plymouth
MOST STARTS:	17—Buck Baker, Lee Petty
MOST LAPS LED:	356—Buck Baker
MOST TOP FIVES:	13—Buck Baker
BEST AVERAGE START:	5.4—Lee Petty, 5.5—Buck Baker
BEST AVERAGE FINISH:	5.8—Buck Baker, 6.8—Lee Petty

23

Tar Heel Speedway, Randleman, North Carolina

It is north of Randleman on Route 220 about four miles past Branson Mill Road, where the Petty compound is located, and then east on Davis Mill Road. At the sharp left-hander, go straight onto to a gravel road and past a sign that reads "Frank Millikan 6223." Beyond Frank Millikan's house is a facility that has not heard the roar of Grand National engines in over 40 years. The rough asphalt of the entrance sprouts weeds from every seam and crack like the speedway itself. Atop the wall on the homestretch a fence protects nobody as the stands are gone without a trace. It is magnificent in its rundown state, a perfect example of the *Silent Speedways of the Carolinas*. A silent sentry stands towering in the brilliant azure sky with a menacing countenance that glares madly through wild shocks of dirty black hair from a pair of clear eyes sunken back into their white sockets. Its tentacles dare victims to come closer at the risk of permanent entanglement. Actually, it is a vine-covered light pole. The pit entrance is a sharp left-hander off turn four and is a small oval within the racing oval. A concrete wall runs from the crossover at the end of turn four all the way around to the middle of the backstretch. The track is littered with old farm implements, a dead truck, and the skeletal remains of some sort of game bird in quiet repose on a tire. The spectator gate in the grandstand fence is at the start/finish line, bound shut by years of vine growth, a portal opening only for those misty night visitors. There is slight banking in the first turn conducive to hard beating and banging with a hay shed squarely in the groove. The concrete wall is in the side of a hill of fertile Guilford County. The hay shed and another structure at the head of the

Staring down like a space alien, a vine-choked light pole creates an eerie image.

Old farm implements, trucks, and weeds reign over the homestretch where the checkers flew three times during the 1963 Grand National season.

weed-choked backstretch bracket turn two. Farm implements are scattered down the backstretch and after another infield crossover, the retaining wall changes to wood. At its newly built best, it is doubtful this fence could hold a roaring Grand National stocker thundering along at nearly a hundred miles an hour. Into turn three, sections of angled metal drape over the wooden railing that might slow a racecar down a little. If not, vaulting or plowing through means a steep drop of 20 or 30 feet to lush pasture, livestock, and a sure ambulance ride. The weeds have almost won the war against the asphalt on this end. Sweeping off turn four, back past the silent sentry on the homestretch, and a tour of the quarter-mile at Frank's house is complete. There were some scenes filmed here in that great 1974 Hollywood epic 43–*The Petty Story*, which starred The King as The King and recently departed Darren McGavin as Lee Petty. It is a fact that three times during the 1963 Grand National season, it hosted 200-lap battles that counted as much as the Daytona 500 in the points race. Here then are the stories of the Tar Heel Trilogy.

It was November 22, 1962, and there was good news as President Kennedy announced Cuba's missile bases had been dismantled and the naval blockade lifted. Richard Nixon said that we would not have him to kick around anymore and four mop-tops in Liverpool sat down together for the first time to record. A couple of miles as the crow flies north of Petty Engineering, the Turkey Day 200 roosted on the tight little quarter-mile asphalt oval. Of course there was a catch ... a Petty Mayflower gets to win the race, but which one of the trio would it be? Nearly 4,000 fans stuffed their way in and delayed their feasts, braving the frigid air under overcast skies to watch a plump field of two dozen drivers dish it out for 200 laps, 50 miles, for $575. That is not much bread at any rate.

Glen Wood, running one of his last races, took the 12th of his 14 career poles, shar-

23. Tar Heel Speedway

Turn Two is bracketed by a hay barn and storage shed.

ing the front row with Paschal in a '62 Petty Plymouth. Other souped-up stars on hand driving Spartanburg Iron Indians were defending champion Weatherly in Moore's 8 and Pearson in Cotton's 6. Also at the table were Jarrett in the Burton-Robinson '62 Chevy 11, Irwin in a '62 Ford 44, and another pair of '62 Mayflowers for the Petty Boys, Richard and Maurice. When the green napkin waved, the flock flew off and Wood gobbled up the laps as the competition wilted. Jarrett was excused first after six laps with handling trouble, finishing 24th and last, while Larry Thomas failed to finish the first course with a bum transmission, nabbing 23rd. Charlotte's John Hoffman completed a 51-lap career for 22nd and Spencer retired Floyd Powell's '62 Chevy 18th. Then on lap 173, with a chokehold on the lead, Wood had a flat and chose not to ask for seconds, ending his day in 15th. By the time he would have received new rubber, he would have been too far behind. That moved Petty Plymouth pilot Paschal to the head of the table just before his boss' tranny cooked and Richard settled for 11th. Paschal led the final 27 bites and rolled on the gravy train to victory by basting the competition by two laps. There was no beef as the leftovers went to Weatherly, who took seconds, Tommy Irwin thirds, Pearson fourths, and Maurice a rare fifth. Others getting their just desserts were Crawfish *Etouffe* Crider sixth while Bluff City, TN's Sherman Utsman salted away a four-year, 21-race career with seventh after running the first three races at Birmingham, Tampa, and here. Pardue was eighth and Sgt. George Green peppered an eight-year career of 116 starts, following the same path to retirement as Utsman, entering the first three events and parking after a ninth here. Tenth was Wendell, Arlington, VA's Jack "Venison" Deniston polished off a two-race career 12th, and Ray Hughes ran the last

Between the Third and Fourth turns, weeds own every crack in the racing surface.

of seven over two years, going home to Asheboro 13th. Columbia's Sonny Fogle launched an eight-race career 17th and Herman "The Turtle Soup" Beam disappointed no one by feathering it around the inside in his '60 Ford for 21st, the last car running, only 89 laps behind. The whole blessed affair took 63 minutes. Everybody must have been in a hurry to get home and feast. And for Jim Paschal ... *well done!*

The planet was mostly happy around May 1963. Except for a race riot in Birmingham, "Puff the Magic Dragon" was high on the charts, Koufax was fanning 'em and Mantle was launching 'em. Speaking of launches, Telstar II went up, as did Gordo Cooper, the last man to go into space alone ending the Mercury program. *The Dick Van Dyke Show* won an Emmy and Bruno Sammartino became wrestling champion. On the fifth, race 22 of the '63 campaign was held at Tar Heel and Richard Petty, being the clever guy that he is, swapped cars with Paschal for this one, not to be fooled twice in his own sandbox. There were only 15 entries and the top two were the same as before. It was déjà vu all over again as Jim Paschal decided to lay back and watch Jarrett pace the field for the opening 130 laps until he had a flat a la Glen Wood in the Turkey Day 200 six months earlier. Paschal inherited the lead according to plan as Ned lost a mile getting fresh rubber. High Point's Paschal cruised away, taking 43 to his second win in a row at Tar Heel and sixth straight on the season for a Petty Plymouth. Weatherly was second again, this time in Cliff Stewart's Pontiac 2, because Bud often declined to go to the lesser events. Therefore, for only $570 to win, Weatherly's main ride stayed parked. However, as the defending champion, Joe got $675 for second, $105 more than Paschal. Jarrett improved on his last place last time with third this trip. Pardue was fourth, Larry Thomas fifth, Spencer seventh, Wendell eighth, Massey ninth driving for old-timer Hubert Westmoreland, and Crawfish tenth. Joe Jones ended a three-year, 12-race career

23. Tar Heel Speedway

Off Turn Four is the track entrance on the right and the pit area on the left.

with 11th, Herman Beam did much better this time 12th, and Richard's brilliant car switch backfired as he finished the last man running 13th, 29 laps behind after a fuel pump was replaced. Buck brought his two red 1962 Chryslers, copping next-to-last and last for himself and Soapy, the only guys that did not beat Richard. As for Paschal's strategy in winning the two races at Tar Heel Speedway is concerned, he took the advice in Little Peggy March's number-one hit "I Will Follow Him" by running second until the leader's tires failed, allowing him to take both victories. Four thousand watched the 62-minute sprint.

They saved the best race at Tar Heel for the third and last appearance for 1963 and history. October 5th will be best remembered as the Saturday the Dodgers completed their sweep of the Yankees in the 60th World Series. However, nineteen teams showed up in Randleman and a two-man war broke out. The field was star-studded as Fearless Fred Lorenzen parked his pearl-colored Galaxie 28 on the pole with archrival and hometown favorite Richard Petty to his right. Weatherly had Bud's Mercury third beside Jarrett's Bondy Long Ford in row two, with Pearson's Dodge 5 and Welborn's Petty Plymouth 42 behind them. Sprinkled on back were race winners Paschal seventh, Dieringer ninth, Pardue 11th, Scott 12th, Buck 14th, and Daytona 500 champ Lund 18th. A line-up worthy of a bigger venue and more than a $550 first prize rumbled under green for 200 laps on a cool fall afternoon. Lorenzen scooted away to a solid lead as fighting broke out just behind. Jarrett and Pearson went into the first turn on the first lap and the inside lane moved up. David got inside Ned and applied the chrome horn. In 1963, cars really had chrome. So David put Ned in the

Thirty-eight lined up in perfect formation over in Turns One and Two.

concrete and it took Jarrett's crew several laps to get his Ford race-worthy. This was also the 51st race of a 55-event season and chances are nerves and patience were in short supply all through the field. It took about 90 laps or so, then "Gentleman Ned" was a gentle man no more. He drew a bead on the Fox (he was not Silver yet) and returned the favor in spades. On lap 107, Pearson was neutralized as he chased the fleet Freddy, and Cotton's demolished Dodge was done for 14th. A war of words ensued afterwards, but it was no big deal. "Gentleman Ned" was a misnomer anyway as the drivers and some fans knew what the press did not write. Lund dropped out for 17th and two-time Tar Heel winner Paschal, now driving for Cliff Stewart, had tranny trouble for 16th. Finally giving his family and friends something to shout about, Petty slammed past Lorenzen on lap 160 and beat, you guessed it, Weatherly to the checkers by just a few ticks. Welborn was third, Dieringer fourth, and Lorenzen fifth, although he lost the rear end and parked with six to go. Baker finished sixth, Massey seventh, a battered but game Jarrett ninth, and youngster J.D. McDuffie tenth. Others were Pardue 12th, Scott 13th, Crawfish 15th, Thomas 18th, and Tyner 19th and last. Lorenzen had made a rarer-than-rare very short track appearance during that historic season when he became the first Grand National driver to win over $100,000. Of course, the $275 he won here really did not help much. Fred's rear end ills and Petty's "It's my yard!" rule finally took over and Richard won a race there. Petty Engineering won all three, but Freddy must have lost a bet to have even raced there in the first place.

Three races, 600 laps, 150 miles, and $1,725 paid out to the winners. Tar Heel Speedway was all done in one season. But when darkness blankets the rolling hills and meadows north of Level Cross, that monster-like light standard comes to life, beaming down so Weatherly, Scott, Pardue, Lund, Thomas, Dierenger, and old Buck can strap in and bang away.

With the holiday race and the intimate crowds, it is the place to race after hours on Thanksgiving.

Track History by the Numbers

RACES:	3—All in 1963 season
YEARS OF RACES:	1962, 1963 (2)
WINNERS:	Jim Paschal (2), Richard Petty
MOST POLES:	1—Glen Wood, Ned Jarrett, Fred Lorenzen
RACE RECORD:	48.605 mph—Jim Paschal, 1962 Plymouth (5/5/63)
QUALIFYING RECORD:	51.933 mph—Glen Wood, 1962 Ford (11/22/62)
WINS BY MAKE:	Plymouth (3)
MOST STARTS:	3—Crider, Jarrett, Pardue, Paschal, R. Petty, Scott, L. Thomas, Weatherly
MOST LAPS LED:	173—Glen Wood
MOST TOP FIVES:	3—Joe Weatherly
BEST AVERAGE START:	3rd—Ned Jarrett, Richard Petty
BEST AVERAGE FINISH:	2nd—Joe Weatherly

24

Tri-City Speedway, High Point, North Carolina

This is another of the *Silent Speedways of the Carolinas* of which there is nothing left to find. Tri-City Speedway was northeast of High Point, located off the intersection of Johnson Street and Old Skeet Club Road behind Immaculate Heart of Mary Catholic Church. The entrance was off Old Skeet Club Road and beside the subdivision under construction.

Paths in the woods where everyone said Tri-City Speedway used to be yielded no solid clues in two visits.

A wire fence, a very swampy terrain, thick underbrush, and briars make for a rabbit's paradise, but very hard to explore. There is an old fence, about a dozen golf balls, a pond, but no topography, or light poles, or anything positively indicating a speedway was ever there. Trails are cut in the woods all over and each of them leads to nothing. However, there are stories to tell about two races in the fifties and one extremely wacky happening.

On Friday, June 26, 1953, they ran the first of two Grand Nationals at this half-mile dirt oval. It would be two seasons before they came back. The inaugural 100-mile challenge saw 23 stockers take the green with Herb Thomas starting first, and he was still there an hour and 43 minutes later when the checkered flag fell over the chrome hood ornament of his Smokey Yunick FABULOUS Hudson Hornet. Indy vet Dick Rathmann was runner-up in his familiar Walt Chapman Hudson 120. Dick was in the midst of six races with finishes of second, second, first, this second, second, and oddly enough, a second. Eubanks took third, Buck fourth, and Petty rounded out the top five. Further back came Paschal sixth, Slick Smith seventh, Lewellen eighth, Martinsville driver Buck Smith in his first of five career starts ninth, and Andy Winfree tenth. Leaksville, NC's Carl Burris in his first of ten career races was 11th, and Ermon Rush's first of four starts spanning seven years was 12th. This event saw the Flock Brothers lay a collective egg with Tim next-to-last and Fonty last. The big excitement of the day took place when Petty pitted for service and got more than he bargained for. As his 15-year-old kid Richard jumped up on the hood to clean the windshield, Lee charged back on the track with the eager crewman *still attached!* Lee got the black flag and pitted again to have the "riding mechanic" removed. He *probably* would not have tried to go the distance with Richard on the hood, so the black flag was *probably* not necessary. It was not an inspired race. Team owner and occasional driver Frank Arford became the second Grand National fatality the previous Sunday at oily Langhorne.

Two weeks after the 1954 season ended, the Grand National circus got off to a frigid start for 1955 here for their final visit. Sunday, November 7, 1954, found 21 drivers attempt to break the ice and get another yawner for their efforts. Herb Thomas took the pole in Smokey's Hornet 92 with Rathmann's Blue Crown Spark Plug Hudson outside. Behind them were Petty in a Chrysler and Gober Sosebee in the famous black Cherokee Garage Olds 51 with the big Native American heads adorning its sides. Row three contained Buck Baker in an Olds flanked by Junior Johnson in Paul Whiteman's Cadillac 7. Spots seven through ten were Elton Hildreth's Nash, Bud Harless' Hudson, Joe Eubanks in Bud Moore's Hudson, and Donald Thomas in another Yunick Hudson. Rathmann led six laps until Petty snatched it away for the final 194. Lee had the only Chrysler, but more were on the way. In race four of this landmark season, the Kiekhaefer invasion began and did not stop for nearly two years.

Another invasion was beaten back and died at High Point that nippy Sunday: the glamorous team owned by Paul Whiteman. Most renowned as "The King of Jazz," Whiteman was no stranger to the big time. In the 1920s, he had the most popular band in America. Paul Whiteman commissioned and introduced George Gershwin's "Rhapsody in Blue" in 1924, Whiteman's signature song. Members of his band were Tommy Dorsey and Jack Teagarden on trombones, Red Nichols and Bix Biederbecke blowing cornets, and the Rhythm Boys with Al Rinker, Harry Barris, and the heartthrob of the group, a crooner named Harry Lillis Crosby, later known as Bing. Whiteman gave Hoagy Carmichael his break by first recording his songs, such as "Georgia on My Mind," "Up the Lazy River," and "Stardust." Paul had an eye for talent with drivers, too, choosing Al Keller, Gwyn Staley, and Junior Johnson to push his buttons. Paul chose his racecars with equal panache, fielding Jaguars and Cadillacs! He ran mostly in one season, a handful of races in 1954 and High Point to open '55, but what a trip it was. In Paul's first outing on June 13, 1954, open-wheeler Al Keller, "The Dirty Indian" as the Indianapolis crowd knew him, beat Eubanks, giving the Whiteman Team their only Grand National win. But they were one for one! It happened in NASCAR's first road race, which took place at the Linden Airport in New Jersey, and was the first and only Grand National victory by a sports car, a Jaguar! The 1954 campaign continued as Staley in the Caddy survived for seventh in Whiteman's next race, the prestigious Southern 500. Langhorne was their third start and a long repair stop made Junior Johnson drive like a moonshiner to place 15th. In the Mid-South 250 on the killer mile and a half high-banked dirt in Lehi, AR, Junior put the Coupe de Ville on the pole only to blow it up in ten laps for 51st. A bad day followed for Johnson and Whiteman at Martinsville, hardly suited for a Cadillac, netting 33rd. The season-ender at North Wilkesboro with Staley aboard was not much better with a 31st. When the 1955 season started at High Point, Whiteman coaxed Johnson away from his daddy's still long enough to pilot the Cadillac one final time to a dismal 17th. That was it for the seven-race Whiteman Era, but everyone knew he had been there. Truth be told, it was actually a feather in Bill France's hat to have someone of

Paul Whiteman's international entertainment-world stature race at all in his fledgling series. "The King of Jazz" Paul Whiteman stayed around as an ambassador for NASCAR well into the 1960s.

This track has most assuredly made it all the way back to nature because no trace of it could be found by speedway archeology. However, this one has a history beyond the two Grand National races described here. Even the great pre–World War II legend Lloyd Seay of Dawsonville, GA, stopped by to win on August 31, 1941, and then won the next day in the big Labor Day race at Lakewood in Atlanta. Unfortunately, the next day, his cousin Woodrow Anderson started a fight with Lloyd over a sugar debt for the still and put a bullet right through the 21-year-old's pump. Speaking of hearts, if you are in the area behind the Immaculate Heart of Mary Catholic Church northeast of High Point in the wee hours, chances are that faint rumble you hear is likely to be a Hudson, Cadillac, or maybe even Lloyd Seay. Back he comes to join in on the fun he did not live long enough enjoy the first time around. For sure, "The King of Jazz" Paul Whiteman and his Orchestra are on hand with Bing and the Rhythm Boys crooning the National Anthem.

Track History by the Numbers

RACES:	2
YEARS OF RACES:	1953, 1955
WINNERS:	Herb Thomas, Lee Petty
MOST POLES:	2—Herb Thomas
RACE RECORD:	62.882—Lee Petty, 1954 Chrysler (11/7/54)
QUALIFYING RECORD:	71.942—Herb Thomas, 1954 Hudson (11/7/54)
WINS BY MAKE:	Hudson, Chrysler
MOST STARTS:	2—Tied by 12 drivers
MOST LAPS LED:	193—Lee Petty
MOST TOP FIVES:	2—Buck Baker, Lee Petty, Herb Thomas
BEST AVERAGE START:	1st—Herb Thomas
BEST AVERAGE FINISH:	2nd—Herb Thomas

25
McCormick Field, Asheville, North Carolina

Finding this member of *Silent Speedways of the Carolinas* is the same as finding the home of the Asheville Tourists Baseball Club and is a breeze. Take U.S. 25 north from I-40 and it is about a mile on the right at McCormick Place. Nothing looks like a racetrack, but it is a beautiful stadium with a rich hardball history and a Grand National tale easily forgotten. Down the left field line there is a mural painted on the front of the clubhouse facing the outfield that depicts five baseball players in various action poses under which it states "Historic McCormick Field." Historic as in the Tourists playing and defeating Ty Cobb's

The beautiful home of the Asheville Tourists had the spotlight for a Grand National race on July 12, 1958.

Detroit Tigers in a 1920s exhibition game. But behind the clubhouse towers the ghostly relic immediately recognizable as part of the long-gone past. It is the massive, cinder block grandstand built into the hillside a la Occoneechee. It is gorgeous in its decrepit, overgrown state. A treacherous set of iron stairs that appears to be from some ghost ship rises 13 steps to the landing at the base of the stands about six feet above field level. The stands have an ever so slight curve inward, stopping abruptly where the new grandstand starts. The ancient concrete seats are almost totally filled in with eroded dirt and are grass-covered from the curved end toward home plate to the other end at the left field wall. Some, but not all, of the brush and trees popping out of the stands were recently chopped, mowed, and removed. The 13 steps actually lead to where the pit area was, with the racing surface beyond that in the current outfield. Over behind the right field baseball fence is the old speedway retaining wall, which still has advertisements painted on it. Near the right field foul pole where it is seen easily, the wall ends cleanly, is kept freshly painted bright blue, standing about three feet high and running for as far one can see behind the curving hardball fence. It is backed up by a substantial piece of Buncombe County as the wall is literally at the base of another hillside every bit as imposing as the one supporting the ghostly stands across the way. In fact, they built the ballpark into the sides of a big, crater-like bowl formed by the surrounding hills. Large beams bolted to the tall wooden utility poles backing and holding up the hardball wall stretch across to the hillside where the other ends are buried about eight feet away. Neither the hardball nor the speedway walls are likely to budge. The race wall runs all the way from the right field foul line to right center, where it ends as if the rest had been chewed off and left as ragged as the opposite end is clean. It has writing painted on it, but it's very hard to see only inches from the ball wall. Although remodeled since 1958, the dugouts, one of them anyway, played an interesting role in McCormick's one and only Grand National. It is the only race to report from this most unusual of all *Silent Speedways of the Carolinas*.

Thirteen rusty steps up to the old grandstand look as if they came from a ghost ship.

Is it a silent speedway if it was located inside a baseball park that is still very much alive? *Of course!* On a sultry Friday night, July 12, 1958, that is where they played, uh, raced. The Grand National hotdogs ran 150 rotations around the playing field in the main event, a grand total of 37.5 miles. It was tied for the shortest race in Grand National history, a record that fell twice within the next week, bottoming out with a 25-mile marathon, actually a little shorter than a marathon, in Buffalo, NY, on July 19th, won by Jim Reed. Although only 15 cars popped up, there were some pretty big hitters there. Among those on deck were league-leading

Recently cleared of foliage, the grandstand runs the length of the left field foul line.

Lee Petty, but Jim Paschal led off from the pole. Heavy-hitters Junior Johnson and Tiny Lund warmed up, as did rookie sensation Shorty Rollins. Exhibition race winners Barney Shore and Whitey Norman had to contend with the Murderer's Row out of Spartanburg of Buck Baker, Jack Smith, Cotton Owens, and Rex White. Rex was only 5'2" tall and played short, of course. You cannot throw out Asheville's own homer Banjo Matthews and the very popular mascot, Herman "The Turtle" Beam. Add a couple of diamonds in the rough like Billy Rafter and R.L. Combs and you have cleaned up the whole roster. This race needed a Fireball in the lineup for sure, but he was riding the pines in Florida. Every inning was close, but Paschal covered all the bases by shutting out the field, leading all the way in a bang-bang finish with Owens, who stole second. Rex was safe at third and Petty, who was bunted into the dugout by Cotton in the prelim, had to be dug out of the dugout in order to finish fourth. Jack Smith bagged fifth, Johnson caught sixth, and Baker wound up seventh. Crowd favorite Matthews got a hit against the wall and watched the last 96 laps from the bleachers. Tiny had a foul race and beat only Banjo and the Turtle, who finished in the cellar. Maybe it was an error to stage a big-league race in a minor league ballpark because another silent speedway, Asheville-Weaverville Speedway, had a hit when they staged a Cracker Jack event up the line only two Sundays earlier.

So if you see something really wacky on the base paths watching the Asheville Tourists play some hot July night, maybe Lee slid into the dugout again. Maybe Fireball showed up and decided to take the mound after all. Or better yet, maybe Tigers Ty Cobb and Heinie

In right field, the speedway wall was cut off with the ball wall about two feet in front. Huge poles support the ball wall with horizontal braces buried into the mountainside.

Manusch are gliding around left and center as a grand congress of ghosts holds sway at historic McCormick Field.

Track History by the Numbers

RACES:	1 (7/12/58)
YEARS OF RACES:	1958
WINNERS:	Jim Paschal
MOST POLES:	Jim Paschal
RACE RECORD:	46.440 mph—Jim Paschal, 1957 Chevrolet
QUALIFYING RECORD:	50.336 mph—Jim Paschal, 1957 Chevrolet
WINS BY MAKE:	Chevrolet
MOST STARTS:	Tied by 15 drivers
MOST LAPS LED:	150—Jim Paschal
MOST TOP FIVES:	Paschal, Owens, White, L. Petty, J. Smith
BEST AVERAGE START:	1st—Jim Paschal
BEST AVERAGE FINISH:	1st—Jim Paschal

26

Asheville-Weaverville Speedway, Weaverville, North Carolina

Kids scream and run at this old ghost! Not from some underworld horror, but North Buncombe High School sits squarely on top of where the third most prolific of the *Silent Speedways of the Carolinas* lived. Between July 29, 1951, and August 24, 1969, the Grand National circuit ran through the picturesque setting of the Asheville-Weaverville Speedway 34 times. First on dirt, then on the black top, some wacky happenings took place, lots of great racing history was written, and nary a trace remains. There is a track there all right, but instead of Flocks and Pettys running hurtling machines around it for Grand National glory, there are teenage boys and girls running hurdles around it for the glory of the NBHS

The third most prolific of the *Silent Speedways of the Carolinas* is beneath the campus of North Buncombe High School.

Blackhawks. North up Highway 19, the Old Mars Hill Highway, north past Weaverville, left at Clark's Chapel Road, wind up and down, left and right, beyond two stone columns marking Gene Sluder's rock house, twist up, then down and around to the right, and you come to the entrance to the sports fields at North Buncombe High. If there is any physical evidence remaining, it is down the hill between Gene Sluder's house and the running track where the first turn was. However, a great legacy of hard-nosed stock car racing on dirt and asphalt exists and it went like this...

On Sunday, July 29, 1951, a solid field of 30 stockers lined up for the first in a long run of big-league races at the scenic oval. After Billy Carden time trialed the Red Devil Olds 14 on the pole, he gave way to the late-arriving Fonty Flock, who was probably held up deciding which Bermuda shorts to wear. Flock then took the green and bested an outstanding field to notch his fifth career win, second only to Curtis Turner's eight. Runner-up went to Gober Sosebee, third to Herb Thomas, fourth was Frank "The Rebel" Mundy in a Studebaker, and Speedy Thompson brought another Studebaker Commander home fifth. Others were Billy Myers eighth, Bob Flock in the Gray Ghost Olds tenth, Tim Flock in The Black Phantom Olds 11th, Jack Smith 13th, Paschal 15th, Bobby Myers 16th, and Joe Eubanks 19th. Lee Petty, Carden, and Marshall Teague fell out early. Fonty, red-hot on the season, pocketed $1,000 for the win. He went on to lead the season with eight wins and finish right behind Thomas in the points chase, the closest Fonty ever got to the crown, except when little brother Tim let him hold one of his.

August 15, 1952, was a muggy Sunday, but *the race that day was arguably the toughest to achieve of an absolutely incredible three-link chain.* A field of 19 arrived for 200 laps on the dirty half-mile and Herb Thomas captured the pole in Smokey's Hudson. Eubanks put a Hornet outside and there were three Flocks, Baker, Rathmann, and another Thomas, to name those entered. A sweaty, gritty hour and 45 minutes later, elder brother Bob Flock and a Hudson carrying his familiar number 7 sat in Victory Lane with a two-lap win over brother Tim. Herb was third, Gene Comstock fourth, Herschel Buchanan hustled a Nash Ambassador fifth, Buck was tenth, Fonty 12th, Eubanks 14th, and Rathmann 15th.

What is so incredible? Bob Flock was beat up, having had a rash of serious crashes over the previous few years that cut his driving down to infrequent at best. In the embryonic days before NASCAR, it was the N.C.S.C.C., or the National Championship Stock Car Circuit. Good name, great drivers, terrific racing! Bob Flock was said to be the best of the Flocks. However, the temper and driving style that made Junior Johnson look like a Miami Beach snowbird kept Bob on the sheets a lot. In October of 1947, Bob, Fonty, and Ed Samples, the '46 Champ, were virtually tied for the N.C.S.C.C. points lead when they came to the Piedmont Interstate Fairgrounds in Spartanburg. Bob drove the powerful Raymond Parks Ford and crashed so violently that he broke all the bones he had, especially those in his back. He recovered to get in enough seat time to win the pole for the very first Strictly Stock Car race in Charlotte on June 19, 1949. He was even getting stronger when he won Strictly Stock Car race number three at Occoneechee Speedway in Hillsborough and the inaugural season curtain dropper, race eight, at North Wilkesboro. Bob was third in the first point championship and tied Champ Red Byron for wins with two. The season of 1950 saw no wins and 20th in points in four starts. Then in the season finale of 1951 at Mobile, Bob Flock destroyed the Gray Ghost and limped out of the speedway after a cursory medical exam. He crossed the Florida line and when the pain got unbearable, he had himself admitted to a Pensacola hospital where he was found to be suffering from multiple fractured ribs *and a broken neck!* Bob Flock was done, most thought. In 1952, he returned for the Asheville-Weaverville race and won it. Remarkable, right? Here is the amazing part *never* to be equaled. Two nights earlier on Friday in Rochester, NY, Brother Tim won in Ted Chester's Hudson 91. Bob won on Sunday. And in the next race on Labor Day, September 1st, Brother Fonty donned those famous "Bermooda" shorts and dominated the Southern 500 to win from the pole. Three straight races saw three different brothers in Victory Lane. Tim's career was peaking, as was Fonty's. But old Bob was barely able to get around, and this was his third and final Grand National win; two checkers in 1949 and one in '52. In addition, speaking of Fonty's Southern 500 win, Bob was there driving team Blackburn's Garage Hudson 7 to Tim's 91. Bob started a distant 55th, and finished 29th, still running at the finish, 62 laps behind. Bob never strapped in to run a Grand National again and Tim crashed out for 33rd. The Flock Brothers never finished one-two-three in a Grand National race. Nevertheless, winning three in a row is even more remarkable, made so by Bob's shaky condition. Can anyone imagine another three-sibling combination winning three big-league races in a row, ever? The Bodines? The Wallaces? The Greens never even had a chance. The brothers, or sisters, that could pull it off are not even on the radar screen yet. Asheville-Weaverville 1952 was the middle link in the Flock Feat that is never to be equaled. The Flock Brothers are all dead now. Did the magnitude of this accomplishment ever cross their minds? Has anybody ever thought of it? It is unreachable! As are they, except when they race and win on the *Silent Speedways of the Carolinas*.

Sunday, August 16, 1953, was a typical summer day with a chance of showers when 19 stockers took the green for 100 miles on the mountain dirt. Curtis Turner put his Eanes Motor Co. '51 Olds on the pole, but promptly crashed and for the third straight year, a Flock, Fonty again, scooted home first over Herb Thomas, Blair, Baker, and Lewellen. On back were Petty seventh, Tim tenth, Paschal 13th, Rathmann 14th, Donald Thomas 15th, and Turner 18th. Fonty's second win netted him a grand in Frank Christian's Hudson 14.

The coveted July 4th date went to Asheville-Weaverville from Spartanburg in 1954, but Spartanburg's promoter extraordinaire Joe Littlejohn, who held a 100-miler the night before, made history. By some hook or crook, the former driver had a passenger seat added to Herb Thomas' Smokey Yunick–built Fabulous Hudson Hornet 92 and rode shotgun as Herb broke the track record for the pole. How and why this happened is a mystery. Then Herb won his third in a row for '54, beating Lewellen for the second straight race, with Rathmann third, Petty fourth, and Sosebee fifth. Others were Eubanks sixth, Paschal tenth, McGriff 13th, Baker 14th, and Speedy Thompson 18th. In the first non–Flock win here, Herb pocketed $1,000 for a dusty day's work.

As if perturbed by Thomas' win in '54, the Flocks returned with a vengeance on July 10, 1955, armed with a pair of gleaming-white shiny-new Kiekhaefer Chrysler 300s, numbers 300 and 301. At the pinnacle of their dual ownership of the keys to the kingdom, Tim and Fonty finished one-two for the second time that week over Paschal third, Donald Thomas fourth, Eddie Skinner fifth, Staley sixth, Baker ninth, Lewellen tenth, Welborn 14th, Johnson 15th, Carden 16th, and Petty 18th and last. Tim's flag-to-flag win was worth $1,000. The next day, the first true rock and roll song became number one in America, and the Flocks did "Rock Around the Clock," making it look easy.

The factory wars raged as 29 took the green on July 1, 1956, when Commandant Kiekhaefer entered four big white Mopars, three Chryslers and a Dodge. As incredibly successful as they were, none of them were factors. Fireball nailed the pole in a De Paolo Ford and a star-studded field chased him. He led over three quarters of the race until a blowout ended his run. When the checkers fell, it was across the nose of another Mopar, that of Lee Petty, with the red and silver CU Later Alligator Mercury of Jim Paschal second, Eubanks' Ford third, Gwyn Staley fourth, and two Kiekhaefers fifth and sixth with Thomas and

Mundy. Johnny Allen was 12th, Carden 17th, Roberts 18th, Rex White 19th, Johnson 20th, Baker 21st, Billy Myers 22nd, Moody, 23rd, Thompson 26th, and Jack Smith 29th and last. A paltry $850 was Petty's take-home pay this scorching summer Sunday.

The 1957 season was the first in which Asheville-Weaverville got two races, and as an added twist, this was the last run here on dirt, as the track would be paved for the return visit. With the Flocks and Kiekhaefer gone, it was wide open for the Sunday, March 31st 100-miler when only 18 entries showed up. But they were quality teams as Pete De Paolo brought four factory Fords, Hugh Babb–Bud Moore had two Chevies, Bill Stroppe came with a pair of Mercurys, Petty had two Oldsmobiles, and Spook Crawford brought a lone Plymouth. Panch had a Ford on the pole, but fell out just past the quarter mark and his stablemate Roberts led until he blew around halfway. That gave it to Buck and Speedy to run one-two to the checkers with Paschal third. Fourth was independent Dick Beaty in a year-old Ford, fifth was Allen, Billy Myers was eighth, Petty tenth, Roberts 13th as the best finisher of De Paolo's Fords, Earnhardt in Petty's other Olds 14th, Goldsmith 15th, Panch 16th, and Moody 17th. It took just over an hour and a half for Buck to win the $850 first prize in front of about 6,000 fans.

The second visit was Sunday, September 8, 1957, and immensely more entertaining than the previous rout. There were two more entries, $150 more in the winner's purse, and the surface was black. Californian Bill Amick put his Ford on the pole and led the first nine laps before giving it up to Cotton for 130. Owens was looking like a winner when a tire popped on lap 141 and he stuffed the Pontiac into the fence for the day's only caution. Amick, Baker, and Petty swapped the lead until the laps ran out and Lee and his Olds were leading. Buck was about a second behind with Amick and Rex White all completing the 200 laps. Fifth was Smith, Beaty sixth, Panch seventh, Frankie Schnieder eighth, Allen ninth, Roberts tenth, hometowner Banjo Matthews 11th, Paschal 13th, George Parrish's Studebaker 15th, Owens 16th, Thompson came down to Earth after his Southern 500 win six days earlier for 18th, and Lewellen 19th. The race took less than 90 minutes.

June 29, 1958, was a sunny summer Sunday with a packed house of over 9,000 on hand to watch 25 battle. Rex White put Max Welborn's Chevy on the pole and fought it out with Owens' '57 Pontiac. The two shortest drivers on the circuit, with Tiger Tom not around, fought bumper to bumper and door to door early until Owens burned a bearing and Rex was home free. Buck was second a lap back, Thompson third, Paschal fourth, and Eddie Pagan fifth. Others were Petty sixth, Welborn seventh, Rollins ninth, Herman Beam tenth, Junior Johnson 12th, Owens 14th, and Smith 25th and last. Winner White won an embarrassing $800.

Seven weeks later on Sunday, August 17, 1958, the tour was back again with a whopping field of 38 set to go in a sweepstakes 250-miler as the blisteringly hot weather made a ragtop the racecar of choice. Surprise pole-sitter Jimmy Massey in the Brushy Mt. Motors Pontiac hardtop paced the star-studded field. Fireball was outside in a '57 Chevy convertible and was holding a big lead when he pitted on lap 370 and was helped from the scorching 22. Local boy to the rescue was Banjo Matthews, who drove the final 130 laps and brought Frank Strickland's Chevy to Victory Lane. It was the closest Matthews ever got to a win in Grand National racing himself. He beat convertible circuit champ Welborn by a lap with Petty third, Thompson fourth, Baker fifth, Jim Reed seventh, Weatherly eighth, Frank ninth, and Irwin in one of his first starts was tenth. On back came Lund 11th, Beam 14th, Lewellen 15th, Wood 24th, Massey 30th, Smith 31st, Carden 33rd, Owens 36th, and White 37th. An SRO crowd of over 10,000 saw Fireball and Banjo collect the $2,650 first prize in a lengthy three and three-quarter hours.

In 1959, Asheville-Weaverville got a generous three Grand National dates. The first came on Sunday, June 28th, two days after Ingemar Johansson pummeled Floyd Patterson for the heavyweight title. A slim field of 20 entered with Glen Wood on the pole. But for the second race in a row, Rex White captured the win, having taken the checkers the day before at Bowman-Gray Stadium. Lee Petty finished on the same lap with Johnson third, Roy "The Wild Injun" Tyner fourth, and Herman "The Turtle" Beam fifth. Owens was sixth, rookie Buddy Baker seventh, Welborn 11th, Wood 13th, Thompson 14th, Lund 16th, and G.C. Spencer 19th. Rex escaped with $900, a nifty $1,575 in 24 hours.

The second event of 1959 was another blockbuster 250-mile sweepstakes seven weeks later on a hot Sunday, August 16th. A gigantic field of 41 lined up, over twice as many as seven weeks earlier. Of course, the addition of the ragtops made it possible. White grabbed the pole and shot away at the start, but the track started breaking up under the heat and pounding. Car after car dropped out with suspension and axle problems. Nearly three and a half hours later, two-time convertible champion Bob Welborn romped by three laps over Lee Petty with Jack Smith third, Joe Lee Johnson fourth, and White fifth. Further back came Frank sixth, Owens seventh, Buck eighth, Johns ninth, Spencer 12th, Lund 14th, Jarrett 17th, Richard Petty 26th, Wood 28th, Pistone 34th, Matthews 35th, Thompson 37th, and Weatherly 40th. Welborn pocketed a hefty $3,200 for the scorching Sunday ride.

Another two moons passed and the boys were back for the third visit as autumn crept into the Blue Ridge. October 11, 1959, saw a solid 29 stockers on the grid with Inman's Tommy Irwin on the pole, but his T-Bird blew on lap 96 of 200. Lee Petty edged within one of Herb Thomas' 48 career victories, besting Wood, Smith, White, and son Richard. Others were Frank sixth, Joe Lee Johnson seventh, Jarrett eighth, Junior ninth, Tyner tenth, Owens 11th, Buck 12th, Thompson 13th, Lewellen 17th, Johns 21st, Lund 27th, Irwin 28th, and Welborn 29th and last. It took less than 80 minutes to run the 100-miler.

Sunday, April 24, 1960, and spring was bustin' out all over. Unfortunately, so was the asphalt at A-W. Twenty stockers pounded the pavement that afternoon as Jack Smith's Bud Moore Pontiac slipped by the front row teammates Junior Johnson and Glen Wood in Wood Brothers' Fords. As the track started coming apart, Smith's oil pan was punctured, and he was gone at lap 35, having led them all. A similar fate awaited Smith and his unlucky "Red Fox" Bonneville 47 in less than two months in the first World 600. Banjo took over, then Welborn, until the red flag flew. Crews tried to patch the holes by filling them with the asphalt that had come loose. Lee Petty promptly took the lead when the green waved, only to have the event called 104 laps later, 33 short of the scheduled distance. Joe Lee Johnson was second and stayed there despite his beef that he won. Jarrett was third, Welborn fourth, Spencer fifth, White seventh, Buck eighth, Richard Petty ninth, Matthews 13th, Pardue 14th, Junior Johnson 15th, Wood 16th, and Smith 17th. The 5,000 fans did not like the 33-lap shortchange, but did not cause a stink ... *this time.*

Sunday, March 5, 1961, was the seventh race of the season and held under a cold, sunless sky. A meager 15 entrants took the green and an even duller race took place. Duller unless you were a fan of the gold, white, and red Chevy 4 of Rex White and Louis Clements. The Spartanburg duo hammered the field from the pole, leading all 200 laps for White's third A-W victory since 1958. Rex out-dueled Cotton, who ran second, Jarrett third, Richard Petty fourth, and Zervakis fifth. Notables were Pardue sixth, the Turtle ninth, Johnsons Junior and Joe Lee 11th and 12th, Paschal 13th, Irwin 14th, and Crawfish 15th and last. A good crowd of 8,500 watched on an uncomfortable afternoon as Rex copped $900.

It should have been Friday the 13th instead of Sunday the 13th and was probably the ugliest spontaneous moment in NASCAR history. Not counting grisly deaths like Myers and Roberts, or a calculated incident like the Turner-Flock unionization attempt, the second race of 1961 at A-W was as bad as it gets. It started out as the Western North Carolina 500, 250 circuits of the half-mile asphalt with a history of breaking up. A huge nonsweepstakes field of 38 was gridded with stock car's Illustrated Man Jim Paschal on the pole in J.H. Petty's Pontiac. Junior Johnson started second, shocking Fred Harb was third, flanked by Jack Smith fourth. Big names were sprinkled throughout and Junior jumped out front as the track, for the third time since its paving, started breaking up. On lap 208, Dick Behling crashed and the caution bled to red. NASCAR announced that due to the terrible track conditions, 50 more laps would be run to pass the 250-lap halfway point and make it an official race. Repairs were made as best as possible and Johnson led those last 50 laps, too, beating Weatherly by three. Meanwhile, NASCAR officials slipped away like thieves before the fans could direct their anger towards them. Most of the 10,000-plus left, but hundreds of "fans" stayed around to protest the decision. They blocked the infield exit and sporadic fighting broke out. Police found themselves helpless until a mountain of a man from Spartanburg named Pop Eargle decided enough was too much. Pop was a giant. He and his boss, the tall and lanky Bud Moore, looked sort of like a king-size Laurel and Hardy. The standoff lasted awhile until some unfortunate rioter made his last mistake of the day by poking Pop in his ample belly with a two-by-four. The thug was relieved of the lumber and Mr. Eargle clobbered him with it. The infielder hostages were free and a major riot avoided, but not by the Buncombe County Sheriff's Department, not by the North Carolina Highway Patrol, and not by NASCAR. It was avoided by a giant with an ever-present cigar stub clenched in his teeth named Eugene "Pop" Eargle, who returns here nightly, twisting wrenches and keeping order.

Finishing behind Johnson and Weatherly were White third, Jarrett fourth, Zervakis fifth, Paschal sixth, Irwin seventh, Allen eighth, Smith ninth, Stacy tenth, Richard Petty 11th, Beam 13th, Buddy Baker 16th, Pardue 19th, Wendell 24th, Buck 28th, Fireball 31st, and Matthews 34th. It was an embarrassing incident for everyone except the competitors that risked their lives to perform for the "fans" that day. Still, the A-W promoter, staff, and NASCAR should have solved the problem of the track's delicate surface long before scheduling another event. All in all, this was a most forgettable day in racing history.

Trying to win back the fans, race two of 1962 was on Sunday, November 12, 1961. Just over 6,000 came, mostly getting in free with their stub from the last abbreviated race, to see a solid field of 27 compete on a cool autumn afternoon. Weatherly had the pole and led early until he gave way to White. Then Paschal led, as did Buck in a Chrysler, before Rex took it back and stormed home a winner over Baker, Weatherly, Smith, Jarrett, and Irwin, all of whom were in the lead lap. Petty was sixth, Paschal seventh, Beam 12th, Pardue 13th, Crider 14th, and Johnsons Junior and Joe Lee were 26th and 27th. The stands were not as full as the bad taste still in the public's mouths from the debacle three months earlier.

March 4, 1962, was a cold, nasty Sunday as 21 crews braved not only the weather, but the memory of the earlier hostilities. Spartanburg teams swept the first four starting spots with White on the pole, Irwin a surprising second, Weatherly third, and Smith fourth. White charged out front for 119 laps, but was hounded by Irwin, who took over on lap 120. After White retook the lead, he pounded the wall in the only caution. Irwin inherited the lead only to lose it again with a botched pit stop under caution. When the green fell, it was all Weatherly and he sailed home the winner in Moore's Pontiac by three laps over Paschal in second, Buddy Baker third, Maurice fourth, and Smith fifth. Further back came Earnhardt sixth, Irwin seventh, Richard eighth, the Turtle 11th, Scott 12th, Crawfish 14th, Jarrett 16th, Joe Lee 17th, White 18th, and Junior Johnson in a Baker Chrysler 21st and last. About 5,000 non-violent spectators saw Weatherly win $1,000.

The Fifth Annual Western North Carolina 250 ran on Sunday, August 12, 1962, under beautiful summer skies. The question was whether the track could handle 500 summertime laps. A field of 25 took the green, led by pole-sitter Jack Smith, who paced the field for 163 laps until tire troubles gave the lead to Paschal. Unchallenged in a Petty Plymouth, Jim led 337 circuits for his fourth win of the year at a race record of over 77 miles per hour. Weatherly was three back in second, White third, Jarrett fourth, and Smith fifth. On hand were Pardue sixth, Petty seventh, Crawfish and Turtle 11th and 13th, Scott 14th, out of retirement in Dick Getty's Chevy was Eddie Pagan taking 15th, Irwin 18th, Welborn 19th, and Bakers Buck and Buddy 23rd and 24th. Maybe this track still had not recovered from the fiasco a year ago because only a meager 6,000 fans attended. It is worth mentioning that this was Pagan's next to last race and his last on the *Silent Speedways of the Carolinas*. In 62 starts since his first in 1954, he captured six poles and four checkered flags, three in 1957. Pagan's wins were on the left coast and he was solid in the east. Probably his best-known feat was the spectacular crash in the 1958 Southern 500 when pole-winner Pagan plowed through 100 feet of first turn guardrail, turning it into twisted metal and splinters and leaving the grounds with a demolished Ford, a broken nose, and $240 in cash. He partnered with retired racer Dick Hutcherson to form Hutcherson-Pagan Enterprises in Charlotte. Eddie Pagan left the grounds again on his 66th birthday, August 1, 1984.

On Sunday, March 3, 1963, the A-W fans finally decided to make up and be nice. Over 10,000 jammed their way in, forcing a delay of the start. Junior Johnson had the famed Chevy 3 on the pole with a new track record of nearly 83 miles per hour. Outside row one in a shocker was Buck Baker in a year-old Chrysler. Even more shocking was that Buck kept that big red Chrysler at or near the front the entire 200 laps. He was not quite good enough to beat winner Richard Petty, but was good enough to outrun the fleet Johnson and Weatherly as the first four finished all 200 laps. Jarrett was fifth in the Turtle's car, sportsman ace Bobby Isaac sixth, Billy Wade in Cotton's Dodge seventh, Stick Elliott ninth, and Floyd Powell tenth. Others were Crawfish 11th, Scott 12th, Pearson in Cotton's other Dodge 18th, and Paschal 19th. The crowd was back, the race was good, and all was well in Weaverville. In a side note, word out of Spartanburg was that Tommy Irwin, badly hurt the day before while practicing there for the 100-miler, was going to be fine after some sheet time.

The Sixth Annual Western North Carolina 250 occurred Sunday, August 11, 1963, and surprises abounded. Nearly 15,000 flowed in despite rainy skies that washed out qualifying. They came to see the Golden Boy, Fred Lorenzen, make a rare short-track appearance. Sign-in set the 27-car field and Bud Moore was angered when told his car for point leader Weatherly would have to start mid-pack instead of first. Bud was there first to sign in, but no one was there to receive him and Joe was nowhere around, so Bud hauled back to Spartanburg. The cars lined up as they signed up with Jarrett first, Lorenzen second, Tommy Irwin all healed up third, and G.C. Spencer driving for Jack Smith fourth. Jarrett led early, and then Freddy and Richard swapped it until the Elmhurst Express took off for good, leading the final 276 laps. Petty was second, teammate Paschal third, and teammates Pearson and Wade fourth and fifth in Cotton's Dodges. Further back came Smith sixth, Buck seventh, Weatherly in a borrowed car eighth, Jarrett ninth, Buddy Baker tenth, Scott 11th, Yarborough 14th, Isaac 18th, and Tommy Irwin in his final Grand National race 19th. Irwin started his career here on August 17, 1958, with a tenth and ended right back here August 11, 1963. In between, Irwin left a mark on stock car racing as spectacular, competent, and hard-luck. G.C. Spencer finished 21st, Johnson 23rd, and Pardue 25th. It took three and a quarter hours for Lorenzen to continue his relentless march to the unthinkable $100,000 mark for one season. After this win, he was only $5,000 short.

A crisp, sunny Sunday greeted teams on February 28, 1965, and Ford's free-for-all continued without those pesky hemis around due to the Chrysler boycott. In fact, this was the day that Richard Petty crashed 43 Jr. in Georgia and the little boy died. At Weaverville, the crowd of nearly 7,000 settled back as Jarrett, Johnson, and Hutcherson duked it out for $1,150. G.C. and Cale made it interesting in year-old Fords and that was it for racing. The track did not break up and there was no near riot. There was a fire, though, shades of Wilson in 1959, only this time it was not the grandstand, but the grassy area outside the backstretch. As the big three (plus two) raced, firefighters and fans joined in to douse and pound out flames, creating a caution when Hutcherson led a lap. The green returned long enough for the stockers to energize the embers and ignite the conflagration all over again. Berry Brooks stuffed a burgundy '64 Pontiac into the wall for another caution, then Jarrett took off for the last quarter of the race. Hutch was second, Cale third, Spencer fourth, and Danny Byrd, who started last here as he did the day before, clawed his way to fifth, a four-race career best. Others were Lund tenth, Johnson 12th, Dieringer 16th, Wendell 17th, and Buddy Baker 21st and last.

The second visit of '65 was Sunday, August 8th, for another edition of the Western North Carolina 500, a punishing 250 miles around the asphalt oval. A field of 27 including Chryslers took the green with Petty on the pole and Jarrett alongside. Almost three and half hours later they were still one-two. In between, Jarrett, Johnson, and Pearson led and Johnson even crashed ... again. It was boring as Richard won by a mile. Third was Hutcherson, Buddy Baker fourth, Cale fifth, Buck sixth, Wendell eighth, Pearson 15th, Johnson 18th, Yarbrough 19th, and Dieringer 20th. It was a forgettable day for 7,500, epitomized by the fact that the most famous number in stock car racing did not adorn Petty's blue Plymouth as he won numberless.

The Fireball 300, not to be confused with the horrible Funicello-Avalon-Fabian celluloid atrocity *Fireball 500* released four days earlier, was held on Sunday, June 12, 1966. This time, all the good Fords were gone and it was a couple Mopars against independents and a gambler. Again, Petty had the pole with Pearson outside. But inside row two was a little red, black, and white Mercury Comet 16 ("The Vomit") of Bud Moore piloted by Darel Dieringer. Bud was gambling with a lightweight, short wheel-based, small-engined Mercury to run with the big hemis ... and it did. This day was all about the classics, Petty and Pearson. Call it Act I of their career rivalry because there would be a period for Pearson, after he left Holman-Moody in 1971 until he found the Wood Brothers in 1973, that some thought he was washed up. Later, the Petty-Pearson Wars left the dirt for national television and Act II. This Sunday, Richard led the most, occasionally giving way to David. Then Pearson took over on lap 183 and combined with Petty's bad luck, raced to a one-mile lead. With victory in sight, Pearson had a flat and he and Cotton rolled the dice that the white Dodge 6 could limp home a la Pearson's first win in the 1961 World 600. Petty drove like a man possessed as Pearson's lead melted like an ice cream in July. With a quarter of a half-mile lap to go, Richard passed David in turn four and came home a winner with the crowd of more than 6,000 going berserk. Who needs the Fords! NASCAR did, but this was a great race anyway. Paul Lewis was third in a Plymouth, old Buck's Olds was fourth, and Sears took fifth in a Ford. Others were Hylton sixth, Stick Elliott eighth, Elmo 11th, Wendell 12th, Lund 15th, Buddy Baker 23rd, Dieringer in the Comet went only 180 laps for 24th, and Jarrett driving Henley Gray's 97 was 26th. Petty got the $1,400, the hardware, and smooch.

The 1966 often-wacky Western North Carolina 500 was presented under the summer sun on Sunday afternoon, August 21, 1966. The packed house of nearly fifteen thousand was thrilled to see the newly unretired Junior Johnson back behind the dash of the yellow 26 Holly Farms Ford. Two weeks earlier, Lorenzen piloted Junior's famed "Banana Boat" into the third turn rail during the Dixie 500 at Atlanta in one of the most infamous instances of NASCAR playing favorites in history. They cleared Johnson's Ford and Yunick's Turner-driven Chevelle, both much closer to modifieds than stockers, to race while virtually disqualifying the Dodges of Owens for Pearson and Jon Thorne for LeeRoy Yarbrough, and the Henley Gray Ford for Jarrett. Eleven days later, another Johnson Ford was "semi-formally" driven by Curtis Turner sporting a coat and tie at Columbia. A full two weeks after these consecutive legendary races, the Ol' Moonrunner himself squeezed through the window to drive for the first time since Halloween 1965 at Rockingham, when Turner won. To the delight of the mountaineers, Johnson scorched his way to the pole and Dieringer put Bud's Comet outside. Spicing up the grid, Curtis Turner, Junior's recently released driver, put a privateer Chevelle 47 in the field third with Petty starting fourth in 42. At least Richard had a number this time, albeit the wrong one. The field of 30 was accented with characters taking the green and showing no signs of rust. Junior took charge leading 118 laps. An exchange of pit stops saw Dieringer, Petty, and Hutcherson lead, before Junior got it back. Then engine woes cost Johnson too much time for him to continue, so he rehired "The Old Reinstated Blond Blizzard," who blew his Chevelle in only a mile and half. Curtis parked the Ford about 100 laps after taking over. With Johnson's Ford gone, Petty led for about 100 laps until his kettle boiled over. With Hutcherson long since retired, none other than Double D, Darel Dieringer, made his laid-back style pay off and inherited a huge lead, only padding it over the final 158 laps to the checkers. Moore's Mercury finally came through after a close-call second at the Firecracker 400 in Daytona a month and a half earlier. A distant runner-up was Inman's G.C. Spencer eight laps back, with third to neighbor James Hylton, making it a happy and prosperous haul back to Spartanburg County for the win, place, and show men of the WNC 500. Sears was fourth, Hassler fifth, Wendell sixth, Bobby Allison eighth, non-factors Pearson 13th, Jarrett 15th, Petty 18th, Johnson 19th, two-time 1966 winner Langley 296 laps behind in 22nd, Hutch 25th, Buddy Baker 28th, and Curtis Turner 30th and last.

No longer deserving "The Vomit" moniker after becoming a confirmed winner, Bud and Darel's little 16 took on all the giants 15 days later on a blazing hot Labor Day at Darlington when it was the toughest race in America. There were no turn walls, much less soft ones. Just strips of elastic steel that when used properly could be an ally in negotiating the mile and a quarter. When rudely slapped, not massaged, that silver ribbon would treat an offensive suitor in kind, as it did Jack Smith and Eddie Pagan in '58, Mitch Cooper in '59, Johnny Allen in '60 and '62, Cale Yarborough in '65, and Earl Balmer in '66. When caressed with a fender, it would set you straight and propel you through the turn faster than if you had not touched it at all. The great ones like the Bakers, the Flocks, the Pettys, Thomas, Turner, Thompson, Roberts, Owens, Weatherly, Stacy, Lorenzen, Pearson, Yarbrough, Yarborough, White, and others knew how to treat this track. Today, Darlington is called "The Lady in Black," but back then, she was no lady at all. On September 5, 1966, under scorching South Carolina skies, Bud Moore was packing a loaded Dieringer, who made like Donavan's number-one song of the day, "Sunshine Superman." All the top stars were there and that little red, white, and Black Beauty beat all 43 of them.

March 5, 1967, was the date of the Fireball 300 on the following Sunday after the Daytona 500 won by Mario Andretti. Mario stayed away from A-W, as did most top cars, drivers, and fans. The race was not that bad as 22 teams competed. Front row starters Dieringer in Junior's Fairlane and Petty battled it out, joined up front by Bobby Allison in his famous Chevelle 2. In the end it was a romp for Richard, beating Darel by a mile, with Allison third, Pearson fourth, and Sears fifth. Others in the mostly starless field were Elmo eighth, Wendell tenth, Tyner 16th, Castles 18th, Daytona third-placer Hylton blew for 20th, and two veterans of that first race in 1949, Buck Baker and Jim Paschal, were top-seven starters and finished 21st and 22nd, next to last and last. Petty pocketed $1,800 for less than two hours of driving.

The 49-race grind concluded on cool Sunday, November 5, 1967, in the Western North Carolina 500. Lots of stars came out, but hardly anyone came to see. A generous estimate of 3,500 witnessed Petty crowned champ for the second time whether he raced or not. The race was electrifying as 30 stockers started, with 22 lead changes, ten cautions, crashes, and fender-banging stopping just short of fisticuffs. Bobby Allison was fastest in one of three Holman-Moody Fords entered. With Lorenzen managing the handpicked team, Bobby was coming off a Rockingham win a Sunday earlier in the team's first outing. When the green fell, Bobby jumped out front and stayed there for nearly the first quarter of the race. As Bobby A. ran away, Paschal retired, followed by front row starter Yarbrough in Junior's Ford. Wendell crashed, Dieringer blew Cotton's Dodge, and local sportsman ace Bosco Lowe parked Banjo's Fairlane. Hutcherson led in his first, and last, effort away from Bondy Long's 29s as they had split. The Iowan drove the Holman-Moody 66 that Grand Prix Champion Jimmy Clark drove to 30th at Rockingham. Pearson led for 90 as European road racer Don Schissler crashed, Cale stripped the gears in Moore's Comet, and Pistone had a pow-wow with the Wild Injun, wrecking both beyond return. The big three, Petty-Pearson-Allison, swapped the lead around furiously as competitors fell around them. Much of the passing was less than polite, but rudeness took over for the finish. Having shown for years that he was no pushover, Allison squared off with Petty in a classic display of take and don't give. With three miles left, Allison slammed his way past Richard and beat him to the checkers as Richard was tagging the Ford's back bumper all the way. Pearson was third, waiting for the leaders to take each other out. On pit road, Maurice's boys charged Freddy's guys in anger, yet a brawl never occurred. Petty's team lost the race, won a title, and must not have felt like fighting. Both were winners. Fourth in what was his final race was the Keokuk Comet Dick Hutcherson. Hassler blew and took fifth with Sears sixth, seventh 104 laps behind was Max Ledbetter, Pistone was tenth, Tyner 11th, Yarborough 12th, Dieringer 23rd, Scott 25th, Yarbrough 27th, and Paschal 27th. Why the fans stayed away in such staggering numbers is a mystery. They missed an outstanding race that may go down as the best race nobody saw.

Dick Hutcherson was a great driver. He strolled in early in 1964 on March 28th at Greenville-Pickens Speedway and stunned everyone, winning the pole. Dick ran more short tracks, then attacked the full schedule in 1965. He broke records, won nine races, and finished second to Jarrett in the standings. In 1966, the Fords were out most of the season, but he still won thrice in 14 starts for 28th in the rankings. In 1967, Hutcherson ran 33 of 49, finished third in the chase winning twice, one of them the Dixie 500, which was his lone major victory. When the 1967 season ended at Asheville-Weaverville, so did a big-league career that resembled his comet nickname. He streaked briefly across the Grand National sky, only running two full seasons. Dick has the second highest average finish of those with over 100 starts. With 103, Hutcherson averaged finishing 8.67 behind only Lee Petty. Dick had 14 Grand National career wins and finished in the top three in an amazing 50 of those 103 races. Hutch was not only a great driver, but also a great guy about whom you never heard anything bad. With ex-driver Eddie Pagan, they started Hutcherson-Pagan Enterprises in 1971, building top-notch racers. On November 6, 2005, driving through Columbia on his way from Florida to his home in Elk Creek, VA, Dick passed away of a heart attack. The Comet burned out at 73.

May 5, 1968, was a forgettable Sunday at A-W unless you were David Pearson. The Fireball 300 had maybe a half dozen drivers with a chance to win, but Pearson in his blue and gold Holman-Moody Ford took the pole and led all except the 87th lap to crush the field of 28, breezing to victory. Isaac was second, Petty third, Hylton fourth, and Elmo fifth. Others were Pete Hamilton 12th, Buddy Baker 18th, Pistone 20th, Wendell 23rd, Buck 24th, and Spencer 27th. Less than 8,000 saw the two-hour yawner.

The 11th Western North Carolina 500 ran on sticky Sunday, August 18, 1968. Around 11,000 sweltered as they watched the Not Yet Silver Fox smoke a field of 29 from second spot. David Pearson swapped the lead early with pole-sitter Dieringer, Goldsmith, and Isaac before leading the last 350-plus laps. Again, Isaac was second, Castles third, Tyner fourth, and Bill Seifert fifth. The rest were Spartanburg's Ervin Pruitt seventh, Wendell ninth, Hamilton tenth, Allison 12th, Goldsmith 17th, Hylton 18th, Dieringer 22nd, Tiny 23rd, and Petty 26th.

It was 364 days before he hung up the goggles for good, but this was the final *Silent Speedways of the Carolinas* and short track start for a legend second to none in skill, guts, and luck. Paul Goldsmith was a winner in the American Motorcycle Association years before he came to NASCAR. He rode against Weatherly, tutored Joe Leonard, and gave Harley-Davidson five major wins at killers like Milwaukee, Langhorne, and the Daytona 200 on the Beach in 1953. If you think of Roberts, Thomas, Teague, and Turner as Smokey Yunick's drivers, better add Goldsmith, too. Goldy rode Smokey-tuned Harleys in '53, drove Smokey's Fords in '57, and won the last beach race with him in a Pontiac in '58. Paul drove the Indianapolis 500 six times with a fifth in '59 and a third in 1960 for Norm Demler, the apple juice king. Paul Goldsmith won nine Grand National races and none by accident. His involvement in Bobby Myers' fatality in the 1957 Southern 500 was followed up at Indy in '58 with Jerry Unser using Goldy's Yunick Offy for a ramp, clearing the third turn wall in the first lap fiasco that killed Pat O'Connor. Goldy sported Unser's tire track on his headgear after that one. He led that last A-W race for 41 laps, the only racer challenging Pearson before the throttle broke. That was Paul Goldsmith ... breaking the throttle. He was a winner in AMA, NASCAR, and USAC. *He was a winner!*

Sunday, May 4, 1969, was the penultimate visit and the final Fireball 300. The race was another bore with Bobby Isaac to blame. Except for 17 laps led early by Pearson, Isaac's Dodge mowed the field down and had over a lap on Hylton after the checkers. Hits were the story of the day and the first was a big one as Richard Petty in a Ford pounded the wall on lap 52. A Goodyear popped and Petty veered right, tagging the concrete about as hard as he ever would in his career. The Ford was demolished and there was concern for Richard's health. Pearson tried copying Petty by smacking the wall hard enough to end his day. Third went to Sears, Castles fourth, Earl Brooks fifth, Rookie of the Year lock Dick Brooks seventh, McDuffie ninth, Scott tenth, Elmo 19th, Pearson 21st, and Petty 23rd. Only 5,500 saw the Sunday snoozer.

It was a summer to remember with man on the moon, music festivals most notably at Woodstock, slaughter in Vietnam matched in California by the Manson Family, Hurricane Camille slamming the Gulf Coast claiming 250, race riots rocking Ft. Lauderdale, Jim Palmer and Ken Holtzman hurling no-nos, the Stones' "Honky Tonk Women" topping the charts, and the final chapter being written at the Asheville-Weaverville Speedway. Sweltering Sunday, August 24, 1969, saw the 12th and final Western North Carolina 500. A dozen of the wackiest, sometimes coma-inducing, stock car races staged. Over 11,000 fans swamped the

26. Asheville-Weaverville Speedway

A running track now occupies the same real estate the stockers ran on below Asheville-Weaverville Speedway—builder Gene Sluder's house on the hill.

facility north of Weaverville, but they would never see the big boys again. A field of 27 assembled that miserably hot day with Isaac on the pole in his orange Dodge 71 flanked by Petty's Ford. Pearson and Marcis were row two followed by Yarbrough and Castles. Isaac jumped out front, but gave way to Pearson and Petty until his battle with 43 ended with the blue Torino tucked into the wall on lap 120, although not as violently as in May. Soon Bobby's tank ran dry and when he got restarted, he was five laps behind Pearson. That is until Pearson's Ford soured and Bobby made up the five laps, *winning by four!* Pearson's Holman-Moody boys protested to no avail. Pearson was second, rookie Dick Brooks third, Elmo fourth, and Hylton fifth. Further back were Scott 12th, Marcis 15th, LeeRoy blew Junior's Ford for 22nd, Petty took 23rd, and Hoss Ellington was 27th and last.

There were 12 WNC 500 races and a dozen winning faces. There were the Fireball 300s. There were huge sweepstakes races of the fifties, track break-ups, a near riot, and 34 races in all. Remember Herb Thomas with Joe Littlejohn riding shotgun during a record-breaking time trial. Bob Flock winning way past his prime, linking up the Flock Brothers Trifecta in '52. Rex White dominating for years. Bud and Darel's Comet and the Golden Boy's win when he was unstoppable. Now kids wait on buses, sneak smokes, steal kisses, play ball, and probably none of them have a clue as to what took place for 18 years on those hallowed grounds ... and still takes place in the cool misty mountain nights down from Gene Sluder's rock House on Haunted Hill.

Track History by the Numbers

RACES:	34
YEARS OF RACES:	1951–1956, 1957 (2), 1958 (2), 1959 (3), 1960 (2), 1961 (3, one the 1st race of '62), 1962 (2), 1963 (2), 1964 (2), 1965 (2), 1966 (2), 1967 (2), 1968 (2), 1969 (2)
WINNERS:	White (5), L. Petty (4), R. Petty (4), F. Flock (2), Isaac (2), Jarrett (2), Pearson (2), B. Allison, Buck Baker, Dieringer, B. Flock, T. Flock, Junior Johnson, Lorenzen, Panch, Paschal, Roberts, H. Thomas, Weatherly, Welborn
MOST POLES:	4—Junior Johnson, Rex White
RACE RECORD:	83.860 mph—Richard Petty, 1967 Plymouth (3/5/67)
QUALIFYING RECORD:	90.407 mph—Bobby Allison, 1967 Ford (11/5/67)
WINS BY MAKE:	Chevrolet (8), Ford (7), Plymouth (7), Dodge (3), Hudson (3), Oldsmobile (2), Pontiac (2), Chrysler, Mercury
MOST STARTS:	23—Buck Baker
MOST LAPS LED:	1,254—David Pearson
MOST TOP FIVES:	10—Rex White
BEST AVERAGE START:	10.7—Buck Baker, 6.3—Richard Petty (22)
BEST AVERAGE FINISH:	10.7—Buck Baker, Richard Petty (22)

27

New Asheville Speedway, Asheville, North Carolina

This one is easy to find. On I-40 in Asheville, take I-240 and get off on Amboy Road. This member of *Silent Speedways of the Carolinas* is all painted and shined up as the Asheville Bicycle Racing Club, part of gorgeous French Broad River Park. It is a third-mile asphalt square with rounded corners where on June 10, 1988, Shawna Robinson became the first woman in history to win a NASCAR touring series event, taking the checkers in a Daytona Dash feature. But the park crews had to work hard repairing the damage wrought in late summer 2004. Asheville and the surrounding area was double sucker punched, first on September 8th by Tropical Storm Frances, then, before the water had a chance to recede, by

Paved, painted, and ready for action, bicycle action, by the French Broad River.

remnants of Ivan a week later. Floods devastated this track and submerged it under eight feet of water, even more in some spots. The pedestrian bridge support to the infield had a line marking where the water crested. The track would be ready for racecars except it needs a pit area and grandstand. The concrete wall backs a steel guardrail, and upon closer examination, it is evident they built a new retaining wall in front of an old one with a small gap visible in between. Those walls have traces of peeling red and white Winston Cup paint and were built around old wooden posts. The backstretch to the south is only yards away from the very powerful French Broad River. Crews repaired a backstretch section that washed away from next to the gate where entered stock car racing's biggest stars. Turns three and four back to the homestretch, including the start/finish line, are also ready for action. The pedestrian bridge offers a great panoramic view, although it was not there for the auto races. It is easy to imagine the stockers of 1962 lined up on the asphalt. New Asheville Speedway never went to seed like Columbia Speedway because it morphed almost directly from stock car racing to the pedal pushers. But that does not matter to the unknowing, uncaring spirits in the nightly programs there. The mortals came once a year for seven straight from 1962 to 1968 with a curtain call in 1971. That, along with two stops a year at Asheville-Weaverville, made "The Land of the Sky" a busy city for race fans in the '60s. Wild happenings took place over those eight events at New Asheville.

The inaugural race on the four-tenths mile asphalt was on unlucky Friday, July 13, 1962. However, that mountain summer night was very lucky for Spartanburg's Jack Smith and his year-old Pontiac 47. It was Jack's fifth win of the season and last of an outstanding career. He beat out Weatherly, Petty, Buck Baker, and Jarrett in a caution-free race.

Jack Smith finished the season fourth in points, gave it a half-hearted effort in 1963 in a Plymouth, and ran three early races prior to Speedweeks in 1964 before hanging it up, but not for good. He moved to Spartanburg around 1959 after hooking up with Bud Moore, then came back from retirement to run sportsman races in the Piedmont in the summer of 1970. It was something seeing him cocking it through the turns at the Fairgrounds a couple of times that summer just like back in the '60s. He won hundreds of modified races in the '40s and '50s, especially the big one on The Beach in 1951 against the best drivers in the country. In 1952, he finished tenth in the one and only year of NASCAR's open wheel Speedway Division, with two seconds and two more top tens in only four starts. Jack drove for Spartanburg's Roy Shoemaker in *the original* Kurtis Kraft Indy car. Jack had Bud Moore's Boomershine Pontiac "The Red Fox" out front by more than six laps in the first World 600 in 1960, leading nearly half the race before parking with a gaping hole in the gas tank. He made some amends by taking the Firecracker 250 a couple of weeks later at Daytona, edging Cotton Owens. Smith finished his career with 21 Grand National wins and was *amazingly* excluded from NASCAR's 50 Greatest Drivers list, an embarrassing omission that reeks of favoritism by those that left off Jim Paschal, too. Smith was a contender from that first Strictly Stock Car race in Charlotte on June 19, 1949, where he finished 13th, until his last race in Savannah, a second, on December 29, 1963. He retired at just 39 years old to a still-booming Spartanburg transmission business. His slogan, heard all over local radio and television, was, "You can trust Jack Smith!" He was a big, burly ex-moonshiner from north Georgia and one of the greatest stock car drivers of all time. Jack Smith crossed over to join the brave racers preceding him on October 17, 2001, at 77 years of age.

They returned on Sunday, July 14, 1963, and the fireworks after the race were not for Bastille Day. The 300-lap, 100-miler had a fine field of only 20 cars, perfect for a third-mile track made slightly shorter since the last trip here. The lead was shared by pole-sitter Pearson, Junior Johnson in that famous 3 1963 Holly Farms Chevy, Petty, and the winner Jar-

27. New Asheville Speedway

Turn Two of the peculiar square-shaped, round-cornered, .333-mile speedway.

rett. After some bumping and grinding of which Petty came out on the short end, Richard confronted Ned, but officials calmed the situation and 4,500, including Ned, went home happy.

Sunday, May 31, 1964, found the racing world reeling. It was the twilight period of 39 days during which the great Fireball Roberts lay in Charlotte Memorial Hospital dying of grotesque burns received a week earlier on lap seven of the World 600. The day before, Eddie Sachs and Dave McDonald died as result of a catastrophic inferno on lap two of the Indianapolis 500. Needless to say, a lot of minds were probably elsewhere, not wanting to run this one. But that is what they do, *they race*. And the winner was the man who a week earlier pulled Fireball from that purple Ford-pyre, Ned Jarrett. The 19 cars racing had some fine drivers like Petty second, Panch third, Pearson fourth, and Cale Yarborough fifth.

Returning on Saturday afternoon, May 29, 1965, the touring pros were in the middle race of a three-races-in-four-days stretch. Two days since Jarrett won at Shelby and the day before a 100-miler at Harris, it was a *Silent Speedways of the Carolinas* trifecta. This was the only race of the three that Junior Johnson entered and the only one Jarrett did not win. Johnson first, Jarrett second, Dick Dixon third, Putney fourth, and Castles fifth. Junior sat on the pole and led all 300 laps in a sleeper.

Thursday night, June 2, 1966, and thunderstorms did not keep 7,000 fans away, but there was a void of top drivers for the Asheville 300. Petty and Pearson took the front row with hometowner and crowd-favorite Jack Ingram of the sportsman ranks starting fourth in a '64 Dodge 00. Petty led the first ten, giving way to Pearson for the next 290, but not without some excitement. With the throttle sticking, Pearson had to cut the ignition off manually, entering the turns, switching it back on for the straights a la Weatherly at Concord four years earlier. If it had not worked, J.T. Putney would have won his first race driving the Louis Clements–tuned Chevy 19. Petty smacked the wall before halfway, making it David's to lose. Sears was third, Hylton fourth, and Hank Thomas fifth in number 92 made famous by another Thomas 15 years earlier.

Exactly one year later on Friday night, June 2, 1967, a slim 18 cars took the green led by Petty on the pole and the return of Jack Ingram outside. Ingram never led and Petty did not win, both mild surprises as Jack crashed and Richard did not have it. Red-hot Jim Paschal made it three out of four, edging Donnie Allison wheeling the Bracken Chevelle 2 usually driven by Brother Bobby. Jim bounced off the rail shortly after halfway while leading and made up five laps to pull off the stunner. He captured the World 600 only five days earlier and won at Beltsville nine days before that. This was the Tattooed One's 24th career win. He got his 25th on June 27th in Montgomery. Twenty-five big time wins, two World 600s, and a 23rd place in the first Strictly Stock Car race ever held on June 19, 1949. The geniuses picking NASCAR's 50 Greatest Drivers left Paschal off the list as noted elsewhere. He was omitted with even better stats than Jack. Both more than deserved to be on that list. Jim drove in every Southern 500 until 1968, when he was driving a factory-backed AMC Javelin on the Grand American tour and winning. He was as tough as or tougher than anybody

An odd mixture of the new wall (lower), old wall (upper), a wooden post between, wildflowers, and a piece of red Fiberglas wedged into it all.

27. New Asheville Speedway

From the post–speedway era bridge, an eastward look past the Start/Finish Line toward Turn Four. The pits were to the right where the hockey rink is located.

was and better than most. Paschal won his penultimate race here and Jack Smith his ultimate. Jim Paschal eased over to the other side on July 5, 2004, at 77 years old ... the same age as Jack Smith.

It was May 31, 1968, Friday night at the fights as 3,500 fans witnessed an extra attraction on the card that evening. A decent field of 23 lost one of its main contenders on lap 39 when Pearson was lapping Stan Meserve, a Canadian who started tenth, and they crashed, sending both to the showers for the night. However, before they got there, pleasantries were exchanged and Pearson got sucker-punched from behind by some brave Meserve flunky. Somebody yelled "*FIGHT!*," and the pits erupted into a brawl as almost everybody with a grudge against anybody took a poke at them. When they restored order, Richard Petty won by a lap over Buddy Baker's Ray Fox Dodge 3 with Isaac third, Hylton fourth, and Langley fifth.

"Joy to the World" by Three Dog Night topped the charts on the evening of Friday, May 21, 1971, Grand National's last call on New Asheville Speedway after three years away. Only 17 teams entered and most of them were angry independents. Petty won in a walkover, although Elmo Langley made it interesting. The independents were miffed about the lack of appearance money and were further insulted when track promoter George Ledford told them all they needed was Petty anyway. It was his version of "Let them eat cake." Well, Petty is about all they had, because seven of the 17, including ringleader James Hylton, parked after the green fell. Hylton, in the thick of the points race, ran one lap and finished last while Petty romped. In the final 1971 standings, Petty won the crown by less than 400 points over Hylton. James Harvey Hylton is a man of principles unafraid to stand up for right and a terrific racer. The farewell crowd of 4,500 booed the finish, not necessarily Petty for winning, but for only five cars finishing. Second was Langley, Flash Gordon third, Jabe Thomas fourth, and old-timer Bill Champion fifth.

It was a very ugly end to an exciting downtown speedway, one of the last to operate during the years of the *Silent Speedways of the Carolinas*. Today, bicycles may rule the old speed plant on the banks of the French Broad by day, but when the stars come out, *the stars come out*, and their names are Jack Smith and Jim Paschal. Joy to the world!

Track History by the Numbers

RACES:	8
YEARS OF RACES:	1962, 1963, 1964, 1965, 1966, 1967, 1968, 1971
WINNERS:	Jarrett (2), R. Petty (2), Jack Smith, Junior Johnson, Pearson, Paschal
MOST POLES:	5—Richard Petty
RACE RECORD:	78.294 mph—Jack Smith, 1961 Pontiac (7/13/62)
QUALIFYING RECORD:	82.285 mph—Jack Smith, 1961 Pontiac (7/13/62)
WINS BY MAKE:	Ford (3), Plymouth (3), Pontiac, Dodge
MOST STARTS:	7—Richard Petty, Wendell Scott
MOST LAPS LED:	702—Richard Petty
MOST TOP FIVES:	6—Richard Petty
BEST AVERAGE START:	1.4—Richard Petty
BEST AVERAGE FINISH:	2.2—Ned Jarrett

28

Greensboro Agricultural Fairgrounds Speedway, Greensboro, North Carolina

The longest name for the shortest of these tracks. The Greensboro Agricultural Fairgrounds Speedway, a.k.a. Central Carolina Fairgrounds Speedway, held three Grand Nationals and they were among the shortest in length of the *Silent Speedways of the Carolinas*. The Greensboro Coliseum and parking lot along the west side of Coliseum Boulevard is the location of this long-ago-razed venue. The speedway ran roughly northeast to southwest and its .333 distance easily fit in the parking area. The first and second turns were in the low end of the huge lot, which was probably graded that way later for drainage. The third turn, at the northeasternmost part, sat just feet from what is now the intersection of Coliseum Boulevard and Holbrook Street. There is not a single trace of the speedway remaining, but this track lies alive and awake beneath its asphalt cover and is in use nightly. The big boys ran here three times and the events were amazing!

The first one was on Sunday, April 28, 1957. The oval was a one-third mile dirt track and the drivers ran 250 laps around that bullring for 83.25 miles. Why they did not schedule another 50 laps and make it a 100-mile event is a mystery. The field was nothing less than spectacular, though, mainly due to the ferocious factory battle in 1957 waged between General Motors, Ford, and to a lesser extent Chrysler. The models offered by those manufacturers also fought among themselves. Buck had the pole in Hugh Babb's Black Widow Chevy tuned by Bud Moore with Goldsmith's Smokey Yunick Ford outside. Row two saw Fireball in a De Paolo Ford and Petty in his Olds. Jack Smith in another Black Widow and Earnhardt in another Petty Olds made up row three. Gridded next was Moody for De Paolo and Billy Myers in Californian Bill Stroppe's red, white, and blue Mercury

Most famous as the usual home of the ACC Men's Basketball Tournament, the Greensboro Coliseum covers a raucous and rowdy .333-mile track.

The east side of the coliseum parking lot was the site of the dirt bullring that easily fit in that space, which is now completely paved over and sloped for drainage.

in the fourth row. The fifth had Panch for De Paolo and Lund in a Pontiac. The sixth row held Paschal for Stroppe and Allen in a Plymouth. A couple of rows back found the third Black Widow for Speedy 15th. Six rows plus one of the very best stock cars and drivers in the country. The race was dominated by Goldsmith, who let Baker lead for 72 laps off and on. The other 178 were Goldy's. Smith was coming hard, but never got close enough to mount a challenge. Baker was third, Moody fourth, and Fireball fifth. Panch crashed on lap 25 and none of the others was any match for Yunick's black and gold rocket.

The second event was another 83.25-miler on a nippy Sunday, October 27th, but a hot dozen more drivers showed up than in April to give the tiny oval a massive *31-car* field for race 53, the finale of the 1957 season. It was a slugfest with a spectacular field involved in spectacular happenings. The pole went to rookie Ken Rush of High Point in Ford 26, normally driven by Turner. It was his Ford audition and it started with a bang. Unfortunately, it ended with a bigger one! Coming out of the second turn, Rush lost it and was clobbered, mainly by Panch, who cartwheeled his Ford. Surprisingly, he continued, only to fall out later. Staley and Possum Jones were also involved. Shortly, the Wild Injun took out the scoring stand, but nobody was scalped. After Turner lost his ride to Rush, he borrowed one from hometown favorite Welborn, but fared poorly. The day and the season belonged to Elzie Wylie Baker, Sr., in Bud Moore's Chevy. Thompson brought Moore's Southern 500 winner home second, followed by Weatherly, Smith, Petty, and Goldsmith. Throw in White and Allen and it was one of the best fields of the year.

They dropped the curtain on the little dirt track on Sunday afternoon, May 11, 1958. A gorgeous day saw 19 entries take the spring green for a quick 150-lap, 50-mile war. Hometowner Welborn, at the peak of his career, went wire-to-wire winning handily over Petty, Johnson, Thompson, and Doug Cox. The event took just over 65 minutes, then Greensboro's speedway slipped into the misty memory of how it was. How it was when the top stockers in the country battled on a third-mile dirt track for less than $1,000 to win. The total winning purse for all three Grand National races run there was an embarrassing $2,200!

The track is long gone. There is no trace at all because the Greensboro Coliseum parking lot sits squarely over this former track where the Central Carolina Fair is still held each September. However, perhaps when a bizarre play takes place during a basketball game at the Coliseum, or at a gun show when someone accidentally cranks off a round, or at the circus when the elephants are spooked, it is because a spirit lies beneath the concrete and asphalt. A spirit in another dimension where the cars are roaring, the crowd is screaming, and dead live to race again.

Track History by the Numbers

RACES:	3
YEARS OF RACES:	1957 (2), 1958
WINNERS:	Goldsmith, Buck Baker, Welborn
MOST POLES:	1—Buck Baker, Rush, Welborn
RACE RECORD:	49.905 mph—Paul Goldsmith, 1957 Ford (4/28/57)
QUALIFYING RECORD:	50.120—Buck Baker, Chevrolet (4/28/57)
WINS BY MAKE:	Chevrolet (2), Ford
MOST STARTS:	3—Austin, Buck Baker, King, L. Petty, J. Smith, S. Thompson
MOST LAPS LED:	184—Lee Petty
MOST TOP FIVES:	2—Buck Baker, L. Petty, J. Smith, S. Thompson
BEST AVERAGE START:	3.5—Buck Baker, L. Petty, J. Smith
BEST AVERAGE FINISH:	3.3—Buck Baker

29

North Wilkesboro Speedway, North Wilkesboro, North Carolina

This brings us to the last, and by no means least, Grand Old Dame of the *Silent Speedways of the Carolinas*. North Wilkesboro Speedway is on every map and easy to find. From Charlotte, go north on I-77 and west on 421 until it looms beside the highway east of town. Turn right off 421 onto Speedway Road and after a few miles, the ragged old track lies on the left across the top of a ridge with a huge field and a couple of houses between it and the road. Take another left at Speedway Lane and wind up and around to the right to the office. The impression is of a facility that was added onto piecemeal, which looks bad enough without all the fading, cracking paint. Knowing where the authorities want to take stock car racing today, it is easy to see why this venue looks better in a rear view mirror. It could never measure up now, but was fine in its day, which was over 30 years ago. It epitomizes the Golden Era of stock car racing in every way, making it the perfect final chapter. She is the Grand Old Dame of the *Silent Speedways of the Carolinas* with the longest run. She held *fifty* major stock car races *after* the Golden Era ended following 1971! This book covers only the first 43, beginning in that infant Strictly Stock year 1949 and ending with death of the good old days in 1971, when the R.J. Reynolds Tobacco Company entered the scene. After they gutted the schedule to 31 races in 1972 from 48 races the year before, lots of drivers, owners, manufacturers, fans, and wonderful old dusty, dangerous, cramped tracks started their death rattles and this old gal died last. The astonishing list of winners in those 43 races is the *Who's Who of Stock Car Racing's Great Golden Age*.

Faded glory marks North Wilkesboro Speedway, the Grand Old Dame of the *Silent Speedways of the Carolinas*.

It had only happened seven times before and the eighth was the last in that historic first and only year of the NASCAR Strictly Stock Championship. They met at a dusty red clay half-mile in North Wilkesboro, NC, the epicenter of the moonshine industry. It was the month Iva Toguri

D'Aquino was sentenced to ten years in the slammer. She is remembered as Tokyo Rose, everyone's favorite DJ in the Pacific during World War Two. It was the week that the Yanks beat dem Bums again in the Series. It was the day after Billy Graham started pitching from the pulpit and picking up saves. It was Sunday, October 16, 1949, autumn in the Brushy Mountains, and a throng of over ten thousand packed the bleachers, fences, trees, and hills to see 22 speed demons going after a $1,500 first prize. Nine makes sat on the grid, led by '49 Lincoln 15 of Ken Wagner from Pennington, NJ, with his first and only pole. Outside front row was Bill Blair in Sam Rice's potent Cadillac in which he had run well earlier. However, the storyline was Red Byron's almost insurmountable points lead going into this finale. So confident was Red that the title was his, the little tail-gunner and car owner Raymond Parks kept that black Olds 22 in Atlanta, skipping the previous 100-miler in Pittsburgh. Flocks Bob, Fonty, and Tim, Lee Petty, Blair, and Turner could catch Byron, but the math was not there. Back in the field that cool Sabbath was Frank Mundy, Herb Thomas, legendary Roy Hall, and female phenom Sara Christian, the real First Lady of Stock Car Racing. Blair blasted by Wagner on the start and was gone, stretching the lead by the lap. Mundy dropped out first for 22nd, but the field stayed intact. Behind Blair's cruising Caddy came a battle between the Flock Trio, Petty, Byron, Thomas, Clyde Minter, Hall, and Turner. The crossed flags flew and still Blair blazed away as Tim's Olds 88 retired eight and a half miles later for 19th. The three-quarter mark came and went, but drama arrived and stayed. On lap 155, point leader Byron blew the mill in the not-so-bulletproof Red Vogt Olds and steamed to a halt in the pits. Then came renewed title hopes for Blair, Petty, and Bob Flock. Was anyone sure that Byron's finishing 16th was high enough to secure the Inaugural Strictly Stock Championship? Pole-sitter Wagner fell out ten laps later for 15th and everything went up for grabs. The crowd was stunned with ten miles to go when Blair's high-flying Caddy, having led every lap, began belching smoke, dropping back into the pack. The race came down to a duel between Petty and Bob Flock, both winners on the tour, as they overhauled Blair, who stumbled on. Entering the last lap, Bob's Olds held the slimmest of margins over Petty's Plymouth, but when the checkers fell, it was Flock over Petty by about two seconds. Quickly the arithmetic was done and 34-year-old warhorse Red Byron out of Anniston, AL, had plenty of points to wear the champion's crown for 1949. Bob Flock's win tied him with Byron for the most in the eight-race season with two, good for third in the standings. Petty's second-place finish slotted him second in the standings. Third a lap behind was Fonty, fifth in the title chase. Fourth went to Martinsville's Clyde Minter, who had another fourth in his only other start. Fifth was Herb Thomas as he absorbed everything in order to dominate the series in a few years for a few years.

And sixth was Roy Hall. Attach every shopworn cliché in the book to this guy and it will not be enough. If 1949 was the birth year of modern stock car racing, Roy Hall was a sperm. He tossed his cousin Raymond Park's speedster across the sand at Daytona to a win over Joe Littlejohn in July 1940 and again in March 1941. Hall was also cousin and teammate to Lloyd Seay, one of the few that could run with him, and a driver of unimaginable potential until blasted through the ticker on September 2, 1941, by Cousin Woodrow, who toted a .32. This was Hall's first start, no doubt wedged between stints in the slammer for various indiscretions almost always involving liquor, legal or otherwise. It was three years before Hall made his second and last Grand National start. (Technically, he made one Strictly Stock start and one Grand National.) His last run was in a DeSoto, starting sixth and retiring for 48th, tucked in the final rundown between Possum Jones and Fireball Roberts in the 1952 Southern 500. In a life of death-defying, moonshining, race-driving, time-serving, hard-drinking, and God knows what-elsing, Roy Hall amazingly lasted until rattling out his final breath on November 14, 1991, at 71 years old, fifty-one years after first winning on the Beach. Hollywood stuff!

Twelfth came winner Bob Flock's teammate Sara Christian, the true First Lady of Stock Car Racing, Louise Smith notwithstanding. Smith gets more ink for crashes, but she never had a better major finish than 16th, which was at Langhorne in the fourth Strictly Stock race ever. In a field of 45, that is truly outstanding, except for the fact that Sara Christian was sixth that same day, just ahead of Lee Petty and Al Keller. Sara's performance was so brilliant that Curtis Turner insisted she join him in Victory Lane. Her next outing in Pittsburgh, the race before North Wilkesboro, she finished fifth. Those two races produced what are still the two highest female finishes in Strictly Stock, Grand National, Winston, or Nextel Cup history. Sara buckled up one more time after North Wilkesboro. In 1950 at Hamburg, NY, Mrs. Christian finished 14th. Sara had great equipment because she chauffeured for her husband Frank Christian, who was top-notch all the way. Sara raced on The Beach before the war and in 1949 won six of 17 on the modified circuit before a Lakewood Speedway crash cracked her back in a couple of places. She was voted Female Driver of the Year in 1949. Head-to-head with Louise Smith, Sara won four to nothing in the big time. Smith is in the International Motorsports Hall of Fame at Talladega, but Sara Christian belongs, too.

At the Wilkes opener, H.F. Stickleather (great name!) from Charlotte was 14th in his only start. Red Byron clinched the one and only 1949 Strictly Stock Car Championship with 16th, Bobby Greene from Siler City, NC, wrapped up a two-race career with 17th, and Bluefield, WV's Bill Greever began an uneventful two-race career with 18th. The opener at North Wilkesboro was full of drama and stories, and the longest run of the *Silent Speedways of the Carolinas* had only just begun.

It was nearly a year before they returned on Sunday, September 24, 1950, and a couple of racing firsts took place. It was the month UN forces landed at Inchon and recaptured Seoul. Ezzard Charles retained his heavyweight crown, decisioning a fading 36-year-old Joe Louis in Yankee Stadium. This was the 15th race of the season held at a track now promoting itself at five-eighths mile instead of a half. There was no mention of the elevation change on the straightaways. Twenty-six nearly stock cars lined up to battle for $1,000 in the 23rd big-league race ever. After Johnny Mantz's Southern 500 win in a Plymouth 20 days earlier, the pits were lousy with them. Since Johnny was looking for open wheel fame with J.C. Agajanian, owner Hubert Westmoreland turned the 500 winner over to a 26-year-old modified pilot from Winston-Salem named Leon Sales. Points leader Fireball Roberts grabbed the first of his 32 career poles in Sam Rice's Olds 88. Even though he only ran a couple of dozen races in the meantime, Fireball would not take another pole until the 1955 Southern 500. This autumn Sunday, the great Red Byron flanked him in a Parks Cadillac. Other stars were the Flocks times three, Jack Smith, Baker, Turner, Blair, Herb Thomas, and Daytona victor in his first start, Harold Kite. The air was thick with red dust as the pack roared through the opening laps of the 200 scheduled. Byron led for three until Fonty gunned his Olds to the point for 103. During the first half, Turner's Olds broke for 22nd and Slick Smith had a Nash crash for 20th. Byron took the lead from Fonty until lap 137, when the heavy Caddy lost a spindle on the bumpy dirt and settled for 19th. Fonty blew immediately thereafter for 18th. With those departures, fellow Georgian Jack Smith was up front and cruising to his first win. Cruising, that is, until the hemi in his Plymouth soured in the final ten miles and the black 98 Jr., the same Southern 500 winner twenty days earlier, motored by and first-time starter Leon Sales became a first time, only time, winner. That little black Plymouth was two for two! Smith smoldered home second, first-timer Ewell Weddle (another great name) brought Lincoln 78 in third, Thomas was fourth in yet another Plymouth, and

29. North Wilkesboro Speedway

Tickets were available here every single year of the Golden Era from 1949 to 1971.

Gayle Warren was fifth in, you guessed it, a Plymouth. Others included Welden Adams sixth, Jerry Wimbish eighth in his first start, Bob Flock ninth, and Tampa's Herbert Burns tenth in his first of two starts. Blair claimed 11th, Kite 12th, Baker 14th, and pole-sitter Roberts blew for 16th, but held the point lead over unentered Bill Rexford. Boston's Dick Shuebruk was 17th, and Jim Cook 23rd in their only career starts, and a couple of guys closed out two-race careers: Jack Carr 25th and Tex Keene 26th and last. A little kid was hit in the pits, recovering later, but it was a sobering event, to say the least. For winner Sales, he never had another top ten in his nine-race career. Nevertheless, Leon sailed along in a car that could not lose and was on top of the sport.

The third trip to North Wilkesboro occurred on Sunday, April 29, 1951, springtime in the mountains. It was the month President Truman fired General McArthur, who then addressed the cadets at West Point, had a ticker tape parade in New York, and just faded away. Also in the Big Apple, the Mick stepped to the dish for the first time in pinstripes and went one for four. And in Kannapolis, NC, Martha Earnhardt had a son and named him Ralph Dale Earnhardt, Jr., after his father, Ralph, Sr. Seventy-nine miles to the northwest, a field of 38, the largest ever here, jammed the five-eighths dirt oval, but this was going to be more like war. Nearly eight thousand spread themselves on every vantage point to witness the mayhem as Fonty put the Frank Christian Red Devil Olds 14 on the pole. He already had three poles and a win in the first six races. Frank Mundy was outside in Perry Smith's Studebaker, and Fireball lined up in row two with Lou Figaro. Row three saw Tim Flock and Pepper Cunningham, four had Turner and Minter, and row five found Bill Blair and Bill Holland. Holland ran the Indianapolis 500 only four times, every year since 1947, and had to show for it second, second, first, and second. He could have won all four if his luck had been as good as it was bad. He finished every lap possible up there, yet was given the heave-ho by the AAA, the dopes that ran the 500 back then. As was detailed in the Charlotte Speedway chapter, Holland was down south because the AAA banned their hottest star for the three-lap Lions Charity Race he ran gratis in Opa-Locka, FL, during the winter of 1950–51. So ever the genius, Bill France dialed him up, got him to bring his driving suits south, and slipped him behind the wheel of Hubert Westmoreland's unbeatable Southern 500–winning Plymouth 98, Jr. The green silk fell and Fonty dashed away ... away ... *and away!* In fact, nobody could catch him and he won a laugher, leading every lap. Behind the flying Olds, there was a real thriller going on and every time somebody looked ready to challenge Fonty, they were slapped from contention. Fireball gave it less than two miles before he parked for dead last, 38th. Minter retired for 37th and Figaro figured in his first crash, taking 36th. Near the quarter mark, Mundy's shocks broke for 28th and the circuit's winningest driver with six, Curtis Turner, had wheel trouble, sending him to cocktails early for 27th. Blair blew for 24th and interesting Pepper Cunningham parked his new Hudson 23rd. Trenton's Pepper ran a ten-race career, including all six ever held at deadly Langhorne, and drove for Marshall Teague at Daytona in 1952. Pepper averaged qualifying in the top ten for his career, even if for only ten events. Fonty kept a relentless pace as Bub King rolled and Shorty York crashed for 21st and 22nd, '50 Champion Rexford got 14th, and Herb Thomas crashed in Figaro's second miscue of the day, relieving Dale Williams and finishing 13th with the hood up. Numerous other spins and slides occurred, unknown cautions flew, and the average speed is lost forever. Finally, Fonty Flock flew beneath the checkers after 150 laps and the hottest guy on the tour stayed that way. Teague led in points, but did not show and for the second race here in a row, the point leader passed on running the mountain oval. Brother Tim was second, Petty third, and the flashy Holland was rock solid in 98, Jr., for fourth.

It was Bill's last *Silent Speedways of the Carolinas* entry and his best finish in a seven-race NASCAR career. Two more years of barnstorming ended for the dashing Holland and the numbskulls at the AAA reinstated him for the 1953 season, but his prime was gone. Imagine that happening today. There would be so many lawsuits flying around that Holland would not have even missed a single practice session! His first real ride back was too slow to qualify for the 500, but he squeezed into the field driving Ray Crawford's Offy at 28th place. Being a seasoned veteran at age 43, he pushed it to the top ten before a cam gear failed 23 laps from the end and he retired for 15th place. Bill never tried Indianapolis, NASCAR, or anything of substance again. Arguably, America's top racer in 1950 had his career dashed against the rocks inside the heads of the AAA officials for charity! The great Bill Holland left us at 77 in 1984. What a waste!

Donald Thomas was fifth at Wilkes, Lewellen seventh, and Dunnaway eighth. Ninth was hometowner Dale Williams, who was unable to complete his only start, being relieved by the crash-happy Figaro. According to racing-reference.com, Williams came back over 40 years later to run five Busch Grand National races in 1994 and '95. Herb Thomas was crashed out by Figaro for 13th, Birmingham's Ed Massey's first start yielded 15th, and Irwin, PA's Ed Schade's last of two starts got a 16th. Martinsville's Paul Stanley's first was good for 19th, Kernersville, NC's Claude Joyce's only race netted 30th, Salisbury, NC's Bob Walters six-race 1951 career ended with 33rd, and Shelby, NC's Ben Dixon took 35th in his only event. It was the North Wilkesboro race with the largest field (38) and the shortest distance (94 miles, 150 laps). It was a crash-fest and the last hurrah for Bill Holland, but 79 miles to the southeast, it was the first hurrah for a baby named Dale.

It was October 1951. *"The Giants win the pennant! The Giants win the pennant! The Giants win the pennant!"* screamed Russ Hodges when Bobby Thomson connected off Dodger Ralph Branca. Marciano had target practice on the face of aged Joe Louis in the Brown Bomber's last fight. And *I Love Lucy* hit the air on CBS. On the 21st, they ran a second yearly Grand National at North Wilkesboro for the first time. It was not the massive 38-car field as before, but a healthy 26 with different faces and a lot less back markers. Herb Thomas had the pole in the Fabulous Hudson Hornet 92 of Smokey Yunick. He was chalking up poles and wins with a regularity that would continue for over three years. Bob Flock put a Hudson, the first of the three-car all–Flock Ted Chester Team, outside row one. Behind them sat Joe Eubanks in the Phil Oates–owned, Bud Moore–tuned Hornet and Fonty Flock in Ted Chester's great Gray Ghost Olds 7 normally chauffeured by Bob. Scattered through the pack were Shuman, Owens, Petty, Billy Myers, Staley, Blair, Paschal, Dunnaway, Tim Flock, and former winner Sales in the old, tired Southern 500–winning 1950 Plymouth 98, Jr. The two dozen plus two sent red dust choking the blue autumn sky as they charged off for 200 laps. Herb led as the stars fell quickly. Staley, in his second start, retired for 25th and Blair was right behind him. Shortly after Salisbury's Bob Walters rolled his Hudson, ending a six-race career with 23rd, the radiator looked more like Old Faithful and Herb went from first to 21st on lap 82. Inheriting the lead was red-hot Fonty and he led the next 117 laps. While he was out front, the excitement continued as Greenville's Leonard Tippett flipped his Hornet for 20th and Jack Wade went back to Charlottesville after a rollover in his Olds brought his two-race career to an end in 19th. One of the things interesting about this age were the brief careers that went only a few races as guys, *and gals*, got a taste of the big time and went home, where lots of old wrecked stock cars rusted away in backyards across the South. Billy Myers retired for 18th and Dunnaway's Ambassador broke for 17th. Glenn had one more race left at Atlanta a couple of weeks later, but this was it on the *Silent Speedways of the Carolinas* and the career that might have been. It was Glenn's 17th of an 18-race career. Who could ever forget his first start? It was *everybody's* first start, June 19, 1949, the genesis of it all. And it was so close to being Glenn's only win that it took the state court to decide the outcome. Glenn Dunnaway instead has the dubious honor of being the first racer to finish last in series history as well as the first disqualified. The Gastonia, NC, racer with four Ns in his moniker crossed over to the other side on the Ides of March 1964.

Less than two hours after the start and despite all the flipping and slipping, Fonty took checkers for his eighth win of the year. He had the career lead in wins and poles at this point in the sport's history and narrowly lost the '51 title to Thomas. Fonty Flock had many wins left, including the '52 Southern 500, and was simply the best. Runner-up was Petty, Eubanks third, Tim Flock fourth in Ted Chester's Black Phantom, and Cotton Owens fifth with his best finish to date in a Studebaker. Seventh was Lewellen, eighth Shuman, tenth Bob Flock, and 11th was one-time winner Sales again driving the historic 98 Jr. It was Leon's last race on the *Silent Speedways of the Carolinas*, although he ran West Palm and Daytona in '52. On April 27, 1981, Leon passed away at the age of 57. Dell Pearson's eight-race career ended after this 12th and he went back to Portland. Donald Thomas was 13th, after relief by his big brother and car owner before halfway so Herb could get points toward his first title. Paschal was 14th looking for that first win and 15th was Bill Widenhouse. Nearly 8,000 saw Fonty complete his '51 Wilkes sweep and it seemed the only way to win there was to be a Sales or Flock.

That is until Sunday, March 30, 1952, when 24 Grand Nationals invaded the mountain track for a 200-lapper. Also that month, Humphrey Bogart and Vivian Leigh won Oscars, Alan Freed held the first rock concert in Cleveland (part of one, anyway), and Sun Records began pressing wax. The Wilkes County 24 were led by big names Fonty, Tim, Buck, Lee, Herb, Donald, Marshall, Dick, Joe, Bill, and Curtis. Herb and Buck had the front row and at the green, Herb moved off to another level altogether. It was a race for second as the most Fabulous of all the powerful Hudson Hornets led the entire 125 miles. Augusta's Harold Mays crashed a Chrysler on the first lap, ending his two-race career with a 24th and last. Circuit sophomore Dick Rathmann parked a *really* hot Hudson with a leaky radiator for 23rd, Tim Flock's Hornet blew for 21st, and Turner had a third potent Hudson pop a radiator for 20th. The worst crash occurred as Jersey's Frankie Schneider had just lapped Perk Brown and lost it, flipped back into Brown's path, and got clobbered. Both were uninjured and took 18th and 19th places. Marshall Teague withdrew for reasons probably no one except his lovely Mitzi knew and placed 16th. The bad day for Hudsons and radiators continued as Buck's also spouted and the man less than two weeks from his first win retired for 15th place. Eubanks lost his brakes in an Olds for 11th, Petty's Plymouth went out not handling for ninth, Paschal the Sailorman's Ford followed with a dead battery for eighth, and Shuman exited his Ford for seventh with bum shocks. It was a car-killing Sunday as only seven of 24 starters finished. Following the lone-surviving Hudson of Herb and Henry (Yunick) was Fonty second, Blair third, Donald Thomas fourth, and Newton, PA's Dave Terrell fifth in his first start. Neil Cole sixth and Otis Martin tenth were the other two finishers. It took 128 minutes for Thomas to nab the grand before ten times that many onlookers.

A field of 27 blended their colors with those splashed across the Brushy Mountains on Sunday, October 26, 1952. Herb Thomas and Fonty Flock, the recent Southern 500 winner, had the front row. When they roared off for 200 laps, Flock jumped out front and stayed there for about four miles until Herb stormed by, and that is how they finished nearly two hours later. Paul Richardson had a 39-lap career, crashing out for 25th. Paschal wrecked his Olds for 18th, as did Bub King in the final laps for ninth. The interesting finish went Thomas, Flock, Thomas, Flock, Rathmann. Herb and Donald swapped Yunick Hudsons 92 and 9 as the first three went the full 200 laps. Sixth was Lewellen, modified star Perk Brown seventh, Fred Dove peacefully landed a Packard eighth, J.C. White ended a five-race career 11th, Welborn was 12th, Petty 13th, and High Point's Coleman Grant ended a six-race, three-year career 15th. Buck was 16th, Eubanks 19th, Blair 26th, and last was Greenville's Joe Staton in Louise Smith's Ford 94. At this point in the sport's history, Tim Flock held a one-win margin over Herb Thomas in victories, 16 to 15. Over 6,000 fans watched Thomas win a grand at an average of 67.044.

March 1953 marked the deaths of mass murderer Josef Stalin, Queen Mary, and athletic icon Jim Thorpe. Countless television stations took to the air, a B-47 accidentally dropped a dud atomic bomb over Florence, SC, and Gary Cooper won an Oscar for *High Noon*. It was cold the 29th when 34 Grand Nationals took to the dirt for 125 miles in the fourth race of the season. They were gridded Thomas, Flock, Rathmann, Flock, Baker, Brown, Shuman, Turner, and others all the way to Otis Martin in 34th. This actually was a *cold* war as Tim Flock took the point and stayed for the first half of the race. Behind Tim's Ted Chester Hudson 91 was Fonty, Herb, Petty, Eubanks, Baker, Lewellen, Shuman, and Rathmann swapping spots, fenders, and gestures. June Cleveland fell out first in a

The peeling paint and piecemeal additions give the track a rustic, cobbled look that has no place in the modern, glitzy NASCAR of today.

Stude for 34th, Donald Thomas crashed for 33rd, and Wally Campbell parked his Dodge for 32nd.

Wally Campbell deserves more mention. Wally hustled through 11 Grand Nationals, was always a contender, but never won. He started 60th in the first Southern 500 even though he was the fastest qualifier at 82.4. Ironically, 500 winner Johnny Mantz was the slowest qualifier at 73.460. Go figure. Campbell captured a pole at Langhorne in the next race, lost again, and never had a top ten finish. A 32nd place at North Wilkesboro ended it for the Trenton Terror as far as the stockers go. In 1952, NASCAR's only year with the Speedway Division, Wally finished second to Buck for the title. Campbell tied for most wins with two. His AAA sprint car career was doing OK until he took to the high banks of Salem the day before his 28th birthday on July 15, 1954. A horrifying crash took Wally over to the other side during a test session.

Back at the race, Elton Hildreth destroyed a '51 Nash for 29th and Tim surrendered the lead to Curtis for nine laps until Rathmann took the lead for ten more. Perk Brown nabbed 27th after his gas tank fell off, Ray Duhigg wrecked a Plymouth for 30th, and Fonty led until Blair's crash brought out another caution. Engine failures sidelined Tim for 23rd and Turner for 22nd, before Fred Dove nested a Plymouth, claiming 21st. Rathmann paced the field for 60 circuits and looked like a cinch until Hustlin' Herb plowed by in his Hornet. Thomas tore home first over Dick, Fonty, and Lee. Rounding out the top ten were Lewellen, Baker, Eubanks, Slick Smith, Dick Passwater, and Bub King. Others were occasional Don Oldenberg's Packard 16th, Passwater's pal and car owner Frank Arford 17th with less than three months to live, and Shuman 31st. Herb won his third straight here, covering the 125 miles in just under an hour and three-quarters for $1,000.

Transcontinental jet service began in October 1953, the Yanks beat the Dodgers again for the Series, and Arthur Godfrey humiliated Julius La Rosa, firing him in front of the whole country for his crooner's "lack of humility." Up in 'shine country on Sunday the 11th, a field of 31 was set to see if someone besides a Flock or Thomas could visit Victory Lane at the mountain oval. Buck Baker put his Southern 500–winning Olds 88 on the pole, scorching the clay at over 71 miles an hour. There were some hot shoes on the grid named Turner, Eubanks, Paschal, Blair, Petty, Welborn, Sosebee, Thompson, Rathmann, and Lewellen, and double doses of Thomas and Flock. However, the courage award went to veteran Ray Duhigg, who returned from a broken neck suffered at Langhorne on June 21st in the race for which Frank Arford was killed qualifying. The field took the green and a furious battle broke out. Turner led the opening six rounds until Buck wrested it away for a lap. Then it was Curtis for one, Buck for two, and Curtis for eight. While war raged, Statesville Pete Stewart opened a 17-race career by dropping out for 30th. Baker assumed command for 52 laps, during which Slim Rominger of Clemmons, NC, ended his two-race career 26th. Fonty slammed his Vogt Hudson past Baker on lap 70 and stayed there until Buck swiped it back on the 89th for 15. Rathmann retired for 24th while Paschal parked 80 in 23rd. The second half was no less frantic as Fonty banged by Baker for two, then Turner took it from him until his engine soured and he was done for 22nd. Buck led for ten laps until Fonty stole it back for 16. Then while nobody was looking, Speedy Thompson driving Buckshot Morris' Olds powered by Flock and thundered away to win by a mile. Fonty claimed second and continued a remarkable streak here of seven top threes in eight chances. Third was the story of the day with Ray Duhigg's gutsy performance in his comeback start. Fourth was Welborn, fifth Lee Petty, with Baker sixth, Blair seventh, Eubanks eighth, Lewellen ninth, Bub King tenth, Don Thomas 11th, Tim Flock 12th, Sosebee 13th, Herb Thomas struggled to 15th, and Ralph Liguori took 16th. A measly throng of 2,000 witnessed a terrific battle for 84 minutes.

In April 1954 Elvis cut his first single, "That's All Right," and Swanson introduced America to the TV dinner in time for Sam Snead's Masters victory and the Army-McCarthy hearings. Sunday the fourth found wintry conditions in the mountains as two dozen stockers performed before a fine crowd of nearly 6,000 under a low overcast for 160 laps. Gober Sosebee won his third career pole, putting his Cherokee Garage 1954 Olds 51 inside the front row with Baker, Thomas, Petty, Paschal, Rathmann, Eubanks, and Welborn behind him. The 39-year-old Atlantan led for 94 laps before giving way to Rathmann's Pure Hudson for a mile. Rocky Mount's Blackie Pitt retired for 24th and last in his maiden voyage. He sailed along for five years and 81 races. Salem, IN's Stan Kross ran his only *Silent Speedways of the Carolinas* event with a 23rd-place finish. Ted Rambo from New Bloomington, OH, crashed what had to be one of the last new Lincolns to race in the Grand National Division for 20th. Ralph Dutton of Chilhowie, VA, ended his five-race career placing 18th. The second half saw Harry Ranier's Hudson pound the fence with Gilbert, WV, Chief of Police Bud Harless driving for 17th. Gober snatched the lead back from Rathmann for 18 rounds and hung tough until Rathmann passed with 45 to go and was gone. It did not help much that Sosebee's right front spindle snapped with eight left and dashed his chance for a final run at Rathmann, which most certainly would have been successful. Because with just over a mile left, the right front blew on Hudson 3 and Dick forged ahead without stopping. He had built up enough cushion to hold off the fast-closing Hornets of Thomas and Eubanks, and rimmed home first as Gober settled for 12th. It was the handsome 30-year-old Californian's 12th career checkers and the first for car owner John Ditz. Dick beat Herb's Hudson by nearly a lap and behind him charged Eubanks in a three-year-old Hornet. Fourth went to Turner, fifth Petty, sixth Liguori, seventh Al Keller, eighth Andy Winfree, ninth Paschal, and Lewellen tenth. Top threats Welborn drove a Petty entry to 11th and Buck was 18 laps down in 15th. It took the LA chauffeur nearly 88 minutes to cop the $1,000.

The New York Giants won the World Series and the TV season saw the premiers of *Father Knows Best* on CBS and *Disneyland* on ABC. It must have been October. Hazel also premiered, but not on NBC. She was in the sky! Hurricane Hazel was the most destructive named storm in U.S. history until then and got a running start in the eastern Caribbean, absolutely clobbering the South Carolina—North Carolina border, where she hit at 140 miles per hour. Hazel ripped a path all the way past Toronto. The month ended with a racing tragedy not of a stock car nature, but infamous nevertheless. On the day before his 52nd birthday on Halloween, the great three-time Indianapolis 500 winner and President of the Indianapolis Motor Speedway, Wilbur Shaw, perished when his private plane nosed into the rich Indiana soil just outside Decatur. Shaw recruited wealthy Hoosier industrialist and sportsman Anton Hulman to purchase the Speedway in its dilapidated state from World War I air ace Eddie Rickenbacker after they made the next world war number two. When preparing to start that first postwar 500 on May 30, 1946, Wilbur had struggled for days for something memorable to say in order to send the drivers on their journey. Then when the time came, Wilbur clutched the microphone to his lips and uttered those seven syllables worldwide that are unique to this great sport, "Gentlemen, start your engines!" It has been repeated thousands of times each week since.

At North Wilkesboro on Sunday, October 24, 1954, the *Silent Speedways of the Carolinas* gathered the *only* soul lost while pursuing glory and fame in the heat of Grand National competition. It was race 37, a number not that different from today's last race of the season. There was brilliant sunshine this crisp, colorful, autumn Sabbath. But the Grim Reaper crept around in the shadows on a day most unlikely for Death to play his hand. On the grid, Bridal Veil, OR's Hershel McGriff copped his fifth pole of the year mostly in Frank Christian's Air Lift Olds 14 with Dick Rathmann's Hudson outside. Lee Petty's Chrysler lined up third, having clinched the '54 Grand National Championship a week earlier in Martinsville. Those last races of the year usually have star-studded fields and this one of 32 entries had just that. Salting the grid were Baker, Owens, two Thomases, Jarrett, Panch, Sosebee, Figaro, Lewellen, Blair, Liguori, Eubanks, Widenhouse, Staley, Paschal, and 16 others. One will feel the cold touch of death. The green fell and the metallic maelstrom thundered into turn one with Hershel and Dick banging away. By the time they got back to the stripe, it was Rathmann out front with McGriff, Petty, Thomas, and Baker in tow. Champion Petty had sufficient cushion to enable him to fall out first for 32nd place. The King of Jazz Paul Whiteman's Cadillac of Gwyn Staley retired next for 31st and Dink Widenhouse was close behind in his famous B-29 Olds 30th. Rathmann whistled along out front as Gober Sosebee parked his Olds in 27th. McGriff, Baker, Figaro, and Panch continue to chase Rathmann's Hudson until the 83rd lap, when Hershel slipped by for a lap. Dick took it back for one and Hershel slammed back by on lap 85. The pace was too much for hometowner Jim Frey's Hudson that ended his one-race career in 25th. Cotton's Hornet blew soon after for 23rd, Lewellen's Mercury suspension broke for 22nd, and young Ned Jarrett's spindle popped for 21st. Rathmann's Hudson began to fade during the final laps and it was Hershel, Buck, and Herb duking it out for the win when it happened. It had never occurred before in the Carolinas and never did again. Scores of thundering, metal-wrenching, car-rending fatal crashes took place, but only once on the *Silent Speedways of the Carolinas* during a Grand National race. As the flagman hunted for the white and checkers, as the nearly 9,000 fans stood and cheered the warriors towards the finish, as the sun sank behind the Brushy Mountains and the shadows lengthened over the half-mile plus of red Carolina clay, the unthinkable struck. Only once before during the actual running of a Grand National event had Death ever swung his scythe at a driver and that was on September 14, 1952, when Larry Mann bought it in his Green Hornet Hudson at bloody Langhorne. On this sorry Sabbath, the 1954 Hudson Hornet number 187 launched into a sickening series of hard flips, the last of which came down with enormous impact, pancaking the roof nearly flat with the car's body. Strapped in the seat of this ill-fated Hornet was a little Inglewood,

CA, racer 13 days past his 37th birthday named Lou Figaro. The nearly nine thousand on hand looked on in horror as rescue workers pried Figaro from his demolished racer and carried the limp body to the ambulance for a trip to Wilkes County Hospital. There it took an extra swing of the scythe on Monday afternoon finally to put Lou away. Lou Figaro's head was crushed, but he hung in there as he had in nearly all of his starts in the big time.

Lou Figaro was no bum. In 1951, he ran 13 of 41 races and on June 30th, in his eighth career start, Lou won the pole and led all 200 laps in Gardena, CA, for his lone Grand National victory. In 1954, he had only run two other races, which had been the two previous where he took eighth at lethal Lehi and ninth at Martinsville. Lou's final career totals showed 16 races (13 in 1951 and 3 in 1954), a pole and a win, three top fives, six top tens, and $2,560 in winnings. The race that killed Figaro found him 11 laps behind in lucky 13th place with three to go and in no danger of improving or losing that position at the finish. His heirs won a hefty $25 for his effort that deadly day. Nonetheless, he was still driving hard enough to kill himself at that point and the obvious severity of the crash prompted the starter's search for the white and checkers to become the hunt for red that October afternoon.

This one ended at 157 laps, about a mile and a half short of the advertised distance. Figaro's fellow west-coaster Hershel McGriff was declared the winner. For Hershel, this was his ninth and final event on the *Silent Speedways of the Carolinas* and *great* does not begin to describe this legend's career. He ran 85 Grand National races beginning with a ninth-place finish in the first Southern 500 in 1950 at age 23, the same year he won the Pan American Road Race. He ended his big-time career finishing 43rd and last on May 16th, 1993, at Sonoma on one of his beloved road courses at 66. (That race was also the last ever won by a Bud Moore car, driven that day by Geoff Bodine.) Hershel raced in 24 of 37 events in 1954, the only year he tried for the Grand National title and he did not really try then. He won all four of his career victories that season, but wound up sixth in points, sandwiched between Eubanks and Paschal, both of whom ran more races. In no other season did he race more than five times, which happened in both '74 and '75. After 1954, he concentrated on his lucrative lumber business and the NASCAR West circuit until he retired. He owns the career wins mark out west with 34, although he only won the title in 1986. McGriff ventured back to the Winston Cup in 1971 and made his biggest splash coming home fifth in the '73 Daytona 500. He ran stockers at Le Mans for 24 hours, hopped over to Australia to the Thunderdome, and attacked Japan's Twin Rings. On April 27, 2002, he pulled into the pits during a 200-miler in Fontana, CA, and retired. No fanfare, no farewell tour, no fuss. Hershel McGriff's inclusion as one of NASCAR's 50 Greatest Drivers was one they *did* get right!

Behind McGriff came Baker second, Herb third, Slick Smith fourth, Rathmann fifth, Panch sixth, Liguori seventh, Blair eighth, Clyde Minter ninth, and Eubanks tenth. Paschal sailed in 12th, poor Lou died for 13th, Hooker Hood (great name) from Memphis in his only *Silent Speedways of the Carolinas* start finished 14th, and in 15th came Clyde Minter's brother Billy in the last of four dismal races. The star-crossed Lou Figaro *still* has three laps to go and he is out there regularly trying to complete them.

It was springtime across the planet in April 1955 when Winston Churchill resigned as British Prime Minister. Dr. Cary Middlecoff took the Masters, the Syracuse Nationals beat the Ft. Wayne Pistons for the NBA title, Jonas Salk discovered the polio vaccine, Ray Kroc opened the first McDonald's in Des Plaines, IL, Congress ordered all currency to include "In God We Trust," and Perez Prado's "Cherry Pink and Apple Blossom White" topped the charts. Peaceful stuff, unlike what took place on Sunday the third at North Wilkesboro

The backside of the main grandstand area is as obviously downhill as the track's homestretch.

Speedway. An overflow crowd of more than 10,000 packed in as 22 stockers lined up for 100 miles. Winning his first pole in his ninth start was the Concord Comet Dink Widenhouse in Olds B-29. Outside was Baker in an Olds and dotting the field were Johnson in an Olds, Tim in a Kiekhaefer Chrysler, Fonty in a Chevy, Turner in an Olds, Rathmann and Herb in Hudsons, Petty in a Chrysler, and Paschal in an Olds. These boys were about to create a little history. Baker jumped out front, but could never pull away. Fonty broke an axle in Christian's Olds and retired for 20th. Dink's hopes of victory evaporated on lap 56 when his engine blew for 19th and Johnson parked two laps later like Dink for 18th. While Baker tried to shake Rathmann, Paschal vapor locked for 16th and past halfway, Herb packed up for 14th. A lap later on the 106th, Kiekhaefer watched Tim drive the white 300 to the truck with electrical problems. Attrition sucked up contenders and Buck and Dick led Lee and Curtis as the laps wound down. With the checkers in sight, the crowd roared and watched in awe as Rathmann tried everything in his arsenal of tricks to squeeze past Baker, but it was nothing doing. Slamming, banging, and dispatching lapped cars as if they were stopped, the Olds and Hudson screamed off the fourth turn side by side and hammered each other to the line with smoke and dust flying. By less than a yard it was Bob Griffin's Olds 88 number 87 of Buck Baker nipping the John Ditz Blue Crown Spark Plug Hudson Hornet 3 of Dick Rathmann at the wire. It was the closest finish in the 184-race history of the Grand National series. The limp throng did not notice Turner beat Petty for third with Eddie Skinner slipping home fifth, Dave Terrell sixth, Lewellen seventh, Gene Simpson eighth, Joel Million ninth, and Blackie Pitt tenth. Others were Catlettsburg, KY's Tommy Ringstaff ending his three-race career in 11th driving a Packard. Also, one of the earliest father-son teams, John Dodd Sr. and Jr., drove Hudsons to 12th and 17th. It was Buck's tenth career win for $1,000 and he did it in a very fast, caution-free 82 minutes.

The second visit occurred October 23, 1955, before another overflow crowd of over ten thousand. The penultimate race of the year found Tim Flock assured of the points crown, having an incredible 17 checkers in the bulletproof Kiekhaefer Chrysler. The autumnal gathering of 28 battled to see who would be best in their class, which was the class without Tim Flock. Kiekhaefer brought three Chryslers, but they did not time trial well. The stellar field found Buck on the pole in De Paolo's Ford and Herb Thomas in Yunick's robin's egg blue, Southern 500–winning, Motoramic 1955 Chevy 92 on his right. Panch had a Ford and Petty a Dodge in row two, Dink's Ford and Fonty's Kiekhaefer held row three, Turner's Ford and Welborn's Chevy held the fourth, and Weatherly's Ford with Thompson's Kiekhaefer completed the top ten. On back were Eubanks, Johnson, Lewellen, Paschal, Staley, Blair, and a diminutive 26-year-old in his first start out of Chi-town named Pistone. Green silk flew and, as in April, Buck was gone. Even though this edition had three cautions, the boys managed to cover the 100 miles 47 seconds faster than before. The 20,000-plus attending the North Wilkesboro races of 1955 saw the closest race in history, but no lead changes. Buck Baker pushed Pete's Ford from the pole to pace the pack all 160 laps this time, too. Two poles, two wins, and all 320 laps led by Buck Baker, who obviously had the clay figured out in Wilkes County. Trailing Buck by half the home stretch was Petty second, Staley third a lap back in Hubert Westmoreland's Chevy, as was Weatherly in his Team Purple Pig Ford fourth, and the trio of Kiekhaefer Chryslers that swept fifth though seventh with Tim, Fonty, and Speedy three laps back. Others were Dink eighth, Dave Terrell ninth, Paschal tenth, Lewellen 12th, Welborn 13th, John McVitty with about six months to live safe at 17th, Liguori 18th, and Blair 19th. Curtis Turner in the other Purple Pig squeaked in 20th, and 500 winner Thomas tumbled to 21st after leaving the grounds between turns three and four on lap 90. Twenty-three-year-old Ned Jarrett was 22nd, not having cracked the top ten in seven starts, Panch 23rd, Eubanks 24th, Concord's Banks Simpson closed out a seven-race career 25th, and a tough little Chicagoan named Tom Pistone made his inaugural big-time start finishing 27th in the 28-car field. He would soon become Tiger Tom and one of the most popular and tenacious drivers on the circuit, winning twice in his 15th and 18th starts during a career spanning 14 seasons and 131 races. Nevertheless, Buck Baker crushingly dominated the '55 season at North Wilkesboro, so much to the chagrin of Carl Kiekhaefer that the Commandant hired the Charlotte chauffeur for 1956.

It was April in the Brushy Mountains for 1956 and 29 speed-happy thrillsters. Jack Burke, Jr., won the Masters, Nat King Cole was attacked on stage in Birmingham, six Marine recruits died at Parris Island, and Grace Kelly married Prince Rainier of Monaco. America's King Elvis Presley had "Heartbreak Hotel" hit number one and Ring King Rocky Marciano retired undefeated. On race day, WSPA TV, Channel 7, signed on for CBS in Spartanburg, becoming one of the first television stations in South Carolina. At the track, the factory war was in full swing and it was the universe against Kiekhaefer's Chryslers. Although not officially factory backed, Kiekhaefer's wealth, technical skill, and iron-fisted rule demonstrated in 1955 that he was more than a match for anything Detroit could throw at him. On Sunday, April 8, 1956, two of Carl's Chryslers and a Dodge went toe-to-toe with 26 others, but the boss would get a gut shot later that afternoon. Junior Johnson, Wilkes County's pride and joy, romped to the pole in his Brushy Mountain Motors '56 Pontiac 55 with Speedy outside in Mr. K's Dodge. Behind them in row two were Tim in the 300 Chrysler and Rex White in his fourth start, driving Chevy "number" X. The Ford factory showed in row three with Moody and Roberts followed by Smokey's Chevy for Herb Thomas and Paschal's Mercury. Six different makes in the first eight starters. Stacking the rest of the deck were Staley, Allen, Eubanks, Baker, Blair, Billy Myers, Lund, Petty, and Dink Widenhouse. Almost 8,000 roared their approval as the metal tornado swept into the first turn at the green. Pole-sitter and clear crowd favorite Junior Johnson stormed to first, staying there for

17 laps until his Iron Indian grenaded the engine, coasting to a smoky halt in the pits for 28th. Thompson took over and on lap 22 Allen wrecked Spook Crawford's Plymouth for 26th. Fireball dropped a drive shaft in De Paolo's Ford on the 38th circuit for 25th and Rex broke the front suspension on lap 112th for 19th. Thompson's lead was shaky at best and on lap 115, Tim Flock pulled off a classic pass of his stablemate and took the lead in a never-to-be-repeated scene! Thompson fell out a dozen laps later with a broken fuel line for 18th, Eubanks snapped an axle for 17th, and Staley cooked the tranny, winding up 15th. Flock was unable to bury the competition, but won by a comfortable margin over the factory Mercurys of Billy Myers and Jim Paschal with Thomas fourth on the lead lap. Fifth, a lap down was Moody, Widenhouse sixth, Clovis, CA's Allen Adkins seventh, Petty eighth, Blair ninth, and Winston-Salem's Whitey Norman tenth on his maiden voyage. Further back were non-factors Buck Baker in Mr. K's other Chrysler 11th, Lund 14th, and Startex, SC's Dick Blackwell in his third start 21st.

The next Sunday night, April 15, 1956, at 10 P.M. on CBS TV, Tim Flock took on John Daly's astute panel of Celeste Holm, Elsa Maxwell, Robert Q. Lewis, and Bennett Cerf on *What's My Line?* He signed into Game Four as T.F. Flock, self-employed "Champion Stock Car Race Driver," but time ran out and he won by default. He stated his next race was the following Sunday at Langhorne. His fellow contestants that night were Italian dress designer Mircol Fontana, Sing Sing Warden Wilfred L. Denno, and mystery guests "Debbie Reynolds and friend" who was, of course, hubby Eddie Fisher.

But alas, this one had a twist of tragedy as another young man had just raced his final Grand National event. John McVitty, from Mamaroneck, NY, had recently moved to Raleigh to make it in the big time and ran his 11th and final Grand National race, dropping out for 20th with a broken fuel pump on his '55 Chevy. He finished eighth in his first two career starts in 1955 at Fonda and Plattsburg, NY, and earned tenth at West Palm Beach in '56. However, when he walked into oily, spooky, deadly old Langhorne 13 days later, he did not walk alone. McVitty went out for his time trial on Saturday, April 21st, just one of 42 on hand for the same purpose. As he roared around the greasy circle, the Dark Rider on the Pale Horse curled his crooked finger at young John and beckoned him to the other side. The terrified onlookers went limp as the flipping Chevy 27 disgorged its pilot through the air and sent him tumbling onto the grimy track like a rag doll. Poor John never lasted until the race day Sabbath when his 41 adversaries carried on for 150 laps without him. They always do. Death is *always* there, but does not always pick a partner. At Langhorne, though, he very often did.

Back to North Wilkesboro, there was the conquering hero that fine Sunday afternoon. Tim Flock was without a doubt at the top of his game with no end to the winning in sight. Driving Carl Kiekhaefer's white 300 to his 21st win, he had notched 20 poles and 18 victories in 1955 for Mr. K and had three of each in the first ten races of '56. Tim had the ride of a lifetime. Then he went to visit Kiekhaefer that afternoon ... *and quit!* He also had stomach ulcers and the cure was going to work for Chevrolet, and he did. Commandant K tried to persuade him otherwise, but it was no go and Tim was gone. That never-to-be-repeated scene was Tim Flock taking the lead in his Kiekhaefer Chrysler. It had happened scores of times since 1955, but it never happened again! That left Baker to move up to the first chair at Kiekhaefer with Thomas and Thompson in the other two seats. Thomas would last until after Spartanburg three months later and he too would go Chevy. The post–Kiekhaefer years saw Tim win one more race later in '56 at Elkhart Lake in a Bill Stroppe Mercury, then drive unremarkably for 15 races spread thinly over the next five years. He hung it up after the 1961 World 600 and Bill France promptly kicked him out of the sport along with

Curtis Turner in the unionization fiasco. At 31, he quit, and at 36, *he was gone!* Tim Flock still holds the best winning percentage of anyone ... *a shocking 21.2 per cent, 39 for 187.* Tim Flock left us on March 31, 1998, at the age of 73.

Three hundred and sixty-four days later, they returned on April 7, 1957, along with about 8,000 fans and a skinny field of 20. The Kiekhaefers were gone, but there was a fantastic factory battle underway and most of the names were entering even the smallest events. North Wilkesboro was not small and of the 20 starters, at least a Buck Baker's dozen had a decent chance of winning in first-class Detroit-area iron. And the heaviest load came from Dearborn with Pete De Paolo's five, count 'em, *five* new Fairlanes for Roberts, Goldsmith, Moody, Panch, and Allen Adkins. Chevrolet countered with Hugh Babb's Bud Moore–wrenched Black Widows of Baker, Thompson, and Smith. Californian Bill Stroppe had his red, white, and blue Mercurys for Billy Myers and Jim Paschal, while Lee Petty had new Oldsmobiles for himself, Tiny Lund, and Ralph Earnhardt. Even Spook Crawford's factory Plymouth was there with Johnny Allen up. A slim, hot line up took the green for what promised to be a real scramble for those watching. What they got was a slaughter led by Fireball, who led all 160 laps, and the next three spots went to the next three Fords as listed earlier. Only Baker queered the deal of a total sweep for De Paolo by beating Adkins for fifth. Seventh was Petty, Mel Larson eighth, ninth Allen, Brownie King tenth, and Lund 11th. The only non-finishers were Thompson 16th, Myers 17th, Smith 18th, Earnhardt 19th, and Paschal 20th. There was finality to this event, but not many, if any, knew what. This was the 14th and final race on the mountain clay. When the gentlemen returned six months later for the penultimate race of the year, it would be on the asphalt ... and darkness would again shroud the event.

The title was decided a week earlier at Concord Speedway and Buck Baker was the Grand National Champion for the second year in a row. The very dashing Baker had driven Bud Moore's Chevy Bel Air 87 to nine wins and the flashy Roberts was next closest with eight. The factories were gone. There was no more De Paolo, no more Babb, and Kiekhaefer was a fading memory. There were great drivers matched with great mechanics racing on historic speedways. North Wilkesboro received a facelift, which was the first step in separating it from tracks in places like Spartanburg that looked healthy, but died quickly in the mid–'60s. North Wilkesboro took action to ensure its security on the schedule into the mid–'90s. On October 20, 1957, a field of 26 with nothing to lose set the grid for 100 miles, 160 laps, on the fresh asphalt. The pole went to none other than Fireball Roberts as he blistered the new surface barely a tenth of a mile an hour *faster* than on the dirt. Go figure. Flanking him was modified star and occasional Grand National driver Banjo Matthews. Behind them were Panch and Smith, Massey and Owens, Thompson and Petty, and Lund and King. However, the most popular man in the field was just returning from a government-ordered holiday in Chillicothe, OH, in federal stir. Hometown boy Junior Johnson was back from nearly a year off the trail and had his familiar Brushy Mountain Motors Pontiac 55 inside Baker in row six. It promised to be a doozy. At the drop of the green, Roberts had already blazed through turn one with 25 others in tow when Roy Tyner lost the handle on his Ford and was creamed by the Studebaker of George Parrish and the Mercury of Max Berrier. The new surface wasted no time claiming cars. Fireball took the next big hit when his front-running Ford vaulted the third turn fence on lap 61 and made a wheels-down landing on the mountain sod of the surrounding countryside. The 28-year-old speedster was unhurt for 21st and Jack Smith took the point in his Chevy 47 until Banjo Matthews led for 18. Junior Johnson was next out as his Pontiac blew for 20th. Then the fun ended on this cool Sunday afternoon.

On his 118th circuit, Tiny Lund's '57 Pontiac lurched sideways off the fourth turn and a wheel with the axle shaft still attached bounded off the blacktop, over the flimsy catch fence, and into an unsuspecting W.R. Thomason, up from Gaston County for the day. The poor man joined the ranks of the spectators worldwide who annually used to give their lives for the sport they loved. These doomed souls do not attend races with any expectation of their dying. The drivers definitely, the crewmembers maybe, but the paying public never fears dying at the races. It began when the first speed trials and long-distance events were run before the turn of the 20th century. It happened to 12-year-old Wilbur Brink, playing in his front yard at 2316 Georgetown Road across the street from the Indianapolis Motor Speedway on May 30, 1931, when leader Billy Arnold's errant tire and wheel took him out. It happened at Le Mans in the worst auto racing crash in history when 83 died on the spot and uncounted others later as the engine and suspension of Pierre Leveigh's Mercedes carved a horrific human trench through the main grandstand in 1955. Wolfgang Von Tripps took 14 with him while leading at Monza in 1961. Another died at Indy in '87, hit by a tire and wheel as he sat in the *top row* of the stands between turns three and four. Three more bought it by the deadly T & W combo watching a CART event at Michigan in '98. Another trio at Lowe's Motor Speedway, using free tickets, paid the ultimate price during an IRL race in '99. Only that time the show did not go on. But it will happen again ... and again ... and again. The Grim Reaper sits in the stands, too, and swings his scythe, sometimes taking heads in basketfuls. It is a wonder it has not happened a hundred more times than it has, especially at most of these *Silent Speedways of the Carolinas*. So at North Wilkesboro Speedway, Death visited for the second time in three years. A man was cut down and the race went on. And until Lowe's Motor Speedway in '99, it always did.

As it did this Sunday, when Jack Smith got it back for one round, then Banjo slipped by for 38 more until Smith seized it for good with ten to go. Banjo faded and Petty got runner-up a few seconds back in his Olds with Matthews third, his best finish until 1962. Fourth was Thompson in Bud Moore's Southern 500–winning Chevy, fifth Owens, sixth Baker, Panch seventh, White eighth, Bill Morton ninth, and tenth Massey. Others were future Chief Inspector Dick Beaty 12th, Allen 13th, and two guys that had cups of coffee in the big time. Jack Marsh's career ended here with 16th and Odessa, TX's Jim Russell took 17th. Tiny placed 19th in the fatal Pontiac 80 that was only a pawn in the ice-cold hands of the darkest of all powers that tragic afternoon. Over 5,000 fans were on hand that day and one less made it home that night.

May 18, 1958, was a gorgeous Brushy Mountain spring Sunday as 24 Grand Nationals took for the second time to the blacktop .625-mile oval. Jack Smith and Lee Petty had the front row, followed by crowd-pleaser Junior Johnson and Eddie Pagan, who crashed after time trials. Speedy and Rex had row three with Cotton and Whitey in four. Rounding out the top ten were Buck and Shorty. What great nicknames the drivers had back then, and what a great race 6,000 folks witnessed! Smith jumped out front and led the first mile and a half until Petty put his old Olds out front for about 20. Jack came back and led until giving it up to Junior on lap 79 as the almost non-existent attrition rate grabbed the first of only three that day. He was Cecil Grubbs, who had a 79-lap career and needed relief from E.J. Brewer to get credit for that much. The crossed flags flew over Johnson's Paul Spaulding '57 Ford 11 and he paced the field the rest of the way, winning by about a straightaway over Smith. It was Junior's sixth career win and his first in nearly three years when he won in Altamont, NY. Rex White was third in the lead lap with Baker fourth one behind, and Pagan fifth despite his time trial woes. On back came Owens sixth, Turner seventh, Doug Cox eighth, Wood ninth, Rollins tenth, Petty 11th, the Turtle 12th, Thompson 14th, and Norman 22nd. It took just over 75 minutes for the Ronda Roadrunner to win $800.

Panoramic view of the north end, Third and Fourth Turns, from Speedway Road.

October 1958 saw the Yankees beat the Braves in the Fall Classic. BOAC launched trans–Atlantic jet service. NASA was created and the first manned space shots, still several years away, were named the Mercury missions. And on the 19th, two dozen stockers gridded at North Wilkesboro on an autumn Sunday in race 50 of the 51-event season. Petty had already clinched the point title and brought along a kid in '57 Olds 2 making his eighth start, the future King Richard. Also in the field was pole-sitter Glen Wood with local superstar Johnson outside. Owens and Thompson held row two. Massey and Lund in three. Lee and Buck started seventh and eighth, while rounding out the top ten were Barney Shore and Richard Petty. There is not much to know about this one. Wood led early and the after-church crowd went wild when Junior put that unstoppable Spaulding Ford out front and in Victory Lane in a blistering 71 minutes. That is sizzling the asphalt at almost 85 miles per hour for 100 miles, a record that stood until 1962. It was Junior's tenth career win and fifth of the year, matching 1955. Wood was second a lap back, Thompson third, Cotton picked fourth, and fifth motored Smith. Others were Massey sixth, Wilbur Rakestraw seventh in the third of six career top tens, Lee ninth, Baker tenth, and Sosebee 11th in his *Silent Speedways of the Carolinas* finale. Newcomer Larry Frank was 12th, Lund 14th, Beam 16th, Rock Hill's Johnny Gardner made his 13th of 14 unimpressive career starts finishing 22nd, and Richard Petty overheated after 35 laps for 23rd. Junior hauled the $800 top prize down the road to the chicken farm.

Gober Sosebee ran the season finale at Lakewood in Atlanta a week later and in 1959 was part of the 21-car convertible contingent in the opening qualifier for the first Daytona 500. Then he took part in that amazing inaugural in a ragtop and lost the transmission after only 44 laps, taking 49th in a field of 59. At 44 years of age, but looking 64, Sosebee retired after helping usher in the super speedway era. He was special. Sosebee was a major cog in that famed Atlanta area moonshine/stock car clique that included the three Flocks, Jack Smith, Raymond Parks, Red Vogt, Roy Hall, and Lloyd Seay. He missed that Strictly Stock Charlotte opener in 1949, but sat on the pole in history's second race, held on the Beach. He drove in 71 Grand Nationals from 1949 to 1959 and used the number 14 once, 22 once, 44 once, 50 twelve times, and 51 a whopping 56 times. In an appropriate 51 starts, he was in a black Cherokee Garage–liveried racer with the famous Indian in the headdress portrait. Sosebee won twice and notched four poles, the last in the race before this one in the one and only event at the Salisbury Super Speedway. With 17 top fives and 33 top tens, Gober Sosebee was proven an outstanding racer that had a career worthy of numerous halls of fame. Gober the Great left this dimension on November 11, 1996, at the fabulous age of 81. Gober died in a farm tractor accident.

Innocent April 1959 arrived and the world was peaceful. Art Wall won the Masters, the Celtics won the NBA title, and Oscars went home with Susan Hayward and David Niven. They could not muster two dozen cars for the hundred-miler at North Wilkesboro on the fifth, missing it by one. However, top drivers entered as Speedy Thompson won his 19th and last pole with Glen Wood alongside. In row two were '58 Rookie of the Year Shorty Rollins and '58 Grand National Champion Lee Petty. Two of the all-time great throttle stompers, Junior Johnson and Curtis Turner, sat in the third row, followed by Spartanburg's Owens and Smith in four, and Lund and Fred Harb rounding out the top ten. At the green, Thompson sped away, pacing the field for the opening half of the race plus eight laps until a wheel bearing fried and Turner took over. Curtis was also done after 19 more laps and quit when lengthy repairs cost him too much time to contend. T-Bird team driver Tom Pistone soldiered on in relief. It was Old Man Petty back on top in his two-year-old Olds and he won by less than a lap over Smith, who won the night before in Columbia. Owens was third, Lund fourth, and Harb fifth. Others were Herman the Turtle sixth, Pistone 11th in Turner's T-Bird, Pardue 14th, Spencer 15th, Paul Walton of High Point ended a two-year, two-race career 16th, pole-sitter Speedy 17th with front row mate Wood 20th, Buck 21st, and Johnson's worn-out Ford 22nd. Over ten thousand witnessed the 83-minute show.

October 1959 saw the new LA Dodgers take the White Sox in six in the Series, the premiers of television classics *The Untouchables* and *The Twilight Zone*, and the death of the once dashing, but lately just dashed, Errol Flynn. The number-one song was Bobby Darin's "Mack the Knife." At North Wilkesboro on the 11th, 26 stockers went to the post led by Wood's '58 Ford and Petty's '59 Plymouth. Bob Welborn spiced up time trials by tumbling down the front stretch in his blue '59 Impala 49. In the race, the other two dozen did not much matter as Papa Lee led all 160 laps, winning handily over White and son Richard, both also doing all 100 miles. For the Old Man, it was his 48th career victory, tying him for the all-time lead with Herb Thomas, who won his last on June 3, 1956. Pistone was fourth, Johnson fifth in Paul Spaulding's new Dodge, Frank sixth, Wood seventh, Buck eighth, Smith 11th, Beam 14th, Thompson 15th, Irwin 23rd, Startex's Dick Blackwell ended a bleak two-year, six-race career 17th, and Jarrett in the reliable now number 38 ex–Spaulding Ford 25th. Three minor cautions flew in front of less than 6,000 fans.

The sixties roared onto the scene and by March, Lucy and Desi were divorcing, Elvis was on his way home from the Army, Ohio State won the NCAA basketball crown, and the U.S. Court of Appeals declared *Lady Chatterley's Lover* not obscene. For the first time, a major league baseball team, the Chicago White Sox, popped out of the dugout with names over the players' numbers on the backs of the uniforms. On the 27th, it got really ugly in North Wilkesboro. Nearly 10,000 fans poured into the stands that brisk, sunny Sunday as 22 Grand National aces hit the black top at the Brushy Mountain facility. Lee Petty, defending series champion, had his blue, high-finned 1960 Plymouth 42 tuned to take his third in a row here, but time trialed only eighth. The pole had gone to the fans' neighbor, Junior Johnson, piloting the Ray Fox '59 Chevy 27 he put in Victory Lane at Daytona six weeks earlier. Outside was none other than Glen Wood with Jarrett and Richard Petty in row two. Buck and Rex had new Chevies out of Spartanburg in row three, with Weatherly and the Old Man in the fourth, followed by Banjo and Joe Lee taking the fifth. Glen took the lead for a lap until Junior went past with the crowd roaring its approval. Joe Lee dropped out first for 22nd and last, joined shortly on the trailer when Rookie of the Year candidate David Gene Pearson, in his fourth start, hammered the wall in his red '59 Chevy 67 and loaded up for 19th. Richard Petty, coming off his first career win a month earlier, lost the engine for 18th. Banjo was next, bringing out the caution when he wrecked his new Ford 94 for 17th with Cotton losing the rear gears in a borrowed Ford for 16th. After Buck blew for 14th with 16 left, Lee laid some heavy iron on leader Johnson with 14 remaining, causing a quick ricochet off the fence, and the 500 winner lost too much time to make up. It is probably just as well because had Johnson caught Old Man Lee, he might have been looking at more jail time! As it was, amid a shower of more than just boos, Lee Petty stole home first followed closely by White, Wood, Jarrett, Johnson, and surprising Doug Yates, all in the lead lap. Tyner was one back in seventh, with Pardue eighth, youngster Buddy Baker ninth, and Weatherly tenth. Nearly 10,000 Junior Johnson fans witnessed the mugging of their favorite driver, and the reaction to Petty taking the checkers bordered on riotous. Risking bodily injury from the missiles raining down on him, Lee addressed the natives to no avail. It was impossible to find anyone outside the Petty camp that sided with the veteran who had just moved into sole possession of first place in the all-time victory column with his 49th win. Others were Paul Lewis from Johnson City, TN, in his first start 12th and Fayetteville's Bunkie Blackburn was right behind him in his second try. The Battle of Brushy Mountain took 26 ticks over an hour and a half in the last race there scheduled for less than 200 miles.

Try remembering October 1960 because many memorable moments occurred. Bank Americard charged onto the scene for the first time, an Eastern Airlines Lockheed Electra plunged into Boston Harbor taking 61 souls to the muddy bottom, and the tube saw *Route 66* premier on CBS Friday nights. On the diamond, Bobby Richardson's grand slam in the World Series was overshadowed by a solo blast five days later from Bill Mazeroski to win it all. The Yankees canned Casey Stengel and Dallas Cowboy Eddie LeBaron threw the shortest TD pass ever, *two inches*. Khrushchev pounded his shoe at the UN and the third and fourth Kennedy-Nixon debates aired. They arrested Martin Luther King in Atlanta, electric wristwatches hit the shelves, 16 of Cal State's football team perished in an air crash, and Cassius Clay pounded out his first pro fight, beating up Tunney Hunsucker. On Sunday the second, the Wilkes 200 was held, and two dozen Grand Nationals showed up to run for the first time longer than a hundred miles. This was scheduled for 320 laps, 200 miles around the .626-mile oval. Rex White in Louis Clements' gorgeous gold and white 1960 Impala sporting the red fours on the doors headed a nice field. He had the pole, flanked by Richard Petty's 1960 Fury, followed by Paschal in another Petty ride 44 and Buck Baker in his own white Chevy 87 in row two. Weatherly drove an obsolete Wood Brothers '58 Ford with Possum Jones in Tom Daniels' white '60 Chevy 2 in the third row ahead of Jarrett's red Galaxie 11 and Old Man Petty in row four. Doug Yates' year-old red Plymouth 23, alongside Junior Johnson lined up dead behind Lee Petty, who had nailed him for the win back in the spring, rounded out the top ten. Other good pilots were further back and one was going to come hard. The green flew and so did 11th placer Cotton Owens in his white 1960 Bonneville 6. While White and Petty battled up front, Cotton was ripping through the field toward the point. When he got there, he wasted no time dispatching Rex and motored way with authority. Meanwhile behind him, stockers were stacking up as the yellow bunting waved for a number of nasty incidents. Much to the approval of the packed house, Petty the Elder pummeled the concrete on lap 129 for 20th place with Johnson no doubt grinning through the grime like the proverbial cat. All was quiet until over a hundred laps later when Yates popped the wall for 19th, racing for leftovers as Cotton had checked out on the field. Owens put distance between himself and White and then the caution would fly and erase his advantage. It happened again on lap 241, only the yellow was for Owens. A left front ball joint snapped, sending the little Spartan slamming the wall, then rolling behind it for an unfair 18th-place finish. The final 78 rounds saw a decent battle twixt White and the challenges of Johnson, Paschal, and a Jones who was not playing possum. Then with about seven miles to go, Paschal's bid flattened like his right front tire, causing him to whack the fence and relegating the High Point hotshot to his trailer. When the green waved for a final shootout, the Impalas of Johnson and Jones were no match for Rex's as the other little Spartan powered home first with an easy spread over Junior and Possum, who toured all 320 circuits. Fourth, a lap back, was Weatherly, fifth Buck, sixth Richard, seventh Jarrett, eighth to Rookie of the Year shoo-in Pearson, ninth the Chevy of Pistone, and tenth Paschal. Further back roared the other hometown boy Jimmy Pardue 12th, Buddy Baker 13th, the Turtle 14th, the Crawfish 15th, Spencer 17th, Frank 22nd, Elmo 23rd, and 24th and last Paul Lewis. Rex was a race away from clinching the Grand National Championship of 1960 at Charlotte in the National 400 a fortnight hence, winning a hefty $2,200. And no missiles were launched at the winner this time.

Sunday, April 16, 1961, was the day the Chicago Black Hawks won a Stanley Cup and the day before the Bay of Pigs invasion. On this perfect spring Sabbath, almost 13,000 people filled North Wilkesboro Speedway for the biggest race there ever. The 400-lap, 250-mile spectacular promised nearly $2,500 to the victor. A fine field of 25 lined up with favorite Junior Johnson on the pole in his Holly Farms '61 Pontiac 27 and outside the Chevrolet of Rex White coming off consecutive finishes here of eighth, third, second, second, and first. The second row found Richard Petty revving it up beside Curtis Turner in the Wood Brothers 21 Ford. Row three sat budding Ford superstar Fred Lorenzen in his third start in the white Holman-Moody 28 that was to become a mainstay on the tour for two weeks short of the next *six years*. Beside Fred was Inman's Tommy Irwin in Tom Daniel's '60 Chevy 2, determined to prove he belonged with the top-shelf chauffeurs. Behind them came Greenville's Johnny Allen and local Jimmy Pardue in Chevies, and Jarrett's Chevy with Buddy in Buck's Chrysler 87. Two to be reckoned with among the other 15 starters were Buck in Buddy's Chrysler 86 gridded 11th and Fireball Roberts 19th in Yunick's 1960 Pontiac 22, although it was 20 when Panch drove it to victory in the Daytona 500 less than two months earlier. On the start, Junior jumped out front with Rex White hot on his heels. Gremlins foiled the rear end of Buck's big-finned Chrysler on lap 27 for 25th and last. Jarrett lasted two laps longer for 24th. Then as Junior showed them the way, his tranny went up in smoke and the crowd darling was stuck with 22nd after pacing the field for the opening 62 laps. Taking over from Johnson was Fearless Freddy, who settled in for 61 tours until he blew the motor in the Lafayette Ford for 19th and White regained his familiar top spot. Rex led until Turner slipped past on the 241st round and looked like he would notch his first win since March of 1959. Out of the clear blue, his Wood Brothers differential fried and Curtis parked for 14th. With that, White cruised back to the lead and rode home to a two-lap bulge over second-placer Irwin in his unheralded year-old Impala. Irwin tied his previous best finish and proved he could hang with the big boys by beating out third-placer Richard Petty, Fireball fourth, and Allen, who crashed with a few laps, left fifth. On back came Zervakis sixth, Buddy seventh, Harb eighth, Beam ninth, and with his first top ten in his 11th start, Reb Wickersham in his 1960 Flying Rebel Racing Team Oldsmobile 33. Crawfish was 11th, Scott 15th, Pardue 17th, Spencer 18th, and Lewis 21st. The longer distance took three hours and 11 minutes to complete and Rex White padded his point lead while cramming $2,455 into his wallet.

The old and the older. The wooden fence may pre-date paving the track in 1957.

The largest field in this race since 1954 greeted a crowd of more than 9,000 for the Wilkes 200 on the October 1, 1961. Thirty entries lined up for over $3,100, led by defending Grand National Champion and the winner of the last two in a row here, Rex White, in his Louis Clements '61 Chevy. Although starting this one behind crowd favorite Junior Johnson and Banjo Matthews, White owned North Wilkesboro with an incredible record since 1957 with consecutive finishes of eighth, third, second, second, first, and first. To his right was Paschal, followed by teammates for the day in matching Bud Moore Pontiacs, Joe Weatherly in 8 and Fireball Roberts in 22. Rows four and five held Smith and Irwin, then Buck and Ned. For the first quarter, it was all Johnson, taken by Weatherly for a lap. In the meantime, Buck blew his Chrysler after only 28 laps for 27th. Junior battled back past Weatherly on the 81st round and stayed there until White finally found the point on lap 120, remaining the leader for the rest of the way. A caution came out due to a two-car crackup involving Allen and Spencer just past halfway. The race had just lost Owens and Smith to engine trouble for 25th and 24th places. When the green reappeared, it was a fight for second as Rex checked out again, leaving Roberts as the only guy within a mile of him. A late crash knocked Irwin out with a solid finish in hand, but the yellow was not enough to thwart Relentless Rex. When the checkers fell, the gold and white Impala had a lap on Fireball in second, four on Petty in third, and five on Johnson and Jarrett in fourth and fifth. On back came Zervakis sixth, Pardue seventh, Weatherly eighth, Bill Morton ninth, and Yates tenth. Irwin took 11th in spite of the crash, Larry Thomas 12th, Wendell 13th,

Crawfish 14th, the Turtle 15th, Lewis 16th, Banjo lost his Wood Brothers rear end for 20th, and Paschal snapped his drive shaft for 21st. White notched his 20th career win and edged closer to championship leader Jarrett in his quest for two titles in a row, which he would fall 830 points short of after the last four events of the 1961 season.

Tax Day, April 15, 1962, was bitterly cold for the inaugural Gwyn Staley 400. The next Day, Walter Cronkite took over the *CBS Evening News with Douglas Edwards*. On the Sabbath, a whopping field of 35, topped only by the 38 cars in April of 1951, hit the blacktop determined to break Rex White's stranglehold on the mountain venue. It turned out to be anything but routine. Rex was blazing hot with consecutive wins at Hillsborough March 18th and Richmond April 1st. At North Wilkesboro, where *he* was the King, Rex had 12th on the starting grid. The five rows ahead of White held pole-sitter, as usual, Junior Johnson paired with Weatherly. Shocking Billy Wade was third in James Turner's old Pontiac 24 inside of Fireball in Banjo's Warrior Motel Pontiac 22. Roberts had just left Smokey's black and gold Bonneville that swept everything in sight two months earlier at Daytona. Row three found Pardue in his own Pontiac flanked by Lorenzen in the powerful Holman-Moody Ford. Row four held Irwin's Chevy 27 from Monroe Shook and Holman-Moody's yellow 29 of Nelson Stacy of Cincinnati. The top ten filled out with Owens' Pontiac alongside the Wood Boys' 21 of Panch. Bobby Johns of Miami had his beautiful blue and white Bonneville 72 inside Rex, and with a lineup like that, there was no doubt that the winner would come from the first six rows. As outstanding as the top dozen were, others loomed back in the field not to be discounted, like Smith, Jarrett, Petty, Dieringer, Frank, Baker, Pearson, Paschal, and in his first start in almost four years, the legendary Herb Thomas. Others with a ghost of a chance were Scott, Turtle, and Crawfish. As always, Johnson sped away, but Fireball ran Junior down, dashing off for the next 95 laps while Pearson retired Julian Petty's 1962 Pontiac 44 for 33rd. Joe Weatherly in Moore's 8 fought around Roberts and paced the field for 90 laps as Panch lost his rear end for 32nd and Rex's torrid streak ended as he retired for 31st just ahead of his neighbor Cotton Owens. The excitement level got a boost on lap 198 when Jimmy Pardue crashed out for 28th. Little Joe was locked in desperate combat with Fireball when Roberts whacked Weatherly into the rail, allowing Richard Petty to take the point. Weatherly lost laps galore while Bud repaired the Pontiac, then compounded his woes by passing under a caution. Petty was in control until Jarrett nipped ahead for 54 rounds and Roberts made an unscheduled stop, knocking him from contention. A bizarre shortage of Pure Firebird fuel, caused by the large field and lack of attrition, brought out a caution so a tanker, gasoline, not a moonshine hauler, could go to town for more. No doubt, a few folks probably ran dry on their way home after being secretly visited by crew members with siphon hoses and buckets. Transmission failures eliminated Paschal for 26th, Stacy for 25th, and a telltale trail of smoke signaled the end of the line for Jarrett on lap 318. Petty took the lead with Lorenzen shadowing his every move, surviving a late caution when Wade crashed with 18 left. The handsome Chicagoan was unable to get by and Petty motored to his sixth career victory. Freddy was second, Johnson a lap back got third, Roberts did a fabulous job getting back all but two laps for fourth, and fifth was surprising Darel Dieringer in Bob Osiecki's red '62 Dodge 90. Buck took sixth, Frank seventh, Weatherly padded his point lead with eighth, Smith ninth, and Houston youngster Billy Wade salvaged tenth in spite of crashing. Further back was Spencer 11th, J.C. Hendricks of Griffin, GA, ending a three-year, six-race career 13th, Larry Thomas 15th, Johns 16th, Irwin 18th, Crawfish 19th, Turtle 20th, and Gerald Duke of College Park, GA, in his last race on the *Silent Speedways of the Carolinas*, 21st in the 16th of a 17-race, four-year career.

The 14th place finisher deserves *extra special* recognition. Starting 23rd and finishing

23 laps behind, was the old trucker out of Olivia, NC, Herbert Watson Thomas. It was his 228th and last start. A *horrific* crash in Charlotte in 1955, his near-death at the hands of Speedy Thompson in Shelby in 1956, and his Fonty Flock–driven car's tragic Darlington in 1957 were detailed previously. But until that fateful Shelby Saturday night, Herb was in his prime at 33 years old and batting .213 with 48 wins and Tim Flock next closest at 39 checkers. Piloting Yunick-wrenched Hudsons, Buicks, and Chevies, he nabbed most of those wins. He was almost always number 92, except when driving as a Kiekhaefer clone, and was only 39 years old when he retired after this Brushy Mountain Sunday. Lee Petty won 47 races after his 39th birthday! Dale Earnhardt won 37 and Richard Petty won 23. And Harry Gant won all 18 of his victories after he was 39! It was 179 races before Lee Petty tied Thomas for the career win total in October 1959 at North Wilkesboro and 187 before Lee surpassed it the very next time they returned in March of 1960. Herb Thomas grabbed 39 poles, making the top ten 68 per cent of the time. He was 29th in the first Strictly Stock Car race in Charlotte, won three Southern 500s, and two Grand National Championships. There is absolutely no telling how many wins and titles Herb Thomas might have captured if he could have continued in top equipment for another five or six years. Herb raced only three times after the Shelby ambush and not at all from 1957 until this frigid April in 1962. On August 9, 2000, Herb Thomas left this dimension to race again in the twilight, probably in a Hudson number 92. And just like his contemporaries Bill Holland, Jack Smith, and Jim Paschal, Herb Thomas was 77 years of age at the time of his passing.

Thirty days hath September, and one was race day in 1962. That month, the population of the planet hit three billion, Maury Wills of the Dodgers stole his 100th base of the season, and Sonny Liston flattened Floyd Patterson in the first round for the heavyweight title. *The Beverly Hillbillies* premiered on CBS Wednesdays, ABC introduced color with *The Jetsons*, and the U.S. Supreme Court ordered James Meredith's admission to the University of Mississippi. Over 11,000 of the three billion inhabitants on Earth settled into the picturesque speedway off Highway 421 for 320 laps of stock car action. Another big field of 31 entered for the Wilkes 320 on Fireball Roberts Day. Fred Lorenzen grabbed the pole and with him was Holman-Moody's Nelson Stacy on the front row. Row two had Panch in a Wood Brothers Ford and Paschal driving for the Pettys followed by Richard Petty and Johnny Allen in the Holly Farms Pontiac 46. The fourth row found Johnson and the man of the day Roberts with Weatherly and Buck Baker's Chrysler right behind. It was all Lorenzen at the start as he paced the pack for 124 rounds. The first car out was one of those that goes into the record books as existing on the very fringe of the history of the sport. Wilkesboro's George Fox started 29th in hometowner Bobby Waddell's 1960 Dodge 5, raced his heart out for 1.875 miles, and parked for 31st and last, ending a promising career after three laps. Waddell was saddled with a pair of soon to be ineligible 1960 goats because his number 50 only went 50 laps further than number 5 for 30th. Waddell's 37-race, seven-year career ended that day, too. Roberts soon found out that although it was his day, it was not his day as the Matthews Pontiac blew for 29th place. Then motor woes terminated Wendell in 28th, Buck 27th, Tiny 26th, and Buck's boy Buddy crashed for 23rd. Back at the front, Junior slipped past Lorenzen and stayed there until the cross flags flew, when Petty took over and checked out. Sherman Utsman and Tom Cox were involved in heavy wall bangers, bringing out yellows, but nothing could stop Petty's potent Plymouth. Panch and Weatherly were in the same lap, but unable to challenge, with Johnson and Paschal a lap back in fourth and fifth. Others were Lorenzen sixth, Stacy seventh, White eighth, Allen ninth, Pardue tenth, Jarrett 11th, Dieringer 12th, Smith 13th, recent Southern 500 winner Larry Frank 14th, Welborn 15th, and finishing in tandem for the third straight time here were, in reverse of the usual, Turtle 20th and Crawfish 21st. Even though Petty chipped away at Weatherly's point lead here, Joe beat Richard in the final two events at Charlotte and Atlanta to bring the Grand National title to Spartanburg after a two-year absence and to Bud Moore's Garage for the first time since 1957.

Big car counts and ever-bigger crowds marked the April 28, 1963, Gwyn Staley Memorial 400 under threatening spring skies. Elsewhere, Jack Nicklaus won the Masters and the Mets bought Duke Snider for $40,000 from the Dodgers. Anne Bancroft and Gregory Peck went home with Oscars and the U.S.S. *Thresher* was lost with all hands aboard off Boston. Pete Rose tripled in his first at-bat and Bob Cousy retired the day the Celtics won the NBA title. Nearly 14,000 fans packed North Wilkesboro Speedway for the 250-miler. Lorenzen had the pole again with shocking Daytona 500 winner Tiny Lund outside in the Wood Brothers 21. Champion Weatherly had Moore's Pontiac third beside Junior Johnson's Ray Fox Chevy 3. Rows three through five found Baker's Pontiac and White's Chevy, Petty's Plymouth and Jarrett's Ford, then Paschal's Plymouth with Isaac's Ford. In a big hurry due to the moisture-laden clouds hanging low over the Brushy Mountains, Lorenzen took off, pacing the field for the 19 laps until Johnson powered by in the Chevrolet that was by far Ford's chief rival. But as Junior was pouring it on out front on the 98th lap, the 427-horsepower engine exploded like a bomb, as did a large section of the fence Junior crashed into while trying to control the careening monster. All he got was $250 and 27th place. A 24-year-old named LeeRoy Yarbrough fell out right after Johnson for 26th, as did Jarrett for 25th and Weatherly in 23rd. Freddy took command after Johnson's crash, but gave it up to Lund until Petty gained the upper hand. Richard was still there when the rains finally came, halting the event after 257 of 400 laps. Try as they might to finish the advertised distance, it was no go and Petty was the winner for the third consecutive race here, matching back-to-back three-peats by Papa Lee and Rex White. Second went to Lorenzen with Lund third, Paschal fourth, and Buck Baker fifth. Others were Pearson sixth, White seventh, Isaac eighth, Wade ninth, and Smith tenth. Larry Thomas 11th, Crider 12th, Buddy Baker 13th, Jimmy Massey in Hubert Westmoreland's Chevy 14th, Beam 15th, and Scott 21st. The huge, soggy crowd filed out after nearly two hours of collectively trying to will away the rain.

September 1963 was a busy time with some good, some sad, and some very bad happenings. In sports, the Professional Football Hall of Fame opened in Canton, OH, and Major League Baseball played its 100,000th game. Stan the Man had his last at-bat, as did the Polo Grounds, and San Fran sent three Alous to the outfield at once. On TV, network news went from 15 to 30 minutes and *The Outer Limits* and *The Fugitive* hit the air. Politically, George C. Wallace stood in the doorway of Tuskegee High and four little black kids were killed in the bombing of a Baptist church in Birmingham. On race day, the Rolling Stones' first concert tour ever had them opening in England for Bo Diddley and the Everly Brothers. In the cool mountain air of the 29th, 28 stockers lined up for 400 laps in the Wilkes 250. Fred Lorenzen, streaking on his astonishing assault of the $100,000 mark in winnings for the year, snagged the pole with teammate and recent Southern 500 winner Fireball Roberts to his right. Row two found courageous Marvin Panch, in his tenth start since life-threatening injuries in February at Daytona, alongside the third Holman-Moody Fastback of Nelson Stacy. Rows three through five housed Weatherly and Smith, Jarrett and Petty, and Johnson and Pearson. When the green fell, Fireball led the opening 153 laps. During that stint, Junior parked the popular Holly Farms Chevy after only four laps as brake problems relegated him to 28th and last. Two Petty Plymouths blew up, saddling Richard with 26th and Massey with 25th. Jack Smith's Plymouth lost its rear end next, prompting a 24th for the burly veteran. Lorenzen and Stacy swapped the lead for the next 70 circuits until Roberts and Lorenzen fought it out later. Dr. L.L. Reitzel ended a 29-race, three-season career, crashing for 23rd. The Charlotte driver curiously passed away on September 24, 1965, ten days after his 33rd birthday. On lap 231, Panch, who had been hanging around the top five watching his Ford friends duke it out, decided it was time to go ... *and went!* He led 82 laps, during which time Pardue retired for 22nd, Johns blew for 21st, Frank lost the binders for 20th, and uncharacteristically, Buck Baker crashed and was credited with 19th. Lorenzen edged past Marvin to lead for 39 laps, but bad rubber stymied Freddy's plans and with 49 to go, Pancho retook the lead, and that was that. Lorenzen was a good quarter-lap behind in second, Stacy was two back in third, Roberts, Jarrett, and Weatherly crossed the line three laps in arrears in fourth, fifth, and sixth. White's new Louis Clements Mercury was seventh, ten laps down. It took going back to eighth place to find a non–Ford product as Pearson put Cotton's Dodge there, Tiny had Ford ninth, and Thomas was tenth in an old goat. Dieringer was 11th, Welborn 12th, Crawfish 13th, Wickersham 14th, and dependable Wendell 15th.

For seventh-placer Rex White, this was his final race on the *Silent Speedways of the Carolinas.* Rex transplanted about 1959 from Silver Spring, MD, to Spartanburg. He was a little guy and the rumor around town was that he had failed his driver's license test at least once and had to sit on a phone book finally to pass it. Rex was a winner, a champion, and retired way before it was necessary. He was not yet 35 when the 1964 season arrived and he split with his partner of many years, Louis Clements, for cross-town owner Bud Moore. Rex ran third at Charlotte the day Fireball burned and was the fastest qualifier in his final Grand National start at Atlanta for the Dixie 400 in June. Because he did not time trial on the first day, he lost the pole. Rex finished fifth a lap behind and called it a career, a big-time career anyway. Rex White ran and won an ungodly number of limited sportsman races (parent of the current Busch Series) in 1965 in a '55 Chevy 4 dolled up in his familiar gold, white, and red livery. In his late 70s, Rex looks 50 and could not be friendlier. How good was he? The big time saw him race 229 times from 1956 to 1964, nabbing 28 victories with 36 poles and the 1960 Grand National Championship. He averaged starting nearly eighth and averaged finishing exactly ninth. Solid, charismatic, and towering over the competition at five feet four, he was a great driver and remains a great guy living in Atlanta. As of this writing, Rex White is the oldest living Grand National Champion.

As for winner Panch this beautiful autumn day, he won, climaxing a comeback from flesh-gnarling burns received seven months earlier in a Maserati crash at Daytona. Everybody knows that tale, but his return an amazing three months after is another story altogether. Marvin competed a dozen times and his *worst* finish was ninth. Prior to this win, he had back-to-back seconds and in two races after this, he backed up poles with thirds. *Marvin was back!* And in one more sidebar, this was Fireball Roberts' last complete race on the *Silent Speedways of the Carolinas.*

April 19, 1964, was a spectacular spring Sunday with a field of 31 on hand. It had been a brutal week for the boys as *four* Grand Nationals had already been held. Panch won at Weaverville on Saturday the 11th, Pearson the next day at Hillsborough, Jarrett on Tuesday the 14th in Spartanburg, again on Thursday the 16th in Columbia, and finally on Sunday the 19th it was North Wilkesboro. This one paid three times as much to win as any of the others, a whopping $3,950. The stars and stars-to-be were all there, with Fred Lorenzen taking his fourth straight pole here in the white Ford 28 so familiar to everyone. Starting outside was his fiercest rival Richard Petty, making this one even spicier. Behind by rows were Panch and Dieringer, Wade and Johnson, Buck Baker and Pardue, and Pearson and Thomas. The field was salted with Jarrett, Paschal, Yarborough, Yarbrough, Johns, Scott, and Spencer. But the big disappointment was that Fireball Roberts, in boring through the steel guardrail and reducing the board fence behind it to kindling, had so pulverized his Passino Purple Fastback Ford in time trials that the Holman-Moody crew could not get it repaired in time. It was Fireball's last *Silent Speedways of the Carolinas* appearance. More on that later. The green fell on this factory short track battle when the war was at its hottest since the spring of 1957. This was the 18th race of the year and FoMoCo had nine wins to seven for Mopar and one slipped in by GM when Wendell Scott won at Jacksonville, FL. The early stages lived up to the billing as Fred led with everybody hammering away at him and each other in his wake. There were numerous slams, spins, and slides that did not warrant a caution, but seven times they did. Even so, the attrition rate was not that high. Bob Cooper crashed on lap 28 for 27th and LeeRoy Yarbrough's Elmo Henderson Pontiac lost its brakes for 26th. After six laps on top, surprising Darel Dieringer shoved Bill Stroppe's California-based Mercury out front. It was not surprising because of either of their skills or reputation, but because North Wilkesboro was Bud Moore–Billy Wade east coast Mercury territory. After Dieringer's stint leading, it was Lorenzen again for 76 as Thomas parked his Dodge for 24th. Pit stops scrambled the standings and Jarrett led a few laps along with Petty. When everything was sorted out, Fearless Freddy was winning again 30 laps before halfway and managed to stay there for the last 230. Cale Yarborough dropped out in Herman Beam's respectable 19, finishing 23rd. Only 30th and last-place starting Jarrett in Bondy Long's Ford was able to complete all 400 laps of the Gwyn Staley 400 as Lorenzen did. A lap back in third was Pancho in the Wood Brothers Ford, fourth-placer Junior Johnson was five behind in a Ray Fox Dodge, Dieringer was fifth in Stroppe's Mercury, Buck Baker and Petty were sixth and seventh in Petty Plymouths, eighth came Wade in Moore's Marauder, and tenth and 11th were Paschal and Pearson driving Cotton's Dodges. Others were Spencer 12th, Pardue 13th, Crider 14th, Scott 16th, Buddy Baker 17th, and Castles 20th in one of Buck's antique Chryslers. It took Lorenzen just over three hours to pull it off before a throng of over 17 thousand.

Then there was Edward Glen "Fireball" Roberts. His actual last *Silent Speedways of the Carolinas* race was here back on September 29, 1963, when he nabbed fourth. But this was the last time he showed up at one, but crashed too hard to race reaching for the pole, which was all he ever did. There is a good argument that Fireball was the greatest driver ever. The numbers say that Roberts won 33 times in 202 big-time races. He ran only 9 of 19 races in 1950 and would have won the point championship if he had only stroked at Hillsborough in the last race, when eventual champ Bill Rexford fell out early, practically handing the title to Roberts. The only year he tried to win the crown was 1957, when he ran 42 of 53 events, won eight, and had only sixth in the standings to show for it. In '61 and '63, he was fifth in the rankings and did not come close to competing in half the races. He captured his first pole at North Wilkesboro in his seventh start and won his last event on the doomed-after-one race road course called the Augusta International Raceway, a coma-inducing track that was quickly liquidated. Roberts' last season, 1964, was mixed after that initial win at Augusta. He fell out early in the Daytona 500, had a hard crash with Pearson at Atlanta, and had this disaster in the Brushy Mountains. After that, Fireball paired a fifth at Martinsville with a second at Darlington, only to burn in his World 600 horror, passing away 39 days later. Fireball Roberts the greatest ever? Probably not, *but his nickname was!*

A racing season tired of death and just plain tired was coming off the horrifying plunge of North Wilkesboro's Jimmy Pardue three weeks earlier. On October 11, 1964, a large car count gridded for the Wilkes 400 under sunny autumn skies. It was the month Eddie Cantor, Cole Porter, and Herbert Hoover passed away. The Tokyo Olympics opened, Dr. Martin Luther King won the Nobel Peace Prize, Craig Breedlove passed the salt at 526.61 miles

Wonderful contrast of a modern steel grandstand and the ancient, but massive wooden fence behind Turn Two.

per hour, and St. Louis beat the Yankees in the World Series, getting Yogi fired. Also, the Rolling Stones first appeared on *The Ed Sullivan Show*, and Viking Jim Marshall scooped up a fumble and scampered 66 yards the wrong way for a safety. As the 58th race of the year, this was two races beyond the 56 in '56 that held the record as Grand National's longest season. Richard Petty had almost locked up his first championship, but lined up anyway with 31 others for 400 laps on the warped .625 oval. Petty timed third looking at the back bumper of front row starter Junior Johnson in his track record–smashing yellow Holly Farms Poultry Galaxie 27. Junior's pole was the first here at more than 100 miles per hour and was over six and a half miles an hour faster than the previous track record! Pearson's white and red-roofed Polara 6 sat outside of Junior. To Petty's right was Lorenzen, who was off the pole here for the first time since 1962. Behind Petty, playfully rapping his chrome, was Pancho, flanked by Paschal in Petty's other Plymouth. Rounding out the top ten were Jarrett and Dieringer, auditioning Cale Yarborough, and ageless Southern 500–winner Buck Baker. At the start, Junior took off, and the fight was on as mid-packers Doug Cooper and Buddy Arrington crashed before a mile was in the books. Johnson City, TN's Mark Hurley wound up a four-year, 16-race career parking for 30th. Title-chaser Jarrett went only three laps further for 29th, dashing his championship dreams. Paul Lewis overheated for 26th, Buddy Baker trailered Bernie Alvarez's Ford for 22nd, and Paschal blew the World 600 winner for 21st. Meanwhile, Junior led for the opening 91 laps until Dieringer slammed Bud's Marauder 16 by to lead for a couple before Johnson wrested it back. As the crossed flags approached,

Mopar took a triple hit as Petty lost his rear end for 19th, Earl Balmer driving Cotton's 5 DNF'd for 18th, and partner Pearson blew for 17th. The second half saw the Fords of Johnson, Lorenzen, and Panch engage in a spirited duel, swapping the lead seven times down the stretch. Crowd-pleasers Wendell Scott and Junior Johnson blew and were credited with 14th and 13th, and Roberts' replacement Bobby Johns lost the differential, but still took tenth. It came down to Panch and Lorenzen and the Wood Brothers' fuel strategy sent Pancho to Victory Lane by almost half a lap. Behind Freddy were the Moore Mercurys of Dieringer third, three back, and Wade fourth, six behind. Fifth and still a winner, having taken first at least once in 12 of the past 13 seasons, was Buck in Fox's Southern 500–winning Dodge 3. Yarborough was sixth in his fourth outing in a powerful Holman-Moody Ford as he was turning heads with his style and results, which were a 20th, eighth and tenth up until then. On back came Crawfish seventh, Thomas in Turtle's Ford eighth, and Castles ninth in Buck's old Chrysler. It took Marv just under two and three-quarter hours to win $3,225 before over 12,000.

The schedulers had only slightly come to their senses by the spring of 1965. After a 100-miler the day before in Greenville won by Hutcherson, 34 lined up in the Brushy Mountain speed palace for the Gwyn Staley Memorial 400. It was the month of a certain necktie party in Kansas for the *In Cold Blood* boys Perry Smith and Bobby Hickok. Oscars went British with Rex Harrison and Julie Andrews, Jack Nicklaus won the Masters, and the Celtics took the NBA title ... again. In spite of the lack of Chrysler products due to their boycott, cars came out of the woodwork for this one, but the fans stayed home. Junior grabbed the pole to the delight of his neighbors and shared the front row with Fearless Freddy. Row two had Panch and Hutcherson, Jarrett and Johns in three, Arrington and Doug Cooper in four, and the fifth held Junior Spencer and an ill-fated lad from Denton, NC, in his first start, named Buren Skeen. It was obvious that the large field did not consist of the best stockers in the land. In fact, a comparable field of USAC stockers in 1965, where no boycotts existed, included Al and Bobby Unser, A.J. Foyt, Norm Nelson, David Pearson, Paul Goldsmith, Jim Hurtubise, Curtis Turner, Parnelli Jones, Gary Bettenhausen, Mario Andretti, and others. The first 164 laps were all Junior's and of the 13 racers that parked during that time, only Buck was a former winner and his season was looking bleak after a good 1964. Buck's new Olds blew for 23rd. In a yawner, Panch and Jarrett challenged Johnson for first and Marvin settled into the lead on lap 370. With his sights set on two in a row here, Panch popped a right front tire with 11 left, the Wood Brothers Ford hurtled into the rail, and Pancho was done. It was Junior by nearly half a lap over Banjo's Ford of Johns. Third a lap back was Jarrett, Hutcherson fourth, Panch fifth, Dieringer sixth, Lorenzen seventh, G.C. eighth, Tiny ninth, Lewis tenth, Wendell 11th, and Trivette in the first non–Ford finisher in 14th with a year-old Chevy. The deed took two hours and 38 minutes to pull off before a thin gate of 8,000. The hometown boy plucked $4,900 to buy more poultry.

On October 3, 1965, a bulging lineup of 35 stockers paired off for the Wilkes 400 before an SRO crowd of over 15,000 under beautiful blue autumn skies. The surrounding hills were splashed with every color in the spectrum, as was the thundering mechanical herd down on main straightaway. The factory war was on again with Chrysler's midsummer return and entries reflected it. Lorenzen was back on the pole for the first time in the past couple of races here and archrival Petty was outside in his Plymouth. There were not many Mopars on hand, but there was quality. Row two had Hutcherson's Ford and Pearson's Dodge followed by hometowner Johnson, going for two in a row, beside Ford mate Cale Yarborough. Seventh through tenth found Jarrett and Panch in Fords, and a row of Isaac's Dodge and surprising Junior Spencer in an independent '64 Ford. At the start, Lorenzen charged out front trying break a string of five rotten finishes dating back to his World 600 win in May. However, on lap 14, the lap-down Dodge of Arrington blasted the bottom out of its hemi, causing the contending trio of Isaac, Petty, and Hutcherson to bounce off each other and the rail like croquet balls. Two-thirds of the Chrysler threat was erased and they got positions 35th through 32nd as listed. Henley Gray crashed on lap 82 for 29th causing another caution, Sam McQuagg had fuel trouble for 28th, and Johns blew his big white and blue-scalloped Pontiac 7A, getting 25th. On the 191st circuit, Junior squeezed by Freddy and stayed out front for the next 120 laps. The second half found an all–Ford fight between Johnson, Lorenzen, Jarrett, and Yarborough with the Wood Brothers' Fords of Panch and new hire Curtis Turner. Then on lap 219 while shadowing Johnson, Lorenzen's engine blew and he loaded up with a disheartening 19th place. Dieringer fell out 90 laps later in a second-rate Ford for 18th at about the same time Yarborough took the point in search of his second career victory. After six laps, Johnson took control and spent the final 80 laps stretching it out to flash under the checkers two laps ahead of Yarborough and Jarrett with Pearson fourth in Cotton's Dodge, the lone bright spot for Mopar. Fifth and sixth were teammates Panch and Turner, trailed in seventh by impressive independent Junior Spencer, also known as the *other* Junior and the *other* Spencer. Eighth place came Pistone, G.C. Spencer ninth, Buddy Baker in his trusty '64 Dodge 88 tenth, Buck 12th, Wendell 13th, and Langley 14th. Even though the field was huge, only ten teams had legitimate shots to win. Junior Johnson blew them away for win 13 on the season and the 50th of his storied career. It put him one ahead of Jarrett in all-time triumphs and four back of career leader Lee Petty's 54. Everybody knew that both Johnson and Jarrett would surpass The Old Man soon or in 1966. But no one could have dreamed it was Junior Johnson's final win. And nobody thought that after Jarrett's 50th victory at Moyock to cap his championship season 34 days later, he would go winless in '66 and end his career tied at 50 with Johnson.

They ran 38 cars here in 1951 when Fonty won and 37 ran just before the place was shut down by greed in 1996. However, on April 17, 1966, during the Ford boycott, 37 stockers entered at North Wilkesboro for the Gwyn Staley Memorial 400. It was just the opposite of last year when Chrysler sat out. Maybe now, Ford's winning streak would be halted, albeit more by its own hand than by Chrysler's. High Point's Jim Paschal had the pole in Tom Friedkin's Bill Ellis–wrenched Fury 14 with Pearson's familiar 6 to his right. Row two had Ford threat Tom Pistone in his light blue two-year-old Shoney's Ford 59 flanked by Petty. Behind them in rows three through five were Bobby Allison in Betty Lilly's new Ford 24 and Sam McQuagg in his red and white Ray Nichels Charger 98. G.C. had an independent '65 Belvedere 49 paired with Doug Cooper's year-old Fury 02 and Buddy Baker in Gene Black's '64 Ford 74 with Elkin, NC's Eddie Yarboro in his first start in a '65 Dodge 40. There were other threats on back, the biggest of which were Goldsmith, Baker, and Johns. However, a show without Chryslers, such as last year's, gridded a much better field than a Fordless one like this. Of the 37 starters, there were six factory cars and maybe another five with any chance to win. Overall, this was a big, pathetic lineup. They ran it anyway and as Paschal held a slim lead over Pearson, Tiger Tom tangled with the rail and retired on lap five for 37th and last. Concord's Ernest Eury made the first start of a nine-race career, parking for 36th, with James Hylton, the eventual 1966 Rookie of the Year, blowing his Dodge after 30 laps for 35th. Max Ledbetter in his second start, but first on the *Silent Speedways of the Carolinas*, parked with an oil leak in one of Buck's old Oldsmobiles for 34th. Various maladies DNF'd others such as Lewis in 33rd, Yarboro in 32nd, Doug Cooper 30th, Johns 28th, Buck 27th, Allison 26th, and Goldsmith lost his brakes for 24th. Paschal led the opening 117 laps and then swapped it with Petty back and forth until lap 347 when on the point,

Richard's engine blew for 11th and Paschal was home free. For Jim Paschal, it was his 20th win, netting him $4,950 in a career dating all the way back to that first Strictly Stock race in 1949. Pearson was hanging tough until his hemi ventilated with 18 laps left and G.C. got past to claim second, six behind. The field was so shabby that Pearson did not race for the last 20 minutes and still took third. On the other hand, some guys got recognition they had probably been cheated out of somewhere earlier. Like Wendell Scott's fourth-place finish 22 laps behind and Henley Gray's fifth. Henley had five top fives in a 374-race career of 14 years and after 1966, never had another, retiring in 1977. Others were Sears sixth, McDuffie seventh, Castles eighth in Buck's reliable '65 Belvedere 86, Seifert ninth, and Gene Cline tenth. Beautiful day, big field, and barely 6,000 fans watched. There are many Junior Johnson and Ford fans in them thar hills.

As lousy as the grid was for the spring race, autumn's Wilkes 400 on October 2, 1966, had a sparkling field of 35 interesting entrants. The Ford boycott was over and the factory wars declared. For the 46th and final time in his legendary driving career, Junior Johnson won the pole and did it with *another* track record. Lined up to the right of the yellow 26 was Petty, followed by Lorenzen third and Hutcherson fourth. Rounding out the top ten were Dieringer in Moore's little Southern 500–winning Comet and Yarborough in row three, Lewis' Plymouth and Langley's Ford in the fourth row, and G.C.'s Plymouth and Bobby Allison's little Chevelle 2 in the fifth row. Some other stars were out, such as '65 Rookie of the Year James Hylton 15th, row nine with living legends Curtis Turner and Buck Baker, and the last winner here, Jim Paschal, riding shotgun on the field in 35th. Determined to bury the field in what probably only he knew was his next to last start, the Ronda Roadrunner roared away to a comfortable lead and stayed there until lap 76 when Lorenzen passed. During that span, Buck lost the clutch and parked his Olds for 31st, followed by Allison who blew for 30th and Elmo for 29th. Johnson dispatched Freddy after he led a little and was pulling away again when the 427 detonated on lap 129 and Junior smoked to a halt in the pits for the last time on the *Silent Speedways of the Carolinas* for a dismal 28th. Running hard to keep pace, Dieringer slammed the concrete lapping a back marker and loaded up for 24th just past halfway. Lorenzen, fresh off his first win of the year at Martinsville, took over and looked unstoppable for the next 178 until the same fate as befell Junior whacked 28 and the Golden Man (the "Boy" was now 31 years old) parked for 23rd. With nobody having the muscle to mount a challenge, Hutcherson inherited the lead in his gold and white Ford, building up enough margin that his engine problems were not enough to enable a fast-closing Pearson to steal the win. For the Keokuk Comet, it was his dozenth triumph in the big time and third of the year. Hot on Pearson's heels in third on the lead lap was underrated Paul Lewis, who licked Pearson one-on-one back on July 28, 1966, to gain his only career win at Maryville, TN. Fourth came Paschal three laps back, Hylton fifth, Turner in Toy Bolton's Chevelle 47 sixth, Roy Mayne seventh, Sears eighth, Hassler ninth, and Buddy Baker tenth. Others of note were Scott 11th, Pistone 12th, and Yarborough running 19th. Hutch pocketed $4,325 for just over two hours and 48 minutes' work before a fine crowd of 15,000.

What can be said about Junior Johnson? He ran once more after this one and finished fifth at Rockingham in the same race that was curtains for Ned Jarrett, who took third. They are tied forever with 50 wins each. But Junior Johnson *is* stock car racing personified. He was not just a moonshiner; he went to a federal penitentiary for it. He was not just a winner; he won 50 times, including the 1960 Daytona 500. He was not just a charger; he won 46 poles and led over 12,600 laps. He did not just crash; he triggered the one that killed Fireball Roberts. He did not just cheat; he built the infamously outrageous Banana Boat.

Local living legend, the great Junior Johnson, is honored with the Third Turn stands bearing his name.

He was not just storied; he was immortalized by Thomas Wolfe in *Esquire*, leading to the fact that he was not just in a movie; he had one made about him called *The Last American Hero*. And in that so-called Modern Era, as a car owner, he did not just win the Winston Cup Championship; he won three in a row, which has never been done before or since. Robert Glen "Junior" Johnson is an absolute. He is without equal. The greats ran the dirt and some are burned into memory. Owens, Pearson, Baker, the Pettys, the Flocks, Thomas, Jarrett, Weatherly, and Hutcherson are unforgettable. But two men stand alone. Curtis Turner and Junior Johnson were the best of the best every time they went by. Junior Johnson is the greatest overall stock car driver, builder, owner, and personality that ever lived. Today's crowd should bow and kneel in Junior Johnson's presence.

The 1967 Gwyn Staley Memorial 400 ranks as one of the all-time dullest races ever! The lineup of 35 stockers was fine as the factories were back. The weather was a wonderful spring mountain Sunday and the purse was as good as the crowd. The problem was that Junior Johnson entered a lightweight, small-block Ford for Darel Dieringer and they not only won the pole by shattering Junior's old track record, but also led all 400-circuits winning by a lap. Of course, their man Johnson delighted most of the 9,400-plus on hand with the outcome and total domination. Therefore, it is unfair and incorrect to call it a dull, boring race. It was exactly like seeing the home team blow out the opponent in the big game. Who were the opponents that were so helpless that April 16th? Cale Yarborough was second a lap back in the Wood Brothers Ford with Hutcherson third, Paschal's Friedkin Plymouth fourth, and Paul Lewis in A.J. King's deep blue Charger 1 fifth. Bobby Allison in that little J.D. Bracken '65 Chevelle 2 followed in sixth, Petty seventh, Sears eighth, Hylton ninth, and Putney tenth. Other notables routed that Sunday were Buck 12th, Scott 13th,

Lund 15th, Langley 18th, Pearson 26th, Goldsmith 28th, McQuagg 30th, and G.C. 33rd. Johnson and Dieringer zapped 'em in a few ticks over two hours and 40 minutes.

A sidebar of the time found David Pearson and Cotton Owens breaking up Spartanburg's Dream Team the next day on Monday, April 17th. They were together for part of 1962, all of '63 through '66, and ten races into 1967. They had 170 starts, 27 wins, 22 poles, and the 1966 Grand National Championship. It seems that there was a snit between the two over riding arrangements to the Columbia race, Owens' entry withdrawal, and Pearson being stood up at the track. However, today they both live happily ever after on Spartanburg's racing landscape and do so as close friends.

In October 1967 the planet was upside down. War raged in Vietnam and it came into most houses every night on *The CBS Evening News with Walter Cronkite*. The Cardinals beat the Red Sox in the first World Series not involving the Yankees, Giants or Dodgers since 1948. Thurgood Marshall was sworn in as the first African-American Supreme Court Justice. Billy Knight flogged an aging X-15 to a record 4,534 miles per hour at 85 miles up. *Hair* opened on Broadway and Disney released *The Jungle Book*. Additionally, seven rednecks in Mississippi were convicted for the murder of three civil rights workers. On the tracks, Richard Petty was taking Tim Flock's 1955 record of 18 wins to the next level. He had won nine in a row when the tour stopped in North Wilkesboro on October 1, 1967, not having lost since August 12th, a stretch including the Southern 500. As they entered this, the 46th race of the season, Richard was on a tear of 14 wins in 16 events with no Ford boycott to help. There were strong Ford teams and one from Mercury, other strong Dodge and Plymouth teams, and Smokey Yunick even had a Chevelle racing on and off. The boys from Dearborn sent Jacques Passino and the FoMoCo brass to the Brushy Mountains to try to figure out what the hell was going wrong. Time trials were encouraging. Hutcherson had the pole in a Bondy Long Ford with LeeRoy Yarbrough beside him. Ford had ordered Yarbrough from Bud Moore's struggling Cyclones to Junior's underachieving Fairlanes. The second row had Paschal's Friedkin Plymouth and Pearson's Holman-Moody Ford. The third pairing was Petty and Goldsmith in a Nichels Plymouth, followed by Bobby Allison's Bracken Chevelle with Californian Jerry Grant in a second Friedkin ride. The fifth row had Hylton in a two-year-old Dodge and Buddy Baker in a Cotton Owens goat. Other possible spoilers of the Petty onslaught were Swede Savage in another Holman-Moody Ford, Cale Yarborough in Castles' Dodge, Pistone in Turkey Minton's Chevelle, G.C. Spencer's Plymouth, sportsman aces Jack Ingram's Chevelle and Paul Moore in A.J. King's Dodge. It started well enough for the Ford boys as Hutch led 20 laps until Paschal took over and Goldsmith swiped it from him. Pearson, actually the Ford standard-bearer since he was H-M's main man, blew the wedge on lap 17 for 34th and Jacques Passino got that sick feeling that had been haunting him all season. Moore followed later for 33rd and Grant parked after 22.5 miles for 31st. Bobby Allison took over for a solid 58 laps until Petty probably said, "Enough's too much," and decided to ease the Plymouth by Allison quickly. But Bobby must have said "Not so fast," and the Hueytown Hustler was not as polite, popping Petty a few times over the next 36 laps until the tired old number 2 edged ahead once more. Conspirators against Petty were still falling like leaves on this October autumn as Ingram was grounded for 26th and Baker blew, as did Goldsmith, finishing 24th and 23rd. It was akin to a bull swatting a fly with its tail as Petty blasted back past Allison without so much as a hesitation and that was that! Maybe Bobby remembered it during their classic battles of 1972. Whatever the case, Passino and Holman and Moody and all the Dearborn suits made for the exits because Petty was taking his tenth in a row. Richard was on a roll never known before and never to be equaled. When they pulled into the pits and clambered out, Hutcherson's Ford was second two laps back along with Yarbrough third, Allison fourth, and Paschal fifth. Others toiling in Petty's wake were Pistone in a fine run sixth, Yarborough seventh, Savage a swell eighth, Sears ninth, and Melvin Bradley tenth. Melvin Bradley? Old Mel from Richmond ran three races in 1962 and three more in '67. This ended his six-race career with 50% top tens and a top five to his credit. Others unable to stop Petty were Wendell 11th; the Cooper Boys Bob and Doug, who were driving for Buck as The Old Pro missed his first race here, finished 12th and 16th; Hylton 18th; and G.C. finished 19th. The next race was at Charlotte for the National 500 and Petty did not lead a lap. Although his victory tear was over, he romped off with his second Grand National crown, befitting the man who ended up being The King.

A big field of 35 lined up on April 11, 1968, for another Gwyn Staley Memorial 400. Pearson had the pole as he and his H-M crewmates had already logged a pair of poles and wins in the first ten races. David had the pole here and needed the victory to put it all together in one place. He was flanked by Junior's car with LeeRoy Yarbrough aboard. Isaac in the K & K Insurance Dodge was third with Dieringer in Mario Rossi's blue and gold Plymouth 22 outside. Rows three through five were Bobby Allison, now driving for H-M, and Petty, Goldsmith and Grant, and G.C. Spencer with Hylton tenth. Pearson led 32 laps until Catawba's Isaac took over for a lap, then surrendered to Petty for 26. Meanwhile, Leonard Brock from Niota, TN, opened a three-race career with a 35th and last place finish. Goldsmith, Allison, and Petty entered the fray, but by halfway, Pearson was back in charge. The contest lost Allison, who finished 29th, and Goldy in 27th. A furious battle ensued between Petty, Pearson, and Yarborough as the lead toggled between them. LeeRoy finally asserted himself and the big crowd of nearly 14,000 went wild as Junior's white Ford 98 legged it out against the field. After 210 laps, Petty lost the hemi for 26th. With ten laps to go all seemed well until ... that sickening wisp ... then trail ... and finally belches of white smoke poured from 98's exhaust pipes and Yarbrough was through. Pearson gave a grin and his 33rd win was in the bag. Buddy Baker was a lap back in second, Isaac third, Dieringer fourth, and Yarbrough was credited with fifth without finishing. Rounding out the notables were Sears sixth, Grant seventh, Tyner eighth, Soapy ninth, Clyde Lynn tenth, Wendell 14th, Buck 19th, G.C. 22nd, Hylton 23rd, and USACer Jim Hurtubise 24th. It took David just over two and three-quarter hours to pocket the $5,100.

Sunday, September 29, 1968, the smallest field in exactly five years entered the Wilkes 400. Thirty were there, and you had to go back to 1963 to find a field of 28 smaller. Bobby Allison put Friedkin's Plymouth 14 on the pole with Pearson's Ford 17 outside as David closed in on his second championship. Petty and Yarborough's 21 sat right behind, followed by Isaac's 71 with Yarbrough's 98, Buddy Baker in Fox's 3 beside young Hamilton in King's Dodge 1. Row five was Dieringer in Rossi's Plymouth 22 with Charlie Glotzbach in Cotton's Dodge 6. It was a fine lineup, if a little shorter than usual. Allison jammed the Plymouth out front for 69 laps, but not before Walston Gardner crashed for 29th on lap three, bringing out the first of a trio of yellows. Then Richard traded the lead with David and LeeRoy for the rest of the first half and beyond as attrition claimed Glotzbach on lap 224 for 24th and Baker 130 laps later for 17th. As Buddy was unfolding his sizable frame from his dead Dodge, Petty was saying good-bye and the race was for second. A lap behind, point-leading Pearson nipped Yarbrough for second with Allison fourth, Cale fifth, Dieringer sixth, Isaac seventh, Hylton eighth, Sears ninth, and Langley tenth, a dozen laps behind. Others were G.C. 11th, Rookie of the Year in waiting Pete Hamilton 12th, rookie Dave Marcis 13th, and Wendell 16th. Petty's 15th win of the season netted him $5,975 and took a little over two hours 39 minutes in front of a healthy 16,000-plus.

Another 30 Grand Nationals started the Gwyn Staley Memorial 400 on springy April 20, 1969. Bobby Isaac in Harry Hyde's orange 71 K & K Insurance Dodge blasted the track record by over two miles per hour as he and Buddy Baker shared the front row. Row two held James Hylton, who was a two-race interim driver for Spartanburg neighbor Cotton Owens, filling the gap between Charlie and Buddy. New Ford chauffeur Richard Petty joined Hylton as they were ahead of row three's Marcis and Sears, both spoiling for that big springboard to better things. The fourth and fifth rows sported shocking Jabe Thomas and McDuffie, then LeeRoy and David. Exactly how Jabe and J.D. out-timed LeeRoy and David is unclear, but fascinating. Back in the pack were Bobby Allison, rookie contender Dick Brooks, and Sam McQuagg. This one was quite the lead-changing war ... for a while, as Isaac led for the opening 89 laps, then Pearson for two, Allison for 38, Isaac for 34, Allison for ten, Baker for 66, Allison for seven, Pearson for 19, Baker for two, Allison for four, Baker for 27, then Allison. Allison bid adieu for the last 101 tours, and with super service by his Mario Rossi crew, motored the blue and gold Fury 22 to a comfortable straightaway plus victory over Yarbrough, Pearson, and Baker all of whom completed the distance. Fifth went to Hylton, followed by McQuagg sixth, Petty, Arrington, Langley, and Trivette. The supporting cast read McDuffie 13th, Scott 15th, Jabe 16th, Brooks 18th, Sears 20th, Isaac 23rd, Marcis 24th, and Atlanta's Danny Turner in the middle of a three-race career 27th. The event took two hours and 37-plus minutes and paid Bobby A. $5,125 to win before about 13 thousand.

October arrived and autumn enveloped the Brushy Mountains of North Carolina. In the news, Drew Pearson and Ho Chi Minh left us, and unable to *Beat the Clock* himself, Bud Collier got the final buzzer, too, proving he was no Superman after all. Away from the obits, Colonel Moammar Gadhafi gained power after the Libyan Revolution, the trial of the Chicago 8 began, Willie Mays hit number 600, and Steve O'Neal had an NFL record 98-yard punt. For leading the Professional Drivers Association (PDA) boycott at the inaugural Talladega race earlier, Richard Petty was booed and jeered lustily in Columbia at a 100-miler. The week before this one, Petty's Torino was bull's-eyed by a beer can and the resulting caution enabled him to make up a lap, aiding his win over Pearson at Martinsville. Was the missile aimed at Petty because he led the PDA boycott at Talladega three weeks earlier? Probably. October 5, 1969, was the next edition of "Assault on The King" as the disdain approached homicidal levels towards the sport's growing icon. For the third straight race here, 30 stockers lined up, again paced by Isaac, flanked in row one by Pearson. The second pair had Petty's Ford and Baker's Owens Dodge. Row three was Richard Brickhouse, the Talladega boycott-race winner in a Bill Ellis Dodge, and red-hot LeeRoy in Junior's Ford 98. That stupendous stable had already won the Daytona 500, Rebel 400, World 600, Firecracker 400, Dixie 500, Southern 500, and still had the American 500 yet to conquer. Behind them were Marcis in Milt Lunda's Dodge 30 and Rookie of the Year-to-be Dick Brooks in Rossi's hand-me-down '68 Plymouth, followed by Sears and G.C. At the green, Isaac established himself out front and stayed there for 121 laps before Petty and Baker passed and traded the lead back and forth. Hylton engaged in fender slamming with Brickhouse, much to the entertainment of the nearly 12,000 witnesses. Petty got back out front and settled in for 260 laps until he and Pearson squared off in the final few. But Petty got the edge and was heading for a sure win with less than ten laps left when some "Roads Skoller" up in the stands let fly a bottle from some alcoholic malt beverage maker likely from Milwaukee or St. Louis. It shattered on the homestretch, precipitating yellow number three and evaporating Richard's margin of probable victory. When the green flew again, Pearson tucked in behind Marcis' lapped Dodge and shadowed him through traffic, past

Petty, and on to his 11th win of the year, second consecutive Grand National Championship, and third title in four years. Richard was stalking Pearson at the end with Isaac third a lap back, Yarbrough fourth, Baker fifth, Marcis sixth, Brickhouse seventh, Brooks eighth, Spencer ninth, and Hylton tenth. The brain surgeon hurling the bottle was arrested and David copped $5,750 for two hours and 40 minutes'-plus of Sabbath Day labor.

It was April 18, 1970, and the Gwyn Staley Memorial 400 was a real Saturday afternoon drag. Unfortunately, it was not a drag race, but a stock car race partially carried on national television as a live edition of ABC's *Wide World of Sports*. It was a lousy field, not because of the 30 cars entered, but because only five or six had a shot to win and that number quickly shrank to one. Isaac's Dodge took the pole with a new track record and Donnie Allison sat alongside in Banjo's Ford 27. Behind them were Yarbrough in Junior's Ford with Hylton's Ford having finally picked up that first win a month and a half earlier in Richmond. Rows three through five contained Marcis and Brooks, Seifert and Jabe Thomas, and Cecil Gordon with Champion. That is a terrible TV top ten. The big deal was that Richard Petty had time trialed outside Wendell Scott in the eighth row and was supposed to be the star of the show. And he was. Isaac scooted out front on the start, but Petty weaved his way past the other rolling roadblocks and claimed the point in only 51 laps. When the ABC boys joined the race in progress, it was over with 300 laps to go. No crashes, no passing for the lead, and millions of comatose viewers falling asleep on sofas and recliners all over America. When it mercifully ended, Petty had won by a lap-plus over Isaac, with Yarbrough third, Hylton fourth, and Brooks fifth. Bobby Allison was sixth in a borrowed Plymouth, with Seifert seventh, Langley eighth, Gordon ninth, and Bill Dennis tenth. Others were Marcis blowing for 20th, Donnie Allison lost the transmission for 22nd, Scott 24th, Parsons 28th, and G.C. 30th and last. The snoozer took almost two hours and 39 minutes before a sleepy crowd of nearly 12,000.

The 1970 Wilkes 400 ran on Sunday, October 4th, four days after the last Grand National dirt track race went down in Raleigh. That is not all that went down, as plane crashes punctuated the weekend. On Friday, October 2nd, 31 members of the Wichita State football team were flying a "scenic route" into a box canyon between Denver and their destination of Logan, Utah. Unable to climb or turn around, the overloaded twin-engine Martin stalled and went into the side of a mountain. On race day, legendary speedster Curtis Turner and golf pro Clarence King blasted into the Pennsylvania countryside in Turner's plane, killing both, as described in the Occoneechee Speedway chapter. Also on race day, Janis Joplin plummeted from the highest altitude of all, crashing in a Los Angeles hotel room after shooting some heroin just a *tad* too pure. Busy weekend at the morgues, but on the lighter side, *Doonesbury* first appeared in newspapers, Connie Mack Stadium closed, PBS launched, the Orioles took the Series from the Reds, Gary Gabelich naturally gassed the salt in Bonneville with a world record run of 622.4 miles per hour, and the race at North Wilkesboro was not a sleeper this time. Isaac led another field of 30 from the pole, paired with Donnie Allison, who was subbing for LeeRoy in Junior's 98. Petty and Bobby Allison were in row two, followed by Hassler and Brooks in three, Langley and Hylton in four, and Castles and Clyde Lynn in row five. There was a quick drop-off in quality without going very deep into the field. The hot dogs ran hard as Isaac was in a tight points battle with Hylton, who was a race winner and annual title contender. After G.C. crashed on the 63rd lap for 30th and last for the second race here in a row, Isaac and Donnie A. duked it out until the orange Charger took command for 122 laps. Then Petty slipped out front until Isaac swiped it back. This spine-tingling duel went on for a good 250 laps until Bobby's jack sunk down into the soft asphalt when pitting and he lost a lap with only a quarter of the race remaining. Driving like the champion he would soon officially become, Isaac unlapped himself under the green and used a late spin and caution by Bub Strickler to erase Petty's lead. At the sprint to the wire, Isaac dashed past Petty with seven and a half miles to go for his 11th win, nipping Richard by about a second. Third was Donnie a lap back, fourth Bobby A., and fifth Hylton, then only trailing Isaac by 50 points. Parsons took sixth, Castles seventh, Lynn eighth, Hassler ninth, Jabe tenth, Elmo 11th, Marcis 13th, Scott 15th, and Brooks 26th. The 250-mile thriller took just over two hours and 46 minutes to run and nearly 9,000 fans went home awake and happy.

It is 1971 and enter the R.J. Reynolds Tobacco Company, Winston, and the Winston Cup. The Nixon regime kicked cigarette advertising off the airwaves so R.J.R. had tons of dough with nowhere to go to spend it. It has already been expressed what this marriage did for, and to, the sport, what it created, and what it erased. It is what it erased that this book is trying to preserve ... in memory only. As written about Columbia Speedway, North Wilkesboro in 1971 is in the first year of the so-called Modern Era and the last year of this book's "Golden Age." Those are two tracks to operate in both categories. Speaking of categories, the April 18th running of the Gwyn Staley Memorial 400 was another in the yawner category. Defending Grand National Champion Bobby Isaac of Catawba was on the pole for the fifth consecutive time here in the Nord Krauskopf–owned, Harry Hyde–wrenched, K and K Insurance Special Dodge Charger 71. Perched outside of Bobby was three-time champ David Pearson, and behind them were double-title holder Petty with Benny Parsons in L.G. Dewitt's Ford 72. Row three held Dick Brooks, now sitting in Mario Rossi's 1970 red and gold Charger 22, and Bobby Allison in his own red and gold '71 Charger 12. The fourth had Richard Brown in a privateer Chevelle 93 and Elmo Langley just ahead of the duo of Charlie Glotzbach, now scrambling for rides in a Junior Johnson–tuned Monte Carlo, and Bill Dennis in Junie Donleavy's Ford 90. The green fell and except for a lap Pearson led while Isaac pitted, a rout was on. Then a smashed windshield, this time *not* caused by a Milwaukee or St. Louis–brewed malt beverage missile, sent Isaac to the pits for a couple of laps. Petty, Pearson, and Brooks pounced on the vacancy before Richard took over for the last 126 to cop his seventh win in the first 13 races. Actually, he was better than that because he could not run both qualifiers at Daytona, which were points-paying races in those days. Second in the all-green affair was Pearson a lap back with Brooks third, Parsons fourth, Allison fifth, Hylton sixth, Dennis seventh, old Bill Champion eighth, Spencer ninth, and Cecil Gordon tenth. Others of note were Isaac 13th as he blew the hemi trying to get back to the lead lap, Brown 16th, Wendell 21st, and Glotzbach lost the tranny for 26th. The two hour and 32-plus minutes sizzler was worth $4,545 for Petty.

There were six races at the end of the 1971 season where the Grand Am stars and pony cars were allowed to compete on small tracks with full-sized stockers. Although it diminished the stature of NASCAR's primary product, it gave a last gasp to a few Grand National veterans toiling on the inferior, unappreciated, and under-attended Grand American tour. The sixth and final event took place with the November 21, 1971, running of the Wilkes 400. Never had the second race here been so late in the season. Except for a few March and September dates, this speedway held its races in April and October. This was the first time ever that a Strictly Stock, Grand National, or Winston Cup race was held here in November. It is the last race on the *Silent Speedways of the Carolinas* and the last of the goofy mixed races. This was the month sportscaster Bill Stern died, the LA Lakers started a 33-game winning streak, the NY Rangers scored eight goals in one period, China got a spot on the UN Security Council, the inmates went ape at Rahway State Prison in New Jersey, and Daniel "D.B." Cooper hit the silk from a Northwest Orient 727 over Washington State with

$200,000 and neither has been found. Across the country, 31 teams lined up strangely in North Wilkesboro for the 47th of 48 races of the 1971 campaign. On the pole was Charlie Glotzbach in the Richard Howard–backed, Junior Johnson–tuned Monte Carlo 3, with Richard Petty, cruising to his third title, the first called "The Winston Cup," resting to his right. The second pair were Bobby Allison in one of the last Holman-Moody Fords and Richard Brown in a pesky Junior Fields Chevelle 91. Row three included Marcis in a Dodge and Tiny Lund in his Pepsi Camaro 55, the first of the pony cars on the grid. The fourth had James Cox, who had never even breathed a decent finish in 20 starts, and Cecil Gordon in a Cyclone. The race itself was as wacky as the concept of mixing the pony cars with the full-sized jobs, but perfect for this book finisher. Glotzbach had the win-hungry Chevrolet *and* Junior Johnson fans screaming as he led the first 41 laps before Allison took over for seven. Petty got into the act by leading 26 until Allison and Lund split up the next five. With the crowd finally sitting down, Petty commanded for 280 laps as Glotzbach dogged him and Lund dropped four behind. With the end in sight, the Petty-blue hemi started losing steam and Charlie charged by for the lead, looking permanently in command with 40 laps remaining. But what was this? Tiny had inconspicuously gained a couple of laps back here, stole two back there, and was on the lead lap as Glotzbach encountered suspension woes. With six left, the Big Fisherman from Cross thundered past shaky Charlie and outlasted a puny Petty to romp home first from four laps back late and win going away. Final score of the "Mixed Races": Pony Cars 3, Winston Cuppers 3. Behind Lund, Glotzbach, and Petty were Marcis fourth, Parsons fifth, and sixth The Old Pro, 53-year-old Buck Baker. Behind Buck were Hylton seventh, Langley tenth, Scott 17th, Allison 21st, and Richard Brown 30th.

This was the last race ever run on the *Silent Speedways of the Carolinas*, event number 276. These pages recall the careers of some of the greats as significant moments came up, such as last race, injury, death, or retirement. Many were missed, but some got their due. However, one man and one man only stands out above all the others ... Elzie Wylie Baker, Sr. Buck Baker had it all: two-time champion, prolific winner, and dashingly handsome. It could not be more appropriate that he did something on the *Silent Speedways of the Carolinas* done by no one else. Buck Baker started the first Strictly Stock Car race in Charlotte on June 19, 1949, and finished the last Winston Cup race of this track's "Golden Age" on November 21, 1971. No one else, but Buck. In giving these glorious drivers their well deserved tributes, one and only one transcends the entire 8,565 days covered in this book ... Buck Baker.

There has been much written about the man and stories are all over the Internet and in books. Buck Baker was born in Richburg, SC, some references say Hartsville, on March 4, 1919. Buck was a sailor in World War II and rumor has it ran a little shine, too. He was a Trailways bus driver and supposedly started racing in 1939 in Greenville, SC, where he was practically unbeatable in a modified. He ran that first Strictly Stock Car race and finished 11th in Kaiser number 87, of course. He won his first of 44 Grand National poles on May 21, 1950, at Martinsville in a Ford number 87. The inaugural win came on April 12, 1952, at Columbia Speedway in Hudson number 89. He also ventured off in '52 to win easily the championship in the only year of the NASCAR Speedway Division, driving the Cadillac Special number 87. He won his first of three Southern 500s in 1953 in the Griffin Motors Olds number 87. He chauffeured Griffin Motors Oldsmobiles in '53 through '55, winning 11 times, ending the period on De Paolo's factory Ford team. In 1956, Buck drove for Carl Kiekhaefer and won 14 of 45 starts and the Grand National Championship in Chryslers usually numbered 300 or 300B. In 1957, he moved from Charlotte to Spartanburg, teamed

"The Old Pro" Buck Baker (left) transcends the entire Golden Era, seen here with Jack Burnett in the pits at Darlington on Saturday, April 10, 1976, after his qualifying 13th.

up with Bud Moore, and won ten of 40 races, including the first ever at Watkins Glen, and his second title partially in the famed Black Widow Chevrolet Bel Air number 87. He was the first to win the Grand National Championship in consecutive years. In 1960, he subbed in Jack Smith's Bud Moore–wrenched Boomershine Pontiac "The Red Fox" number 47 and won his second Southern 500 running the last two laps on the left rear rim. Back to Chrysler for '61, he had some success giving that marquee its first victory since 1956 and last to date on June 23rd in Hartsville. He also won his 44th and final pole at Greenville on October 28th. Buck Baker returned to Charlotte and was winless in 1962, his first season without a victory since 1951. Ditching Chrysler for Pontiac in 1963, he started winning again and was signed for the whole 1964 season by Chrysler factory teams, first driving Petty's number 41, then Ray Fox's Dodge number 3. It was in that seat he won at Valdosta, GA, and on a scorching hot Labor Day, September 7, The Old Pro outlasted everybody to take his third Southern 500 and final Grand National win. Only Herb Thomas had three Southern 500 wins at that time, which was, and still is, a huge accomplishment. Success started falling off with his return to Olds in '65 through '67 and an assortment of other tired iron. Buck took second in the 1965 Southern 500, 14 laps behind winner Jarrett, with relief help from Buddy in Plymouth number 86, which was a pretty good car. Buck's stable of castoffs and oddballs actually took fifth, sixth, and tenth in the 1966 World 600 with Buck tenth. He drove the

Buck Baker was 57 years old and on his way to sixth in the 1976 Rebel 500 on April 11. Teammate Dick Brooks later relieved Buck's last run in a top-notch ride.

Grand Am circuit from 1968 until 1972 and had a few wins against some healthy competitors like Lund, Paschal, and the Allisons. In the 1976 Rebel 500 at Darlington on April 11th, the 57-year-old clocked Junie Donleavy's top-flight Truxmore Ford number 93 to a 13th place on the grid and brought it home sixth with some relief help from Dick Brooks. Driving scattered also-ran rides unlike the Donleavy Ford in 1976, Buck called it a career on October 10, 1976, with a 24th-place finish in a car sponsored by Hall of Famer-to-be Louise Smith's Smith's Auto Parts/Hadacol Chevy number 59. Buck Baker was great, lucky, and blessed. He was great to have a record like the one he compiled. He was lucky not to have had a big crash that everyone remembers. He had crashes, though it is hard to single one out. The 1962 Daytona 500 was maybe the worst and the only one with an injury. He broke a rib or two and took out some guardrail, but did minimal sheet time. Best of all, Buck was blessed. He undoubtedly missed scores of crashes with split-second reflexes and without the help of one single spotter in his whole career! His account of taking the path not chosen by Fireball Roberts on that horrible Charlotte Sunday in 1964 was documented the day after by the wire services. Even though he definitely stayed in the show too long, he retired a very healthy 57-year-old living legend. Moreover, he still had 26 years to live! Buck started his famous driving school, where no less than Jeff Gordon and hundreds of others got their first taste of stock cars. Buck might have lived to read this book, but The Old Pro could not wait and left us on April 14, 2002. He was 83 when he crossed over, but he was surely driving 87. Buck Baker was the best!

As for North Wilkesboro Speedway, it held *Silent Speedways of the Carolinas* races three and 276. It spanned all 23 silent speedways years and was the only one to host races under all three names, Strictly Stock, Grand National, and Winston Cup. Now, as a chill breeze moans and caresses the huge empty silver stands and the moon plays tag with the clouds, everybody that raced and mattered comes back. That is why North Wilkesboro epitomizes the entire Silent Speedways Era. What is written about this place holds true for the whole period. Some come back here to race on the dirt in what they drove to the grounds, like Roy Hall, who's haulin' a little something extra in the back. Red Byron, the sport's first

The Final Lap. Buck Baker took his last competitive trip around the Charlotte Motor Speedway on October 10, 1976, pulled in, and retired after 636 starts. He was 31 laps behind in 24th, beating Al Holbert, Gordon Johncock, A.J. Foyt, Neil Bonnett, Coo Coo Marlin, Johnny Rutherford, and Dave Marcis in his finale.

champ, limps by with that ever-present stogie clenched in his teeth. A spirited wolf whistle means the real First Lady of Stock Car Racing, Atlanta's Sara Christian, has arrived, still claiming as hers alone the two best female finishes in big-time stock car racing history, both recorded over 55 years ago. But watch those cat-calls, her husband Frank Christian is a powerful car owner not to be insulted. There is Leon Sales, victorious in his first start here or anywhere in that Southern 500–winning Plymouth, only to never visit the top five again. Also leaning on that famous Plymouth 98 Jr. is the most dashing of them all, resplendent in his white uniform, 1949 Indianapolis 500 winner Bill Holland, who also drove it to his best career finish, a fourth here. Harold Kite has his Lincoln that won his first start on The Beach in 1950 before racing eight more times, dying in the last one at Charlotte in 1965. The Flock Brothers stand next to their winning mounts: Bob with his Olds 7 that captured the very first race here; Fonty, winner of two straight in the Red Devil and Gray Ghost Oldsmobiles that Red Vogt is tuning; and Tim, who finally took the checkers in his 11th and final try in Kiekhaefer's 300A. Of course, North Wilkesboro's original three-peater Herb Thomas stands with Smokey Yunick beside their Fabulous Hudson Hornet 92 and recall how Herb came here to run his last mortal laps in 1962. And speaking of mortality, Speedy Thompson, the man who very nearly killed Herb at Shelby in '56, rests near his '53-winning Olds. Dick Rathmann peers from the cockpit of his Pure Sensitized Hudson 3, the winner here in '54. Clean-cut Fireball Roberts chats with fellow 1957 winner Jack Smith about how he took the last checkers here on dirt that season while Jack the first on pavement. Roberts' mechanic Paul McDuffie, cut down in the Darlington pit crash of 1960, reaches under the hood for adjustments. Nearby, Lee Petty, who took three in a row here in '59 and '60, and Tiny Lund, winner of that mixed-race swan song in '71, finally let bygones be bygones after a furious four-on-one fight in '57 when Lee, Elizabeth, Richard, and Maurice jumped teammate Tiny for leaking secrets. There is a trio of hot newcomers: Wilkesboro winners Bobby Isaac, Darel Dieringer, and Dick Hutcherson share smokes and prepare to buckle up again.

The great Harry Hyde is tweaking Isaac's orange Charger 71. All around his great white fleet, Carl Kiekhaefer is barking orders as his nattily clad crewmen hop to it. The wrenches clang and the air guns whirr under the ghostly gazes of car owners and mechanics like 1960 champion owner-builder Louis Clements as others fade eerily into the shadows. Even Commissioner Cannonball Baker made a run here to see his old pals and the new arrivals.

Of course, there are the suited, dapper promoters smoking, smiling, and getting contracts inked, lining up the talent, which is always in abundance in this underworld. The purses are ungodly while driver and spectator safety is not an issue. Naturally, the leader among this group, towering above the rest, is William Henry Getty France, the force that made it all happen. He is young, happy, and going in 50 directions at once. However, this is North Wilkesboro and Gwyn Staley's big brother Enoch built the place and is calling the shots. Mixing among the stars and cars are Spartanburg's Joe Littlejohn, who never drove on the *Silent Speedways of the Carolinas* in this "Golden Age," but rode shotgun with Herb Thomas once to the pole at Asheville-Weaverville. Joe's still promoting as he did at the Piedmont Interstate Fairgrounds for 22 big-time races. Also out there, contract in hand, is Gene Sluder, who bulldozed and promoted historic Asheville-Weaverville Speedway out in his own backyard. Roy Harris, Concord Speedway's owner, jumped on Bill France's bandwagon and started touting the stockers before Red Vogt came up with the name NASCAR. Promoter Charlie Combs from the Spindle Center Fairgrounds is glad-handing the racers, as is Alvin Hawkins, who handled the stocks all over the Carolinas. Parks Williams, promoter of the neat-as-a-pin Starlite Speedway in Monroe, held only one race, but he is there making sure the boys come back, especially Darel Dieringer, his race's winner. Paul Sawyer and Joe Weatherly have a laugh about putting on the Wilson show and the grandstand burning down. There are others like Sam Nunis and forgiveness is begged for not naming them all. Many more, like the drivers, owners, and mechanics, have not crossed over.

There is a pair of Rays on the scene and they are behind a mike. Ray Melton, the Voice of the Darlington Raceway for over 30 years, is the natural choice to direct the activities on the track. His booming voice is synonymous with Darlington, but he had other gigs across the *Silent Speedways of the Carolinas*, as he hailed from nearby Virginia Beach. He probably saved lives and spared injuries with his calm crowd control during the Wilson grandstand fire. He appears prominently in *Thunder in Carolina*. The other Ray is Raymond Caddell, who also stars in that movie playing the dirt track announcer at those races filmed at Hartsville Speedway. Caddell may have been in Hollywood shooting his scenes, but he looks and sounds great calling Mitch Cooper's and Les York's races in 1959 and stands by to spell Mr. Melton. Over the airwaves at the now defunct 950 AM WSPA in Spartanburg, there was only one man and one source: "This is Bob Montgomery... Universal Racing Network." Bob's baritone voice delivers the races once more from the *Silent Speedways of the Carolinas* as his no-nonsense style is realized anew by the security his audiences feel.

There are other racers that did not win here or make a big splash, but race in the dark like the rest. Their faces are not as clear, but their resolve to win just as strong. Joe Weatherly, lost at Riverside in '64, discusses his setup with the giant wrench-twister Pop Eargle. Bob Welborn's here with Marshall Teague, killed testing an experimental car at Daytona in '59. Jimmy Pardue, erased at Charlotte Motor Speedway while testing in '64, bats the breeze with driver and mechanical genius Banjo Matthews. Preparing to go out for practice are Gober Sosbee, Bill Blair, '50 Champ Bill Rexford, and the Myers Boys, Bobby, lost at Darlington in '57, and Billy of a heart attack while racing at Bowman-Gray in '58. Curtis Turner, who bored into the mountains of Pennsylvania in '70, laughs it up with Ford factory boss Pete De Paolo. The promoter's kid brother Gwyn Staley, lost at Richmond in a ragtop in

'58, had the spring race named after him here. He is prepared to make music in his boss' Cadillac 7. His boss is none other than "The King of Jazz," bandleader Paul Whiteman. Buddy Shuman, burned alive in '55 in a Hickory hotel fire, goes three on a match with Joe Eubanks and Wally Campbell, who perished on the high banks of Salem, IN, in '54. John McVitty ran his last full race here, then went to die at oily Langhorne in '56. Ralph Earnhardt, who dropped dead in his garage while working on his sportsman number 8 in 1973, is scouring the pits for a ride. Herb Thomas' brother Donald and Speedy's brother Jimmy discuss the curse of having a successful big brother. "The Wild Injun" Roy Tyner walks with Elmo Langley, who went to Japan to drive the pace car and died there. Tank driver Nelson Stacy and his bosses John Holman and Ralph Moody discuss the Fords. Larry Thomas, who died on a dark, rainy Georgia highway, and Billy Wade, lost blowing tires for Goodyear at Daytona, seem amused at running their last races together, then crossing over 20 days apart in January 1965. LeeRoy Yarbrough is relaxed now after dying in a Florida madhouse in '84. Buren Skeen, who started here and died after a Darlington Labor Day crash in '65, is back, as is Wendell Scott, Shorty Rollins, and Friday Hassler, who left us on the backstretch at Daytona in '72. J.D. McDuffie, taken out on national TV at Watkins Glen in '91, joins outsiders Jim Hurtubise and California's Swede Savage, who lingered a while in '73 before succumbing to horrible Indy injuries, dying on a July 2nd just like Fireball. Fresh arrivals Dick Brooks and Bunkie Blackburn get to try for Rookie of the Year with a new crowd.

Two ghosts in the gathering get special recognition. The first is Lou Figaro. Lou is the *only* racer among the scores of others that raced here, sweated here, and lost here that died here, or on any of the *Silent Speedways of the Carolinas*. His Hudson was number 187. He added the 1 because another fellow had 87. That other special driver is Buck Baker. In addition to all written in these pages about Buck, he ran here 34 times, more than anywhere else he raced in the big time. He drove in the very first Strictly Stock Car race ever in Charlotte in 1949. He raced his first event here in 1950, dominating twice in 1955, winning both races from the pole and leading every lap. Buck finished sixth in the last race of the Golden Age in 1971, which was held in this Brushy Mountain venue. In that one, Buck was piloting his own Pontiac Firebird 87, Jr. sponsored by Brushy Mountain Motors of North Wilkesboro.

North Wilkesboro Speedway and Buck Baker ... Alpha and Omega. They were both there at the start and they were both there at the finish. They were both there in between. The only ones. It was an era of the toughest races on the roughest tracks with the greatest drivers, crews, owners, promoters, announcers, and fans that ever lived, and died. But when they lived, they did so with gusto unmatched today. They are not gone and they are not forgotten. They will race on and on and their numbers are ever increasing. As for their living peers, their roll calls are getting shorter and shorter as they cross over frequently, joining long lost comrades, renewing friendships, and rekindling ancient rivalries. *We, too, are on our way.*

Track History by the Numbers

RACES: 43
YEARS OF RACES: 1949, 1950, 1951 (2), 1952 (2), 1953 (2), 1954 (2), 1955 (2), 1956, 1957 (2), 1958 (2), 1959 (2), 1960 (2), 1961 (2), 1962 (2), 1963 (2), 1964 (2), 1965 (2), 1966 (2), 1967 (2), 1968 (2), 1969 (2), 1970 (2), 1971 (2)
WINNERS: R. Petty (7), Junior Johnson (4), L. Petty (3), H. Thomas (3), White (3), Buck Baker (2), F. Flock (2), Panch (2), Pearson (2), B. Allison,

Farewell to the North Wilkesboro Speedway and the Golden Era of Stock Car Racing, and greetings to the *Silent Speedways of the Carolinas* as they continue on ... forever!

	Dieringer, B. Flock, T. Flock, Hutcherson, Isaac, Lorenzen, Lund, McGriff, Paschal, Rathmann, Roberts, Sales, J. Smith, S. Thompson
MOST POLES:	8—Junior Johnson
RACE RECORD:	98.479 mph—Richard Petty, 1971 Plymouth (4/18/71)
QUALIFYING RECORD:	107.588 mph—Charlie Glotzbach, 1971 Chevrolet (11/21/71)
WINS BY MAKE:	Ford (13), Plymouth (11), Oldsmobile (7), Chevrolet (4), Hudson (4), Dodge (2), Camaro, Chrysler
MOST STARTS:	33—Buck Baker
MOST LAPS LED:	2468—Richard Petty
MOST TOP FIVES:	13—Richard Petty
BEST AVERAGE START:	10.8—Buck Baker, 5.5—Junior Johnson (21)
BEST AVERAGE FINISH:	12.5—Buck Baker, 7—Lee Petty (20)

Sources

Books

Edelstein, Robert. *Full Throttle, The Life and Fast Times of Curtis Turner.* New York: The Overlook Press, 2005.
Fielden, Greg. *Forty Years of Stock Car Racing. Volume One: The Beginning, 1949-1958.* Surfside Beach, SC: The Galfield Press, 1987.
____. *Forty Years of Stock Car Racing. Volume Two: The Superspeedway Boom, 1959-1964.* Surfside Beach, SC: The Galfield Press, 1988.
____. *Forty Years of Stock Car Racing. Volume Three: Big Buck and Boycotts, 1965-1971.* Surfside Beach, SC: The Galfield Press, 1989.
____. *Rumblin' Ragtops: The History of NASCAR's Fabulous Convertible Division.* Surfside Beach, SC: The Galfield Press, 1990.
Fox, Jack C. *The Indianapolis 500.* Cleveland: The World Publishing Company, 1967.
Shaw, Wilbur. *Gentlemen, Start Your Engines.* New York: Coward-McCann, 1955.

Films

Thunder in Carolina. Howco International Pictures, 1960.
1957 Southern 500. Rare Sportsfilms, Inc., n.d.

Inquiries

Greensboro, NC, Public Library—Arthur Erickson, Genealogy Librarian; Greensboro, NC, maps from 1943, 1957, and 1959
High Point, NC, Public Library—Jackie Hedstrom, North Carolina Collection Librarian
Horry County, SC, Public Information Office—Kelly Lee Brosky, Supervisor I
Monroe, NC, Public Library—Cheryl Hinson, Librarian
City of Newberry, SC—B. Brannon
State Library of North Carolina—Bonnie Spiers, Librarian
Wilson, NC, Visitors Bureau—Sandra Homes

Magazines

Stock Car Racing, Volume 5, Number 1, January 1970, "Baker & Son Racedrivers" by Bob Myers, Eastern Publishing Co.
Stock Car Racing, Volume 5, Number 8, August 1970, "Ray Melton" by Jim Hunter, Eastern Publishing Co.

Newspapers

The Charlotte Observer: 6/18/49, 5/23/92
The Concord Tribune: 5/5/56, 5/7/56, 5/8/56, 6/10/64
The Fayetteville Observer: 11/2/57
The Gastonia Gazette: 9/11/58, 9/12/58, 9/13/58
NASCAR Winston Cup Scene: 10/31/02

The Salisbury Post: 10/4/58
The Spartanburg Herald-Journal: 11/11/39, 7/3/53, 7/5/53, 7/6/55, 7/7/55, 9/3/57, 3/5/60, 3/2/63, 3/3/63, 6/27/64, 8/15/65, 6/4/66, 5/1/83, 6/30/83
The Union Observer: 6/13/02

Websites

www.abrc.com Asheville Bicycle Racing Club
www.cyclecenter.com Columbia Speedway information
www.dcfair.com Dixie Classic Fair, Winston-Salem, NC
www.dogpile.com Maps
www.google.com Search engine
www.goupstate.com The Spartanburg Herald-Journal online
www.IMDb.com Motion picture information
www.jayski.com Racing information
www.m-w.com Miriam-Webster Online
www.mapquest.com Maps and aerial photographs
www.mountainx.com Gentlemen, Start Your Memories
www.nascar.com Racing information
www.ncstatefair.org State fairgrounds map and photo
www.presnc.com Poet's Walk, Occoneechee Speedway
www.racingone.com Racing information
www.racing-reference.com Racing information
www.scopesys.com Historical events
www.terraserver.com Maps and aerial photographs
www.tricklefan.topcities.com Racing deaths
www.tv.com/episode-306 *What's My Line?* # 306 with Tim Flock
www.visitfayettevillenc.com Fayetteville, NC, maps
www.vukovichaccident.com Bill Vukovich death
www.webprosolutions.com Southern Dirt Tracks Past
www.wiskit.com Perpetual calendar
www.zwire.com *The High Point Enterprise* online (1/12/03)

Index

AAA 34, 36, 103, 109, 154, 173, 178, 244, 247
Aaron, Hank 105
ABC 73, 248, 262, 274
ABC's Wide World of Sports 116, 150, 274
Acton, Marvelous Marv 78–80
Adams, Weldon 103, 173, 243
Adkins, Allen 253, 254
Aero-Commander 67, 123, 151
Agajanian, J.C. 242
Alabama (AL) 120, 121, 241; Anniston 241; Birmingham 59, 146, 205, 206, 244, 252, 263; Hueytown 67; International Motorsports Hall of Fame 39, 106, 156, 165, 242; Mobile 35, 44, 219; Montgomery 234; NASA 120; Talladega 72, 131, 273; Talladega 500 72, 121, 139; Tuskegee High 263
Alfred Hitchcock Presents 55, 105
Ali, Muhammed (Cassius Clay) 67, 69, 258
Allen, Donnie 1, 2, 30
Allen, Johnny 8, 9, 10, 48–50, 76, 91, 92, 106, 108, 127, 129, 138, 139, 141, 155, 156, 161–163, 181–183, 185, 191, 196, 198, 221, 223, 226, 238, 239, 252–254, 259, 262
Allison, Bobby 39, 66–70, 73, 75, 79, 80, 121, 122, 151, 226–228, 230, 234, 268–276, 281
Allison, C.C. 39
Allison, Donnie 234, 274, 275
The Allisons 278
The Alous 263
Alvarez, Bernie 66, 266
AMC (Javelin) 80, 81, 234
American Bandstand 47, 198
American Football League 97
American Motorcycle Association 228
American Red Ball Special 116
Amick, Bill 8, 10, 39, 50, 92, 127, 129, 138, 155, 156, 161, 162, 195, 196, 221
Anderson, Cousin Woodrow 212, 241
Andrea Doria 47
Andretti, Mario 97, 226, 267
Andrews, Julie 267
Andrews, Wayne 80
Angel, Don 51
Apollo 13 73
Apple Records 70
Apt, Milburn 49
ARCA 75, 122
Archer, George 71
Arford, Frank 36, 60, 154, 157, 211, 247, 248
Arkansas (AR) 38, 48, 49, 53, 106, 211; Lehi 38, 48, 49, 53, 106, 211; Memphis-Arkansas Speedway 53
Army 12, 67, 133, 257
Army-McCarthy Hearings 45, 248
Arnold, Billy 255
Arrington, Buddy 21, 27, 28, 62, 97, 118, 119, 266–268, 273
Ascari, Alberto 177
Auerbach, Red 64
Austin, L.D. 11, 52, 53, 58, 129, 182, 193, 239
Austin-Healy 45
Australia Thunderdome 250
Avalon 225
Ayulo, Manny 178

Babb, Hugh 108, 139, 162, 221, 237, 254
Bachelor Father 49
Bailey, H.B. 80, 81, 83
Baker, Cannonball 280
Baker, Elzie Wylie, Sr. ("Buck") 1–3, 6–14, 18–21, 23, 24, 27–31, 33–39, 42–52, 55–65, 68–70, 73, 80–83, 85, 87–92, 94, 95, 97, 103–106, 108–112, 114, 115, 118, 119, 124, 127, 129, 130, 132, 133, 135, 136, 138–142, 145–148, 150, 154–158, 160–166, 168–170, 176, 179, 181–183, 185, 186, 189–196, 198–202, 207, 208, 210–212, 215, 219–225, 227, 228, 230, 232, 237–239, 242, 243, 246–270, 272, 276–279, 281, 282
Baker, Elzie Wylie, Jr. ("Buddy") 2, 10–13, 20, 21, 27, 30, 51, 52, 55, 57–61, 63–68, 70, 82, 88, 114, 116, 119–122, 135, 136, 139–141, 164, 169, 170, 186, 198–200, 222–226, 228, 235, 258, 259, 262, 263, 265, 266, 268, 269, 271–274, 277
The Bakers 3, 164, 226
Bakker, Jim 56
Baldwin, Roger 156
Ballard, Walter 78
Balmer, Earl 226, 267
Bancroft, Ann 263
Bank Americard 258
Barker, John 34
Barron, Bob 57
Batman 65
Baumel, Larry 73
Beam, Herman "The Turtle" 10, 11, 13–17, 20, 50–53, 55–58, 60, 87, 108, 109, 111, 112, 114, 115, 132, 141, 156, 157, 164, 167, 168, 185, 199, 200, 206, 207, 215, 221–224, 255–257, 259, 261, 263, 265, 267
Beat the Clock 273
The Beatles 23, 61, 63–67, 70, 73, 112, 119
Beaty, Dick 92, 221, 255
Beauchamp, Johnny 55, 110, 199, 201
The Beverly Hillbillies 262
Behling, Dick 223
Bell X-2 47, 49
Ben Casey 112
Bennett, Jim 58
Berrier, Max 254
Beswick, Arnie 26
Bettenhausen, Gary 267

Index

Bewitched 65
Biederman, Don 67
Bill Comet and the Comets 105
Billboard Hot 100 47, 67, 163
Black, Gene 135, 268
Blackburn, Ronald "Bunkie" 11, 55, 56, 111, 169, 258, 281
Blackwell, Dick 253, 257
Blair, Bill 7, 32–37, 39, 42, 45, 83, 101–106, 109, 138, 150, 154, 155, 160, 173, 194, 220, 241–250, 252, 253, 280
Blevins, Bill 156, 157
Bodine, Geoff 250
The Bodines 220
Bogart, Humphrey 246
Bolton, Toy 65, 269
Bond, Ward 199
Bonnett, Neil 279
Booth, Shirley 59
Bottinger, Rodney 20
Bowani 18
Bowman, Bill 179
Boyd, Johnny 177
Bracken, J.D. 66, 68, 70, 234, 270, 271
Bradley, Mel 15, 168, 272
Branca, Ralph 245
Branson, Don 63
Brantley, Bruce 17
Breedlove, Craig 60, 265
Brewer, Gay 67
Brewington, Leroy 17
Brickhouse, Richard 273, 274
Brigance, Buck 53
Brink, Wilbur 255
Britt, Manley 50
Brock, Leonard 272
Brooks, Berry 24, 225
Brooks, Dick 5, 75, 78–80, 82, 228, 229, 273–275, 278, 281
Brooks, Earl 72, 122, 228
Brooks, Elmer 45
Brooks, Garth 136
Brosky, Kelly Lee 180
Brown, Perk 246, 247
Brown, Richard 275, 276
The Browns 52
Bruce, Lenny 65
Burdick, Bob 52
Burke, Jack, Jr. 252
Byrd, Danny 19, 225
Byrd, Tracy 136
Buchanan, Herschel 36, 45, 173, 175, 219
Buddy Holly and the Crickets 49
Buesink, Julian 34
Buick (Roadmaster) 7, 32–34, 37, 39, 42, 48, 102, 155, 158, 179, 201, 262
Burnett, Jack 277
Burns, Dick 34

Burns, Herbert 243
Burris, Carl 211
Burton-Robinson Racing Team 20, 97, 186, 205
Byron, Red 3, 32, 34, 39, 42, 43, 83, 101, 102, 219, 241, 242, 278

Caddell, Raymond 280
Cadillac (Coupe de Ville) 33, 42, 211, 212, 241, 242, 249, 276, 281
Cadillac Records 138
Cain, Scotty 199
The Caine Mutiny 45
Calhoun, Rory 86–88
California (CA/Californian) 15, 36, 38, 50, 78, 92, 108, 115, 127, 139, 145, 228, 237, 248, 250, 253, 265, 271, 281; Cal State 258; Carrell Speedway 37; Chalome 155; Clovis 253; Disneyland 111; Eureka 38; Fontana 250; Gardena 36, 37, 250; Golden State 37; Hanford 44; Hollywood 59, 87–89, 101, 242, 280; Inglewood 249; Lancaster 161; Los Angeles (LA) 248, 274; Merced 8, 38, 92; Napa 400 61; Poor Man's 500 37; Porterville 78; Riverside 61, 115, 141, 142, 186, 189, 280; Sonoma 250; Watts 64
Cambodia 73
Campbell, Wally 247, 281
Canada 65; Ontario, Niagara Falls 37, 195; Toronto 249
Cantor, Eddie 265
Capps, John 105
Captain Kangaroo 105
Carden, Billy 7, 10, 35, 39, 47, 49, 91, 138, 155, 161, 162, 179, 195, 198, 219–221
Carmichael, Hoagy 211
Carr, Don 49
Carr, Jack 243
Carrigg, Lee Roy 75
CART 255
Casper, Billy 73
Castles, Neil "Soapy" 18–20, 23, 28, 30, 49, 50, 60–65, 68–73, 75, 78, 79, 94, 99, 120, 122, 135, 136, 150, 168, 170, 186, 207, 227–229, 233, 265, 267, 271, 272, 274, 275
Cat Ballou 64
CBS 64, 97, 104, 245, 248, 252, 253, 258, 262
CBS Evening News with Douglas Edwards 261
CBS Evening News with Walter Cronkite 271
Cerf, Bennett 253

Chamberlain, Ted 109, 132
Chamberlain, Wilt "The Stilt" 67, 108, 112
Champion, Bill 72, 75, 79, 236, 274, 275
Chance, Dean 68
Chapman, Walt 173, 210
Charles, Ezzard 242
Chesapeake Bay Bridge-Tunnel 61, 116
Chester, Ted 43, 154, 220, 245, 246
Chevrolet (Bel-Air/Camaro/Chevelle/Chevy/Impala/Monte Carlo) 7–13, 15, 16, 17, 18, 21, 26, 27, 31, 37–39, 46–51, 53, 55–58, 60, 65–68, 70, 72, 74, 78, 81–83, 85, 87, 89, 91, 95, 106, 108, 110–112, 114, 115, 123, 124, 127, 132, 133, 135, 138–140, 143, 146, 147, 150, 154, 155, 158, 160–165, 169–171, 173, 179, 181–183, 185, 189–192, 196, 198, 199, 201, 202, 205, 217, 221, 222, 224, 226, 227, 230, 232, 234, 237–239, 251–255, 257–264, 269–271, 275–277, 282; "Black Widow" 8, 92, 108, 139, 162, 196, 237, 238, 254, 277; Cherokee Garage 132; Daytona Beach Kennel Club 11, 55; Holly Farms 16, 114, 168, 232, 263; Honest Charley 53; Louise Smith's Auto Parts/Hadacol 278; Lowe's 57; Motoramic 47, 252; Pepsi (Camaro) 80, 81, 276; Piedmont 10; Thor 10, 88, 198, 199
Chichester, Francis 65
Chico 140
Childress, Richard 81
China 275
Christian, Frank 6, 45, 104, 154, 173, 220, 242, 243, 249, 251, 279
Christian, Sara "The First Lady of Stock Car Racing" 33, 39, 101, 124, 241, 242, 279
Chrysler (Great White Fleet/300) 1, 7, 8, 12, 13, 20, 23, 24, 27, 31, 33, 36–39, 46–49, 57–65, 85, 87, 89–92, 94, 95, 105, 108, 109, 114, 119, 124, 134, 138, 141, 143, 150, 155, 158, 161, 162, 165, 176, 178, 179, 181, 194, 195, 202, 207, 211, 212, 220, 223–225, 230, 237, 246, 249, 251–253, 259, 260, 262, 265, 267, 268, 276, 277, 282; Mercury Outboards 1, 105, 150, 162

Churchill, Winston 250
Cilloniz, Raul 110
Civil Rights Act (Bill) 69, 199
Claren, Bill 46
Clark, Dick 47, 198
Clark, Jimmy "The Flying Scot" 69, 97, 227
Classical American Homes Preservation Trust (CAHPT) 123
Clements, Johnny 16, 17
Clements, Louis 10, 11, 56, 65, 112, 135, 199, 222, 234, 258, 260, 264, 280
Cleveland, June 34, 246
Cline, Gene 269
Cline, Patsy 114
Clothier, Millard 33
Cobb, Ty 57, 212, 215
Cole, Ed 108
Cole, Nat King 252
Cole, Neil 103, 246
Collier, Bud 273
Colvin, Bob 142
Combs, Charlie 280
Combs, R.L. 215
Como, Perry 47, 50
Comstock, Gene 6, 36, 219
Concorde 71
Conrad, Pete 64
Cook, Jim 243
Cook, Sam 138
Cooper, Bob 20, 24, 65, 67, 265, 272
Cooper, D.B. 275
Cooper, Doug 20, 23, 26, 30, 62, 66, 99, 115, 186, 239, 266–268, 272
Cooper, Gary 246
Cooper, Gordo 59, 64, 206
Cooper, Mitch 87, 88, 226, 280
Copas, Cowboy 114
Cousy, Bob 263
Cox, Doug 50, 91, 109, 132, 255
Cox, James 276
Cox, Tom 15, 141, 262
Cracker Jack 215
Crane, H.T. "Pappy" 53
Crawford, A.M. "Spook" 9, 11, 50, 55, 91, 108, 111, 127, 138, 146, 163, 182, 191, 221, 253, 254
Crawford, Ray 244
Creature from the Black Lagoon 45
Cregar, Charlie 163
Crider, Curtis "Crawfish" 11, 13–15, 17–20, 23, 52, 55–58, 60, 61, 88, 97, 112, 114–116, 118, 119, 141, 142, 168, 186, 200, 205, 206, 208, 209, 222–224, 259, 261, 263–265, 267
Crisler, Al 33
Crockett, Larry 178

Cronkite, Walter 261
Crossfield, Scott 49
Cuba 57, 204; Bay of Pigs Invasion 56, 259; Castro 50; Havana 50
Cunningham, Briggs 16, 17
Cunningham, Pepper 244
Czechs 199

Daly, John 253
Daniel Boone 65
Daniels, Tom 258, 259
D'Aquino, Iva Toguri "Tokyo Rose" 240–241
Darrin, Bobby 257
Davis, Joel 30, 60, 67, 68, 135
Davis, Nelda Jean 134, 136
Davis Ranch 134
Dean, James 155
Dean, Paul 120
Death ("Angel of Death," "Dark Rider on the Pale Horse," "Grim Reaper," "Lord of the Underworld," "Pale Rider," "Reaper") 11, 16, 17, 46, 49, 115, 116, 118, 119, 154, 157, 177, 178, 189, 249, 253, 255
De Gaulle, Charles 71
Demler, Norm 228
Democratic National Convention 61, 70
Deniston, Jack 205
Dennis, Bill 274, 275
Dennis, Lloyd 35
Denno, Warden Wilfred 253
Denver 274
De Paolo, Pete 8, 9, 47, 91, 106, 108, 138, 139, 155, 161, 162, 195, 196, 220, 221, 237, 238, 252–254, 276, 280
De Paolo Engineering 181
Derrington, Bob 26, 28, 64, 135
Desi (Arnaz) 257
De Soto 241
De Witt, L.G. 70, 78, 275
De Zalia, Clarence 193
Diamond, Neil 62
Dibos, Eduardo 110
The Dick Van Dyke Show 112, 206
Diddley, Bo 263
Dieringer, Darel 13, 14, 17, 25, 27, 49, 63, 64, 97, 118, 119, 135, 136, 155, 156, 169, 170, 185, 189, 198, 207, 208, 225–230, 261, 262, 264–272, 279–281
DiMaggio, "Joltin'" Joe 103
Dimeo, Jim 62
Disney 271
Disneyland 248
Ditz, John 248, 251
Di Vicenzo, Roberto 69

Dixon, Ben 245
Dixon, Dick 99, 233
Dodd, Johnny, Jr. 177, 251
Dodd, Johnny, Sr. 251
Dodge (Charger/440/Polara/Super Bee) 6, 8, 11, 16–21, 27–31, 34, 37, 46–49, 53, 56, 58, 60, 62–73, 75, 78, 80, 82, 85, 90, 94, 97, 106, 108, 111, 116, 119–122, 124, 135, 136, 138, 142, 150, 152, 154, 161, 168, 169, 171, 173, 178, 179, 186, 207, 208, 220, 224, 225, 227, 229, 230, 234–236, 247, 252, 261, 262, 264, 265, 267, 268, 270–277, 279, 282; Free Lt. Calley 78; K&K Insurance Special 70, 121, 150, 272, 273, 275; Lowe's 56
Dominican Republic 63
Donavan 226
Donavan, Jim 8
Donleavy, Junie 34, 155, 165, 275, 278
Doonesbury 274
The Doors 68
Dorsey, Tommy 211
Dove, Fred 246, 247
Downing, Al 68
Duhigg, Ray 35, 45, 173, 247, 248
Duke, Gerald 11, 111, 261
Dunbar, John 109
Dunn, George 50, 51, 132, 133
Dunnaway, Glenn 33, 34, 39, 101, 103, 244, 245
Dutton, Ralph 248
Dye, Wayne 27
Dylan, Bob 59

Eargle, Eugene "Pop" 223, 280
Earnhardt, Martha Coleman 243
Earnhardt, Ralph Dale, Sr. 177, 197, 243, 245, 262
Earnhardt, Ralph Lee 9, 20, 58, 61, 114, 116, 138, 141, 196, 221, 223, 237, 243, 254, 281
Earth Day 73
Eastern Airlines 258
The Ed Sullivan Show 59, 195, 266
Edelstein, Robert (*Full Throttle*) 142
Edsel 49
Edwards Air Force Base 49
Eichmann, Adolf 56
Eisenhower 49
Elliott, Stick 17, 19, 20, 30, 65, 141, 224, 225
Ellis, Bill 268, 273
Ellis, Jimmy 69

Emmy 50, 59, 206
England (British) 60, 263, 267; BBC 112; BOAC 256; Liverpool 204; Queen Mary 246
Engle, Joe 64
Epstein, Brian 68
Epton, Joe 139, 168
ESPN 33
Esquire 270
Etheridge, Jack 71, 72
Eubanks, Joe 6–8, 10–12, 17, 35, 36, 38, 39, 42, 44, 45, 47, 48, 52, 55–57, 60, 83, 88, 91, 104, 105, 108–112, 124, 132, 133, 138, 139, 154, 155, 157, 160, 161, 164, 173, 181, 194–196, 198, 199, 210, 211, 219, 220, 245–250, 252, 523, 281
Eulenfeld, Rod 24
Eury, Ernest 135, 268
Evans, Sue 138
The Everly Brothers 263
Exxon Valdez 164

Fabian 225
Father Knows Best 54, 248
Faye, Tammy 56
Female Driver of the Year 242
Fiberglas Special Offenhouser 122
Fields, Junior 276
Figaro, Lou 3, 244, 249, 250, 281
Fireball 500 225
Fisher, Eddie 253
The Fleetwoods 53
Flock, Bob 32–35, 42, 43, 48, 49, 101–103, 124, 160, 219, 220, 229, 230, 241–243, 245, 279, 282
Flock, Fontello Truman "Fonty" 1, 6, 7, 32–37, 42–45, 47, 60, 85, 92, 101–105, 109, 124, 150, 154–156, 158, 160, 165, 173, 176, 178, 179, 196, 197, 211, 219, 220, 230, 241–248, 251, 252, 262, 268, 279
Flock, Frances 5
Flock, Timothy F. 1, 5, 7, 8, 31, 32, 34–37, 40, 43, 45–49, 57, 69, 83, 97, 101, 102, 110, 124, 138, 150, 152, 154, 155, 158, 160, 161, 173, 176, 178, 179, 195, 202, 211, 219, 220, 223, 230, 241, 244–247, 251–254, 262, 271, 279, 282
Flocko, Jocko 154, 157
The Flocks (Brothers/Fabulous) 3, 39, 42, 44, 49, 83, 101, 104, 105, 108, 154, 157, 218, 220, 221, 226, 245, 246, 256, 270, 279

Florian, Jimmy 35, 103
Florida (FL/Floridian) 71, 72, 103, 215, 219, 227, 244, 265, 281; The Beach 34, 65, 71, 102, 110, 132, 164, 232, 242, 256, 279; Bradenton 57; Daytona (Beach) 5, 9–13, 34, 35, 46, 53, 58, 63, 65, 67, 70, 88, 91, 97, 101, 102, 110, 118, 119, 122, 131, 139, 141, 154, 156, 181, 189, 191, 197, 201, 226, 227, 232, 241, 242, 244, 245, 257, 261, 263, 264, 275, 280, 28; Daytona 200 228; Daytona 500 (The 500) 12, 16, 17, 24, 53, 63, 64, 73, 74, 77, 110, 111, 115, 123, 141, 164, 165, 168, 186, 192, 199, 201, 204, 207, 226, 250, 256, 258, 259, 263, 265, 269, 273, 278; Daytona Qualifying Races 24, 52, 60, 81, 165, 201, 256; Ebony Room 5; Firecracker 250/400 15, 57, 58, 63, 88, 135, 226, 232, 273; Ft. Lauderdale 228; Green Cove Spring 139; Halifax Hospital 12; Jacksonville 65, 72, 115, 142, 201, 265; Lake Lloyd 17; Liberty City 70; Lions Charity Race 244; Miami (Miamian) 1, 2, 34, 38, 51, 70, 156, 170, 219, 261; Opa-Locka 34, 244; Pensacola 154, 219; Permatex 300 122, 169; Speedweeks 53, 55, 141, 169, 201, 232; Streamline Hotel 5, 142; Tampa 186, 205, 243; West Palm Beach 245, 253
Flynn, Errol 257
Fogle, Sammy 59, 64, 206
FoMoCo 29, 99, 108, 265, 271
Fontana, Mircol 253
Ford (Galaxie/Fairlane/Fastback/Mustang/Torino) 3, 8, 9–11, 13, 14, 16, 18–21, 25, 27–29, 31–35, 39, 42, 45, 47–50, 53–55, 57, 59–68, 70–73, 78–80, 83, 85, 88, 91, 92, 94, 99, 101–103, 105, 106, 108–111, 115, 116, 119–122, 124, 127, 134–136, 138, 139, 142, 143, 146, 150, 152, 154, 155, 158, 161–165, 168, 170, 171, 173, 181, 183, 186, 189–192, 195–199, 202, 205–209, 219, 200, 221, 222, 224–230, 236–239, 246, 252–259, 261–276, 278, 280–281; "Banana Boat" 66, 226, 269; Courtesy 11, 21, 22, 55, 61; Elizabeth City Motors 11; Hallmark Homes 63; Holly Farms 25, 64, 66, 119, 226, 266; Lafayette 16, 259; Police Special 34; "Purple Pig" 252; Shoney's 65, 119, 135, 268; Truxmore 278; "Turtlemobile" 116, 142; What-A-Burger 10, 110; "Wild Hog" 48
Forry, Sam 26
43–The Petty Story 204
Foster, John 49
Four Seasons 115
Fowler, Danny viii
Fox, George 262
Fox, Jackie 69
Fox, Ray 13, 15, 20, 60, 70, 111, 114, 142, 169, 235, 257, 263, 265, 267, 272, 277
Foyt, A.J. 63, 81, 267, 279
France, William Henry Getty "Bill" 5, 27, 34, 91, 122, 123, 139, 142, 150, 211, 244, 253, 280
Frank, Larry 10, 11, 17, 50, 109–111, 116, 155, 168, 198, 221, 222, 256, 257, 259, 261, 262, 264
Frazier, "Smokin'" Joe 71
Freed, Alan 246
Frey, Jim 249
Friedkin, Bill 68, 268, 270–272
Friel, Norris 66
F-Troop 65
Fuel Injection Special 177
The Fugitive 68, 263
Funicello 225

Gabelich, Gary 274
Gable, Clark 199
Gadhafi, Colonel Moammar 273
Gahan, Ernie 13
Gant, Harry 262
Gardner, Johnny 51, 256
Gardner, Walston 71, 272
The Garry Moore Show 55
Gemini 5 64
General Motors 237
Georgia (Georgian) 10, 11, 17, 97, 115, 212, 225, 242, 277, 281; Atlanta 10, 11, 17, 42, 45, 66, 101, 104, 123, 132, 189, 191, 198, 232, 245, 256, 258, 263–265, 273, 279; Atlanta 500 52, 78, 103, 142, 212, 226; Atlanta Motor Speedway 33; Augusta 28, 29, 60, 70, 97, 168, 186, 189, 246, 265; Augusta International Speedway 115, 265; College Park 261; Dallas 26; Dawsonville 45, 212; Dixie 400/500 11, 15, 66, 226, 227, 264, 273; Ft. Benning 78; Griffin 261; Jonesboro 58; Lakewood Speedway 10, 45, 54, 103, 191, 198, 212, 242,

256; The Masters 50, 61, 64, 67, 71, 73, 116, 248, 250, 252, 257, 263, 267; NAPA 500 33; Ringgold 65; Savannah 46, 112, 115, 142, 168, 232; Southeastern International Dragway 26; Thomasville 186; Tifton 189; Tucker 17; Valdosta 20, 277
Germany 69; Hockenheim 69
Gershwin, George 211
Getty, Dick 15, 224
Ghost, Paul 96
Glotzbach, "Chargin'" Charlie 13, 70, 71, 78, 79, 272, 273, 275, 276, 282
GM 265
Goalby, Bob 69
Godfrey, Arthur 247
Goldsmith, Paul 9, 53, 64–66, 92, 106, 108, 138, 155, 156, 158, 163, 191, 196, 197, 221, 228, 237–239, 254, 267, 268, 271, 272
Goldwater, Barry 186
Goodyear 75, 97, 118, 119, 228, 281
Gordon, Cecil "Flash" 72, 73, 79, 80, 151, 236, 274–276
Gordon, Jeff 278
Graham, Billy 241
Graham, Frank 186
Grammy 59
Grand American Racing Association (GARA) 142
Grand Prix 69, 177
Grant, Coleman 246
Grant, Gogi 47
Grant, Jerry 271, 272
Gray, Henley 30, 135, 136, 225, 226, 268, 269
The Great Train Robbery 60
Greek Money 15
Green, Sgt. George 15, 52, 56, 111, 168, 185, 205
Greene, Bobby 242
The Greens 220
Greever, Bill 242
Griffin, Bob 251
Griffith, Charlie 191, 192
Grilliot, Hank 44
Grissom, Gus 57
Grossman, Bob 46
Groucho 140
Grubbs, Cecil 255
Gunsmoke 50
Gurney, Dan 115

Haberling, Harold 97
Hagerty, Royce 53
Hair 271
Hale, Alan, Jr. 86

Halford, Johnny 72, 73
Hall, Roy 241, 256, 278
Hamilton. Pete 74, 228, 272
Hamby, John 50
Harb, Fred 13, 14, 50, 52, 57, 147, 191, 193, 223, 257, 259
Harden, Jack 120
Harless, Bud 211, 248
Harley-Davidson 228
Harpo 140
Harris, Roy 137, 280
Harrison, Rex 267
Hartje, Bud 135
Hassler, Friday 66, 67, 226, 227, 269, 274, 281
Hawaii 52
Hawkins, Alvin 6, 33, 280
Hawkins, Hawkshaw 114
Hawkins, Jeff 63
Hayes, Bill 105
Hayward, Susan 257
Hayworth, Frank 91
Hege, Gene 50
Hege, Harvey 147
Helms, Buddy 102
Helms, Jimmy 20, 61, 119
Helper, Russ 36
Helton, Mike 39
Hemingway, Ernest 57
HemisFair 69
Henderson, Elmo 12–14, 17, 20, 61, 88, 265
Henderson, Harvey 108
Hendrick, Rick 154
Hendricks, J.C. 261
Henry J 34, 35, 42
Hepburn, Katharine 69, 71
Hersey, Skimp 33
Hess, Larry 66, 67
Hickok, Bobby 267
High Noon 246
Hildreth, Elton 211, 247
Hines, John 86, 87
Ho Chi Minh 273
Hobby, Gene 19, 23, 26, 119, 120
Hodges, Russ 245
Hoffman, John 205
Hogan, Ben 42
Holbert, Al 279
Holland, Bill 34, 34, 39, 42, 103, 244, 245, 262, 279
Hollis, George 189
Holloway, B.G. 15, 56
Holm, Celeste 253
Holman, John 281
Holman-Moody 10, 19, 25, 28, 55, 61, 70, 108, 110, 121, 127, 150, 151, 164, 198, 199, 225, 227–229, 259, 261–263, 265, 267, 271, 272, 276
Holtzman, Ken 228

The Honeymooners 105.
Hood, Hooker 250
Hoover, Herbert 265
Howard, Richard 81, 276
Hoyt, Jerry 178
Hudson (Fabulous/Hornet) 3, 6, 7, 31, 32–36, 39, 42, 44–46, 85, 102–105, 109, 124, 150, 154, 158, 160, 165, 173, 175, 176, 179, 210–212, 219, 220, 230, 244–249, 262, 276, 279, 282; Blackburn Auto Service (Garage) 173, 220; Blue Crown 46, 211, 251; Fabulous 173, 245, 246; Green Hornet 249; Oates Motors 173; Pure 105, 160, 248; Pure Sensitized 45, 194, 279
Hughes, Ray 205
Hulman, Tony 154, 249
Humphries, Preston 96
Hunsucker, Tunney 258
Hurley, Mark 168, 266
Hurricane Camille 228
Hurricane Connie 195
Hurricane Hazel 248, 249
Hurtubise, Jim 267, 272, 281
Hutcherson, Dick "Keokuk Comet" 19, 20, 25, 27–29, 31, 61, 63–68, 83, 94, 95, 99, 116, 119, 120, 124, 169, 171, 224–228, 267–271, 279, 282
Hutcherson-Pagan Enterprises 224, 227
Hutchins, Sonny 169
Hyde, Harry 72, 121, 150, 273, 275, 280
Hylton, James Harvey 5, 29, 66–73, 75, 78–82, 119–122, 135, 136, 150–152, 170, 225–229, 234–236, 268–276

I Love Lucy 104, 245
Illinois (IL) 76, 250; Chicago (Chicagoan/Chi-town) 35, 44, 65, 70, 252, 261; Chicago Black Hawks 259; Chicago 8 273; Des Plaines 250; DuQuoin 76; McDonald's 250; Springfield 76; Waukeegan 65; West Chicago 64
IMCA 19, 35, 46, 109
In Cold Blood 267
Indiana (IN) 249, 281; Brickyard 400 81; Decatur 249; Greensburg 35, 44; Indianapolis 32, 36, 45, 87, 122, 154, 155, 178, 211; Indianapolis 500 (Indy/ International Sweepstakes/ Motor Speedway) 8, 34, 36, 42, 59, 97, 99, 103, 116, 139, 154, 173, 177, 178, 186, 195, 210,

228, 233, 244, 249, 255, 279, 281; Salem 247, 248, 281
Ingram, Jack "The Iron Man" 76, 233, 234, 271
International Speedway Promotion 142
Into, Bubba 186
Iowa (IA/Iowan) 61, 119; Harlan 146; Keokuk 19
IRL 255
Irwin, Tommy 10, 11, 13, 15–19, 52, 53, 55–57, 109–112, 114, 132, 141, 191, 198–200, 205, 221–224, 257, 259–261
Isaac, Bobby 3, 16–18, 29, 59, 60, 62, 63, 65, 70–75, 83, 85, 97, 114, 115, 121, 150–152, 170, 186, 189, 224, 228–230, 235, 263, 267, 268, 272–275, 279, 280, 282
Italy (Italian) 253, 255; Monza 255

Jaguar (Jags) 36, 45, 46, 211
Japan 250, 281; Tokyo Olympics 265; Twin Rings 250
Jarrett, Ned 3, 11–29, 31, 37, 39, 51–66, 85, 88, 94, 95, 97, 99, 111, 112, 114–116, 119, 124, 139, 141–143, 155, 164, 165, 168–171, 186, 189, 198–202, 205, 207–209, 222–226, 230, 232, 233, 236, 249, 252, 257–266, 268–270, 277
The Jetsons 262
Johansson, Ingemar 222
Johncock, Gordon 279
Johns, Bobby 10–12, 19, 38, 48, 53, 55, 56, 97, 106, 138, 156, 157, 170, 199, 222, 261, 264, 267, 268
Johnson, Dick 68, 72
Johnson, Flossie 115
Johnson, Hubert 53
Johnson, Joe Lee 10–12, 52, 53, 55, 164, 191, 199, 222–224, 257, 258
Johnson, President Lyndon B. 61, 69, 186
Johnson, Robert Junior "The Rhonda Roadrunner" 3, 7, 10–14, 16–19, 24, 37, 38, 47, 48, 50–57, 60, 62, 64, 66, 67, 71, 81, 85, 88, 89, 99, 105, 106, 109–112, 114–116, 119, 120, 124, 140, 150, 152, 155, 156, 161, 164, 165, 167–170, 176, 179, 191, 192, 195, 196, 198–201, 211, 215, 219, 221–227, 230, 232, 233, 236, 239, 251, 252, 254–276, 281, 282
Jones, Joe 206

Jones, Lewis "Possum" 10, 11, 50, 56, 155, 186, 191, 238, 241, 258, 259
Jones, Parnelli 59, 267
Jones, Pee Wee 197, 206
Joplin, Janis 274
Joyce, Claude 224
The Jungle Book 271

Kagle, Reds 10, 163
Kaiser 33, 34, 276
Kansas (KS) 32, 267; Belleville 33; Friendly Acres Retirement Community 33; Great Bend 32, 33, 102; Newton 33; Salina 33; University of Kansas Jayhawks 108; Wichita State 274
Katona, Iggy 35
Keck, Bobby 19, 108, 116, 147, 156, 182
Keene, Tex 243
Keller, Al "The Dirty Indian" 36, 39, 45, 60, 155, 160, 177, 211, 242, 248
Kelly, Grace 252
Kennedy, President John F. (JFK) 142, 199, 204, 258
Kennedy, Robert 71
Kentucky 251; Catlettsburg 251; Kentucky Derby 47
Keselowski (Kaye), Ron 73, 75, 78, 80
Khrushchev 111, 258
Kiekhaefer, Carl "Commandant" "Mr. K" 1, 7, 8, 9, 35, 37–39, 46–49, 87, 91, 92, 95, 105, 106, 108, 124, 138, 139, 150, 155, 160–164, 176, 181, 195, 196, 211, 220, 221, 251–254, 262, 276, 279, 280
Kieper, John 38
King, A.J. 270, 271
King, Brownie 8, 50, 108, 127, 129, 163, 193, 239, 254
King, Bub 244, 246–248
King, Clarence 123, 274
King, Reverend Martin Luther 60, 65, 69, 258, 265
The Kingsmen 60
Kite, Harold 34, 44, 91, 119, 242, 243, 279
K-Mart 112
Knight, Billy 271
Korea: Inchon 242; Seoul 242
Koufax, Sandy 58, 61, 206
Krauskoph, Nord 275
Kroc, Ray 250
Kross, Stan 248
Kurtis Kraft 232

Lady Chatterley's Lover 257
Lamphear, Sonny 30

Langdon, Shep 53
Langley, Elmo 27–31, 64, 66–73, 75, 79, 80, 82, 119, 120, 122, 135, 136, 150, 151, 155, 168, 170, 186, 189, 200, 225–229, 235, 236, 259, 268, 269, 271–276, 281
LaRosa, Julius 247
Larson, Mel 139, 161, 254
The Last American Hero 270
Laugh In 121
Laurel and Hardy 223
LaVois, Harry 26
Leake, Harry 13, 57
LeBaron, Eddie 258
Ledbetter, Max 30, 227, 268
Ledford, George 235
Leigh, Vivian 246
Le Mans 46, 177, 250, 255
Leonard, Joe 228
Levegh, Pierre 177, 255
Lewellen, Jimmy 7, 10, 33–37, 39, 43, 45, 47–49, 101, 103–105, 109, 111, 154–156, 160, 161, 192, 194, 195, 210, 220–222, 244–249, 251, 252
Lewis, Emory 105
Lewis, Paul 11, 99, 119, 120, 225, 258, 259, 261, 266, 267, 269, 270
Lewis, Robert Q. 253
Liberty Bell 7 57
Life 177
Liguori, Ralph 6, 39, 45, 47, 48, 105, 138, 154, 160, 161, 248–250, 252
Lilly, Betty 268
Lincoln 32–34, 39, 101, 102, 105, 142, 154, 241, 242, 248, 279; Mecklenburg Motors 33
Linder, Dick 102
Liston, Sonny 262
Littlejohn, Joe, Jr. 5
Littlejohn, Joe, Sr. 5, 6, 7, 12, 13, 23, 25, 27, 29, 31, 220, 229, 241, 280
Livingston, Ed 60
Long, Bondy 16, 60, 67, 70, 168, 207, 227, 265, 271
Long, Sterling 103
Lorenzen, Fred "Elmhurst Express" "The Golden Boy" 48, 65, 66, 138, 141, 168, 207–209, 224, 226, 227, 229, 230, 259, 261–269, 282
Lotus 97; Pure Firebird Special 186
Louis, Joe 42, 242, 245
Louisiana 101
Lowe, Boscoe 227
Lowe's 11
LPGA 37; Betsy Rawls Peach

Blossom Invitational Golf Tournament 37
Lucky Teeter's Hell Drivers 42
Lucy 257
Luna 10, 64
Lund, Tiny "The Big Fisherman" 8, 9, 10, 25–30, 39, 48–53, 58, 61, 63–68, 71, 73, 80, 81, 83, 85, 91, 92, 108, 109, 111, 115, 116, 120, 121, 132, 133, 135, 136, 138, 139, 142, 146, 147, 155–157, 161–164, 168–170, 185, 186, 189, 191, 192, 196, 198, 199, 207, 208, 215, 221, 222, 225, 238, 252–257, 262–264, 267, 271, 276, 278, 279, 282
Lunda, Milt 273
Luptow, Frank 34, 35, 103
Libyan Revolution 273
Lymon, Frankie 69
Lynn, Clyde 28, 65–66, 78, 135, 135, 272, 274, 275

MacArthur, Douglas 56, 61, 243
Maddox, U.S.S. 61
Mahoney, Chuck 34
Major League Baseball 57, 263; All Star Game 57; Atlanta-Fulton County 64; Baltimore Orioles 105, 274; Braves 64, 256; Candlestick Park 57, 65; Detroit Tigers 214; Dodgers (LA/Dem Bums) 50, 64, 68, 71, 105, 207, 241, 245, 247, 257, 262, 271; Ebbets Field 49; Fenway 57; Giants (SF) 50, 64, 245, 248, 263, 271; Mets 58, 61, 263; National League 1; Nationals 57; Phillies 57, 58; Polo Grounds 49, 263; Red Sox 271; Reds 64, 114, 274; St. Louis Cardinals 266, 271; Shea Stadium 61, 64; Tigers 121; Twins 68; White Sox 257; World Series (Fall Classic/Series) 105, 112, 207, 247, 248, 256, 258, 266, 271, 274; Yankee Stadium 59; Yankees 112, 207, 241, 242, 247, 256, 258, 266, 271
Maloney, Jim 64
Mandeville, Roger 5
Mann, Larry 249
Manning, Larry 99, 186
Mansfield, Jayne 101, 110, 114, 115, 124
Manson Family 228
Mantle, Mickey "The Mick" 58, 206, 243
Mantz, Johnny 34, 35, 103, 109, 242, 247

Manusch, Heinie 215, 217
The Many Loves of Dobie Gillis 55
March, Little Peggy 207
Marciano, Rocky 245, 252
Marcis, Dave 72, 73, 75, 151, 229, 272–276, 279
Marichal, Juan 64
Maris, Roger 57, 112
Marlin, Coo Coo 279
Marsh, Jack 129, 255
Marshall, E.G. 59
Marshall, Jim 266
Marshall, Thurgood 271
Marshman, Bobby 97, 116, 186
Martin, Otis 6, 32, 102, 246
Martin, Pee Wee 33, 103
Marvin, Lee (Kid Shelleen/Tim Strawn) 64
Mary Poppins 61
Maryland (MD) 264; Beltsville 234; The Preakness 15; Silver Spring 264
Maserati 264
Massachusetts (MA) 165, 243; Boston 243, 263; Boston Harbor 258; Norwood 165
Massey, Ed 244
Massey, Jimmy 11, 13, 47, 59, 106, 109, 111, 115, 155, 191, 198, 206, 208, 221, 254–256, 263
Matthews, Banjo 7, 47, 198, 215, 221–223, 227, 254, 255, 257, 258, 260–262, 267, 274, 280
Maxwell, Elsa 253
May, Dick 73
Mayne, Sgt. Roy 16–17, 19, 269
Mayor Pat McCrory 39
Mays, Harold 246
Mays, Willie 45, 273
Mazerowski, Bill 258
McCarthy, John 66, 78, 136
McCartney, Paul 71, 73
McClain, Jim 46, 121
McDonald, Dave 97, 116, 186, 233
McDonald's 124
McDuffie, J.D. 30, 60, 66, 72, 79, 81, 135, 136, 168, 208, 228, 269, 273, 281
McDuffie, Paul 12, 279
McGavin, Darren 204
McGinnis, Pop 36, 160
McGrath, Jack 178
McGriff, Hershel 7, 36, 45, 154, 155, 194, 195, 202, 220, 249, 250, 282
McGuire, Frank 108
McHugh, Clint 49
McMahon, Bill 169
McMillion, Worth 20, 122

McQuagg, Sam 170, 268, 271, 273
McVitty, John 49, 252, 253, 281
Mediterranean 64, 177
Meisenhelder, Ken 74
Melton, Major 17
Melton, Ray 164, 197, 280
Mercedes 177, 255
Mercury (Comet/Cougar/Cyclone/Marauder/Montego) 7, 8, 9, 10, 15, 20–24, 27, 33, 34, 42, 50, 57, 59, 60, 66, 67, 70, 71, 80, 81, 91, 92, 97, 99, 102, 106, 108, 109, 115, 116, 136, 138, 139, 154–156, 161, 163, 165, 168, 181, 182, 189, 197, 207, 220, 221, 225–227, 229, 230, 237, 249, 252–254, 264–267, 269, 271, 276; Bristol Lincoln-Mercury 62; CU Later Alligator 220; "The Vomit" 225, 226
Meredith, James 262
Meserve, Stan 235
MG 45
Michigan (MI) 60, 66, 197, 255; Champion Spark Plug 400 60; Dearborn 92, 254, 271; Detroit (Motor City) 9, 42, 106, 108, 109, 162, 252, 254; Lansing 65; Michigan State Fairgrounds 109; Motor City 250 109, 119; Troy 73; Yankee 600 197
The Mickey Mouse Club 105
Middlecoff, Dr. Cary 250
Midkiff, Jesse 156, 157
Midnight Cowboy 72
Miller, Bill 35
Milliken, Frank 203
Million, Joel 46, 105, 251
Minter, Billy 250
Minter, Clyde 34, 103, 241, 244, 250
Minton, Turkey 271
The Misfits 57
Mississippi (MS) 53, 61, 154, 271; Long Beach 53; University of Mississippi 262
Mr. Ed 112
Monaco 252; Monte Carlo 177
The Monkees 119
Monroe, Marilyn 199
Montgomery, Bob "The Voice of Stock Car Racing" 115, 116, 280
Moody, Ralph 8, 9, 31, 38, 39, 49, 91, 95, 106, 108, 138, 155, 161–163, 165, 181, 183, 196, 198, 202, 221, 237, 238, 252–254, 281
Moore, Bunk 108, 136
Moore, Doug 62

Moore, Lloyd 34, 35, 102
Moore, Paul "Little Bud" 25, 63, 64, 70, 94, 119, 186, 271
Moore, Walter "Bud" 5, 6, 8–13, 15, 16, 18, 19, 22, 24, 27, 36, 42, 45, 49–51, 53, 57, 58, 60, 62, 63, 66, 92, 97, 108, 109, 112, 114–116, 118, 119, 127, 136, 139–142, 146, 154, 155, 162, 168, 173, 185, 189, 196, 198, 199, 205–207, 211, 221–227, 229, 232, 237, 238, 245, 250, 254, 255, 260, 261, 263–267, 269, 271, 277
MoPar 7, 47, 63, 65, 91, 135, 155, 220, 225, 265, 267, 268
Morgan 45
Morris, Buckshot 248
Morton, Bill 115, 255, 260
Mounts, Arden 7, 179
Mundy, Frank "The Rebel" (Frank Menendez) 33–35, 42–44, 57, 58, 81, 82, 85, 103, 155, 219, 221, 241, 244
Muni, Paul 68
Murphy, Paula 186
Murrow, Edward R. 63
Musial, Stan "The Man" 15, 263
My Three Sons 65
Myers, Billy 8, 9, 10, 35, 37, 46–50, 91, 92, 104–106, 108, 138, 139, 142, 155, 156, 161–163, 179, 181, 185, 189, 195–198, 219, 221, 228, 237, 245, 252–254, 280
Myers, Bobby 24, 50, 116, 139, 161, 163, 182, 196–198, 219, 222, 228, 280
Myers, Chocolate 197
The Myers (Brothers) 140, 157, 280
Myler, Kenny 28

NASA 256; Mercury 59, 206, 256
NASCAR 1, 5, 6, 12–14, 27–30, 33, 35–37, 39, 43–45, 60, 63, 64, 66, 67, 72, 73, 91, 96, 97, 109, 119–122, 134, 139, 142, 150, 151, 154–157, 168, 173, 201, 211, 212, 219, 222, 223, 226–228, 231, 232, 234, 240, 244, 247, 250, 280; Busch Series 1, 76, 244, 264; Daytona Dash 231; Fifty Greatest Drivers 82, 232, 234, 250; Grand American 79, 81, 142, 234, 275, 278; Grand National 1, 2, 19, 20, 22–24, 26, 28–30, 33–37, 41–43, 45–55, 57–61, 63–67, 69–73, 76, 79–82, 87, 90–92, 96, 97, 99, 103, 105, 109–112, 114–116, 119, 121, 122, 125, 127, 129, 131, 132, 134, 135, 137–140, 142, 146, 147, 150, 154, 156, 159–165, 168, 170, 176, 177, 179, 181, 182, 186, 190, 191, 194–199, 201, 203, 204, 208, 210–214, 218, 220–222, 224, 227, 228, 232, 235, 237, 239, 241, 242, 245–251, 253–260, 262–265, 271–278, 281; Nextel Cup Series 1, 43, 55, 160, 242; Speedway Division 232, 247, 276; Strictly Stock Division 1, 3, 33, 38, 42, 43, 49, 52, 60, 71, 82, 101, 122, 132, 151, 160, 192, 201, 219, 232, 234, 240–242, 256, 262, 269, 275, 276, 278; West 250; Winston Cup Series 1, 41, 43, 82, 83, 160, 232, 242, 250, 270, 275, 276, 278
Nash (Ambassador) 34–36, 39, 45, 103, 109, 154, 173, 179, 219, 242, 245, 247
National Anthem 178, 212
National Championship Stock Car Circuit (N.C.S.C.C.) 219
National Football League (NFL) 97, 108, 258; Chicago Bears 147; Cleveland Browns 147; Dallas Cowboys 258; Viking 266
Native American 211
Navy 82
Nazuruk, Mike 178
NBA 250; Celtics 64, 257, 263, 267; Ft. Wayne Pistons 250; LA Lakers; 76ers 67; Syracuse Nationals 250
NBC 97, 195, 248
NCAA 257
Nebraska: Omaha 52
Needles 47
Negre, Ed 73
Nelson, Norm 267
Nelson, Ricky 51, 87
Netherworld 145
Nevada (NV): Las Vegas 49, 139, 161
New England 97
New Jersey (Garden State, Jersey) 45, 155, 211, 241, 246; Atlantic City 61; Elizabeth 61; Linden (Airport) 45, 211; Northern 300; Old Bridge 53, 182; Paterson 61; Pennington 241; Rahway State Prison 275; Trenton 53, 244, 247
New York (NY) 64, 214, 220, 243, 253, 255; Altamont 255; Broadway 49, 271; Buffalo 214; Columbia (University) 70; Fonda 253; Hamburg 132, 242; Lake Placid 199; Mamaroneck 253; New York City (Big Apple) 6, 60, 243; Plattsburg 253; Rochester 6, 34, 103, 220; Sing Sing 253; Syracuse 182; Watkins Glen 201, 277, 281; West Point 243; Woodstock 228
New York Rangers 275
Newport Pop Festival 70
Nichels, Ray 9, 268, 271
Nichols, Red 211
Nicklaus, Jack 64, 263, 267
Niven, David 257
Nixon, Richard Milhous 72, 78, 121, 199, 204, 258, 275
Nobel Peace Prize 265
Norman, Whitey 127, 129, 147, 148, 196, 215, 253, 255
North Carolina (NC/Old North State) 1, 3, 7, 12, 32, 36, 37, 87, 90, 96, 99, 101, 131, 134, 136, 137, 144, 149, 151, 153, 154, 156, 159, 167, 169, 170, 172, 176, 184, 185, 189–191, 194, 196, 203, 210, 211, 213, 218, 231, 229, 237, 240, 243–245, 248, 249, 262, 267, 268, 273; ACC Tournament 237; American 500 122, 273; Asheville 3, 14, 69, 213, 218, 231; Asheville 300 233; Asheville Bicycle Racing Club 231; Asheville Tourists Baseball Club 213, 215; Asheville-Weaverville Speedway (A-W) 7, 11, 17, 19, 26, 27, 29, 195, 215, 218–229, 232, 280; Ayr Mount 123; Belmont Raiders 146; Blue Ridge 12, 94, 97, 222; Bowman-Gray Stadium 1, 11, 17, 54, 55, 65, 79, 112, 139, 140, 156, 164, 168, 176, 201, 222, 280; Brushy Mountains 195, 241, 246, 252, 255, 258, 262, 263, 265, 267, 271, 273, 281; Bumcombe County 213; Bumcombe County Sheriff's Office 223; Burlington 191; Cabarrus County 138; Carolina 500 77; Carter-Finley Stadium 149; Catawba 70, 72, 272, 275; Champion Speedway 190, 191; Chapel Hill 55, 62; Charlotte (Queen City) 1, 2, 7, 12, 20, 29, 32, 33, 35–39, 42, 45, 49, 52–54, 59, 63, 90, 97, 101, 103, 118, 122, 131, 135, 151, 154, 179, 186, 189, 194, 197, 199, 201, 205, 219, 224, 240, 242, 259, 262–264, 272, 276–

279, 281; Charlotte Carousel Queen 138; Charlotte (Memorial) Hospital 142, 161, 233; Charlotte Motor Speedway (CMS/Lowes) 118, 119, 122, 194, 199, 255, 279, 280; Charlotte Speedway 1, 32–39, 201, 244; Clemmons 248; Cleveland 63; Cleveland County 161; Cleveland County Fairgrounds 39, 90, 91, 93, 94; Comfort Inn 39; Concord 47, 49, 53, 54, 75, 109, 115, 137, 139, 141, 191, 199, 252, 268; *Concord Tribune* 138, 142; Currituck County 167; Deep Gap 78; Denton 267; Dixie Classic Fairgrounds 176; Dog Track Speedway 167–169; Dorton Arena 150; Elkin 268; Eno River 100, 101, 108, 110–112, 114, 116, 119, 120, 122, 123; Fayetteville 163, 169, 172, 190, 191, 258; Fayetteville Steel Erectors and Metal Buildings, Inc. 190; Fireball 300 225–229; Forsyth County Fairgrounds Speedway 176–179; Ft. Bragg 173, 175; Franklin 69; French Broad River 231, 232, 236; Gaston Christian School 144; Gaston County 147, 255; Gastonia 3, 33, 62, 65, 144, 146, 245; *Gastonia Gazette* 146; Greensboro 33, 53, 190, 192, 198, 237, 239; Greensboro Agricultural Fairgrounds Speedway (Central Carolina Fairgrounds) 237, 239; Greensboro Coliseum 237, 239; Guilford County 203; Gwyn Staley 400 261, 263, 265, 267, 268, 270, 272–275; Harnett County 172; Harnett County Speedway 3, 96, 97, 172, 173, 175; Harris 96, 97, 189; Harris Speedway 94, 96, 97, 99, 167, 233; Harris Speedway (Concord/Concord International/ New Concord) 137–139, 141–143, 234, 254, 280; Hickory 7, 37, 53, 54, 65, 69, 138, 141, 154, 164, 195, 281; Hickory Speedway 1; High Point 14, 147, 195, 206, 210–212, 238, 246, 257, 259, 268; Hillsborough 13, 19, 20, 61, 99, 101, 103–105, 107–112, 114–116, 118–123, 132, 142, 151, 155, 191, 201, 219, 261, 264, 265; Home State 200 151; Immaculate Heart of Mary Catholic Church 210, 212; Indian Trail 136; Jacksonville 97, 184, 185, 186, 189; Jacksonville Speedway 184, 185, 187, 189; Joe Weatherly Memorial 150 116, 119; Kannapolis 243; Kernersville 244; Kill Devil Hill 170; Kitty Hawk 170; Laurinburg 71; Leaksville 211; Level Cross 208; Lowell 144; McCormick Field 213–215, 217; Mebane 16; Mecklenburg 35; Mecklenburg Rebels 146, 147; Monroe 3, 73, 134, 195; Mt. Holly Hawks 146; Moyock 167, 168, 268; National 400/500 12, 97, 119, 186, 199, 259, 272; NBHS Blackhawks 218, 219; New Asheville Speedway 94, 99, 168, 231–233, 235; Newton 116; North Buncombe High School 218; North Carolina Highway Patrol 223; North Carolina Speedway 1; North Carolina State Fairgrounds 149; North Carolina State Fairgrounds Speedway 149, 151; North Carolina State Wolfpack 149; North Raleigh Industrial Park 153; North State 200; North Wilkesboro (Wilkes) 19, 33, 53, 61, 67, 92, 118, 119, 123, 135, 136, 139, 151, 168, 201, 211, 219, 240, 242, 244, 245, 247, 249, 252–254, 256, 257, 260–262, 264, 265, 268, 271, 274–276, 278–281; North Wilkesboro Speedway 1, 240–243, 245–247, 250, 251, 253, 255, 257, 259, 261, 263, 265, 267, 269, 271, 273, 275, 277, 278, 281, 282; Occoneechee Speedway 1, 2, 100–106, 108, 109, 111–115, 117–123, 214, 219, 274; Olivia 37, 160, 262; Onslow County 184; Park 'n Shop 194; Preservation North Carolina (PNC) 123; Raleigh 8, 92, 149, 151, 153, 155, 15; Raleigh 250 36, 73, 195, 253, 274; Raleigh Speedway 150, 153, 156, 157; Randleman 28, 132, 203, 207; Rockingham 1, 77, 122, 226, 227; Rocky Mount 248; Salisbury 131–133, 244, 245; Salisbury Confederate Prison 132, 133; Salisbury National Cemetery 133; Salisbury Super Speedway 3, 131, 133, 257; Shelby 8, 26, 36, 39, 90, 61, 94, 96, 99, 106, 155, 161, 233, 245, 262, 279; Siler City 80, 242; South Business Park 190; Southern Home Show 151; Southern States Fairgrounds 37, 52, 54, 55, 194–199; Spindle Center Fairgrounds 3, 144–147, 280; Spring Lake 3, 172; Stanley Blue Devils 146; Starlite Speedway 3, 73, 133, 135, 136, 280; Statesville 248; Tar Heel Speedway 203–209; Textile 250; Tidewater 300 170; Tri-City Speedway 210; Turkey 200; University of North Carolina Tar Heels 108; Weaverville 24, 47, 54, 55, 61, 116, 122, 219, 224, 225, 229, 264; Western North Carolina 500 (WNC 500) 223–229; Wilkes County "The Bootlegging Capital of the World" 195, 252; Wilkes County Hospital 250; Wilkes 200/250/400 258, 260, 262, 263, 265, 267, 268, 272, 274, 275; Wilson 47, 54, 87, 159, 160, 161, 164, 165, 191, 225, 280; Wilson County (American Legion) Fairgrounds Speedway 159, 161, 163, 165; Wilson Fire Department 163; Winston-Salem "Tobaccotown" 1, 17, 62, 164, 176–178, 242, 253; World 600 10–15, 28, 29, 57, 81, 82, 88, 94, 97, 109, 164, 197, 222, 225, 232–234, 253, 265, 266, 268, 273, 277

North Vietnam 61, 64; Haiphong 67
Northern Tour 182
Northwest Orient 275
Nottebart, Don 58
Nunis, Sam 280

Oates, Phil 245
O'Connor, Pat 228
Offy 228, 244
Ohio (OH) 50, 53, 263; Canton 263; Chillicothe (Federal Reformatory) 50, 195, 254; Cincinnati 261; Cleveland 246; Dayton 35, 103; Ohio State University 70, 257; New Bloomington 248
Oklahoma (OK): Oklahoma City 178
Oldenberg, Don 37, 173, 247
Oldsmobile (Olds/88) 3, 6, 7, 9, 12, 28, 31–37, 39, 42, 45, 46, 50, 65, 68–70, 85, 91, 92, 94, 102–105, 108, 109, 124, 132, 133, 135, 138, 139, 143, 146, 150, 152, 154, 155, 163, 165,

170, 173, 175, 179, 191, 194, 196, 198, 202, 211, 219, 221, 225, 230, 237, 241–249, 251, 254–257, 267, 268, 277, 279, 282; Air Lift Special 104, 249; Black Phantom 42, 43, 219, 245; Cherokee Garage 36, 45, 102, 211, 248; Eanes Motors 34, 220; Flying Rebel Racing Team 259; Gray Ghost 42, 160, 219, 245, 279; Griffin Motors 276; Helzafire 47, 105, 179; Red Devil 42, 160, 219, 243, 279
O'Neal, Steve 273
Ord, Jim 37
Oregon (OR) 249; Bridal Veil 249; Portland 37, 38, 53, 182, 194, 245
Oscar (Academy Award) 61, 69, 71, 72, 116, 246, 257, 263, 267
Osieki, Bob 261
Osmond, Marie 136
Oswald, Billy 60
Outer Mongolia 112
The Outer Limits 263
Owens, Everett "Cotton" 5, 7–20, 27, 29–31, 34, 35, 37, 43, 51, 52, 56–58, 60, 63–70, 72, 73, 85, 92, 97, 104, 106, 108–112, 114, 116, 119, 120, 124, 132, 133, 138–141, 143, 151, 154–158, 164, 168, 170, 186, 194, 196, 198, 199, 205, 208, 215, 217, 221, 222, 224–227, 232, 245, 249, 254–261, 264, 265, 267, 268, 270–273

Paar, Jack 112
Packard 34, 37, 46, 109, 173, 246, 247, 251
Pagan, Eddie 10, 50, 108, 127, 129, 139, 156, 182, 191, 198, 221, 224, 226, 227, 255
Palmer, Arnold/Arnie 50, 61, 116
Palmer, Clyde 38
Palmer, Jim 228
Pampers 63
Pan American Road Race 250
Panch, Marvin "Pancho" 8, 9, 10, 12, 19, 20, 29, 31, 39, 44, 49, 50, 61, 65, 92, 105, 108, 116, 127, 129, 130, 138, 139, 141, 143, 155, 156, 161–164, 182, 195, 196, 198, 199, 202, 205, 221, 230, 237, 238, 249, 250, 252, 254, 255, 259, 261–268, 281
Pardue, Jimmy 8, 10, 11, 13, 14, 17–20, 52, 56–58, 60–62, 97, 111, 112, 114–116, 118, 168, 171, 186, 191, 200, 207, 208, 222–224, 257–262, 265, 280
Parks, Raymond 32, 102, 219, 241, 242, 256
Parnell, Bud 53
Parrish, George 179, 221, 254
Parsons, Benny 73, 75, 78, 79, 151, 274–276
Parsons, Goldie 170
Paschal, Jim "The Illustrated Man/Tattooed One" 3, 6–10, 13–17, 31, 33–39, 42, 45, 47–50, 54, 57, 58, 65, 67, 68, 80–83, 85, 91, 92, 103–106, 108, 112, 114, 119, 124, 138, 139, 141, 150, 154–158, 160–163, 165, 170, 177–179, 181, 182, 185, 194–196, 198, 199, 202, 205–207, 209, 210, 215, 217, 219, 220, 223, 224, 227, 230, 232, 234–237, 245, 246, 248–254, 258–266, 268–272, 278, 282
Passino, Jacques 265, 271
Passwater, Dick 36, 39, 154, 175, 247
Patterson, Floyd 222, 262
Patterson, Johnny 6, 175
PBS 274
Pearson, David Gene "The Silver Fox" 3, 5, 10–15, 17–21, 24, 27–30, 55–57, 60–67, 70–73, 82, 85, 87, 89, 94, 95, 97, 111, 115, 116, 118–122, 124, 135, 142, 143, 150, 152, 168–171, 186, 199, 200, 205, 207, 208, 224–230, 233–236, 258, 259, 261, 263–275, 280
Pearson, Dell 245
Pearson, Drew 273
Peck, Gregory 263
Pedrick Piston Rings 197
Penland, Joe 58, 63
Pennsylvania (PA) 37, 53, 67, 92, 123, 151, 244, 246, 274, 280; Abbottstown 37; Bloomsburg 160; Bradford 53; Connie Mack Stadium 274; Heidelberg 201; International 200 60; Irwin 244; Langhorne 45, 49, 50, 60, 122, 154, 178, 182, 191, 211, 228, 242, 244, 247–249, 253, 281; New Oxford 53; Newton 246; Pittsburgh 241; Puke Hollow 178; Punxsutawney 123; Reading 53, 54
Perdue, Lt. Governor Beverly 39
Perry Mason 49, 70
Peter, Paul, and Mary 59
Petre, Joan 135
Petty, Julian (J.H.) 146, 182, 191, 192, 223, 261
Petty, Lee "Papa" "The Old Man" 3, 6–14, 17, 26, 31, 33–40, 42–50, 52, 53, 56, 83, 85, 91, 92, 94, 97, 101–106, 108–112, 124, 127, 129, 132, 133, 138–140, 142, 143, 145, 147, 148, 154–158, 160–166, 169, 171, 175–179, 181–183, 185, 189–196, 198–202, 210–212, 215, 217, 219–222, 227, 230, 237, 239, 241, 242, 245, 247–249, 251–258, 262, 263, 268, 279, 281
Petty, Maurice 13, 14, 17, 26, 28, 59, 112, 114, 116, 141, 142, 205, 223, 227
Petty, Richard 10–24, 26, 27, 29, 31, 50, 53, 55–62, 64–75, 77–83, 85, 88, 97, 102, 109, 111, 112, 114–116, 118–122, 124, 131, 132, 135, 141–143, 146, 150–152, 164, 168–171, 186, 191, 192, 198–202, 204–209, 211, 222–230, 232–236, 256–259, 261–276, 281, 282
Petty Compound/Engineering/Mayflower/Oldsmobile/Plymouth 16, 17, 19, 24, 60, 114, 115, 122, 151, 163, 196, 198, 203–205, 207, 208, 221, 224, 232, 265, 266, 277
The Pettys 3, 24, 28, 30, 33, 55, 56, 151, 164, 218, 226, 262, 270
Phoenix 36, 97, 178, 186
Pike's Peak Hill Climb 122
Pistone, "Tiger" Tom 10, 29, 30, 53, 64–66, 110, 111, 119, 120, 135, 136, 140, 164, 69, 170, 199, 200, 221, 222, 227, 228, 252, 257, 259, 268, 269, 271, 272
The Pit and the Pendulum 57
Pitt, Blackie 10, 38, 161, 248, 251
Pless, B.A. 44, 45
Plymouth (Fury/Barracuda/Mayflower) 8–17, 19, 20, 23, 24, 26–29, 31, 34, 35, 42, 50, 52, 55, 57, 60, 61, 63, 65, 66, 68, 70, 71, 73, 75, 77, 78, 80, 85, 91, 94, 97, 99, 102, 102, 106, 108, 114–116, 119, 121, 122, 124, 127, 135, 138, 139, 143, 146, 151, 152, 154, 161, 163, 171, 173, 181–183, 186, 189, 191, 199, 201, 202, 205, 206, 209, 221, 225, 230, 232, 236, 237, 241–247, 253, 254, 257, 258, 262, 263, 265–273, 277, 279, 282; Friedkin Enterprises 122, 123
Pontiac (Bonneville/Firebird/Iron Indian/Pony) 8–18, 24, 31, 47, 56–58, 60, 80, 81, 85,

88, 92, 106, 108, 110, 112, 114, 115, 124, 138, 141, 143, 154, 156, 158, 169, 195, 196, 199, 200, 206, 221–223, 225, 228, 230, 232, 236, 238, 252, 254, 255, 258–263, 265, 268, 277, 281; Alemeda Auto Parts 81; Boomershine 10, 12, 232, 277; Brushy Mountain Motors 8, 49, 195, 195, 221, 252, 254, 281; Dirt Dauber 15, 58, 112, 140, 141; Hedges 10, 11; Holly Farms 12, 111, 112, 259, 262; Home Depot; Justus 12; "The Red Fox" 53, 222, 232, 277; Warrior Motel 261
Poor, Bill 198
The Pope 178
Porsche (Spyder) 45, 155; "Little Bastard" 155
Porter, Cole 265
Portier, Sidney 61, 116
Powell, Floyd 16, 17, 114, 205, 224
Prado, Perez 37, 250
Presley, Elvis 38, 47, 49, 56, 195, 248, 252, 257
Price, Lloyd 140
Priddy, Cotton 49
Procter, Vicki Harris 137, 142
Professional Drivers Association (PDA) 72, 273
Professional Football Hall of Fame 263
Pruitt, Ervin 73, 228
Pruitt, Ray 34
Pure (Firebird) 17, 57, 162, 164, 186, 261
Putney, J.T. 20, 21, 27, 30, 64, 65, 99, 135, 233, 234, 270

Quarry, Jerry 69

Rafter, Billy 50, 215
Ragon, Lloyd 53
Rakestraw, Benny 52
Rakestraw, Wilbur 50, 256
Raley, Tom 69
Rambler (Ambassador) 66, 67
Rambo, Ted 248
Ramsey, E.C. 45
Randolph, Amanda 68
Ranier, H.B. 6, 78, 248
Ranier, Prince 252
Rathmann, Dick 6, 7, 35–37, 42, 45, 46, 104, 105, 150, 154, 155, 157, 160, 173, 175, 177, 194, 195, 210, 211, 219, 220, 246–251, 279, 282
The Red Skelton Show 55
Reed, Jim 35, 155, 214, 221
Reeder, Ann 138

Reitzel, Dr. L.L. 57, 112, 264
Rexford, Bill 3, 34, 60, 103, 243, 244, 265, 280
Reynolds, Debbie 253
The Rhythm Boys 211, 212; Crosby, Harry Lillis "Bing" 211, 212
Rice, Sam 103, 241, 242
Richardson, Bobby 258
Richardson, Paul 246
Rickenbacker, Eddie 249
The Rifleman 55
Riley, Richard 52, 53
Ringling and Barnum and Bailey Circus 47
Ringo 112
Ringstaff, Tommy 251
R.J. Reynolds Tobacco Company (R.J.R.) 240, 275; Winston 275
Robbins, Marty 136
Roberts, Doris 5
Roberts, Glen "Fireball" 2, 5, 8–10, 13, 17, 20, 22, 23, 34, 39, 43, 45, 49, 50, 53, 55, 57, 58, 83, 91, 92, 95, 97, 103, 105, 106, 108, 109, 112, 116, 118, 122, 124, 125, 127, 129, 130, 138, 139, 141–143, 154–158, 160, 161, 163, 181–183, 185, 186, 189, 195–198, 202, 215, 220, 221, 223, 226, 228, 230, 233, 237, 238, 241–244, 252–254, 259–265, 267, 269, 278, 279, 281, 282
Robertson, Cliff 71
Robertson, Don 73
Robinson, Shawna 231
Rodgers, Dave 197
Rodgers, Truett 135
The Rolling Stones 228, 263, 266
Rollins, Shorty 10, 50–52, 109, 132, 146, 156, 164, 198, 215, 221, 255, 257, 281
Rominger, Slim 248
Roper, "Alfalfa" Jim 32, 33, 39, 101, 102
Rose, David 58
Rose, Pete 114, 263
Rose, Mauri 8, 48, 49, 138, 155
Roseboro, John 64
Rossi, Mario 73, 78, 82, 272, 275
Route 66 258
Rush, Ermon 211
Rush, Ken 20, 50, 127, 129, 132, 139, 164, 238, 239
Russell, Jim 255
Ruth, Babe 112
Rutherford, Johnny 279

Sachs, Eddie "The Clown Prince" 97, 116, 233
Sadler, Sgt. Barry 64
Safer, Morley 64
Sain, Gary 16, 17
St. Louis 273, 275
Sales, Leon 242, 243, 245, 246, 279, 282
Salk, Jonas 250
Sammartino, Bruno 206
Samples, Ed 219
Savage, Swede 271, 272, 281
Saverance, Ed 43
Savold, Lee 42
Sawyer, Paul 163, 280
Scarborough, Carl 154
Schade, Ed 244
Schissler, Don 227
Schneider, Frankie 45, 60, 155, 156, 158, 191, 193, 221, 246
Schneider, Leo 34
Schrader, Ken 76
Schultz, Volney 176
Scott, Oliver Wendell 13, 15–20, 23, 25–30, 57, 58, 60–73, 75, 79, 82, 88, 97, 99, 112, 114–116, 119–121, 135, 136, 139, 141, 142, 150, 151, 168–171, 186, 189, 205–209, 223–228, 259–265, 267–270, 272–276, 281
Sears, "Big" John 30, 65–70, 72, 73, 75, 79, 120, 122, 135, 136, 150–152, 170, 225–228, 234, 269, 270, 272, 273
Sears, James 73, 136
Seay, Jim 83
Seay, Lloyd 212, 241, 256
Seifert, Bill 228, 269, 274
Senna, Ayrton 177
Sessoms, Frank 58
Setzer, Ned 25, 26
Sexton, Buster 66, 67
Shannon, Del 13
Shaw, Graham 61
Shaw, Reid 135
Shaw, Wilbur 249
Shirey, Bill 80
Shoemaker, Roy 232
Shook, Monroe 164, 165, 261
Shore, Barney 215, 256
Shuebruk, Dick 243
Shuman, Louis "Buddy" 35–37, 39, 42, 45, 104, 157, 160, 195, 245–247, 281
Simpson, Banks 252
Simpson, Gene 251
Singer, Bill 71
Sirhan, Sirhan 71
Skeen, Buren 267, 281
Skinner, Eddie 179, 220, 251
Skinner, Mr. 86
Sluder, Gene 219, 229, 280

Smilin' Jack 33
Smith, Betty 5
Smith, Bob 102
Smith, Bruton 131, 132, 138
Smith, Buck 210
Smith, Jack 3, 5, 9–17, 31, 33, 38, 39, 45, 49–51, 53, 57–60, 83, 85, 88, 89, 92, 106, 108, 111, 112, 115, 127, 129, 130, 138–143, 155–157, 161–163, 165, 182, 185, 189–192, 196, 198, 199, 202, 215, 217, 219, 221–224, 226, 232, 234–239, 242, 254–257, 260–263, 277, 279, 282
Smith, Louise 5, 45, 101, 103, 242, 246, 278
Smith, Perry (car owner) 34, 35, 42, 44, 82, 244
Smith, Perry (murderer) 267
Smith, Robert 141
Smith, Sam 64
Smith, Slick 33, 154, 158, 210, 242, 247, 250
Smith, Wayne 28
Snead, Sam 248
Snider, Duke 263
Snowden, Bill 34, 102, 160
Soares, John 37
Some Like It Hot 163
Sosebee, Gober 3, 6, 35, 36, 37, 39, 42, 44–47, 50, 83, 101, 102, 104, 105, 108, 109, 132, 133, 160, 194, 211, 219, 220, 247–249, 256, 257, 280
South Carolina (SC/Palmetto State) 1, 3, 5–11, 27, 41, 42, 52, 55, 57, 63, 66, 70, 86, 87, 125, 139, 180, 186, 195, 226, 246, 249, 253, 276; Arclite (100/200) 47, 58; Brewington Ambulance Service 16; Camden 63; Carolina Power & Light 42; Carolina Velo 42; Cayce 58, 63; Charleston 13, 15, 63; Charleston Heights 186; Cherokee Springs 139; Coastal Speedway 180–183; Columbia 3, 10, 11, 17, 19, 27, 35, 41–55, 57, 59–61, 63, 65–67, 70–75, 78, 81, 105, 106, 108, 116, 138, 164, 205, 228, 257, 264, 271, 273, 275; Columbia Speedway 1, 41–45, 52, 55, 64, 66, 68, 69, 73, 76, 77, 79–83, 85, 276; Columbia 200 61, 71, 73, 74, 80, 186, 226, 232; Congaree Mobile Home Sales 41; Conway 181; Cross 27, 29; Darlington "The Lady in Black" 11, 12, 29, 43, 44, 50, 58, 73, 87, 92, 122, 139, 142, 153, 154, 156, 164, 201, 226, 262, 265, 278–281; Dorman High School 30; Elloree 75; Eye in the Sky 197; Florence 197, 246; Gamecock Speedway 1; Greenville 9, 19, 45, 53, 54, 57–59, 63, 65, 101, 111, 112, 127, 129, 165, 182, 198, 245, 246, 259, 267, 276, 277; Greenville-Pickens Speedway 1, 227; Hardeeville 186; Hartsville 44, 45, 86–89, 276, 277; Hartsville Rescue Squad 87; Hartsville Speedway 2, 3, 86–89, 280; Horry County Public Information Office 180; Hub City Speedway 5; Inman 10, 16, 27, 29, 55, 63, 119, 135, 150, 222, 226; John Sewell Heating and Roofing 13; Lake Santee 29; Lancaster Speedway 1; Maurice's Piggy Park 41; McLeod Hospital 197; Myrtle Beach (Grand Strand) 17, 54, 58, 180–182, 198; Myrtle Square Mall 180; Newberry 125, 129, 139; Newberry Speedway 3, 125, 127, 129; North Charleston 52; Parris Island 252; Piedmont Interstate Fairgrounds (The Fairgrounds) 1, 2, 5–15, 17–21, 23–25, 27–31, 219, 232, 280; Rambi Raceway 54, 181; Rebel (300/400/500) 11, 14, 29, 122, 164, 201, 273, 278; Richburg 276; Rock Hill 12, 51, 256; Sandlapper 200 60–63, 67, 70, 83; Shaw Air Force Base 16; Southern 500 10, 11, 17, 20, 24, 30, 34, 42–45, 47–53, 56, 63, 81, 92, 103, 104, 109, 110, 115, 116, 118, 119, 122, 123, 127, 135, 136, 139, 145, 146, 151, 154–156, 160, 165, 168, 179, 182, 186, 195, 196, 198, 201, 211, 220, 221, 224, 228, 234, 238, 241, 242, 244, 245, 247, 250, 252, 255, 262, 263, 266, 267, 269, 271, 273, 276, 277, 279; Southern Shops Haynes Freight Yard 1; Spartanburg (County/Spartan) 1, 5–8, 10–12, 15–22, 25–31, 36–38, 42, 53–58, 61, 63–67, 70, 72, 75, 78, 87, 88, 90, 97, 109, 111, 112, 115, 116, 119, 122, 127, 135, 139, 140, 147, 170, 173, 185, 198, 205, 215, 219, 220, 223, 224, 228, 229, 232, 252–254, 257, 259, 263, 264, 271, 273, 276, 280; Spartanburg General Hospital 6, 16, 17; *Spartanburg Herald-Journal* 16, 20, 22, 197; Spartanburg High School 30; Spartanburg Racing Museum 31; Startex 253, 257; Sumter 1; Sun 'n Sand Motel 12; Timmonsville 27; Union 64; West Columbia 41; Whitney Mills 13; WSPA AM 280; WSPA TV 252
Spaulding, Paul 10, 50, 51, 53, 54, 83, 109, 111, 164, 198, 255–257
Spell, Tom 20
Spencer, G.C. 10–16, 18, 19, 25–29, 52, 53, 55–58, 63, 99, 111, 112, 121, 122, 141, 186, 199, 205, 206, 222, 224–226, 228, 257, 259, 261, 264, 267–269, 271–275
Spencer, Junior 267, 268
The Spirit of America 60
Sputnik 50, 198
Stacy, Nelson 14, 114, 115, 223, 226, 261–264, 281
Staley, Enoch 123, 280
Staley, Gwyn 7, 8, 37, 38, 39, 47, 48, 50, 91, 92, 105, 106, 127, 129, 130, 138, 139, 150, 155, 156, 161, 162, 176, 179, 182, 183, 190–193, 195, 211, 220, 238, 245, 249, 252, 253, 280
Stalin, Josef 246
Stanley, Hank 34
Stanley, Paul 244
Stanley Cup 259
Star Trek 65, 119
Staton, Joe 246
Steiger, Rod 69
Stelter, Lyle 70–72, 135
Stengel, Casey 64, 258
Stern, Bill 275
Stewart, Cliff 206, 208
Stewart, Pete 19, 168, 248
Stewart, Tony 76
Stickleather, H.F. 242
Stockton, Harold 69
Stokes, Gene 58
Strickland, Frank 156, 221
Strickler, Bub 275
Stroppe, Bill 9, 91, 108, 115, 139, 155, 163, 197, 221, 237, 238, 253, 254, 265
Studebaker (Commander) 10, 34, 35, 42–44, 58, 83, 85, 103, 154, 173, 179, 219, 221, 244, 245, 247, 254
Styrofoam 124
Sullivan, Ed 64
Sun Records 246
Superman 273
Surveyor 3
Swanson 248
Sweatlund, Charles 12

Talman, William (Hamilton Burger) 70
Tatum, Jim 65
T-Bird 10, 11, 13, 14, 17, 52, 53, 55–57, 110, 111, 124, 140, 143, 164, 190, 199, 228, 257; Power Products Division 110; "Thunder Chicken" 111
Teagarden, Jack 211
Teague, Marshall 34, 35, 39, 42, 43, 45, 83, 103, 109, 219, 228, 244, 246, 280
Teague, Mitzi 246
Telstar II 206
Tennessee (TN) 27, 78, 114, 196, 205, 258, 266, 269, 272; Bluff City 205; Bristol 112; Camden 114; Chattanooga 62; Cleveland 169; Johnson City 258, 266; Maryville 27, 78, 269; Memphis 69, 250; Nashville 16, 27, 44, 54; Newport 108; Niota 272; Sweetwater 120
Terrell, Dave 37, 105, 246, 251, 252
Texas (TX) 81; Corpus Christi 146; Houston (Houstonian) 26, 73, 80, 81, 97; Odessa 255; San Antonio 69; Texas Motor Speedway 33; University of Texas 65
That Girl 65, 119
Thomas, Donald 7, 34, 35, 42, 43, 45, 104, 105, 150, 155, 160, 173, 176, 211, 219, 220, 244–248, 281
Thomas, Hank 234
Thomas, Herbert Watson 3, 6, 7, 8, 31, 33–40, 42–49, 83, 91–93, 95–97, 99, 101, 103–106, 108, 124, 138, 150, 154–156, 158, 160, 161, 165, 173, 175, 176, 179, 181, 194–197, 201, 210–212, 219, 220, 222, 226, 228–230, 234, 241, 242, 244–253, 257, 261, 262, 270, 277, 279–281
Thomas, Jabe 71, 73, 82, 236, 273–275
Thomas, Larry 16, 20, 58, 97, 105, 115, 116, 186, 189, 205, 206, 208, 209, 260, 261, 263–265, 267, 281
The Thomases 3, 157, 249
Thomason, H.K. 255
Thompson, Jimmy 33, 52, 132, 139, 191, 281
Thompson, Speedy "The Monroe Motorman" 7–10, 31, 34, 37–39, 45, 48–51, 83, 85, 90–93, 95, 105, 106, 108, 109, 111, 127, 129, 132, 133, 138–140,
143, 146–148, 150, 154–156, 158, 160, 161–164, 181–183, 185, 189, 191, 192, 195, 196, 198, 199, 202, 219–222, 226, 237, 239, 242, 248, 252–257, 262, 279–282
Thompson, Tommy 35, 109
Thomson, Bobby 103, 245
Thorne, Jon 66, 226
Thorpe, Jim 246
Three Dog Night 235
Thresher, U.S.S. 263
Thunder in Carolina 86–88, 110, 280
Tippett, Leonard 104, 245
The Tonight Show Starring Steve Allen 47, 195
Trailways 276
Triplett, Charles 135, 136
Trivette, E.J. 20, 23, 62, 78, 83, 267, 273
Tropical Storm Frances 231
Tropical Storm Ivan 231
Truman, President 243
Tucker, Tanya 136
Turner, "The Blonde Blizzard" Curtis Morton 3, 6, 8, 10, 11, 27–29, 32, 34–39, 45, 48, 51, 52, 64–67, 73, 83, 85, 88, 101–106, 108–111, 122–124, 138–140, 142, 143, 150–152, 154–157, 160, 163–166, 169, 173, 190–193, 195, 196, 198, 202, 219, 220, 223, 226, 228, 238, 241–242, 244, 246–248, 251–255, 257, 259, 268–270, 273, 274
Turner, Danny 273
Turner, James 261
Turnipseed, Donald 155
The Turtles 67
The Twilight Zone 257
Twitty, Conway 191
Tyner, Roy "The Wild Injun" 10, 12, 30, 50–53, 63, 65, 67, 69, 71, 73, 75, 97, 109, 111, 122, 132, 133, 135, 136, 146, 170, 192, 199, 208, 222, 227, 228, 238, 254, 258, 272, 281

Uncle Miltie's Texaco Star Theatre 7
United Nations (UN) 112, 242, 258, 275
USAC (Big Car/Stock Car) 17, 35, 46, 103, 122, 197, 228, 267, 272
U.S. Court of Appeals 267
U.S. Marines 63, 164, 252
U.S. Olympic Team 199
U.S. Open 42
U.S. Supreme Court 262

Universal Racing Network 115, 280
Unser, Al 267
Unser, Bobby 267
Unser, Jerry 228
The Untouchables 257
U.S.S.R. 64, 199
Utah (UT) 65; Bonneville Salt Flats 169, 186, 274; Logan 274
Utsman, Sherman 205, 262

Van Dyke, Dick 59
Vietnam 64, 228, 271; Gulf of Tonkin 61; My Lai Massacre 78
Virginia (VA/Virginian) 8, 12, 13, 34, 58, 140, 163, 164, 167, 198, 201, 205; Arlington 205; Charlottesville 245; Chilhowie 248; Danville 13; Elk Creek 228; Manassas 53; Martinsville 44, 47, 54, 118, 198, 210, 211, 241, 244, 249, 250, 265, 269, 273, 276; Norfolk 8, 168; Richmond 116, 139, 141, 168, 182, 191, 261, 272, 274, 280; Roanoke 34, 45; South Boston 55; Virginia Beach 280
Vogt, Red 6, 29, 241, 248, 256, 279, 280
Von Tripps, Wolfgang 255
Vukovich, Bill "Vuky" "The Mad Russian" 36, 37, 45, 154, 177

Wachovia Bank 180
Waddell, Bobby 262
Wade, Billy 16–24, 28, 60–62, 97, 99, 115, 116, 118, 189, 224, 261, 263, 265, 267, 281
Wade, Jack 245
Wagner, Honus 15
Wagner, Ken 241
Wagon Train 49
Waites, Frank 17
Walden, Bob 147, 198
Wall, Art 257
Wallace, George C. 263
The Wallaces 220
Walters, Bob 244, 245
Walton, Paul 257
Waltrip, Darrell 80
Ward, James 34
Ward, Rodger 177
Warren, David 63
Warren, Frank 60, 72, 73, 75, 79
Warren, Gayle 243
Warren, Jerome 59
Washington 275; Seattle 63
Washington (DC) 60; Congress 178, 250; Lincoln Memorial 60; Senate 199; Supreme Court 271

Watt, Blackie 30
Wayne, John 73
Weatherly, Joe "The Clown Prince" 8, 10, 12, 13, 15–19, 29, 37–39, 48, 52–60, 83, 92, 97, 105, 106, 111, 112, 114–116, 119, 120, 122–124, 138–143, 156, 157, 160–165, 168, 186, 190–192, 195, 198, 199, 202, 205–209, 221–224, 226, 228, 230, 232, 233, 238, 246, 252, 257–264, 270, 280
Weathersby, Louis 63
Weaver, Ray 190
Weddle, Ewell 242
Weinberg, Danny 44
Welborn, Bob 7, 10, 37, 47, 50–53, 83, 105, 110, 115, 122, 141, 146–148, 150, 154–156, 160, 164, 179, 191–195, 198, 199, 207, 208, 220–222, 224, 230, 238, 239, 246, 248, 252, 262, 264, 280
Welborn, Max 50, 91, 221
West, Vernon 146
West Side Story 49, 57
West Virginia (WV) 242, 248; Bluefield 242; Gilbert 248
Westmoreland, Hubert 32–34, 42, 91, 206, 242, 244, 252, 263
What's My Line? 253
Wheeler, Humpy 39, 134
White, Don 46, 103, 105
White, Gene 47
White, J.C. 246
White, Rex 3, 5, 8, 10–14, 17, 38, 48, 55–58, 85, 88, 89, 91, 106, 111, 112, 124, 138, 141, 155, 161, 164, 165, 191–193, 196, 199, 200, 215, 217, 221–224, 226, 229, 230, 238, 252, 253, 255, 257–264, 281
Whiteman, Paul "The King of Jazz" (and His Orchestra) 36, 45, 211, 212, 249, 281
Whitman, Charles 65
Wickersham, Reb 259, 264
Widenhouse, Bill 35, 45, 47, 115, 155, 157, 161, 195, 245
Widenhouse, Dink "The Concord Comet" 37, 47, 105, 138, 150, 194, 195, 249, 251–253
Wilkes, Felix 33, 102
Williams, Dale 244
Williams, Jim 134
Williams, Parks 134, 280
Wills, Maury 262
Wilson, Fritz 110
Wilson, Guy 8
Wimbish, Jerry 243
Winfree, Andy 154, 211, 248
Wisconsin (WI): Elkhart Lake (Road Course) 195, 253; Milwaukee 105, 228, 273, 275
Wolfe, Thomas 270
Wood, Glen 50, 52, 110, 139, 140, 154–156, 164, 191, 192, 196, 198, 204–206, 209, 221, 222, 255–258
Wood, Hannah 2
Wood, Jake 1, 2
Wood, Jesse L., Jr. 1
Wood, Naomi 1
Wood, Smoke 1
Wood, Yaneth 1, 2
Wood Brothers 19, 54, 97, 115, 122, 139, 141, 151, 191, 199, 222, 225, 258, 259, 261–263, 265, 267, 268, 270
Woods, Ernest 45, 47
Woodward, Wayne 65
World War I 249
World War II 197, 212, 241, 276
Wright, Orville 170
Wright, Wilbur 170
Wynn, Early 58
Wynn, Johnny 66, 67, 135

X-15 49, 60, 63, 112, 271

Yarborough, Cale 18–21, 23, 25, 27, 29, 60, 63, 64, 70, 73, 80, 118, 119, 122, 142, 168, 169, 199, 224–227, 233, 264–266, 268–272
Yarbrough, Eldon 72
Yarbrough, LeeRoy 21–23, 27–29, 60, 61, 64, 66, 70–73, 83, 116, 119, 225–227, 229, 263–265, 267, 271–274, 281
Yates, Doug 11, 13, 55–57, 62, 119, 186, 189, 199, 258, 260
Yogi 266
York, Les 87, 280
York, Shorty 35, 244
Young, Steve 62, 63
Yunick, Henry "Smokey" 6, 7, 9, 11, 34, 37, 45, 47, 66, 67, 104, 108, 122–124, 138, 141, 150, 155, 156, 160, 163, 169, 173, 175, 176, 179, 181, 191, 196, 210, 211, 219, 220, 226, 228, 237, 238, 246, 252, 259, 261, 262, 271, 279

Zaharias, Babe 37, 49
Zervakis, Emanuel "The Golden Greek" "The Greek" 57, 58, 88, 89, 111, 112, 155, 161–165, 222, 259, 260

www.ingramcontent.com/pod-product-compliance
Ingram Content Group UK Ltd.
Pitfield, Milton Keynes, MK11 3LW, UK
UKHW050541150426
5217IPUK00026B/2025